THE PHILOSOPHY OF
BERTRAND RUSSELL

Volume I

BERTRAND RUSSELL

VOLUME I

THE PHILOSOPHY OF
BERTRAND RUSSELL

EDITED BY PAUL ARTHUR SCHILPP

HARPER TORCHBOOKS ❧ THE ACADEMY LIBRARY

HARPER & ROW, PUBLISHERS · NEW YORK, EVANSTON, AND LONDON

TABLE OF CONTENTS

Volume I

TABLE OF CONTENTS
Volume II

PREFACE

EVERY serious student of twentieth century philosophy will welcome the appearance of Volume V in our *Library of Living Philosophers*. For the name of Bertrand Russell has been in the forefront of philosophical discussion for more than forty years. His contributions to mathematical philosophy and symbolic logic have marked him as one of the world's very few really great and seminal thinkers. And the breadth of his interests and variety of his writings have made him at the same time one of the most widely read and critically discussed of our contemporaries.

Yet the present volume is no mere work of supererogation. For, although many of Mr. Russell's philosophical ideas have been the subject of innumerable essays, dissertations, and monographs, they have never before been treated systematically and subject by subject. Still less have most previous criticisms of his ideas been able to elicit from Mr. Russell the careful and studied replies which the reader will find here in his "Reply to Criticisms" (cf. pp. 679-741).

There will be many philosophers, of course, who will not be satisfied with Mr. Russell's "Reply." Some of these will object to the relative brevity of the "Reply." Others, however, will be dissatisfied on more "philosophical"—or is it "temperamental"? —grounds. There is no likely way of meeting the demands of this latter group—unless, indeed, one join their respective camp. As concerns the former, the editor merely desires to say that (only day before yesterday) he discovered what he believes to be the major reason why Mr. Russell did not reply at greater length. In conversation with the editor, Mr. Russell intimated that his greatest surprise, in the reading of the twenty-one contributed essays, had come from the discovery that "over half of their authors had *not* understood" him [i.e., Russell]. This fact amazed Mr. Russell all the more because he always thought that he had been making every effort to write clearly and to express his ideas in the briefest possible and most direct way. In other words, Mr. Russell undoubtedly felt that—not having succeeded in making his ideas clear in the first place by his numerous and varied writings—it was hopeless to expect any better understanding for a renewed attempt in his "Reply," and therefore useless to waste words on anything more than seemed absolutely called for.

Does this prove that the major aim of our Library *is itself doomed to failure?* We shall leave the answer to this question to our readers and reviewers.

However, especially in view of Mr. Russell's thus expressed sentiments, the editor is all the more grateful to him for his never failing kindness, courtesy, and helpfulness throughout the years of work on this volume. Needless to say, without such continued coöperation from Mr. Russell the present volume could not have materialized.

Similar gratitude is, of course, due to the twenty-one contributors, each of whom wrote his essay for this volume at no small cost to himself in time and energy. The editor also desires to express his appreciation and gratitude to Messrs. Lester E. Denonn, of New York City, and Robert S. Hartman, of Lake Forest, Illinois. Mr. Denonn undertook the heroic task of compiling the bibliography of Mr. Russell's published works; and Mr. Hartman was so kind as to do most of the work on the thankless—but for the research-scholar so exceedingly important—job of preparing the index to this volume.

One new feature of the present volume is the appearance of one of the contributed essays in two languages. Professor Albert Einstein wrote his contribution in German. In view of the significance of his "Remarks" (as he modestly calls his paper), it has seemed best to publish his contribution both in the original German and in English translation.

When Professor Harold Chapman Brown was invited to contribute an essay to this volume, little did the editor dream that the paper on "A Logician in the Field of Psychology" would be Professor Brown's last contribution to philosophy. Early last fall Mr. Brown was already too ill to read and make the necessary corrections on the galley-proofs. On November 9, 1943, he passed away in his home at Stanford University, where he had taught for a quarter of a century, and where the editor years ago had the privilege of sitting at Professor Brown's feet in some of the latter's graduate seminars. We are particularly happy, therefore, to have his last philosophical work preserved here.

Rapidly failing health and untimely death also cheated the readers of this volume out of an essay which was to have appeared here. Professor L. Susan Stebbing had promised several years ago to contribute an essay on "Russell's Conception of Philosophy" to our Russell volume. During the early summer of 1943 we received first a cablegram from London, saying that serious illness would prevent her from fulfilling her promise. On September 11, she too passed on, bringing to a sudden end a career which doubtless had been that of the most noted contemporary philosopher of her sex. Fortunately we were able to print her essay on "Moore's Influence" in Volume IV of this *Library*.

From the beginning of this series we knew that at some time we should find ourselves confronted by the fact that one of our great *living* philosophers should be passing off the scene before we had the chance to finish the volume on his philosophy. We greatly regret to have to record the fact that this fear has already been justified by the event. In February of this year (1944) Léon Brunschvicg died at the age of seventy-five. As early as 1939 he had promised his coöperation in the production of a volume which was to have dealt with his philosophy. Consequently a volume on the philosophy of Léon Brunschvicg has been announced in each of our first four volumes. This unexpected death of M. Brunschvicg obviously makes the carrying out of this promise impossible. France and the world have lost another great philosopher.

P. A. S.

DEPARTMENT OF PHILOSOPHY
NORTHWESTERN UNIVERSITY
EVANSTON, ILLINOIS

March 18, 1944

ACKNOWLEDGMENTS

GRATEFUL ACKNOWLEDGMENT is hereby made to the publishers of all of Mr. Russell's books as well as to the editors and publishers of philosophical, literary, scientific, and mathematical journals and magazines for their kind permission to quote from the works of Bertrand Russell. We are particularly grateful for their courtesy in not insisting upon a detailed enumeration of the books and articles quoted. Exact title, name of publisher, and place and date of publication of each of Mr. Russell's works are given in the bibliography, which will be found on pages 743 to 804 of this volume.

Grateful acknowledgment is further made to the publishers of other works quoted in the following pages, who have also been kind enough not to require the specific enumeration of the works quoted.

Bertrand Russell

MY MENTAL DEVELOPMENT

MY MENTAL DEVELOPMENT

MY mother having died when I was two years old, and my father when I was three, I was brought up in the house of my grandfather, Lord John Russell, afterwards Earl Russell. Of my parents, Lord and Lady Amberley, I was told almost nothing—so little that I vaguely sensed a dark mystery. It was not until I was twenty-one that I came to know the main outlines of my parents' lives and opinions. I then found, with a sense of bewilderment, that I had gone through almost exactly the same mental and emotional development as my father had.

It was expected of my father that he should take to a political career, which was traditional in the Russell family. He was willing, and was for a short time in Parliament (1867-68); but he had not the temperament or the opinions that would have made political success possible. At the age of twenty-one he decided that he was not a Christian, and refused to go to Church on Christmas Day. He became a disciple, and afterwards a friend, of John Stuart Mill, who, as I discovered some years ago, was (so far as is possible in a non-religious sense) my godfather. My parents accepted Mill's opinions, not only such as were comparatively popular, but also those that still shocked public sentiment, such as women's suffrage and birth control. During the general election of 1868, at which my father was a candidate, it was discovered that, at a private meeting of a small society, he had said that birth control was a matter for the medical profession to consider. This let loose a campaign of vilification and slander. A Catholic Bishop declared that he advocated infanticide; he was called in print a "filthy foul-mouthed rake;" on election day, cartoons were exhibited accus-

3

ing him of immorality, altering his name to "Vice-count Amberley," and accusing him of advocating "The French and American system."[1] By these means he was defeated. The student of comparative sociology may be interested in the similarities between rural England in 1868 and urban New York in 1940. The available documents are collected in *The Amberley Papers*, by my wife and myself. As the reader of this book will see, my father was shy, studious, and ultra-conscientious—perhaps a prig, but the very opposite of a rake.

My father did not give up hope of returning to politics, but never obtained another constituency, and devoted himself to writing a big book, *Analysis of Religious Belief*, which was published after his death. He could not, in any case, have succeeded in politics, because of his very exceptional intellectual integrity; he was always willing to admit the weak points on his own side and the strong points on that of his opponents. Moreover his health was always bad, and he suffered from a consequent lack of physical vigour.

My mother shared my father's opinions, and shocked the 'sixties by addressing meetings in favour of equality for women. She refused to use the phrase "women's rights," because, as a good utilitarian, she rejected the doctrine of natural rights.

My father wished my brother and me to be brought up as free thinkers, and appointed two free thinkers as our guardians. The Court of Chancery, however, at the request of my grandparents, set aside the will, and I enjoyed the benefits of a Christian upbringing.

In 1876, when after my father's death, I was brought to the house of my grandparents, my grandfather was eighty-three and had become very feeble. I remember him sometimes being wheeled about out-of-doors in a bath-chair, sometimes in his room reading Hansard (the official report of debates in Parliament). He was invariably kind to me, and seemed never to object to childish noise. But he was too old to influence me directly. He died in 1878, and my knowledge of him came

[1] My parents, when in America, had studied such experiments as the Oneida community. They were therefore accused of attempting to corrupt the purity of English family life by introducing un-English transatlantic vices.

through his widow, my grandmother, who revered his memory. She was a more powerful influence upon my general outlook than any one else, although, from adolescence onward, I disagreed with very many of her opinions.

My grandmother was a Scotch Presbyterian, of the border family of the Elliots. Her maternal grandfather suffered obloquy for declaring, on the basis of the thickness of the lava on the slopes of Etna, that the world must have been created before B.C. 4004. One of her great-grandfathers was Robertson, the historian of Charles V.

She was a Puritan, with the moral rigidity of the Covenanters, despising comfort, indifferent to food, hating wine, and regarding tobacco as sinful. Although she had lived her whole life in the great world until my grandfather's retirement in 1866, she was completely unworldly. She had that indifference to money which is only possible to those who have always had enough of it. She wished her children and grandchildren to live useful and virtuous lives, but had no desire that they should achieve what others would regard as success, or that they should marry "well." She had the Protestant belief in private judgment and the supremacy of the individual conscience. On my twelfth birthday she gave me a Bible (which I still possess), and wrote her favourite texts on the fly-leaf. One of them was "Thou shalt not follow a multitude to do evil;" another, "Be strong, and of a good courage; be not afraid, neither be Thou dismayed; for the Lord Thy God is with thee whithersoever thou goest." These texts have profoundly influenced my life, and still seemed to retain some meaning after I had ceased to believe in God.

At the age of seventy, my grandmother became a Unitarian; at the same time, she supported Home Rule for Ireland, and made friends with Irish Members of Parliament, who were being publicly accused of complicity in murder. This shocked people more than now seems imaginable. She was passionately opposed to imperialism, and taught me to think ill of the Afghan and Zulu wars, which occurred when I was about seven. Concerning the occupation of Egypt, however, she said little, as it was due to Mr. Gladstone, whom she admired. I remember an argument I had with my German governess, who said that the English, having once gone into Egypt, would never come out, whatever they might promise, whereas I maintained, with much patriotic passion, that the English never broke promises. That was sixty years ago, and they are there still.

My grandfather, seen through the eyes of his widow, made it seem imperative and natural to do something important for the good of mankind. I was told of his introducing the Reform Bill in 1832. Shortly before he died, a delegation of eminent nonconformists assembled to cheer him, and I was told that fifty years earlier he had been one of the leaders in removing their political disabilities. In his sitting-room there was a statue of Italy, presented to my grandfather by the Italian Government, with an inscription: "A Lord John Russell, L'Italia Riconoscente;" I naturally wished to know what this meant, and learnt, in consequence, the whole saga of Garibaldi and Italian unity. Such things stimulated my ambition to live to some purpose.

My grandfather's library, which became my schoolroom, stimulated me in a different way. There were books of history, some of them very old; I remember in particular a sixteenth-century Guicciardini. There were three huge folio volumes called *L'Art de vérifier les dates*. They were too heavy for me to move, and I speculated as to their contents; I imagined something like the tables for finding Easter in the Prayer-Book. At last I became old enough to lift one of the volumes out of the shelf, and I found, to my disgust, that the only "art" involved was that of looking up the date in the book. Then there were *The Annals of Ireland* by the Four Masters, in which I read about the men who went to Ireland before the Flood and were drowned in it; I wondered how the Four Masters knew about them, and read no further. There were also more ordinary books, such as Machiavelli and Gibbon and Swift, and a book in four volumes that I never opened: *The Works of Andrew Marvell Esq. M. P.* It was not till I grew up that I discovered Marvell was a poet rather than a politician. I was not supposed to read any of these books; otherwise I should probably not have read any of them. The net result of them was to stimulate my interest in history. No doubt my interest was increased by the fact that my family had been prominent in English history since the early sixteenth century. I was taught English history as the record of a struggle against the King for constitutional liberty. William Lord Russell, who was executed under Charles II, was held up for special admiration, and the inference was encouraged that rebellion is often praiseworthy.

A great event in my life, at the age of eleven, was the beginning of Euclid, which was still the accepted textbook of geometry. When I had got over my disappointment in finding that he began with axioms, which had to be accepted without proof, I found great delight in him. Throughout the rest of my boyhood, mathematics absorbed a very large part of my interest. This interest was complex: partly mere pleasure in discovering that I possessed a certain kind of skill, partly delight in the power of deductive reasoning, partly the restfulness of mathematical certainty; but more than any of these (while I was still a boy) the belief that nature operates according to mathematical laws, and that human actions, like planetary motions, could be calculated if we had sufficient skill. By the time I was fifteen, I had arrived at a theory very similar to that of the Cartesians. The movements of living bodies, I felt convinced, were wholly regulated by the laws of dynamics; therefore free will must be an illusion. But, since I accepted consciousness as an indubitable datum, I could not accept materialism, though I had a certain hankering after it on account of its intellectual simplicity and its rejection of "nonsense." I still believed in God, because the First-Cause argument seemed irrefutable.

Until I went to Cambridge at the age of eighteen, my life was a very solitary one. I was brought up at home, by German nurses, German and Swiss governesses, and finally by English tutors; I saw little of other children, and when I did they were not important to me. At fourteen or fifteen I became passionately interested in religion, and set to work to examine successively the arguments for free will, immortality, and God. For a few months I had an agnostic tutor with whom I could talk about these problems, but he was sent away, presumably because he was thought to be undermining my faith. Except during these months, I kept my thoughts to myself, writing them out in a journal in Greek letters to prevent others from reading them. I was suffering the unhappiness natural to lonely adolescence, and I attributed my unhappiness to loss of religious belief. For three years I thought about religion, with a determination not to let my thoughts be influenced by my desires. I discarded first free will, then immortality; I believed in God until I was just eighteen, when I found in Mill's *Autobiography* the sentence: "My father taught me that the question 'Who made me'? cannot be answered, since it immediately suggests the further question 'Who made God'?" In that moment I decided that the First-Cause argument is fallacious.

During these·years I read widely, but as my reading was not directed, much of it was futile. I read much bad poetry, especially Tennyson and Byron; at last, at the age of seventeen, I came upon Shelley, whom no one had told me about. He remained for many years the man I loved most among great men of the past. I read a great deal of Carlyle, and admired *Past and Present*, but not *Sartor Resartus*. "The Everlasting Yea" seemed to me sentimental nonsense. The man with whom I most nearly agreed was Mill. His *Political Economy*, *Liberty*, and *Subjection of Women* influenced me profoundly. I made elaborate notes on the whole of his *Logic*, but could not accept his theory that mathematical propositions are empirical generalizations, though I did not know what else they could be.

All this was before I went to Cambridge. Except during the three months when I had the agnostic tutor mentioned above, I found no one to speak to about my thoughts. At home I concealed my religious doubts. Once I said that I was a utilitarian, but was met with such a blast of ridicule that I never again spoke of my opinions at home.

Cambridge opened to me a new world of infinite delight. For the first time I found that, when I uttered my thoughts, they seemed to be accepted as worth considering. Whitehead, who had examined me for entrance scholarships, had mentioned me to various people a year or two senior to me, with the result that within a week I met a number who became my life-long friends. Whitehead, who was already a Fellow and Lecturer, was amazingly kind, but was too much my senior to be a close personal friend until some years later. I found a group of contemporaries, who were able, rather earnest, hard-working, but interested in many things outside their academic work—poetry, philosophy, politics, ethics, indeed the whole world of mental adventure. We used to stay up discussing till very late on Saturday nights, meet for a late breakfast on Sunday, and then go for an all-day walk. Able young men had not yet adopted the pose of cynical superiority which came in some years later, and was first made fashionable in Cambridge by Lytton Strachey. The world seemed hopeful and solid; we all felt convinced that nineteenth-century progress would continue, and that we ourselves should be able to contribute something of value. For those who have been young since 1914 it must be difficult to imagine the happiness of those days.

Among my friends at Cambridge were McTaggart, the Hegelian philosopher; Lowes Dickinson, whose gentle charm made him loved by all who knew him; Charles Sanger, a brilliant mathematician at College, afterwards a barrister, known in legal circles as the editor of Jarman on Wills; two brothers, Crompton and Theodore Llewelyn Davies, sons of a Broad Church clergyman most widely known as one of "Davies and Vaughan," who translated Plato's *Republic*. These two brothers were the youngest and ablest of a family of seven, all remarkably able; they had also a quite unusual capacity for friendship, a deep desire to be of use to the world, and unrivalled wit. Theodore, the younger of the two, was still in the earlier stages of a brilliant career in the government service when he was drowned in a bathing accident. I have never known any two men so deeply loved by so many friends. Among those of whom I saw most were the three brothers Trevelyan, great-nephews of Macaulay. Of these the oldest became a Labour politician and resigned from the Labour Government because it was not sufficiently socialistic; the second became a poet and published, among other things, an admirable translation of Lucretius; the third, George, achieved fame as an historian. Somewhat junior to me was G. E. Moore, who later had a great influence upon my philosophy.

The set in which I lived was very much influenced by McTaggart, whose wit recommended his Hegelian philosophy. He taught me to consider British empiricism "crude," and I was willing to believe that Hegel (and in a lesser degree Kant) had a profundity not to be found in Locke, Berkeley, and Hume, or in my former pope, Mill. My first three years at Cambridge, I was too busy with mathematics to read Kant or Hegel, but in my fourth year I concentrated on philosophy. My teachers were Henry Sidgwick, James Ward, and G. F. Stout. Sidgwick represented the British point of view, which I believed myself to have seen through; I therefore thought less of him at that time than I did later. Ward, for whom I had a very great personal affection, set forth a Kantian system, and introduced me to Lotze and Sigwart. Stout, at that time, thought very highly of Bradley; when *Appearance and Reality* was published, he said it had done as much as is humanly possible in ontology. He and McTaggart between them caused me to become a Hegelian; I remember the precise moment, one day in 1894, as I was walking along Trinity Lane, when I saw in a flash (or thought I saw) that the ontological argument is valid. I had gone out to buy a tin of tobacco; on my way back, I suddenly threw it up in the air, and exclaimed as I caught it: "Great Scott, the ontological argument is sound." I read Bradley at this time with avidity, and admired him more than any other recent philosopher.

After leaving Cambridge in 1894, I spent a good deal of time in foreign countries. For some months in 1894, I was honorary attaché at the British Embassy in Paris, where I had to copy out long dispatches attempting to persuade the French Government that a lobster is not a fish, to which the French Government would reply that it was a fish in 1713, at the time of the Treaty of Utrecht. I had no desire for a diplomatic career, and left the Embassy in December, 1894. I then married, and spent most of 1895 in Berlin, studying economics and German Social Democracy. The Ambassador's wife being a cousin of mine, my wife and I were invited to dinner at the Embassy; but she mentioned that we had gone to a Socialist meeting, and after this the Embassy closed its doors to us. My wife was a Philadelphia Quaker, and in 1896 we spent three months in America. The first place we visited was Walt Whitman's house in Camden, N.J.; she had known him well, and I greatly admired him. These travels were useful in curing me of a certain Cambridge provincialism; in particular, I came to know the work of Weierstrass, whom my Cambridge teachers had never mentioned. After these travels, we settled down in a workman's cottage in Sussex, to which we added a fairly large work-room. I had at that time enough money to live simply without earning, and I was therefore able to devote all my time to philosophy and mathematics, except the evenings, when we read history aloud.

In the years from 1894 to 1898, I believed in the possibility of proving by metaphysics various things about the universe that religious feeling made me think important. I decided that, if I had sufficient ability, I would devote my life to philosophy. My fellowship dissertation, on the foundations of geometry, was praised by Ward and Whitehead; if it had not been, I should have taken up economics, at which I had been working in Berlin. I remember a spring morning when I walked in the Tiergarten, and planned to write a series of books in the philosophy of the sciences, growing gradually more concrete as I passed from mathematics to biology; I thought I would also write a series of books on social and political questions, growing gradually more abstract. At last I would achieve a Hegelian synthesis in an encyclopaedic work dealing equally with theory and practice. The scheme was inspired by Hegel, and yet something of it survived the change in my philosophy. The moment had had a certain importance: I can still, in memory, feel the squelching of melting snow beneath my feet, and smell the damp earth that promised the end of winter.

During 1898, various things caused me to abandon both Kant and Hegel. I read Hegel's *Greater Logic*, and thought, as I still do, that all he says about mathematics is muddle-headed nonsense. I came to disbelieve Bradley's arguments against relations, and to distrust the logical bases of monism. I disliked the subjectivity of the "Transcendental Aesthetic." But these motives would have operated more slowly than they did, but for the influence of G. E. Moore. He also had had a Hegelian period, but it was briefer than mine. He took the lead in rebellion, and I followed, with a sense of emancipation. Bradley argued that everything common sense believes in is mere appearance; we reverted to the opposite extreme, and thought that *everything* is real that common sense, uninfluenced by philosophy or theology, supposes real. With a sense of escaping from prison, we allowed ourselves to think that grass is green, that the sun and stars would exist if no one was aware of them, and also that there is a pluralistic timeless world of Platonic ideas. The world, which had been thin and logical, suddenly became rich and varied and solid. Mathematics could be *quite* true, and not merely a stage in dialectic. Something of this point of view appeared in my *Philosophy of Leibniz*. This book owed its origin to chance. McTaggart, who would, in the normal course, have lectured on Leibniz at Cambridge in 1898, wished to visit his family in New Zealand, and I was asked to take his place for this course. For me, the accident was a fortunate one.

The most important year in my intellectual life was the year 1900, and the most important event in this year was my visit to the International Congress of Philosophy in Paris. Ever since I had begun Euclid at the age of eleven, I had been troubled about the foundations of mathematics; when, later, I came to read philosophy, I found Kant and the empiricists equally unsatisfactory. I did not like the synthetic *a priori*, but yet arithmetic did not seem to consist of empirical generalizations. In Paris in 1900, I was impressed by the fact that, in all discussions, Peano and his pupils had a precision which was not possessed by others. I therefore asked him to give me his works, which he did. As soon as I had mastered his notation, I saw that it extended the region of mathematical precision backwards towards regions which had been given over to philosophical vagueness. Basing myself on him, I invented a notation for relations. Whitehead, fortunately, agreed as to the importance of the method, and in a very short time we worked out together such matters as the definitions of series, cardinals, and ordinals, and the reduction of arithmetic to logic. For nearly a year, we had a rapid series of quick successes. Much of the work had already been done by Frege, but at first we did not know this. The work that ultimately became my contribution to *Principia Mathematica* presented itself to me, at first, as a parenthesis in the refutation of Kant.

In June 1901, this period of honeymoon delight came to an end. Cantor had a proof that there is no greatest cardinal; in applying this proof to the universal class, I was led to the contradiction about classes that are not members of themselves. It soon became clear that this is only one of an infinite class of contradictions. I wrote to Frege, who replied with the utmost gravity that *"die Arithmetik ist ins Schwanken geraten."* At first, I hoped the matter was trivial and could be easily cleared up; but early hopes were succeeded by something very near to despair. Throughout 1903 and 1904, I pursued will-o'-the wisps and made no progress. At last, in the spring of 1905, a different problem, which proved soluble, gave the first glimmer of hope. The problem was that of descriptions, and its solution suggested a new technique.

Scholastic realism was a metaphysical theory, but every metaphysical theory has a technical counterpart. I had been a realist in the scholastic or Platonic sense; I had thought that cardinal integers, for instance, have a timeless being. When integers were reduced to classes of classes, this being was transferred to classes. Meinong, whose work interested me, applied the arguments of realism to descriptive phrases. Everyone agrees that "the golden mountain does not exist" is a true proposition. But it has, apparently, a subject, "the golden mountain," and if this subject did not designate some object, the proposition would seem to be meaningless. Meinong inferred that there is a golden mountain, which is golden and a mountain, but does not exist. He even thought that the existent golden mountain is existent, but does not exist. This did not satisfy me, and the desire to avoid Meinong's unduly populous realm of being led me to the theory of descriptions. What was of importance in this theory was the discovery that, in analysing a significant sentence, one must not assume that each separate word or phrase has significance on its own account. "The golden mountain" can be part of a significant sentence, but is not significant in isolation. It soon appeared that class-symbols could be treated like descriptions, i.e., as non-significant parts of significant sentences. This made it possible to see, in a general way, how a solution of the contradictions might be possible. The particular solution offered in *Principia Mathematica* had various defects, but at any rate it showed that the logician is not presented with a complete *impasse*.

The theory of descriptions, and the attempt to solve the contradictions, had led me to pay attention to the problem of meaning and significance. The definition of "meaning" as applied to words and "significance" as applied to sentences is a complex problem, which I tried to deal with in *The Analysis of Mind* (1921) and *An Inquiry into Meaning and Truth* (1940). It is a problem that takes one into psychology and even physiology. The more I have thought about it, the less convinced I have become of the complete independence of logic. Seeing that logic is a much more advanced and exact science than psychology, it is clearly desirable, as far as possible, to delimit the problems that can be dealt with by logical methods. It is here that I have found Occam's razor useful.

Occam's razor, in its original form, was metaphysical: it was a principle of parsimony as regards "entities." I still thought of it in this way while *Principia Mathematica* was being written. In Plato, cardinal integers are timeless entities; they are equally so in Frege's *Grundgesetze der Arithmetik*. The definition of cardinals as classes of classes, and the discovery that class-symbols could be "incomplete symbols," persuaded me that cardinals as entities are unnecessary. But what had really been demonstrated was something quite independent of metaphysics, which is best stated in terms of "minimum vocabularies." I mean by a "minimum vocabulary" one in which no word can be defined in terms of the others. All definitions are theoretically superfluous, and therefore the whole of any science can be expressed by means of a minimum vocabulary for that science. Peano reduced the special vocabulary of arithmetic to three terms; Frege and *Principia Mathematica* maintained that even these are unnecessary, and that a minimum vocabulary for mathematics is the same as for logic. This problem is a purely technical one, and is capable of a precise solution.

There is need, however, of great caution in drawing inferences from minimum vocabularies. In the first place, there are usually, if not always, a number of different minimum vocabularies for a given subject-matter; for example, in the theory of truth-functions we may take "not-*p* or not-*q*" or "not-*p* and not-*q*" as undefined, and there is no reason to prefer one choice to the other. Then again there is often a question as to whether what seems to be a definition is not really an empirical proposition. Suppose, for instance, I define "red" as "those visual sensations which are caused by wave-lengths of such and such a range of frequencies." If we take this as what the word "red" means, no proposition containing the word can have been known before the undulatory theory of light was known and wavelengths could be measured; and yet the word "red" was used before these discoveries had been made. This makes it clear that in all every-day statements containing the word "red" this word does not have the meaning assigned to it in the above definition. Consider the question: "Can everything that we know about colours be known to a blind man?" With the above definition, the answer is yes; with a definition derived from every-day experience, the answer is no. This problem shows how the new logic, like the Aristotelian, can lead to a narrow scholasticism.

Nevertheless, there is one kind of inference which, I think, can be drawn from the study of minimum vocabularies. Take, as one of the most important examples, the traditional problem of universals. It seems fairly certain that no vocabulary can dispense wholly with words that are more or less of the sort called "universals." These words, it is true, need never occur as nouns; they may occur only as adjectives or verbs. Probably we could be content with one such word, the word "similar," and we should never need the word "similarity." But the fact that we need the word "similar" indicates some fact about the world, and not only about language. What fact it indicates about the world, I do not know.

Another illustration of the uses of minimum vocabularies is as regards historical events. To express history, we must have a means of speaking of something which has only happened once, like the death of Caesar. An undue absorption in logic, which is not concerned with history, may cause this need to be overlooked. Spatio-temporal relativity has made it more difficult to satisfy this need than it was in a Newtonian universe, where points and instants supplied particularity.

Thus, broadly speaking, minimum vocabularies are more instructive when they show a certain kind of term to be indispensable than when they show the opposite.

In some respects, my published work, outside mathematical logic, does not at all completely represent my beliefs or my general outlook. Theory of knowledge, with which I have been largely concerned, has a certain essential subjectivity; it asks "how do *I* know what I know?" and starts inevitably from personal experience. Its data are egocentric, and so are the earlier stages of its argumentation. I have not, so far, got beyond the earlier stages, and have therefore seemed more subjective in outlook than in fact I am. I am not a solipsist, nor an idealist; I believe (though without good grounds) in the world of physics as well as in the world of psychology. But it seems clear that whatever is not experienced must, if known, be known by inference. I find that the fear of solipsism has prevented philosophers from facing this problem, and that either the necessary principles of inference have been left vague, or else the distinction between what is known by experience and what is known by inference has been denied. If I ever have the leisure to undertake another serious investigation of a philosophical problem, I shall attempt to analyse the inferences from experience to the world of physics, assuming them capable of validity, and seeking to discover what principles of inference, if true, would make them valid. Whether these principles, when discovered, are accepted as true, is a matter of temperament; what should not be a matter of temperament should be the proof that acceptance of them is necessary if solipsism is to be rejected.

I come now to what I have attempted to do in connection with social questions. I grew up in an atmosphere of politics, and was expected by my elders to take up a political career. Philosophy, however, interested me more than politics, and when it appeared that I had some aptitude for it, I decided to make it my main work. This pained my grandmother, who alluded to my investigation of the foundations of geometry as "the life you have been leading," and said in shocked tones: "O Bertie, I hear you are writing *another* book." My political interests, though secondary, nevertheless, remained very strong. In 1895, when in Berlin, I made a study of German Social Democracy, which I liked as being opposed to the Kaiser, and disliked as (at that time) embodying Marxist orthodoxy. For a time, under the influence of Sidney Webb, I became an imperialist, and even supported the Boer War. This point of view, however, I abandoned completely in 1901; from that time onwards, I felt an intense dislike of the use of force in human relations, though I always admitted that it is sometimes necessary. When Joseph Chamberlain, in 1903, turned against free trade, I wrote and spoke against him, my objections to his proposals being those of an internationalist. I took an active part in the agitation for Women's Suffrage. In 1910, *Principia Mathematica* being practically finished, I wished to stand for Parliament, and should have done so if the Selection Committee had not been shocked to discover that I was a free thinker.

The first world war gave a new direction to my interests. The war, and the problem of preventing future wars, absorbed me, and the books that I wrote on this and cognate subjects caused me to become known to a wider public. During the war I had hoped that the peace would embody a rational determination to avoid future great wars; this hope was destroyed by the Versailles Treaty. Many of my friends saw hope in Soviet Russia, but when I went there in 1920 I found nothing that I could like or admire. I was then invited to China, where I spent nearly a year. I loved the Chinese, but it was obvious that the resistance to hostile militarisms must destroy much of what was best in their civilization. They seemed to have no alternative except to be conquered or to adopt many of the vices of their enemies. But China did one thing for me that the East is apt to do for Europeans who study it with sensitive sympathy: it taught me to think in long stretches of time, and not to be reduced to despair by the badness of the present. Throughout the increasing gloom of the past twenty years, this habit has helped to make the world less unendurable than it would otherwise have been.

In the years after my return from China, the birth of my two older children caused me to become interested in early education, to which, for some time, I devoted most of my energy. I have been supposed to be an advocate of complete liberty in schools, but this, like the view that I am an anarchist, is a mistake. I think a certain amount of force is indispensable, in education as in government; but I also think that methods can be found which will greatly diminish the necessary amount of force. This problem has both political and private aspects. As a rule, children or adults who are happy are likely to have fewer destructive passions, and therefore to need less restraint, than those who are unhappy. But I do not think that children can be made happy by being deprived of guidance, nor do I think that a sense of social obligation can be fostered if complete idleness is permitted. The question of discipline in childhood, like all other practical questions, is one of degree. Profound unhappiness and instinctive frustration is apt to produce a deep grudge against the world, issuing, sometimes by a very roundabout road, in cruelty and violence. The psychological and social problems involved first occupied my attention during the war of 1914-18; I was especially struck by the fact that, at first, most people seemed to enjoy the war. Clearly this was due to a variety of social ills, some of which were educational. But while individual parents can do much for their individual children, large-scale educational reform must depend upon the state, and therefore upon prior political and economic reforms. The world, however, was moving more and more in the direction of war and dictatorship, and I saw nothing useful that I could do in practical matters. I therefore increasingly reverted to philosophy, and to history in relation to ideas.

History has always interested me more than anything else except philosophy and mathematics. I have never been able to accept any general schema of historical development, such as that of Hegel or that of Marx. Nevertheless, general trends can be studied, and the study is profitable in relation to the present. I found much help in understanding the nineteenth century from studying the effect of liberal ideas in the period from 1814 to 1914.[2] The two types of liberalism, the rational and the romantic, represented by Bentham and Rousseau respectively, have continued, ever since, their relations of alternate alliance and conflict.

The relation of philosophy to social conditions has usually been ignored by professional philosophers. Marxists are interested in philosophy as an *effect*, but do not recognize it as a *cause*. Yet plainly every important philosophy is both. Plato is in part an effect of the victory of Sparta in the Peloponnesian war, and is also in part among the causes of Christian theology. To treat him only in the former aspect is to make the growth of the medieval church inexplicable. I am at present writing a history of western philosophy from Thales to the present day, in which every important system is treated equally as an effect and as a cause of social conditions.

My intellectual journeys have been, in some respects, disappointing. When I was young I hoped to find religious satisfaction in philosophy; even after I had abandoned Hegel, the eternal Platonic world gave me something non-human to admire. I thought of mathematics with reverence, and suffered when Wittgenstein led me to regard it as nothing but tautologies. I have always ardently desired to find some justification for the emotions inspired by certain things that seemed to stand outside human life and to deserve feelings of awe. I am thinking in part of very obvious things, such as the starry heavens and a stormy sea on a rocky coast; in part of the vastness of the scientific universe, both in space and time, as compared to the life of mankind; in part of the edifice of impersonal truth, especially truth which, like that of mathematics, does not merely describe the world that happens to exist. Those who attempt to make a religion of humanism, which recognizes nothing greater than man, do not satisfy my emotions. And yet I am unable to believe that, in the world as known, there is anything that I can

[2] *Freedom and Organization, 1814-1914* (1934).

value outside human beings, and, to a much lesser extent, animals. Not the starry heavens, but their effects on human percipients, have excellence; to admire the universe for its size is slavish and absurd; impersonal non-human truth appears to be a delusion. And so my intellect goes with the humanists, though my emotions violently rebel. In this respect, the "consolations of philosophy" are not for me.

In more purely intellectual ways, on the contrary, I have found as much satisfaction in philosophy as any one could reasonably have expected. Many matters which, when I was young, baffled me by the vagueness of all that had been said about them, are now amenable to an exact technique, which makes possible the kind of progress that is customary in science. Where definite knowledge is unattainable, it is sometimes possible to prove that it is unattainable, and it is usually possible to formulate a variety of exact hypotheses, all compatible with the existing evidence. Those philosophers who have adopted the methods derived from logical analysis can argue with each other, not in the old aimless way, but coöperatively, so that both sides can concur as to the outcome. All this is new during my lifetime; the pioneer was Frege, but he remained solitary until his old age. This extension of the sphere of reason to new provinces is something that I value very highly. Philosophic rationality may be choked in the shocks of war and the welter of new persecuting superstitions, but one may hope that it will not be lost utterly or for more than a few centuries. In this respect, my philosophic life has been a happy one.

Bertrand Russell

BRYN MAWR, PENNSYLVANIA
JULY, 1943

I

Hans Reichenbach

BERTRAND RUSSELL'S LOGIC

BERTRAND RUSSELL'S LOGIC

I

IT is the plan of this book to open discussions between a philosopher and his critics, benevolent or otherwise, for the purpose of creating an opportunity to clarify opinions and correct misinterpretations. I must confess that this program, welcome as it appears in many other cases, makes it somewhat difficult for me to contribute to the present volume. Bertrand Russell distinguishes himself from many other philosophers by the clarity with which he has always presented his ideas. An attempt to further clarification, therefore, seems to be out of place, and should be reserved for other sorts of philosophy. There are philosophies, indeed, which were so vaguely stated that every school of philosophy was able to give them interpretations corresponding to its own views. Many a philosopher derives his significance from the obscurity of his exposition rather than from the weight of his ideas; and I should like to believe that such ideas would have lost their persuasive power had they been formulated more precisely and coherently. Bertrand Russell is certainly not a philosopher of this sort. He constitutes a fortunate example showing that a philosopher may owe his success to clarity and cogency, to painstaking analysis and the renunciation of the mysterious language of oracles. It seems therefore scarcely necessary to provide for a second edition of his philosophy enlightened for the use of posterity by the criticism of opponents. What makes the present writer even more unsuitable for such a purpose is the fact that he does not even feel himself an opponent, that he agrees very much with most of the fundamental views of Bertrand Russell, to whom he is deeply grateful for the instruction and enlightenment which he has always gathered from Russell's books.

In order that this essay may serve the general purpose of the present volume I shall therefore try to follow another plan. I shall attempt to summarize the contributions which Russell has made to modern logic, hoping that Mr. Russell will correct my summary wherever it is incomplete or where the emphasis is on the wrong point. I hope, in addition, that Mr. Russell will answer some questions as to the genesis of his ideas and thus give us some valuable information concerning the history of modern logic. Finally I am optimistic enough to assume that at least on some points there will remain a diversity of opinion which may supply the reader with the most coveted fruit on the tree of philosophy: a philosophical dispute.

II

Let us have a short view of the situation within the history of logic at the time when Russell entered its field. Aristotelian logic, which for two thousand years had dominated Western thought, had finally been superseded by the symbolic logic constructed by such men as Boole, de Morgan, Peirce, Peano, Cantor, Frege, and Schröder. Boole's work, from which we may date the modern period of logic, was already fifty years old. But the new ideas had not yet acquired any significant publicity; they were more or less the private property of a group of mathematicians whose philosophical bias had led them astray into the realm of a mathematical logic. The leading philosophers, or let us better say the men who occupied the chairs of philosophy, had not taken much notice of it and did not believe that Aristotelian logic could ever be surpassed, or that a mathematical notation could improve logic. Russell, then at the age of twenty-eight, had read the writings of this group and attended a congress of logic in Paris in the year 1900, where he met Schröder, Peano, Couturat and others. A few years later he wrote his *Principles of Mathematics*, followed after some further years by the *Principia Mathematica*, written in coöperation with Whitehead. Why is it that from the appearance of these books we date the second phase of modern logic, the phase which united the various starting points and logistic calculi into one comprehensive system of symbolic logic?

There are several reasons which made Russell's work the beginning of this new phase. The first is given by a number of technical improvements over the symbolic systems of his predecessors. The second is that he combined the creation of a symbolic logic with the claim of including the whole of mathematics, an idea which, controversial as it has always been, has never ceased to excite the minds of mathematicians and logicians alike. The third is that Russell, uniting in his books a skilfully chosen notation with the brilliant style of a writer, drew the attention of philosophers of all camps to symbolic logic, which thus was made palatable for the first time.

III

I shall try to summarize the technical improvements which Russell has contributed to symbolic logic.

There is to be mentioned first Russell's introduction of the concept of *propositional function*. The idea of conceiving grammatical predicates as classes is of course much older and goes back to Aristotle; Boole's algebra of logic makes wide use of it. But Russell's concept of propositional function extends the concept of a *class* to that of a *relation* and thus combines the advantage of the mathematical analogy with a closer correspondence to conversational language. This close relation to conversational language constitutes one of the strong points in Russell's logic. It manifests itself also in his theory of descriptional functions. Using the iota-symbol introduced by Peano, Russell showed the way to the understanding of the definite article "the" and similar particles of speech, and developed Peano's notation into a general syntax of a high degree of perfection. It is surprising to what extent the understanding of the logical nature of language is facilitated by the use of Russell's concepts. In many a logic course I have given I have had the occasion to watch this effect of Russell's logic. Through its clarification of the structure of language, symbolic logic awakens logical abilities till then dormant in the minds of the students.

Next I must mention Russell's decision to use material implication. This sort of implication with its puzzles, it is true, has been known for a long time; Peirce,[1] who himself saw the advantages of this implication, quotes Sextus Empiricus as the first to have pointed out the nature of this relation, and justifies its use by showing that its queer consequences cannot lead to wrong results. But Russell was the first to discover that the whole system of logic can be consistently developed by the use of this sort of propositional operation. He saw that this is a point where the correspondence to meanings of conversational language must be abandoned, if a satisfying logic is to be constructed; and his logic thus was the first which is consciously *extensional*. He was not afraid to use propositions like "snow is black implies sugar is green," since he saw that the meaning of the word "implies" used here can be clearly defined and leads, unreasonable as it appears at first sight, to a reasonable logical calculus. He deliberately postponed the construction of concepts better fitting conversational usage, in the hope that this might be possible within the frame of an extensional logic, by the introduction of more complicated relations. His formal implication represents a stepping stone on this path; Russell saw that it corresponds much more closely to what is usually meant by an implication, although he frankly stated the limitations holding even for this generalized implication. This line of development has later been continued in Carnap's discovery, according to which a reasonable implication can be defined by the use of the metalanguage; a further continuation of this line of thought, which leads from tautological implications to a more general kind of implication corresponding to natural laws, has been given by the present author.[2]

It is the advantage of extensional operations that they permit us to define the notion of tautology. Although the formal definition of tautology on the basis of truth-tables seems to have been an idea of Wittgenstein's, I have no doubt that Russell has always clearly seen this fact and used it for the definition of logical formulae. The necessity expressed by logical formulae de-

[1] Chas. S. Peirce, *Collected Papers*, Cambridge, 1932, Vol. II, 199.
[2] A presentation of these results has, however, not yet been published.

rives from the fact that they are true whatever be the truth-values of their constituents. This tautological character of logical propositions, on the other hand, represents the ground of their emptiness; and Russell has always emphasized that a logical formula states nothing. He saw, at the same time, that this result does not make logic superfluous. On the contrary, the use of logic within all forms of scientific thought is based on the fact that logic is empty. Were it not so, we would not be allowed to add logical formulae to empirical assumptions. Logical transformations exhibit the inherent meanings of such assumptions without secretly increasing their content. Moreover, although a tautology is empty, the statement that a certain formula is a tautology is not empty; and the discovery of new and intricate tautologies will always remain a challenge to the logician or mathematician. The history of mathematics, revealing more and more unexpected tautological relations, represents a proof of this contention.

I should like to add here a remark concerning Russell's distinction between inference and implication. Although at the time he wrote the *Principia* the present distinction between levels of language (with which we have to deal later) was not yet known, Russell clearly saw that inference and implication are of a different logical nature. Whereas implication is an operation connecting propositions and leading to a new proposition, inference represents a procedure, performed on propositions. Russell emphasized that inferences cannot be stated in a formula, a result which may appear somewhat paradoxical, since he symbolized it in the traditional schema

$$\frac{p \supset q}{q}$$

We know today that the correct formulation is to say that the schema belongs to the metalanguage; that the formalization of inference can be given, not in statements of the object language, but only in the metalanguage. This formulation given at a later stage was anticipated by Russell's original distinction of formalizable and non-formalizable parts of logic.

I have mentioned here only a few prominent points among Russell's technical contributions to symbolic logic, since an extensive historical study is not included in the program of my paper. There remains to be given an analysis of Russell's views on the foundations of logic. But we cannot go into this problem without having first outlined his theory of the relation between logic and mathematics.

IV

What Russell claims to have shown is the identity of logic and mathematics, or, more precisely, that mathematics is a part of logic. The proof of this thesis is given in two steps. On the first he gives a definition of the positive integers, or natural numbers, showing that they are expressible in terms of purely logical notions including the operators "all" and "there is." On the second he shows, in correspondence with theories developed by other mathematicians, that the whole of mathematics is reducible to the notion of natural number.

The enormous significance of this theory is evident. If it is true, the whole of mathematics is reducible to logical statements containing only the simplest logical concepts; although the translation of a complicated mathematical formula into such simple notions cannot actually be carried through because of the limitations of man's technical abilities, the statement that such a translation can be carried through *in principle* represents a logical insight of an amazing depth. The unification of mathematics and logic so constructed can be compared to the unification of physics and chemistry attained in Bohr's theory of the atom, a result which also can be stated only in principle, since the actual translation of a chemical reaction into quantum processes involving only protons, electrons, and so on, cannot be carried through. Here, as in the case of Russell's logical theory of mathematics, it is the fact that there is such an ultimate unity which has excited the admiration of scientists and philosophers alike.

I shall not here go into the discussion of the second step. The reducibility of mathematics to the theory of natural numbers is regarded as possible by the majority of mathematicians. The interesting version given to this theory by Russell, according to which the irrational numbers are to be conceived as classes of rational numbers, is a continuation of a principle which in its full import was introduced by him within his analysis of the first step; and we shall discuss this *principle of abstraction* in that connection.

Let us, therefore, enter directly into an examination of the first step. Russell's definition of number is based on the discovery, anticipated in Cantor's theory of sets, that the notion of "equal number" is prior to that of number. Using Cantor's concept of similarity of classes, Russell defines two classes as having the same number if it is possible to establish a one-to-one coördination between the elements of these classes. Thus when we start from the class constituted by the men Brown, Jones and Robinson, the class constituted by Miller, Smith and Clark will have the same number because we can establish a one-to-one correspondence between the elements of these classes. Now the class of all classes which have the same number as the class constituted by Brown, Jones and Robinson is considered by Russell as constituting the number 3. A number is therefore a class of classes.

It may appear strange that a number, which seems to be a very simple logical element, is to be interpreted by so complicated a notion as a class of classes, or a totality of totalities, of physical things; a concept which includes so many classes of unknown objects. But Russell shows that this definition provides us with all the properties required for a number. When we say that there are 3 chairs in this room, all we wish to say is that there is a relation of one-to-one correspondence between the class of these chairs and certain other classes, such as Brown, Jones and Robinson; a relation which can be expressed, for instance, in the fact that, if Brown, Jones and Robinson sit down on these chairs, there will be no chair left, and each of the men will have his chair. It is this property of the class of the chairs which we express by saying that this class has the number 3; and since having a property is translatable into being a member of a certain class, we can state this property also by saying that the class of the chairs is a member of the class of classes which by the above definition is called the number 3.

This definition of number represents an illustrative application of the *principle of abstraction,* which has been made by Russell one of the cornerstones of logic. To define a property by abstraction has usually been interpreted as a rule singling out the common property of the objects concerned. Russell saw that the rule: "consider the property which such and such objects have in common," is in this form of a questionable meaning. He replaces it by the rule: "consider the class constituted by all objects having a certain given relation to each other;" i.e., he defines the common property in extension rather than in intension. Once more we see here the principle of extensionality at work. Russell shows that it is unnecessary to go beyond the extensional definition. All that can be said about the common property can be replaced by the statement that something is a member of this class. Thus in order to say what "green" means we shall point to a green object and define: a thing is green if it has the same color as this thing. The meaning of the word "green" therefore is definable by the statement: something is green if it is a member of the class of things which have the same color as this thing. We see that the principle of abstraction expressed in this sort of definition represents an application of Occam's razor; it would be an "unnecessary multiplication of entities," if we were to distinguish the meaning of the word "green" from the membership in the class defined. In the same sense Russell's definition of number constitutes a standard example of an application of Occam's razor.

Since a definition by abstraction refers to physical objects as determining the property under consideration, the definition of number above given is an ostensive definition. For example, in order to define the number 3 we point to some objects such as Brown, Jones and Robinson and say it is the number of *this* class which we call '3.' Russell has however given another definition of number which is not of the ostensive type, and we must now analyze the nature of this definition.

This *logical* definition of number applied to the number 1 is written in the form

$$(F \, \varepsilon \, 1) =_{\text{Df}} (\exists x)(x \, \varepsilon \, F) \cdot (y)[(y \, \varepsilon \, F) \supset (y = x)]$$

This definition states that a class F has the number 1 if the class has a member so that if anything is the member of the class it is identical with this member. Similarly we can state that a class F has the number 3 by the following formula

$$F \,\varepsilon\, 3 =_{\text{Df}} (\exists x)(\exists y)(\exists z) \cdot (x \,\varepsilon\, F) \cdot (y \,\varepsilon\, F) \cdot (z \,\varepsilon\, F) \cdot (x \neq y) \cdot (y \neq z)$$

$$(x \neq z) \cdot (u)[(u \,\varepsilon\, F) \supset (u = x) \lor (u = y) \lor (u = z)]$$

This is equally a logical definition since it does not refer to three physical objects in an ostensive way. It is true that the definition itself contains three symbols, namely existential operators, which thus represent a class of three physical objects in extension. But the definition does not refer to these objects, since it does not speak about the signs occurring in it. It would be different if, for instance, we were to write the word "green" always in green ink and then to say: green is the color of this sign. Such a definition refers to a property of a symbol occurring in it and is therefore ostensive.

In order to see clearly what is achieved in Russell's logical definition of number let us consider his definition of the number 1. Here the meaning of the term "one" is reduced to the meaning of some other terms including the term "there is a thing having the property F." The meaning of this latter sentence must be known when we wish to understand the definition. It is a primitive term in Russell's sense. Now it is clear that this term practically contains the meaning of "one." For instance, we must know that the sentence "there is an apple in the basket" is true even when there is only one apple in the basket. We could define the existential operator in such a way that an existence statement is true only when there are at least two objects of the kind considered. That this is not the ordinary meaning of the phrase "there is," is something we have to know when we apply existential operators. Therefore the meaning of the term "at least one" is antecedent to Russell's definition of the number 1. This does not make this definition circular, since, as the definition shows, the meaning of the *number* 1 is given by a rather complicated combination of primitive terms, among which the primitive "at least one" is only one constituent.

Let us now consider the relation of Russell's definition to Peano's axiomatic definition of natural numbers.

Peano in his famous five axioms has stated the formal properties of natural numbers. These axioms contain the two undefined concepts "the first number," and "successor." Peano then defines by the use of his axioms what a natural number is.[3] His definition is a recursive definition; therefore we can paraphrase it by saying that something is a natural number if it is derivable from the two fundamental concepts in compliance with the rules stated in the axioms. It is well known that Peano's definition admits of a wider interpretation than that given by the natural numbers. The even numbers, e.g., satisfy Peano's axioms if the interpretation of the term successor is suitably chosen. The series defined by Peano has therefore been given the more general name of a *progression*. This result shows that, as in the case of all axiomatic definitions, or implicit definitions, we must distinguish between the *formal system* and its *interpretation*.

This may be illustrated by the example of geometry. An axiomatic construction of Euclidean geometry, such as that given by Hilbert, though fully listing all internal properties of the fundamental notions, must be supplemented by *coördinative definitions* of these notions when the formal system is to be applied to reality. Thus physical geometry is derived from Hilbert's system by the use of coördinative definitions, according to which straight lines are interpreted as light rays, points as small parts of matter, congruence as a relation expressed in the behavior of solid bodies, etc. This interpretation is not a consequence of the formal system; and there are many other admissible interpretations. But these other interpretations do not furnish what we call *physical* geometry.

Similarly it is only one of the interpretations of Peano's system which represents the series of natural numbers. It is here that Russell's definition comes in: this definition furnishes an interpretation of Peano's system. Russell's definition can be

---

[3] This, at least, is our present conception of Peano's axioms, based on the work of Frege and Russell. Peano himself considered the notion of natural number as a third undefined concept and seems to have regarded all his axioms as synthetic.

used to define the *first number* (it may be advisable to use here the number one, and not the number zero used by Peano, in order to make the definition clearer), and in addition to define the successor relation. All the rest is then done by Peano's axioms; these axioms will lead to the consequence that all numbers are classes of classes in Russell's sense. The system so obtained may be called the Peano system in Russell's interpretation. It is this system which we use in all applications.

The necessity of combining Peano's definition with his own has been recognized by Russell in his discussion of the principle of mathematical induction. This principle, also called the principle of recurrence, is used in the famous inference from n to n + 1, applied in many mathematical proofs. When it is shown that the number 1 has a certain property, for instance that of satisfying a certain equation; and when it is shown in addition that if a number n has this property the number n + 1 must have this property also, then we regard it as proved that all numbers have this property. How do we know the validity of this inference? We can actually perform this inference only for a certain number of steps, and we cannot run through an infinite number of such steps and therefore cannot extend the inference in this way to all numbers. Poincaré therefore regarded the principle of mathematical induction as a synthetic principle *a priori*. It was Frege and, independently, Russell who recognized that a very simple solution to this problem can be found: the principle must be considered as constituting a part of the definition of natural numbers. It thus distinguishes this series from other series which do not have this property, and represents a specific feature which less strictly is expressed by saying that every element of the series can be reached in a finite number of steps, although the number of all elements is infinite.

When this conception is to be utilized for Russell's definition of number we must notice that this is possible only because of a certain peculiarity of recursive definitions. The Peano system contains the three fundamental notions "first number," "successor," and "natural number." But only the first two of these are undefined; the third is defined in terms of the two others. Therefore, only these first two fundamental notions require coördinative definitions; the interpretation of the third notion then is determined by the given two coördinative definitions in combination with the formal system. In other words, the totality of physical objects belonging to the system is defined in a recursive way in terms of the interpretations of the first two fundamental notions.

To make this clear let us consider a similar example limited to a finite series. Let us assume that there is a certain male fly with pink wings, and that there is a law according to which the male descendants of such a fly will also in general have pink wings. The first fly may be called the Adam fly. We now define the term "color family derived from the Adam fly" as follows: 1) the Adam fly belongs to this family; 2) if any fly belongs to the family then each one of its male offspring belongs to it which has the same color of wings as its male parent. These two definitions are sufficient to determine a totality of flies; it is this totality to which we give the above name. The family will presumably be finite, because at a certain stage there will be no male offspring with pink wings or no offspring at all. It is not necessary, however, to give any direct definition of this totality, i.e., a definition which allows us to determine whether a given individual fly belongs to this totality without examining its relations to the Adam fly. In the same sense the totality of natural numbers is defined if the first number and the successor relation are defined, as soon as the limitation of the totality through the inductive axiom has been added.

The interpretation of Peano's axioms given by Russell's definition of number is of a peculiar kind. It does not refer Peano's undefined notions to empirical terms, as is done by the physical interpretation of geometry. When we use Russell's logical definition of the number 1 we do not introduce any new notions into the Peano system. All the notions used in the above logical definition of the number 1 are equally used in Peano's formal system. Thus the statement that each element of the progression has one and only one successor, when formalized, is written in the same way as the definition of the number 1, by the use of an existential operator followed by a qualification in terms of an all-operator and an identity sign. Russell's interpretation of the

Peano system must therefore be called a logical interpretation, to be distinguished from an empirical interpretation.

For this reason it is possible to regard Russell's definition of number, not as an interpretation but as a supplementation of Peano's system. We can simply write Russell's definition of the number 1 as a sixth axiom, to be added to Peano's five axioms. Similarly the definition of the successor relation can be expressed in a purely logical way and then added as a seventh axiom. The Peano system thus is made complete and loses its character as a system of implicit definitions, since the terms "first number" and "successor" are no longer undefined. When used in the first five axioms they stand only as abbreviations for what is said in the sixth and seventh axiom. It then is even possible to prove Peano's axioms, with the exception of the axiom of infinity. The latter axiom seems to be a condition which we must write as an *implicans* before the whole of mathematics, thus conceiving mathematics ultimately as a system of implications.

I think, therefore, that Russell is right when he says a logical definition of natural number can be given. He is also right when he insists that the meaning of the number 1 used in mathematics is expressed by his definition, and that the mathematical number 1 is not completely defined when it is conceived as a term defined implicitly in Peano's five axioms. This is clear also from the fact that Peano's five axioms use the complete meaning of "one," in Russell's sense, within the statement that each element of the series has *one and only one* successor. We saw that the formalization of this expression requires all the means used in Russell's definition of "one." Using this result we can say that, in the formalist interpretation, the Russell numbers are implicitly contained; they occur in such notations as "the first successor," "the second successor," "the twelfth successor," etc. What the formalist uses, when he applies Peano's axioms to arithmetic, are not the undefined elements, but these successor numbers. All that Russell says, then, is that the latter numbers should be used for the interpretation of the undefined elements of the system. To refuse this would simply represent a tactics of evasion.

I should like to add a remark concerning the application of arithmetical concepts to physics. The formalists are inclined to regard this application as being of the same type as the application of geometry, namely as based on coördinative definitions of the empirical kind. The first to express this conception was Helmholtz.[4] He explains that, e.g., the concept of addition can be realized by various physical operations; we then must check whether the operation used actually has the properties required for an addition. Thus, if we empty a bag of apples into a basket containing apples also, this operation has the character of an arithmetical addition. On the other hand, mixing hydrogen molecules and oxygen molecules at a rather high temperature does not have the character of an addition since these molecules will disintegrate into atoms and then combine to water molecules in such a way that the number of water molecules is not the sum of the numbers of hydrogen molecules and oxygen molecules. This conception seems to contradict the logical interpretation of arithmetic, according to which no empirical coördinative definition concerning the arithmetical fundamentals is necessary.

I think this contradiction can be eliminated as follows. We frequently do apply arithmetic in Helmholtz's sense by the use of coördinative definitions of the empirical type. But there is, besides, the purely logical application in Russell's sense. The latter is given only when the arithmetical operations are not connected with any physical change of the objects concerned. Thus adding five apples to seven apples in Russell's sense means that as long as a class of five apples and a separate class of seven apples exist, these two classes can be simultaneously conceived as one class of twelve apples. Russell's conception does not say whether this additive relation holds when the joined class is the result of a physical process to which the original classes are submitted, e.g., by putting the apples into the same bag. A statement that in the latter case we also can speak of arithmetical addition is of the Helmholtz-kind. In this case we leave the sign

[4] H. V. Helmholtz, "Zählen und Messen erkenntnistheoretisch betrachtet," 1887. Reprinted in Schlick-Hertz, *Helmholtz' Schriften zur Erkenntnistheorie*, Berlin, 1921, 70.

of arithmetical addition logically uninterpreted, and interpret it, instead, by means of a coördinative definition of the empirical type. The logical definition of number operations can be conceived as the limiting case of empirical definitions holding when no physical changes are involved. It does not depend on physical assumptions, because its application is empty, like all statements of deductive logic, and leads merely to logical transformations of statements. It is true that the practical value of arithmetic derives from its frequent use in combination with coördinative definitions of the empirical kind. But it is also true that such definitions would be useless if we had no purely logical definition of number: we state, in such cases, that the addition, which has been defined empirically, leads to the same result as an addition which is logically defined. If numbers were not used in the meaning given by the logical definition, arithmetic could not be applied to physical operations. It is the historical significance of Russell's logic to have pointed out this fact.

V

I must turn now to a discussion of Russell's *theory of types*. After having discovered the antinomy of the class of classes which do not include themselves, Russell saw that too liberal a use of functions of functions, or classes of classes, leads into contradictions. He therefore introduced a rule narrowing down such use. This is the rule of types.

It is the basic idea of this theory that the division of linguistic expressions into true and false is not sufficient; that a third category must be introduced which includes *meaningless* expressions. It seems to me that this is one of the deepest and soundest discoveries of modern logic. It represents the insight that a set of syntactical rules—Carnap now calls them *formation rules*—must be explicitly stated in order to make language a workable system, and that it is a leading directive for the establishment of such rules that the resulting language be free from contradictions. We need not ask whether or not a certain expression is "really" meaningful; it is a sufficient condition for absence of meaning when a certain sort of expression leads to contradictions. It is from this viewpoint that I have always regarded the theory of types. This theory is an instrument to make language consistent. This is its justification; and there can be no better one.

In the further development of the theory of types Russell introduced a second form; to the *simple* theory of types he later added the *ramified* theory of types. The simple theory of types states that a function is of a higher type than its argument; it follows that classes which contain themselves cannot be defined. This simple rule has found the consent of most logicians and appears at present so natural to the younger generation of logicians that it has acquired an almost self-evident character. Such is the fate of all great discoveries; artificial and sophisticated as they may appear at the time when they are first pronounced, after a while nobody can imagine why they had not been recognized from the very beginning. "Truth is allotted only a short period of triumph between the two infinitely long intervals in which it is condemned as paradox or belittled as trivial," says Schopenhauer.

The ramified theory of types, on the contrary, has met with much aversion on the side of the logicians. According to this theory every type must be subdivided into functions of different orders so that each order can contain only lower orders as their argument. Russell saw that this restriction excludes too great a part of mathematics. To save this group of mathematical theorems he introduced the axiom of reducibility, according to which to every function of a higher order there exists a corresponding function of the first order which is extensionally equivalent to it. Russell himself seems not to have been too much pleased with this axiom, although he sometimes defended it as being of the same sort as Zermelo's axiom of choice.

Meanwhile a more convenient solution of the difficulties was given by the line of thought which was attached to Ramsey's classification of the paradoxes into logical and semantical ones and which has been continued by Carnap and Tarski. Logical paradoxes are those in which only functions are involved; in semantical paradoxes, on the other hand, we are concerned with the use of *names* of functions alongside of the functions themselves. A paradox of this sort is the statement of the Cretan who says that all Cretans lie. For the purpose of logical analysis, this historically famous paradox is better simplified to the form "this statement is false," where the word "this" refers to the sentence in which it occurs. It was only this sort of paradox which made the introduction of the ramified theory of types necessary; for the paradoxes of the logical sort the simple theory of types is sufficient. Now it has been shown that the semantical paradoxes can be ruled out if in addition to the theory of *types* a theory of *levels of language* is introduced. According to this theory the object language must be distinguished from the metalanguage, a distinction carried on to the introduction of a meta-metalanguage, and so on. Disregarding some exceptions, it is in general considered as meaningless if a linguistic expression refers to the language in which it is contained. This extension of the theory of types to a theory of levels of language was anticipated by Russell himself who, in his Introduction to Wittgenstein's *Tractatus*, referring to the problem of generality, wrote:[5]

These difficulties suggest to my mind some such possibility as this: that every language has, as Mr. Wittgenstein says, a structure concerning which, *in the language*, nothing can be said, but there may be another language dealing with the structure of the first language, and having itself a new structure, and that to this hierarchy of languages there may be no limit.

It seems to me, therefore, that the theories of Carnap and Tarski about the distinction of levels of language represent merely a continuation of ideas originating from Russell himself, a continuation which perhaps also includes ideas derived from Frege and Hilbert. Russell has recently published a statement[6] expressing on the whole his consent to Carnap's exposition of this linguistic solution of the semantical paradoxes. Thus it seems that this is at least a point on which a general consensus of opinion is attainable.

[5] Ludwig Wittgenstein: *Tractatus Logico-Philosophicus*, London, 1922, 23.
[6] In his new Introduction to the second edition of his *Principles of Mathematics*, New York, 1938.

VI

I should like now to discuss a question as to the foundation of logic; a question which has often occurred to me when I was studying Russell's logic.

Russell has emphasized that logic is not purely formal, that it contains some primitive terms whose meaning must be understood before we can enter into formal operations. He has listed these primitive terms, among them propositional operations and the existential operator, or, instead of the latter, the all-operator. Equally, some of the axioms of logic must be understood as necessarily true; then other formulae can be formally derived from them. Later analysis has shown that it is possible to eliminate all material thinking from the object language and to define logical necessity as a formal property of formulae, namely the property of being true for all truth-values of their constituent propositions. But the results of this formalization should not be overestimated, since in performing it we cannot dispense with material thinking in the metalanguage. Russell is therefore justified in that primitive notions and propositions will remain necessary at least on one level of language. Although they can also be eliminated from the metalanguage, they will reappear in the meta-metalanguage and so on. For instance, in the construction of truth-tables, which belong to the metalanguage, we take it for granted that for two elementary propositions only the four combinations "true-true," "true-false," "false-true," and "false-false" are possible. This means an application in the metalanguage of the same sort of tautologies as are formally proved within the object language.

It appears indeed inevitable that the directive of self-evidence has to be followed. In saying so I do not intend to introduce a sort of apriorism into logic. When we use a logical statement as self-evident we do not combine with this use the claim that the statement will always appear evident. If tomorrow we discover that we were mistaken we shall be ready to correct our statement, and shall follow new evidence, once more without the claim of eternal validity. It seems to me that in this sense the concept of *posit*, which I have introduced within the analysis of inductive inference, applies also to deductive logic. It is true, if we make an inductive posit we can very well imagine that it be false; whereas when we state a logical tautology we cannot imagine that the formula be false. But we can imagine that tomorrow we shall *say* that it is false. The procedure of positing is here in the metalanguage. The formula "p ∨ ∼ p" is a tautology; but *that* it is a tautology is not a tautology, but an empirical statement concerning a group of signs given to the sense of sight.[7] The statement about the tautological character has therefore only the reliability of empirical statements, and can only be *posited*.

I should believe that this conception corresponds to Russell's views, and I should like to know whether he considers it as a satisfactory solution of the problem of self-evidence.

The revision of opinion which we reserve with every statement of a self-evident character can be of two sorts. First, we must always envisage the possibility of an error in the sense of a slip of the controls of our thinking. Of this sort are errors made in the addition of numbers, or in the committing of logical fallacies. A second sort of error is of a deeper nature. It consists in not seeing that our statement is true only within certain limitations, that it depends on certain assumptions which we do not explicitly state, but which if once stated can be abandoned. We shall thus arrive at generalizations within which our former statement appears as a special case. It is self-evident for this special case, but outside this usage it is simply false.

An example of this sort seems to me to be given in the *tertium non datur*. This principle has long been considered as one of the pillars of logic; and it is used so not only in traditional logic, but equally in Russell's logic. But modern developments have shown that the principle can be abandoned. That either "p" or "non-p" is true, holds only for a two-valued logic; but if we use, instead, a three-valued logic, the principle is false. An unqualified validity must be replaced by a qualified

---

[7] It is true that we can construct in the metalanguage a tautological statement by *describing* the formula "p ∨ ∼ p" and then saying that such a formula is a tautology. But then it remains an empirical question whether a certain formula written on paper has these properties. We ultimately must always refer to statements which are thus empirically given.

validity; the *tertium non datur* is valid only with respect to certain assumptions about the nature of propositions.

Propositions can be classified in various ways. It is customary to divide them into the two categories of true and false propositions; if this is done the *tertium non datur* is self-evident. But that propositions *must* be divided into these two categories can by no means be asserted. The necessity of the *tertium non datur* is therefore of a relative nature; the formula is necessary with respect to a dichotomy of propositions. This division of propositions, on the other hand, has the character of a *convention*. It therefore can never be proved false; but it can equally be replaced by another convention, e.g., a trichotomy of propositions. Which sort of classification is to be used will depend on the purposes for which the classification is made. When the dichotomy leads to a system of knowledge satisfying the exigencies of human behavior it will be considered as reasonable; this is the ground on which we use a two-valued logic in conversational language and equally in the language of classical science. But it may happen that for certain purposes a dichotomy will appear unreasonable and that a classification of propositions into three categories will seem preferable. We then shall not hesitate to use a three-valued logic and thus abandon the *tertium non datur*.

The reasons determining the usefulness of a classification of propositions will depend on the purposes for which the classification is used and on the means by which it is carried through. To speak of "Truth in itself" and "Falsehood in itself," existing as Platonic ideas, constitutes a method which has no relation to actual procedures of knowledge. We cannot use this sort of truth-value. The notion of truth used in actual knowledge is so defined that it is related to what actually can be done. We have methods to find out the truth, and if no such methods existed it would be no use to speak of true propositions. This does not mean that we are always able to apply these methods; there may be technical limitations to them. But we require that in principle such methods should be given; otherwise the notion of truth would be a castle in the air.

These considerations show that when we speak of truth in ordinary language we actually mean verifiability, i.e., the possibility of verification. Russell has objected that, by a restriction of language to verifiable statements, many statements which we usually regard as meaningful, would be cancelled from the domain of meaning. I do not think that a theory replacing truth by verifiability must lead to these consequences. If the notion of verifiability is defined in a sufficiently wide sense, it will include all sorts of statements which Russell would like to consider as true or false, such as his example "it snowed on Manhattan Island on the first of January in the year 1 A.D."[8] This aim can be reached if the term "possibility," applied within the expression "verifiability," is suitably defined. It certainly would narrow down meanings too much if we should require that a sentence be true only when it is actually verified. In the latter case it is *known* to be true; but "true" is defined in the wider meaning that a sentence is true if it can be shown to satisfy certain conditions, called verification. Similarly, a sentence will be called false if it can be shown that the sentence does not satisfy these conditions.

Are we then allowed to say: for every sentence it is possible to show that it is either true or false? I do not think that a logician can have the courage to assert such a far-reaching statement, if he does not have a proof for it.

Arguments of this sort have first been used by Brouwer in his famous criticism of mathematical methods. His three-valued logic is somewhat complicated because of its application to mathematics. Mathematics is a completely deductive science; its truth is determined by logical methods alone and does not refer to observation. The only way to determine whether a mathematical formula is true, is by deriving it from the axioms of mathematics, whose truth may be regarded as shown by self-evidence. When a mathematical formula of a syntactically correct form is given, is it possible, in principle, either to derive this formula or its negation from the axioms? Brouwer has raised this question; he regards it as unanswerable and there-

[8] Russell's *An Inquiry Into Meaning and Truth*, New York (1940), 347. As to a wider form of the verifiability theory of meaning, cf. the author's *Experience and Prediction*, Chicago (1938), Chapter I. The conception that verifiability is a pragmatic concept is perhaps a consequence of too narrow a definition of verifiability, resulting in particular from reference to technical, instead of physical, possibility in this definition. It may be possible to construct verifiability as a semantic notion.

fore insists on a division of mathematical statements into the three categories of true, false, and indeterminate. If we could give an affirmative answer to that question, Brouwer's trichotomy would be dispensable. But we all know that thus far such a proof has not been given. Gödel's theorem has shown that if we submit mathematical demonstrability to certain limitations there certainly are "undecidable" formulae. But Gödel also shows that the truth or falsehood of these formulae can be found out by methods using the metalanguage. Thus the controversy is still open.

Russell answers considerations of this sort by distinguishing truth from verifiability;[9] he thinks that independently of whether we are able to find the truth we should assert the principle that a sentence is, or is not, true. I do not see what this principle can mean other than a convention. If we are not given any methods to find out a truth, all we can do is to say that we wish to retain the formula "$p \vee \sim p$" for all sorts of statements. But if this convention is established for a purely deductive science such as mathematics, there will arise the question of consistency. If it were possible to show that the postulate of the *tertium non datur* will never lead to contradictions, its establishment would represent a permissible convention. But Hilbert and his collaborators, in spite of ingenious advances in this direction, have so far not been able to give the proof.

For empirical sciences the situation is different. Here the methods of verification are widely dependent on conventions, at least when physical objects which are not directly observable are concerned. It is therefore possible to combine the postulate of the *tertium non datur* with the principle of verifiability, if suitable conventions as to the method of verification are introduced. But if this is done, another problem may arise which represents, for empirical languages, the correlate of the problem of consistency existing for a deductive science: this is the problem whether the use of a two-valued language is compatible with certain other fundamental principles usually maintained for empirical sciences.

A case of this sort has turned up in recent developments in

[9] *Ibid.*, Chapter XVI.

physics, namely in quantum mechanics. We are facing here the question whether we shall introduce rules determining the values of unobserved entities, and thus introduce a two-valued logic in the sphere of the quanta. Now the results of quantum mechanics can be so interpreted that when we insist upon constructing the language of physics in a two-valued manner it will be impossible to satisfy the postulate of causality, even when an extension of causal connections to probability connections is admitted. The violations of the principle of causality are of another kind; they consist in the appearance of an action at a distance. On the other hand, it can be shown that causal anomalies disappear when the statements of quantum mechanics are incorporated into a three-valued logic. Between true and false statements we then shall have indeterminate statements; and the methods by which the truth-values of statements are derived from empirical observations are so constructed that they will classify any quantum mechanical statement in one of the three categories.[10]

This situation resembles very much the development of the problem of physical geometry. After it had been shown that in addition to Euclidean geometry several other geometrical systems can be constructed, the question as to which geometry holds for the physical world could be answered only on the basis of a convention. It could be shown, furthermore, that some of these conventions, if used for the description of the physical world, will lead to causal anomalies. Thus Einstein's theory of general relativity leads to the result that a use of Euclidean geometry for the description of the physical universe leads to causal anomalies. This is the reason that Euclidean geometry has been abandoned and replaced by a Riemannian geometry.[11] Similarly, we must distinguish between various logical systems and make the question of application dependent on the sort of physical system so obtained.

I do not see why this conception of the *tertium non datur*

---

[10] This interpretation of quantum mechanics is given in a book by the author on the *Philosophic Foundations of Quantum Mechanics*, in press at the University of California Press.

[11] Cf. the author's *Philosophie der Raum-Zeitlehre*, Berlin (1928), §12.

should lead to difficulties. I do not quite understand Russell's[12] insistence upon the law of excluded middle; in particular I am not clear whether he considers the law as *a priori* or has other reasons for insisting upon this law. I should be glad to get Professor Russell's opinion on this point.

One argument may be stated in favor of the superiority of the *tertium non datur*. The multi-valued logics introduced by Brouwer, Post, Lucasiewicz and Tarski, including the three-valued logic of quantum mechanics, are so constructed that the metalanguage coördinated to them is two-valued. Thus we can say in the metalanguage of a three-valued logic of this type, "a proposition is either true or it is not true," in the ordinary meaning of the word *not*. That the category "not true" divides into the two categories "indeterminate" and "false," makes for the metalanguage no more difficulties than, for our ordinary two-valued logic, a division say of a country's armed forces into the three categories of army, navy and air force. It is this use of a two-valued metalanguage which makes the multi-valued logical system very simple and easy to handle. I do not think, however, that it is necessary always to use a two-valued metalanguage. Elsewhere I have given an example[13] of a multi-valued logic applied within an infinite series of metalanguages. It is true that the metalanguage in which this theorem is stated, and which is not contained in the denumerable infinity of the metalanguages to which the theorem refers, is two-valued. But it should be possible to define a method by which each two-valued language on every level can be translated into a multi-valued language; this method would then be applicable also to the language in which it is stated.

Our preference for a two-valued logic seems to be based on psychological reasons only. This logic is of a very simple nature, and we shall therefore prefer it to other conventions concerning a classification of propositions. On the other hand, a closer consideration shows that the two-valued logic which we use in all these cases is never strictly two-valued, but rather must be considered as resulting from probability logic by the

---

[12] *An Inquiry Into Meaning and Truth*, Chapters XX and XXI.
[13] *Wahrscheinlichkeitslehre*, Leiden (1935), 371.

method of division, which I have described elsewhere.[14] Such a logic satisfies the usual rules only with exceptions. Thus if "p" is true and "q" is true, it may occasionally happen that "p and q" is false. These discrepancies can be eliminated when the two-valued logic is replaced by a probability logic; the logic of the metalanguage used will then be once more of the approximately two-valued type, but with a higher degree of approximation, i.e., with fewer exceptions. This process can be continued. The replacement of a two-valued logic by a multi-valued logic and the use of a two-valued logic on a higher level, therefore, seems to represent only a method of proceeding to a higher degree of approximation. But a strictly two-valued language is perhaps never used.

VII

Russell's logic is a *deductive* logic. It never was intended to be anything else; and its value derives from the fact that it represents an analysis of the analytic, or demonstrative, components of thought. But Russell has frequently recognized that there are other components which have a synthetic character and which include *inductive* methods.

I think we should be grateful that a man, who has devoted so much of his work to deductive logic and who has given a new foundation to this science, which in its modern form will for ever be connected with his name, has never pretended that deductive operations can cover the whole of cognitive thought. Russell has repeatedly emphasized the need for inductive methods and recognized the peculiar difficulties of such methods. He thus makes it clear that he does not belong to the category of logicians who claim that the cognitive process can be completely interpreted in terms of deductive operations, and who deny the existence of an inductive logic. It is indeed hardly understandable how such utterances can be made, in view of the fact that knowledge includes predictions, and that no deductive bridge can lead from past experiences to future observations. A logic which does not include an analysis of inductive inference will always remain incomplete.

Now it is a perfectly sound method to restrict one's field of

[14] *Experience and Prediction*, Chicago (1938), §36.

work to one sort of thought operations and to leave the analysis of another sort to others. And yet I should like to ask Professor Russell to tell us a little more about his personal opinions in this other field. His books occasionally contain very interesting remarks on induction. Thus we find in one of his writings a well-aimed caricature of a familiar misinterpretation of the inductive inference. The latter is regarded by some logicians as being of the form: p implies q, now we know q, therefore p. Russell[15] illustrates this inference by the example: "If pigs have wings, some winged animals are good to eat; now some winged animals are good to eat, therefore pigs have wings." I should like to add that I do not regard this sort of inference as being improved if the conclusion is stated in the form: "p is probable." I do not think it is probable that pigs have wings. Actually, the calculus of probabilities knows no such inference; and it appears hardly understandable why some logicians try to impose upon scientific method the use of an inference which every mathematician would refuse to recognize. I do not see, either, that the logic of the inference is improved when it is named an inference by confirmation.

I think an analysis of the problem of induction must be attached to the form of inductive inference which has always stood in the foreground of traditional inductive theories: the inference of induction by enumeration. It can be shown that all inductive methods, including the so-called inference by confirmation, are ultimately reducible to this sort of inference; more precisely: it can be proved that what such methods contain in addition to inductive inferences by enumeration, belongs to deductive logic. This is shown by the axiomatic construction of the calculus of probabilities.[16] I should like to believe that Russell agrees with this statement.

As to the analysis of induction by enumeration, the traditional discussion has been greatly influenced by the criticism of David Hume. I think Hume's proof that the conclusion of inductive

---

[15] In his contribution to: *The Philosophy of John Dewey*, Evanston and Chicago (1939), 149.

[16] Cf. the author's *Wahrscheinlichkeitslehre*, and his *Experience and Prediction*, chap. V.

inferences can never be proved to be true, is unquestionable. But I do not think that Hume's interpretation of induction as a habit is able to point a way out of the difficulties. Russell occasionally follows Hume by remarking that, in regarding inductive inference as a method of cognition, we turn *causes* of our belief into *grounds* of such belief.[17] If this were the only answer which could be given to the problem of induction, we should frankly state that modern logic is unable to account for scientific method.

Now it seems to me that Hume's treatment of the problem of induction, apart from its healthy refutation of all sorts of rationalism, has seriously biased later philosophies of induction. Even the empiricist camp has not overcome Hume's tacit presupposition that what is claimed as knowledge must be proven as true. But as soon as this assumption is discarded, the difficulties for a justification of induction are eliminated. I do not wish to say that we can at least demonstrate the inductive conclusion to be probable. The analysis of the theory of probability shows that not even this proof can be given. But a way out of Hume's skepticism can be shown when knowledge is conceived, not as a system of propositions having a determinable truth value or probability value, but as a system of posits used as tools for predicting the future. The question of whether the inductive inference represents a good tool can then be answered in the affirmative by means of considerations which do not use inductive inferences and therefore are not circular.

VIII

It is only within the frame of a system of knowledge which *as a whole* is posited that we can coördinate probability values to individual propositions. Here, in fact, probability replaces truth in so far as no empirical sentence is known to be true, but can be determined only as more or less probable.

Russell has argued that such a usage of probabilities does not eliminate the notion of truth. He contends that even in a probability theory of knowledge every sentence should be regarded as true or false, and that what a degree of probability refers to is

[17] *An Inquiry Into Meaning and Truth*, 305.

the degree to which a proposition is true.[18] I do not think that this conception is necessary. The sentences "p" and "p is true" are equipolent, and therefore it is of course permissible to attach the degree of probability either to the one or to the other. But it appears an unnecessary complication to use the second version; it is simpler to say directly that "p" is probable. Such a semantical interpretation of probabilities can be consistently carried through.[19]

The question may be asked whether the concept of truth is completely redundant. Russell is inclined to say that it is not, and that if it is eliminated from one place it will reappear in another place of the system of knowledge. I think this leads back to what was discussed in section VI. There is no doubt that, if a probability logic is used for the object language, the notion of truth is dispensable for this language. What can be asked is only whether the concept will reappear in the metalanguage. Now it seems that what I said about the approximately two-valued character of this language holds equally whether the object language is conceived as a three-valued system or as following the rules of a probability logic. Actually, what is called truth in conversational language has never had more than a high degree of probability. The truth of statements made under oath, for instance, is certainly not more than a probability of high degree. It seems that truth is a concept which we use only in idealized logical systems, but which in all applications is replaced by a substitute sharing only to a certain extent the properties of truth.

This result, it seems to me, applies also to the problem of basic statements. I think it is an outstanding feature in Russell's philosophy that he attaches so much importance to the empirical nature of basic statements. He has emphasized the necessity of an observational basis of science in discussions with some authors who apparently attempted to discard the notion of observation entirely from the exposition of scientific method. Russell here has carried on the empiricist tradition in opposition to logical

[18] *Ibid.*, 400.
[19] Cf. the author's "Über die semantische und die Objekt-Auffassung von Wahrscheinlichkeitsausdrücken," *Erkenntnis, Journal of Unified Science,* VIII, (1939), 50.

systems which, in spite of their claims to cover the method of empirical science, resemble only too much a modern form of rationalism. But, in spite of this agreement in general, I have to raise some objections to Russell's theory of basic statements as given in one of his recent publications.[20]

It seems to me that Russell's attempt to reduce the content of immediate observations to sense-data springs from the desire to find a basis of knowledge which is absolutely certain. I do not quite understand whether he wishes to say that sense-data statements are absolutely certain, or whether they possess only the highest degree of certainty attainable. But it seems clear that he wishes to construct a system of basic statements of such a kind that no basic statement can ever be shaken by later observations.[21] Now everybody will agree with Russell, I think, when he says that basic statements must be logically independent, i.e., that they must be so formulated that none of them can ever logically contradict another. But I cannot see how such an independence can be maintained when inductive methods are admitted.

Russell has argued[22] that basic statements cannot be empty, because if such statements were empty their sum also would be empty, and no synthetic knowledge could be derived from them. This, I think, is a sound argument. But I should like to use it in reverse also: if by the use of inductive methods basic statements will lead to a prediction of future observations, then such observations conversely will also make the original statements more or less certain. Inductive methods always work both ways. The rule of Bayes represents an inference by which probabilities holding in one direction are transformed into inverse probabilities. If, therefore, the system of knowledge is construed as being derived from basic observations in terms of inductive methods, this will include the admission that the totality of observations can be used as a test for the validity of an individual observation.

If this is once recognized, it appears no longer necessary to

[20] *An Inquiry Into Meaning and Truth,* Chapters X and XXII.
[21] *Ibid.,* 398.
[22] *Ibid.,* 395, 397.

look for basic statements different from statements of simple physical observations, i.e., to regard sense-data as the immediate object of observation. A set of less reliable statements will do, if such statements are of the observational type, i.e., if they are reports about concrete physical objects. If such basic statements have a sufficiently high initial weight, or in other words, if they are at least subjectively true in an approximate meaning of truth, they can be used for the construction of knowledge; and the probability of this knowledge can, on the whole, be even greater than the probability of any individual basic statement. That such possibilities are given by the use of probability methods may be illustrated by the fact that the average error of the mean of a set of observations is smaller than the error of the individual observations of this set. It is the advantage of the probability theory of knowledge that it frees us from the necessity of looking for a basis of data having absolute certainty.

IX

I have tried to outline the major results of Russell's logic; and I have ventured to criticize Russell's views on certain points. But I think that my criticism concerns what, for Russell's logic, are only minor points. This logic is not of a type which needs to be afraid of critique.

My exposition would be incomplete without the addition of some words concerning the influence of Russell's logical work on the present generation of philosophers. Comparing the general level of philosophical writings at the time when Russell wrote the *Principia* with that of today, we find a remarkable change. Studies in mathematical logic, which forty years ago appeared only occasionally and were read only by a small group of experts, today occupy a great part of the space filled by philosophical publications. A school of younger logicians has grown whose work, to a great extent, has been stimulated by the study of Russell's books and who have tried to continue Russell's methods even beyond the goal for which they were created. The knowledge of Russell's symbolism is today a necessary condition to pass any academic examination in logic; the discussion of Russell's theory of mathematics and of his theory of types plays a prominent part in philosophical seminars, and Russell's methods have become the tools by which a younger generation tills the philosophical soil. The logic and epistemology of today is unthinkable without Russell's contributions; his work has been assimilated even by those who in part contradict his views and look for other solutions.

It would be too optimistic an interpretation of this situation if we were to believe that the use of mathematical logic and its methods will always indicate profundity. Some decades ago we hoped, and I think I can include Russell in this "we," that if mathematical logic should some day become a part of general philosophical education, the times of vague discussions and obscure philosophical systems would be over. We cannot help admitting that our belief was based on a fallacious inference. We see today that the knowledge of symbolic logic is no guarantee for precision of thought or seriousness of analysis.

This has been shown, in particular, by some criticisms of Russell's more recent writings. I do not say this with the intention of condemning a critique of Russell's views. But I do think that such criticism should bear the mark of the same seriousness which distinguishes Russell's thought. Who criticizes Russell should first try to understand the major issues which always stand behind Russell's conceptions. It does not make a good show when a critic, who learned his logic from Russell, indicates with friendly condescension between his lines that he regards Russell's recent writings as not quite up-to-date. The reader might be induced to discover that the use of a meta-linguistic vocabulary is not a sufficient criterion for a more advanced state of logical analysis. What use is it to make minor distinctions, if these discriminations are irrelevant for the problems considered? There is such a thing as a fallacy of misplaced exactness; this may be mentioned to those who are inclined to strain out the gnat but to swallow the camel. A truly philosophical attitude will be shown in the ability to balance purpose and means, in the subordination of technical research to the general issue for which it is being undertaken.

It is this balancing of purpose and means which we can learn from Russell himself. The enormous technical work of the

Principia was done by him in the pursuit of a major philosophical aim, the unification of logic and mathematics. Russell's work bears witness that logical analysis can become an instrument for the solution of major philosophical problems. Let us not forget that a display of logical symbolism is not in itself the aim of philosophy. There are philosophical problems still unsolved; let us try to use logical technique in order to solve them. Let us look at Bertrand Russell as a man who, by the precision of his methods and by the largeness of his mind, has opened an approach to a philosophy adequate to our time.

HANS REICHENBACH

DEPARTMENT OF PHILOSOPHY
UNIVERSITY OF CALIFORNIA AT LOS ANGELES

2

Morris Weitz

ANALYSIS AND THE UNITY OF RUSSELL'S PHILOSOPHY

ANALYSIS AND THE UNITY OF RUSSELL'S PHILOSOPHY

IN this essay I shall attempt to prove three related propositions regarding Russell's philosophy: (1) The fundamental element in his philosophy is the method of analysis. (2) This method of analysis has been exemplified by him in four rather distinct ways, in ontology, abstract cosmology, mathematical logic, and in the examination of the symbolism of science and ordinary life. The first exemplification, because it has to do with the "stuff" of reality, I shall label "ontological analysis;" Russell himself calls the second exemplification "formal analysis," the third "logistic," and the fourth, among other expressions, "constructionism." A more adequate term, however, because of the unfortunate associations which have surrounded "constructionism,"[1] is the phrase, "the resolution of incomplete symbols," and I shall use it in referring to the application of analysis to scientific and common-sensical symbolism. (3) By analysis Russell—although he has never systematically said so —means mainly a form of definition, either real definition of a non-Aristotelian sort, or contextual definition, i.e., definition of symbols in use. The first two doctrines are proved together and occupy the first four sections, while the third doctrine is demonstrated in the final section.

Two important consequences result from the demonstration of these three doctrines. The first is that C. D. Broad's remark,[2]

---

[1] For example, many students of Russell seem to think that constructionism is concerned with the making of entities, the way a carpenter builds a house. Such a view is incorrect, but is wholly understandable because of the unfortunate term, "constructionism."

[2] "As we all know, Mr. Russell produces a different system of philosophy every

which he may have uttered in jest, but which many philosophers accept as a serious charge, to the effect that Russell is a flighty philosopher because he has published a new system of philosophy every few years, is absolutely untrue. Most of the changes in Russell's philosophy are minor ones and occur in his application of analysis to ontology. It is shown that these changes are due to a more rigorous application of his analytical method. Once the primacy of analysis is understood, it will become evident that there *is* a basic unity in his work, and that this unity revolves around his method.

The second consequence has to do with Russell's theory of analysis. Many contemporary philosophers[3] seem to regard it as axiomatic that philosophy never analyzes facts, i.e., that which is non-linguistic, but always symbols. Ayer, e.g., maintains that the *entirety* of philosophical analysis is contextual definition.[4] It will be seen, I think, that this is too narrow a view and does not exhaust philosophical analysis, especially as Russell has practiced it. Many of Russell's analyses, I shall show, are concerned with complexes which are primarily non-linguistic, and therefore have nothing to do with contextual definition.

SECTION I. ANALYSIS AS ONTOLOGY

Russell began his philosophical career as an Absolute Idealist, so far as ontological analysis is concerned. That is, he maintained that the fundamental stuff of reality was the Absolute Mind.[5] However, in 1898, G. E. Moore convinced him of the

few years . . . ," in "Critical and Speculative Philosophy," *Contemporary British Philosophy*, First Series, 79.

[3] Especially the logical positivists, Carnap and his followers.

[4] A. J. Ayer, *Language, Truth and Logic*, Ch. IV.

[5] "Logical Atomism" (hereafter L. A.), *Contemporary British Philosophy*, First Series, 360. A full alphabetical list of the abbreviations of Russell's works to be referred to in this essay is as follows: (1) *A. of Matter* = *The Analysis of Matter*; (2) *A. of Mind* = *The Analysis of Mind*; (3) *E. W.* = *Our Knowledge of the External World*; (4) *Inquiry* = *An Inquiry Into Meaning and Truth*; (5) *I.M.P.* = *Introduction to Mathematical Philosophy*; (6) K.A.D. = "Knowledge by Acquaintance and Knowledge by Description" (reprinted in *Mysticism and Logic*); (7) L. A. = "Logical Atomism;" (8) M. T. of C. = "Meinong's Theory of Complexes and Assumptions" (*Mind*, n.s., 1904); (9) M. T. of T. = "The Monistic Theory of Truth" (reprinted in *Philosophical Essays*, 1910); (10) N. of A. = "On the Nature of Acquaintance" (*Monist*, 1914); (11) *Phil.* =

inadequacy of this position.[6] The arguments used by Moore, and accepted by Russell, against Absolute Idealism, did not appear in print until 1903, in Russell's *P. of M.* and in Moore's "Refutation of Idealism,"[7] and 1906, in Russell's M. T. of T. Before 1903, however, Russell read Leibniz and

came to the conclusion . . . that many of his most characteristic opinions were due to the purely logical doctrine that every proposition has a subject and a predicate. This doctrine is one which Leibniz shares with Spinoza, Hegel and Mr. Bradley; it seemed to me that, if it is rejected, the whole foundation for the metaphysics of all these philosophers is shattered.[8]

In 1900 Russell published *P. of L.*, in which he proved that the most popular part of Leibniz' philosophy, the monadology, was a deduction from certain premisses, mainly logical, which Leibniz tacitly accepted as self-evident.[9]

Russell's motivation in his rejection of Absolute Idealism was his desire to establish the irreducibility of relations and a Platonic theory of propositions, which would render them independent of mental activity. He needed these doctrines in order to satisfy his desire to establish the foundations of mathematics.[10] Without these, mathematical philosophy is rendered self-contradictory, hence impossible.[11] Thus, in 1898, when Russell was working on the foundations of mathematics, he was quite willing

---

Philosophy; (12) P.L.A. = "Philosophy of Logical Atomism" (*Monist*, 1918/19); (13) *P. of L.* = *The Philosophy of Leibniz*; (14) *P.M.* = *Principia Mathematica*; (15) *P. of M.* = *The Principles of Mathematics*; (16) *P. of P.* = *The Problems of Philosophy*; (17) P: W. T. A. = "On Propositions: What They Are and How They Mean" (*Proceedings Aristotelian Society*, Suppl. Vol. 1919); (18) R. S. D. P. = "The Relation of Sense-Data to Physics" (*Mysticism and Logic*); (19) R. U. P. = "On the Relations of Universals and Particulars" (*Proceedings Aristotelian Society*, 1912); (20) S. M. P. = "On Scientific Method in Philosophy" (*Scientific Method in Philosophy*); (21) U.C.M. = "The Ultimate Constituents of Matter" (*Mysticism and Logic*).

[6] L. A., 360.
[7] This article first appeared in *Mind* (1903), 433-454.
[8] L. A., 360.
[9] *P. of L.*, 4.
[10] "I came to philosophy," Russell writes, "through mathematics or rather through the wish to find some reason to believe in the truth of mathematics." L. A., 359.
[11] *P. of M.*, xvii.

to accept a philosophy like Moore's dualism, which would give him an adequate basis for the non-self-contradictory character of extant mathematics.

By 1900 Russell was a dualist, contending that mind and matter, and universals and particulars, are ultimate. But before we can adequately discuss his arguments for dualism, we must say something more about his rejection of idealism.

His fundamental objection to idealism of the monistic and monadic sort, represented by Hegel and Leibniz respectively, is logical, whereas his refutation of Berkeley rests mainly upon empirical grounds. Absolute Idealism, Russell maintains, assumes as its basic axiom the doctrine of internal relations, the view that "every relation is grounded in the natures of the related terms."[12] It regards the axiom as equivalent to the assumptions that every relation is really an adjective of the terms taken as a whole and that every proposition has one subject and one predicate; from which it follows, Russell argues, that, for this view, there is only one final and complete truth which consists of one proposition with one subject (the Whole) and one predicate.[13]

Russell has three objections to the axiom: (1) It cannot be carried out, especially in the case of asymmetrical relations. If we try to reduce a relation like "greater than" to adjectives of the related terms, considered as a whole, we cannot then distinguish the relation from its converse; consequently, we cannot give any sense or direction to the relation.[14] (2) It fails to give any significant meaning to the phrase "nature of a term." To mean anything the nature must not be other than its term because there would then have to be an irreducible relation binding them. A term, hence, *is* its nature. But

... in that case, every true proposition attributing a predicate to a subject is purely analytic, since the subject is its own nature. ... If the "nature of a term" is to consist of predicates, and at the same time to be the same as the term itself, it seems impossible to understand what we mean when we ask whether S has the predicate P.[15]

[12] M. T. of T., in *Philosophical Essays*, 160.
[13] *Ibid.*, 163-164.
[14] *P. of M.*, 225.
[15] M. T. of T., 167.

(3) It is absurd on its own grounds. Its fundamental proposition, "There is only one subject and its predicate," is false because it implies a distinction between the predicate and the subject. This calls for the assertion of absolute identity in reality, which is incompatible with the idealist thesis of identity in difference.

The difficulty is that "identity in difference" is impossible, if we adhere to strict monism. For identity in difference involves many partial truths which combine . . . into the one whole of truth. But the partial truths, in a strict monism, are not merely not quite true: They do not subsist at all. If there were such propositions . . . that would give plurality. In short, the whole conception of "identity in difference" is incompatible with the axiom of internal relations; yet without this conception monism can give no account of the world . . . I conclude that the axiom is false, and that those parts of idealism which depend upon it are therefore groundless.[16]

Russell's criticism of monadism differs very little in its broad features from his refutation of monism. His rejection of Leibniz' monadology is directed mainly against Leibniz' treatment of relations. Leibniz, while he recognized relations, attempted to reduce them to predicates of individual substances. Russell objects to this treatment on two grounds: (1) It cannot convey the sense of an asymmetrical relation either;[17] and (2) it is incompatible with Leibniz' belief in a plurality of spirits, which is the essence of his idealism. To maintain any form of pluralism, Russell contends, the ultimacy of relations must be insisted upon. Without such a doctrine, we get either monism or solipsism, where all other individuals are reduced to adjectives of oneself.[18]

Russell's refutation of Berkeley is derived from Moore's distinction between consciousness and the object of consciousness.[19] Fundamentally, Russell contends, Berkeley's argument is based upon the fallacy of equivocation; he uses "idea" in two different senses: (1) as the object of sensation and (2) as the

[16] *Ibid.*, 168-169.
[17] *P. of M.*, 221-224.
[18] *P. of L.*, 15.
[19] Moore, *op. cit.*, 450; Russell, *P. of P.*, 17.

sensation itself. Berkeley's theory that the *esse* of the object
must be mental

. . . seems to depend for its plausibility upon confusing the thing apprehended with the act of apprehension. Either of these might be called
an "idea;" probably either would have been called an idea by Berkeley.
The act is undoubtedly in the mind; hence, when we are thinking of
the act, we readily assent to the view that ideas must be in the mind.
Then, forgetting that this was only true when ideas were taken as acts
of apprehension, we transfer the proposition that "ideas are in the
mind" to ideas in the other sense, i.e., to the things apprehended by our
acts of apprehension. Thus, by an unconscious equivocation, we arrive
at the conclusion that whatever we can apprehend must be in our
minds. This seems to be the true analysis of Berkeley's argument, and
the ultimate fallacy upon which it rests.[20]

Russell's refutation of Berkeley brings us to his dualism of
the mental and the physical, and the universal and the particular. Let us begin with his dualism of the mental and the physical and consider it from 1898 until 1921, in which year he
published his own version of neutral monism in *A. of Mind*,
thereby giving up the earlier dualism.

The earliest statement of Russell's dualism is, I think, in his
articles, M. T. of C., which were published in 1904. There are,
Russell states, certain theses which Moore has led him to accept.
Among these is the view ". . . that every presentation and every
belief must have an object other than itself and, except in certain cases where mental existents happen to be concerned, [the
object is] extramental."[21] The arguments for this thesis are not
fully developed until 1912, in *P. of P.*, i.e., in his refutation of
idealism and his positive statement of mind-matter dualism.

Mind and matter are the ultimate entities of the world of
existence (as against subsistence) in *P. of P.*, so far as ontological analysis is concerned. The argument for matter is based
upon sense-data and certain principles of inference. The argument for mind is based upon immediate experience.

What is matter, according to *P. of P.*? It is, for one thing,

[20] *P. of P.*, 65-66; see also R. S. D. P., in *Mysticism and Logic*, 152; U. C. M.,
in *Mysticism and Logic*, 130; and *E. W.* (First Edition), Ch. III.
[21] M. T. of C., *Mind* (1904), 204.

the assemblage of all physical objects, but it may also be considered, in a narrow sense, as the same thing as a single physical object.[22] As a physical object, it is the cause of our sense-data, i.e., it is that which we regard as the cause of the immediate objects of sense-experience, when we take our sense-experience to be veridical.[23] What reasons are there for supposing matter to be real? Because the hypothesis that it is real is the simplest one which can account for the facts; i.e., the hypothesis that matter exists apart from and independently of our sense-experience can explain (1) certain gaps in our sense-experience and (2) certain causal properties, which no other hypothesis, e.g., solipsism, can do.[24]

Now, granted the hypothesis that matter is real, what is its nature? Here Russell is agnostic. Both idealism and materialism are too dogmatic in their interpretation of matter, since we can know nothing about its intrinsic nature. But it does not follow that we are left with the *Ding-an-sich*, because we can know certain logical properties of matter. These are derived from the assumption that matter exists and the correspondences between matter and sense-data.[25] For example, "If one object looks blue and another red, we may reasonably presume that there is some corresponding difference between the physical objects. . . . But we cannot hope to be acquainted directly with the quality in the physical object which makes it look blue or red."[26]

Russell says little about mind in *P. of P*. But from what he does say, we may derive a picture of what he takes mind to be. In the first place, it is the self, i.e., that which is aware of things in sensation and of universals in conception; and it is also that which believes and thinks and desires: in short, it is *consciousness*.[27] The central problem about mind is whether we know it by acquaintance or by description; i.e., do we know it immediately as an object of experience, the way we know a sense-datum, like a red patch, or by means of a true proposition of

[22] *P. of P.*, 18.
[23] *Ibid.*, 35.
[24] *Ibid.*, 35-36.
[25] *Ibid.*, 54; see also *A. of Matter*, 226-228.
[26] *Ibid.*, 53.
[27] *Ibid.*, 79-81.

the form "The one and only one thing which is acquainted with certain sense-data and universals, etc.?" Russell acknowledges the difficulty of the problem but holds, with hesitation, that we do know the self by acquaintance because we may at times be acquainted with an actual case of acquaintance, in which case the self is a constituent of the total datum "self-acquainted-with-sense-datum."[28]

It must not be supposed that, because we are acquainted with our selves, we are acquainted with *mental substance*. We may be acquainted with our individual consciousness as it functions in apprehending objects other than itself or in apprehending itself but it does not follow that *that* which apprehends or is apprehended is a more or less permanent person which underlies all of our momentary experiences. To prove the existence of mental substance demands further argument and cannot be derived from the single fact that we are aware of our momentary selves.[29]

The distinction between mind and matter is maintained by Russell until 1914. In R. S. D. P. he replaces matter by "sensibilia," thereby reducing the physical in reality to that which resembles sense-data. Before discussing this change, however, we must say something about Russell's contribution to ontological analysis in N. of A.

The major concern of these articles on the nature of acquaintance is to analyze experience. Russell finds, as an empirical truth, that the simplest and most pervading aspect of experience is acquaintance. It ". . . is a dual relation between a subject and an object which need not have any community of nature. The subject is 'mental', the object is not known to be mental except in introspection."[30]

As a matter of fact, "acquaintance," in N. of A., replaces "mind" as the ultimate mental activity. That is, Russell rejects mind as the ultimate mental *entity*, substituting for it acquaintance as the ultimate mental *fact*. The way this comes about is through Russell's rejection of his P. of P. view that we are

[28] *Ibid.*, 79.
[29] *Ibid.*, 29.
[30] N. of A., *Monist* (1914), I, 1.

acquainted with our selves. Under the impact of Hume's analysis of experience and the critique of dualism by neutral monism, Russell is forced to deny that we ever have more than self-consciousness. It follows that we are not acquainted with the self as an isolated entity and, therefore, we do not know its intrinsic nature; from which it further results that we are acquainted only with mental facts. The mental is thus defined as a fact involving acquaintance and relations based upon it:[31] the distinctive characteristic of the mental ". . . is not to be found in the particulars involved, but only in the nature of the relations between them."[32] To sum up: the basic difference between *P. of P.* and N. of A. is that the mental in the latter essays is defined in terms of facts and not in terms of particulars.

The next important essay in ontological analysis is R. S. D. P. Its chief contribution is the replacement of matter by sensibilia as the ultimate physical entities. What are sensibilia? They are ". . . those objects which have the same metaphysical and physical status as sense-data, without necessarily being data to any mind."[33] They become sense-data by entering into the relation of acquaintance. That they exist apart from acquaintance Russell accepts as a metaphysical hypothesis which, like many of his hypotheses, is justified by the principle of continuity:

We have not the means of ascertaining how things appear from places not surrounded by brain and nerves and sense-organs, because we cannot leave the body; but continuity makes it not unreasonable to suppose that they present *some* appearance at such places. Any such appearance would be included among *sensibilia*.[34]

The function of sensibilia in this essay is to replace the "matter" and "physical object" of *P. of P.* Both of these can now be constructed out of sensibilia. Constructionism will be discussed in Section IV, but something must be said about it here. To put it briefly, it seems to me that Russell means by a logical construction the *substitution of a symbol* whose denota-

---

[31] *Ibid.*, III, 442.
[32] *Ibid.*, IV, 583.
[33] R. S. D. P., in *Mysticism and Logic*, 148.
[34] *Ibid.*, 150.

tion is given in sense-experience or is continuous with and similar to something given in sense-experience for a symbol whose denotation is neither given in sense-experience nor is similar to and continuous with something given in sense-experience but is postulated as an unempirical, inferred entity. The justification of this interpretation will be presented in Section IV, and must be taken for granted here.

For constructionism, then, a symbol of a physical object no longer denotes an entity which was postulated as the cause of our sense-data and whose intrinsic nature is a mystery to us. Rather it denotes a whole class of appearances, which includes sense-data and ". . . also those 'sensibilia', if any, which, on grounds of continuity and resemblance, are to be regarded as belonging to the same system of appearances, although there happen to be no observers to whom they are data."[35] Matter is not defined as the whole class of appearances but as the limiting appearances of the thing: "The *matter* of a given thing is the limit of its appearances as their distance from the thing diminishes."[36]

Although Russell says little about the mental in R. S. D. P., he is still a dualist, making references to mental facts as those which involve awareness.[37] Sensation is the simplest kind of mental fact. It is to be distinguished from sensibilia and sense-data. "By a sensation I mean the fact consisting in the subject's awareness of the sense-datum."[38] The subject—and here Russell rejects his thesis of N. of A.—is mental because it is a constituent in a mental complex (e.g., sensation) and the only constituent which is not physical. In N. of A. Russell argued that the subject cannot be known to be either mental or physical because we are not acquainted with it; in R. S. D. P. the subject is inferred as mental because it appears in a mental fact, sensation, which contains no other mental constituent and, therefore, it must be mental in order for sensation itself to be mental. The significance of this argument is that once again we may assert

[35] *Ibid.*, 154.
[36] *Ibid.*, 165.
[37] *Ibid.*, 150.
[38] *Ibid.*, 152.

that there are mental *particulars*, which are defined as those constituents of mental facts that are aware of something.

The last of the 1914 writings pertaining to ontological analysis are Lectures III and IV of *E. W.* These lectures are more concerned with the problem of constructing the notions of physics out of the data of sense-experience than they are with ontology. Nevertheless, they do contain one important alteration: Russell reduces all sensibilia which are not sense-data to "ideal" elements and defines them in terms of "actual" elements, i.e., sense-data.[39]

The final essay on ontology in this period which we must consider is U. C. M. (1915). It contains nothing radically new but represents pretty much the view Russell proclaimed until he presented his version of neutral monism in 1921. The dualism between sense-data and sensation is adhered to. The world of existents Russell regards as consisting of ". . . a multitude of entities [which are] arranged in a certain pattern. The entities which are arranged I shall call 'particulars'. The arrangement or pattern results from relations among particulars."[40] These particulars are like the notes in a symphony which is being played:

The ultimate constituents of a symphony (apart from relations) are the notes, each of which lasts only for a very short time. We may collect together all the notes played by one instrument: these may be regarded as the analogues of the successive particulars which common sense would regard as successive states of one "thing." But the "thing" ought to be regarded as no more "real" or "substantial" than, for example, the rôle of the trombone.[41]

Mind is also a logical construction, constituted by ". . . an assemblage of particulars, namely, what would be called 'states of mind', which would belong together in virtue of some specific common quality,"[42] i.e., consciousness.

This brings us to the close of our description of Russell's dualism of the mental and the physical in the period from

[39] *E. W.*, 111-112.
[40] U. C. M., in *Mysticism and Logic*, 129.
[41] *Ibid.*, 130.
[42] *Ibid.*, 131-132.

1898-1921. His second period, that of neutral monism, extends from 1921 to the present. However, before we can discuss neutral monism, we must complete the dualistic picture of reality which Russell maintained during the first period and say something about his theory of universals and particulars. Russell's dualism is a double one, consisting in the beliefs that the mental and the physical are ultimate and that the universal and the particular are irreducible.

In 1898 Russell became a Platonist as regards universals. His motivation was mathematical, just as it was in his acceptance of mind-matter dualism. His desire was to make mathematics independent of the human mind.[43] This desideratum, which is an integral part of logistic, was in direct revolt against the Kantian intuitionism, which made the truth of mathematical propositions dependent upon mental activity. Once intuitionism was rejected, Russell, in order to guarantee the truth of mathematics, contended that mathematics consisted of analytic *a priori* truths, i.e., truths which are independent of all experience.

This thesis, that mathematics is analytically *a priori,* carried with it certain implications. The two most important were (1) that mathematical ideas, e.g., implication, number, etc., are Platonic essences; and (2) that *any* term, mathematical or otherwise, is a universal which, as a timeless entity, inhabits the realm of being.[44]

P. of M., Russell's earliest work in which universals are discussed, is orthodox Platonism, except for one very curious doctrine, namely, that universal *relations* have no instances.[45]

[43] *P. of M.,* xviii; L. A., 359-361.

[44] *P. of M.,* 42-43.

[45] Russell's argument for this doctrine, somewhat simplified, is as follows: Consider two statements, "A differs from B" and "C differs from D." Assume that the "differs from" in these two statements *are* instances of the universal relation "difference." In order for them to be instances of the relation, they must have something in common with the universal relation. And to have something in common with the universal relation, they must have a common relation to the universal relation. But they cannot have a common relation to the universal relation because that would contradict the first hypothesis, that the relation is one of *difference.* Therefore, the "differs from" in "A differs from B" and "C differs from D" cannot be instances of the universal relation "difference." From which it

However, in his next discussion of universals, in K. A. D. (1910-11), he rejects this view, without offering any reason for doing so, for he is so convinced that universal relations do have instances that he devotes most of his argument to the proof that we are acquainted with universal relations themselves. He writes, e.g., "Thus we must suppose that we are acquainted with the meaning of 'before', and not merely with *instances* of it."[46]

In R. U. P. (1911-12), which is Russell's most brilliant essay on the problem of universals, he contends that dualism (of universal and particular) rests upon the belief that the relation of predication is ultimate, i.e., that there are particulars and that these have qualities or relations which are instances of universals.[47] Nominalism and universalism, which deny universals and particulars respectively, are rejected, the first because it must admit the universal relation "similarity," in its denial of universal qualities and relations other than similarity;[48] the second because it cannot account for our actual experience of numerical diversity of similar universals in perceptual space.[49]

From the point of view of ontological analysis, all the entities in reality, Russell maintains, are divisible into two classes:

(1) Particulars, which enter into complexes only as the subjects of predicates or as the terms of relations, and if they belong to the world of which we have experience, exist in time, and cannot occupy more than one place at one time in the space to which they belong; (2) universals, which can occur as predicates or relations in complexes, do not exist in time, and have no relation to one place which they may not simultaneously have to another.[50]

In *P. of P.*, which is the last of the writings on universals

---

follows that the universal itself appears wherever it is used. And, since the same difficulty confronts every universal relation, no relation, Russell concludes, can have instances. *P. of M.*, 50-52.

[46] K. A. D., in *Mysticism and Logic*, 213 (my italics).

[47] R. U. P., *Proceedings of the Aristotelian Society* (1911-12), 8.

[48] *Ibid.*, 8-9; also *P. of P.*, 150.

[49] R. U. P., 16-17.

[50] *Ibid.*, 23-24.

in this period, Russell uses language to prove the reality of universals and particulars: any sentence contains at least one element, the verb, which symbolizes a universal; and may, if it denotes something with which we are acquainted, contain one element, the proper name, which symbolizes a particular. Besides verbs, prepositions and adjectives also denote universals.[51]

The status of the universal is Russell's final point. The particular, of course, is either mental or physical. "Thus thoughts and feelings, minds and physical objects *exist*. But universals do not exist in this sense; we shall say that they *subsist* or *have being*, where 'being' is opposed to 'existence' as being timeless."[52]

This concludes our discussion of Russell's dualism: of the mental and the physical; and the universal and the particular. It was his position, as regards ontological analysis, from 1898 until 1921, the year of the publication of *A. of Mind*. From 1921 until the present day, so far as I know, Russell has been a modified neutral monist, as far as mental-physical dualism is concerned, and, in regard to universals and particulars, he has either become dubious about or rejected his dualism. Which it is, we shall try to determine later.

Neutral monism is a metaphysical theory which was formulated, independently of each other, by William James and Ernst Mach, and was developed by R. B. Perry, E. Holt and other American new-realists. Russell interprets it as

. . . the theory that the things commonly regarded as mental and the things commonly regarded as physical do not differ in respect of any intrinsic property possessed by the one set and not by the other, but differ only in respect of arrangement and context. The theory may be illustrated by comparison with a postal directory, in which the same names come twice over, once in alphabetical and once in geographical order; we may compare the alphabetical order to the mental, and the geographical order to the physical.[53]

[51] *P. of P.*, 81, 146.
[52] *Ibid.*, 156.
[53] *N. of A.*, II, 161.

When Russell first considered neutral monism seriously in 1914 he rejected it for two important reasons: It could not explain the difference between sensation and sense-data;[54] nor could it make intelligible the fact that each person's experience is partial and not inclusive of all reality.[55]

Notwithstanding his critique of neutral monism, Russell, even in 1914, was much attracted by the view, especially by its use of Occam's razor. "That the things given in experience should be of two fundamentally different kinds, mental and physical, is far less satisfactory to our intellectual desires than that the dualism should be merely apparent and superficial."[56] Also his own attempt to reduce "matter" to a logical construction in *E. W.*, Russell recognized, came close to neutral monism. The great stumbling block in his acceptance of neutral monism was what he regarded as an irreducible distinction: that between the object of experience and the subject of experience. When Russell realized that the subject itself was a construction, and that, consequently, the distinction between sense-data and sensation was illusory, he became a neutral monist.

It is in *A. of Mind* that the distinction between sense-data and sensation is given up. Russell writes: "If we are to avoid a perfectly gratuitous assumption, we must dispense with the subject as one of the actual ingredients in the world."[57] And why is the subject a gratuitous assumption? Because it is not given in experience: "Empirically, I cannot discover anything corresponding to the supposed act [i.e., subject]; and theoretically I cannot see that it is indispensable."[58] When the distinction between the subject and what he is aware of is given up, ". . . the possibility of distinguishing the sensation from the sense-datum vanishes. . . . Accordingly the sensation that we have when we see a patch of colour simply *is* that patch of colour, an actual constituent of the physical world, and part of what physics is concerned with."[59]

[54] *Ibid.*, 185.
[55] *Ibid.*, III, 447.
[56] *Ibid.*, II, 169.
[57] *A. of Mind*, 142.
[58] *Ibid.*, 17-18.
[59] *Ibid.*, 142.

Russell's answer to the second objection to neutral monism is presented, although quite indirectly, in his discussion of the classification of particulars and will be considered when we come to that topic later in this section.

I come now to the basic doctrines of Russell's neutral monism. Orthodox neutral monism, i.e., the theory as expressed by Mach, James and the new-realism, maintains two doctrines: (1) the stuff of the world is neither physical nor mental but neutral; and (2) the dualism in the world is not of entities but of causal laws. It is evident that Russell is a neutral monist as far as (2) is concerned.

> The dualism of mind and matter . . . cannot be allowed as metaphysically valid. Nevertheless, we seem to find a certain dualism, perhaps not ultimate, within the world as we observe it. The dualism is not primarily as to the stuff of the world, but as to causal laws.[60]

However, it is not clear that he accepts the first doctrine. Consider, e.g., the following quotation:

> My own belief . . . is that James is right in rejecting consciousness as an entity, and that the American realists are partly right, not wholly, in considering that both mind and matter are composed of a neutral-stuff which, in isolation, is neither mental nor material [i.e., physical]. I should admit this view as regards sensations: what is heard or seen belongs equally to psychology and to physics. But I should say that images belong only to the mental world, while those occurrences (if any) which do not form part of any "experience" belong only to the physical world. There are, it seems to me, *prima facie*, different kinds of causal laws, one belonging to physics, and the other to psychology. The law of gravitation, for example, is a physical law, while the law of association is a psychological law. Sensations are subject to both kinds of laws, and are therefore truly "neutral." . . . But entities subject only to physical laws, or only to psychological laws, are not neutral, and may be called respectively purely material [i.e., physical], and purely mental.[61]

Our problem, now, is this: how can we reconcile this quotation with the first doctrine of neutral monism? Perhaps it can

[60] *Ibid.*, 137.
[61] *Ibid.*, 25-26. Cf. P: W. T. A., *Aristotelian Society Supplementary Volume* (1919), 18.

be done, with the aid of the theory of types, in the following way: The doctrine that the stuff of the world is neither mental nor physical but neutral is ambiguous and may mean one or both of two things: (a) Mentality and physicality are not first-order properties of ultimate entities, like the properties of redness or roundness, but are second-order properties which accrue to these entities when they have certain kinds of causal relations to each other. Thus, two entities are mental when they have a relation to each other which psychology studies; or two entities are physical when they have a relation to each other which physics studies. This part of the first doctrine, I think, Russell accepts. (b) *Any* entity can be either mental or physical, i.e., any entity can possess the second-order property of mentality or physicality. Here Russell objects because, as our quotation states, some entities, the *unperceived entities of physics*, even though they are neutral—i.e., have no first-order property of mentality or physicality—cannot be brought into psychological causal laws; while other entities, *images*, which are also neutral in the above sense, cannot be considered in physical causal laws. It is only the remaining entities, *sensations*, also neutral, which can be treated causally by both physics and psychology.

If this interpretation is correct, it follows that Russell is a neutral monist, but of a modified sort, accepting the doctrine that the dualism in the world is causal and the doctrine that mentality and physicality are properties of entities-in-relation and not of entities-in-isolation, but rejecting the orthodox neutral monistic doctrine that *any* neutral event can be treated by both psychology and physics.

As an ontological theory, then, Russell's neutral monism revolves around two related doctrines: (1) The world is composed of neutral events, which are sensations in some contexts, images in other contexts, and unperceived events in still other contexts; and (2) the dualism in the world is not between entities, as it is for Descartes and orthodox dualism, but between causal laws.[62] Let us discuss these in turn.

(1) Russell says, in regard to the doctrine of eventism:

[62] *A. of Mind*, 137, 143-144.

"Everything in the world is composed of 'events'; that, at least, is the thesis I wish to maintain."[63] What, then, is an event? For one thing, it is something which occupies a small finite region of space-time.[64] It is also something penetrable and destructible, unlike the matter of traditional physics.[65] We know this empirically; i.e., we experience the overlapping of events and, according to physics, events in the form of "electrons" and "protons" actually annihilate each other. Our usual experience with events is in terms of sensations and images. E.g., "seeing a flash of lightning is an event; so is hearing a tire burst, or smelling a rotten egg. . . ."[66]

The ultimate kinds of events-in-relation are sensations, images and unperceived events. Everything which we recognize as "mind" and "matter" can be built up out of these. "Mind" is constructed out of sensations and images.[67] "Matter" is constructed out of sensations and unperceived events.[68] Indeed, Russell suggests that in a completed science the concepts "mind" and "matter" would disappear, and would be replaced by causal laws concerning events.[69]

Sensations are definable in at least three ways: (1) as the intersection of mind and matter;[70] (2) as the non-mnemic element in a perception, i.e., as that element in a perception which does not depend upon past experience, i.e., habit, memory, etc.;[71] and (3) as events whose causal laws include events which are stimuli *external* to the brain.[72]

Images are defined with the aid of the third definition of sensations, namely, as events whose causal laws include events which are sensations.[73]

Images belong exclusively to psychology because, if they

[63] *Phil.*, 276.
[64] *A. of Matter*, 286.
[65] *Ibid.*, 386.
[66] *Phil.*, 276.
[67] *A. of Mind*, 69, 109, 121, 143.
[68] *Ibid.*, 121.
[69] *Phil.*, 281.
[70] *A. of Mind*, 144.
[71] *Ibid.*, 139.
[72] *Ibid.*, 109.
[73] *Ibid.*

also belonged to physics, they would contradict the laws of physics. Russell uses this argument to refute behaviorism when it denies the existence of images. Behaviorism denies the distinction between images and sensations, regarding images as faint sensations. If this is true, especially for visual and auditory images, physics is contradicted because these images do not have the connections with physical events which visual and auditory sensations actually have.

Suppose, for example, that I am sitting in my room, in which there is an empty arm-chair. I shut my eyes, and call up a visual image of a friend sitting in the arm-chair. If I thrust my image into the world of physics, it contradicts all the usual physical laws. My friend reached the chair without coming in at the door in the usual way; subsequent inquiry will show that he was somewhere else at the moment. If regarded as a sensation, my image has all the marks of the supernatural.[74]

Besides sensations and images there are unperceived events. The argument for them is given in *A. of Matter*. The basic assumption is the causal theory of perception which says, in effect, that any percept[75] is a member of a group of percepts, given and inferred; and that the whole group can be correlated with another group of events which do not enter into perception.[76]

Perhaps the theory may be clarified by being formalized: Let "Px" $=$ x is a percept; "A" $=$ a group of percepts, given and inferred; "B" $=$ a group of unperceived events; and "1-1" $=$ the correlator. Then the causal theory of perception says:

$$(x)(\exists A,B): . \ Px: \supset :x\varepsilon A \cdot A1 - 1B.$$

For example, suppose I am having a blue percept; then the causal theory states (1) that this percept is a member of a class of percepts which includes roundness, hardness, shininess, etc., and which I call a "table;" and (2) that the class itself is related to events which can be correlated with hardness, blueness, roundness, etc. These events psychology calls the

---

[74] *Ibid.*, 153.

[75] A percept is a sensation plus its physiological, as against its psychological, accompaniments. See *A. of Matter*, 189.

[76] *A. of Matter*, Ch. XX.

"stimuli" of our perceptions and physics the "causes" of our perceptions.

According to Russell, both sciences are correct in their belief that there are events which no one perceives or can perceive and which can be correlated with events which we do perceive or are perceptible. The alternatives to this belief are phenomenalism and solipsism, both of which Russell rejects, the second because it is too desperate an alternative[77] and the first because it cannot account for such obvious facts as dictaphones repeating conversations or the hearing of a noise sooner by people who are close to its source than by people farther from its source.[78]

(2) Causal dualism is the theory that the dualism in the world is not of entities but of laws. These two kinds of causal laws are irreducible. Russell calls them the physical and the psychological causal laws.[79] As we have seen, according to Russell, the world is made up of evanescent particulars. Collected in one way they form psychological laws; collected in another way they form physical laws.

For the understanding of the difference between psychology and physics it is vital to understand these two ways of classifying particulars, namely: (1) according to the place where they occur; (2) according to the system of correlated particulars in different places to which they belong, such system being defined as a physical object.[80]

Psychology, thus, is interested merely in the places where different particulars occur, i.e., in *certain* particulars themselves, whereas physics is concerned with the *whole* system of appearances. This method of collecting particulars enables us to suggest what Russell would probably reply to his N. of A. objection to neutral monism. He said that neutral monism cannot account for the partiality or egocentricity of each person's experience. The way in which psychology collects appearances, I think, makes it inevitable that our experiences shall be partial because particulars appear from certain points of view. Partiality, therefore, is explicable by Russell's neutral monism as the

---

[77] *Ibid.*, 198.
[78] *Ibid.*, 214.
[79] *A. of Mind*, Ch. V.
[80] *Ibid.*, 102.

inevitable fact that one person's experience is the resultant of the universe seen from one, not from all, points of view.

This brings us to the question why causal dualism is ultimate. As Russell interprets it, it is, I think, identical with the problem of materialism. One can define materialism in one of two ways: (1) the ultimate stuff of the world is physical, i.e., non-mental; or (2) the ultimate laws in the world are physical, and *all* genuine laws are fundamentally physical. Russell rejects materialism in the first sense as being too dogmatic.[81] And the truth or falsity of materialism in the second sense reduces itself, it seems to me, to the following five problems in Russell's later works.

(1) Can "vital" movements be reduced to "mechanical" ones? Russell says, in answer to this problem of reduction, that our information is too meagre to declare oneself either way on the question.[82]

(2) Are images reducible to sensations? As we have seen, Russell rejects materialism in this sense, arguing that images cannot be brought into the statement of physical laws without falling into contradiction. However, Russell adds: "I am by no means confident that the distinction between image and sensation is ultimately valid, and I should be glad to be convinced that images can be reduced to sensations of a peculiar kind."[83]

(3) Are mnemic phenomena ultimate? That is, does the past operate upon our present experience directly or by means of its modification of the brain? The issue is between the ultimacy of mnemic phenomena and the ultimacy of the "engram," i.e., the modified brain structure. As an empiricist, Russell maintains that we do not have sufficient evidence to reduce mnemic phenomena to physiology, since the engram is an inferred entity, whereas the influence of the past upon a response is given directly in experience.[84]

(4) Is "physicalism" true? Physicalism is the view, advocated by Carnap and his followers, which holds that ". . . every

[81] *A. of Matter*, 382.
[82] *A. of Mind*, 47.
[83] *Ibid.*, 156.
[84] *Ibid.*, 85.

sentence of any branch of scientific language . . . can . . . be translated into the physical language without changing its content."[85] Although Russell does not criticize physicalism directly, nevertheless, we can discover what he thinks of it from his discussion of the sort of thesis it proclaims. Physics, he says, can tell us a good deal about the world, but *nothing* about the most intimate part of it, sensations or perceptions.

To take a simple instance: physics might, ideally, be able to predict that at such a time my eye would receive a stimulus of a certain sort; it might be able to trace the physical properties of the resulting events in the eye and the brain, one of which is, in fact, a visual percept; but it could not itself give us the knowledge that one of them is a visual percept. It is obvious that a man who can see knows things which a blind man cannot know; but a blind man can know the whole of physics. Thus the knowledge which other men have and he has not is not part of physics.[86]

(5) Is determinism true? Russell says no, basing his denial upon the quantum theory, which destroys any form of "mind-brain determinism." That is, Russell argues: assume that the mind and brain *are* causally connected. But,

perhaps the electron jumps when it likes; perhaps the minute phenomena in the brain which make all the difference to mental phenomena belong to the region where physical laws no longer determine definitely what must happen. This, of course, is merely a speculative possibility; but it interposes a veto upon materialistic dogmatism.[87]

I conclude, then, that Russell is a causal dualist, even though he would like very much to reduce all causal laws to physics and thereby accept a causal materialism.

I come now to the final topic of this section, Russell's theory of universals and particulars in the years 1921-40. As a dualist Russell accepted three related doctrines: (1) there are universal qualities; (2) there are universal relations; and (3) there are particulars. In this second period of ontological analysis Russell,

[85] R. Carnap, *Philosophy and Logical Syntax*, 89.
[86] *A. of Matter*, 389.
[87] *Ibid.*, 393.

at one time or another, has either become dubious about, modified, or rejected these doctrines.

(1) In *A. of Mind* Russell expressed doubt about the reality of universal qualities, offering an interpretation of them which is nominalistic. Whiteness, e.g., may be taken ". . . as denoting a certain set of similar particulars or collections of particulars."[88] However, in *Inquiry*, Russell returns to the view that there are universal qualities, basing his argument, as he did in R. U. P. and *P. of P.*, upon the premiss that there are universal relations.[89]

(2) Russell also retains his earlier thesis about universal relations, but he modifies his doctrine somewhat in that he no longer regards them as self-evident. There are, Russell contends in *A. of Mind*, good reasons for believing that universal relations, although not self-evident, are part of the *inferred* structure of the world.[90] These reasons, however, do not appear until *Inquiry*, where Russell employs the causal theory of meaning, i.e., the theory that the words we use are caused by *non-verbal* contexts, to prove the reality of universal relations.[91]

(3) The doctrine that there are particulars was ably defended by Russell in R. U. P., in his criticism of universalism, which is the theory that denies the existence of particulars. It maintains that universals and not their instances exist in all places where they appear. If two places have the same shade of colour, e.g., the shade in both places is identical. It denies the relation of predication: to say "this is white" is really to say "whiteness exists here."[92] Dualism contends, on the other hand, that there are particulars and that predication holds between a universal and a particular. Thus, to say "this is white" is to say "whiteness is a predicate of a particular which I call 'this'." Russell's rejection of universalism was based upon (1) our sense-experience of diversity, i.e., our perception of two similar patches of, e.g., white; and (2) the logical principle that

[88] *A. of Mind*, 196.
[89] *Inquiry*, 436-437.
[90] *A. of Mind*, 228.
[91] *Inquiry*, 429-437.
[92] R. U. P., 8.

existents in different places at the same time cannot be numerically identical.

Russell's rejection of universalism was maintained by him, so far as I know, from 1911-40. In *Inquiry*, however, Russell, in discussing a problem quite remote from that of universals, namely, substance, sketches a theory which, if he really accepts it, makes him a universalist. Stated simply the theory is this: Proper names, like "this" and "that," are regarded by many philosophers as symbols of *particulars*. Thus, when one utters the statement "this is red," one means, on this view, that a given sense-particular, which one calls "this," has the predicate or quality of redness. But, Russell argues, if one construes the proposition in such a way (which, of course, Russell does in his dualistic doctrine of R. U. P.), ". . . one finds that 'this' becomes a substance, an unknowable something in which properties inhere, but which, nevertheless, is not identical with the sum of its properties. Such a view is open to all the familiar objections to the notion of substance."[93] In order to avoid this difficulty with the word "this" as a symbol of an unknowable substance, Russell rejects the doctrine that "this" (and "that") stand for particulars. He suggests that, whenever we have a subject-predicate proposition, like "this is red," we must interpret it as "redness is here." Thus, in the case of a physical object, like an apple, we must not say, "this is an apple," but "redness, roundness, sweetness, etc., are here."[94] A thing, then, is nothing but a bundle of coexisting qualities. All of this follows, unless we wish to get stuck with the substratum of Locke. Now, that this theory is tantamount to universalism is shown by the fact that it denies implicitly the relation of predication, which is basic to dualism and rejected by universalism. The interpretation of "this is red" as "redness is here," i.e., the rejection of subject-predicate propositions, is exactly the way in which universalism interprets propositions of this sort.

Our problem here, of course, is to show how Russell would answer his own objection to universalism, as he expressed it in R. U. P. It seems to me, from a careful reading of Chapter VI

[93] *Inquiry*, 120.
[94] *Ibid.*, Ch. VI.

of *Inquiry,* where this problem is considered (quite indirectly, though), that Russell might say to the dualist: it is true that we do experience spatial diversity, i.e., two similar patches of white; and it is just as true that two patches of white cannot be numerically identical. But—and this would be the vital point—the white in the two patches of white is identical. What makes the white two are not the instances of white but the spatial co-ordinates.[95] That is, two patches of white are two, not because they are instances of white, but because the universal has two separate sets of co-ordinates. The names of the whiteness are, in our example, "Whiteness plus co-ordinates A, B" and "Whiteness plus co-ordinates C, D." Thus, the twoness of two patches of white depends upon the specificity of the co-ordinates, not upon the instances of white.[96]

If this account of Russell's new theory of universals is correct,—and I do not see how else to interpret his discussion in *Inquiry,*—then it is a fact that Russell has rejected (knowingly or not) his earlier dualism of universals and particulars, substituting in its place the doctrine of universalism which denies the existence of particulars.

Section II. Analysis as Formal Analysis

Formal analysis, as Russell has conceived it, is the application of analysis to abstract cosmological problems. As a kind or use of analysis it was developed by him from the very beginnings of his philosophical career, but it reached its climax after the publication of *P. M.,* in a series of articles, P. L. A. (1918-19).

[95] *Ibid.,* 122.

[96] The chief difficulty with this theory, I think, has to do with these co-ordinates: (1) Russell treats them as if they were *qualities* apart from the qualities that they describe. But co-ordinates are no more experienceable separate qualities than the unknowable substratum which forced Russell to give up his dualism in the first place. (2) Granted that co-ordinates are distinct from the qualities which they describe, are they not then *particulars,* not in the sense of being instances of universals perhaps, but in the sense of being the denotation of proper names? Has Russell done more than substitute for "this" and "that" the names of co-ordinates, which denote one quality at one place at one time? If Russell admits that spatial co-ordinates are particulars and their symbols are proper names, the whole point of his universalism is lost, because the relation of predication is readmitted: all qualities become predicates of their co-ordinates.

The easiest way in which to understand formal analysis is to begin with Russell's conception of logic, because it is in terms of. logic that he defines formal analysis. Logic, according to Russell, has two continuous but distinguishable parts, a philosophical and a mathematical part. The philosophical part is concerned, first, with the forms which are abstracted from an examination of the linguistic and non-linguistic aspects of reality, and, secondly, with the foundations of mathematics. The mathematical part of logic comprises the theorems which are deduced from the foundations.[97]

That part of philosophical logic which deals with the forms of reality is formal analysis, whereas the other part, the foundations of mathematics, is logistic. Logistic will be considered in the next section; but it is important to see at the outset the common root of formal analysis and logistic, i.e., to see that both are defined in terms of logic.

Form, which is the basic problem of formal analysis, may be defined in two ways, by an analysis of language or by an analysis of experience. Russell, in the isomorphic tradition of Plato, Aristotle and Wittgenstein, begins with the first way and uses his findings as a clue, but not as *the* clue, in the analysis of non-linguistic form. The best way to define form, according to Russell, is in terms of actual propositions.

In every proposition . . . there is, besides the particular subject-matter concerned, a certain *form*, a way in which the constituents of the proposition . . . are put together. If I say "Socrates is mortal," "Jones is angry," "The sun is hot," there is something in common in these three cases, something indicated by the word "is." What is in common is the *form* of the proposition, not an actual constituent.[98]

From any of these propositions one can derive the others, by

---

[97] "Logic, we may say, consists of two parts. The first part investigates what propositions are and what forms they may have; this part enumerates the different kinds of atomic propositions, of molecular propositions, of general propositions, and so on. The second part consists of certain supremely general propositions, which assert the truth of all propositions of certain forms. This second part merges into pure mathematics, whose propositions all turn out, on analysis, to be such general formal truths." *E. W.*, 61. See also S. M. P., in *Mysticism and Logic*, 112; *I. M. P.*, 1; P. L. A., IV, 48; and *E. W.*, 46.

[98] *E. W.*, 45-46; see also *I. M. P.*, 199 and P. L. A., V, 202.

substitution; that which remains unchanged when one replaces constituents and gets different propositions is the form of these propositions. Propositional form, thus, is that which one gets when one substitutes variables for the constituents of propositions.

The same analysis of factual form can be given:

Two facts are said to have the same "form" when they differ only as regards their constituents. In this case, we may suppose the one to result from the other by *substitution* of different constituents. For example, "Napoleon hates Wellington," results from "Socrates loves Plato" by substituting Napoleon for Socrates, Wellington for Plato, and *hates* for *loves*. It is obvious that some, but not all, facts can be thus derived from "Socrates loves Plato." Thus some facts have the same form as this and some have not. We can represent the form of a fact by the use of variables: thus "xRy" may be used to represent the form of the fact that Socrates loves Plato.[99]

We come now to the different kinds of forms, i.e., to the enumeration of the various fundamental ways in which the ultimate ontological entities can be organized. There are two basic kinds of forms: (1) proper names and logical particulars; and (2) propositions and facts. Let us begin with the form manifested by proper names and particulars.

A proper name ". . . is a simple symbol whose meaning is something that can only occur as subject."[100] It ". . . directly [designates] an individual which is its meaning, and [it has] this meaning in its own right, independently of the meanings of all other words."[101] It is the only kind of word which is theoretically capable of standing for a particular and can only be applied to a particular with which the speaker is acquainted; for one cannot name anything one is not acquainted with.[102]

True examples of proper names are very difficult to find. Most people regard words like "Socrates," "Roosevelt," etc., as proper names. But, according to Russell, they are mistaken, because these words do not stand for particulars, but for compli-

[99] P: W. T. A., 2.
[100] *I. M. P.*, 173.
[101] *Ibid.*, 174.
[102] P. L. A., II, 523-524.

cated systems of particulars, and are really abbreviations for definite descriptions.[103]

The only words one does use as names in the logical sense are words like "this" or "that." One can use "this" as a name to stand for a particular with which one is acquainted at the moment. . . . It is only when you use "this" quite strictly, to stand for an actual object of sense, that it is really a proper name.[104]

Logical particulars are what proper names mean. They are, along with facts, the sort of objects one would have to take into account in any inventory of the world. They have this peculiarity,

. . . that each of them stands entirely alone and is completely self-subsistent. It has that sort of self-subsistence that used to belong to substance, except that it usually only persists through a very short time, so far as our experience goes. That is to say, each particular that there is in the world does not in any way logically depend upon any other particular.[105]

Besides proper names and logical particulars, formal analysis is concerned with another basic dichotomy: propositions and facts. A proposition, for Russell, is an indicative sentence, one which either asserts or denies something. It is that which we believe truly or falsely; i.e., it is the logical vehicle of truth or falsehood. A proposition, Russell points out, differs from a name because its relations are different; there are two relations that a proposition may have to a fact, being true and being false; whereas there is only one relation that a name can have to that which it names: it can just name it, and if it does not, it is a mere noise.[106] It follows that facts cannot be named by propositions but only asserted or denied (or questioned, etc.) by them.

It is as necessary to distinguish between facts and particulars as it is to distinguish between propositions and names. A fact is not a particular, but the sort of thing represented by whole sentences.[107] It is a complex of particular(s) and qualities and

---

[103] *Ibid.*; see also *A. of Mind*, 193.
[104] P. L. A., II, 524-525. But cf. *P. of M.*, 42-43 and *Inquiry*, Ch. VI.
[105] P. L. A., II, 525; see also *A. of Matter*, 199-200.
[106] P. L. A., I, 507-508.
[107] *Ibid.*, 520.

relations.[108] Furthermore, a fact is

. . . the kind of thing that makes a proposition true or false. If I say "It is raining," what I say is true in a certain condition of weather and is false in other conditions of weather. The condition of weather that makes my proposition true (or false . . .) is what I should call a "fact."[109]

Finally, facts are objective, i.e., independent of our thinking about them. Russell regards this as an undeniable datum of formal analysis. It follows that the world ". . . is not completely described by a lot of 'particulars', but that you must also take account of these things that I call facts . . . and that these . . . are part of the real world."[110]

Thus far in our discussion of formal analysis we have defined form and distinguished between the basic forms: proper names and particulars, and propositions and facts. The latter category contains various species which we must discuss next. There are five such species which Russell has persisted in accepting as valid: atomic propositions and facts; molecular propositions and facts; existence propositions and facts; general propositions and facts; and completely general (or logical) propositions and facts. Since these may be either positive or negative, there are also negative facts to be considered.

(1) An atomic proposition is one which ". . . asserts that a certain thing has a certain quality, or that certain things have a certain relation."[111] Examples are: "this is white;" "this is below that;" "this is between that and the other thing." Every atomic proposition has an adjective or verb and a subject, which is the proper name of the proposition.[112]

Corresponding to atomic propositions are atomic facts. They ". . . are what determine whether atomic propositions are to be asserted or denied."[113] They are the simplest kinds of facts, consisting in the possession of a quality or relation by some

[108] P: W. T. A., 1-2.
[109] P. L. A., I, 500-501.
[110] *Ibid.*, 502; see also *E. W.*, 55.
[111] *E. W.*, 56; see also *P. M.*, I, xv.
[112] P. L. A., II, 523.
[113] *E. W.*, 56.

particular(s).[114] In every atomic fact there is one component which is either the quality or the relation and one or more terms (particulars). Thus, there is a perfect isomorphism between atomic propositions and atomic facts: subjects (proper names) correspond to terms (particulars); adjectives correspond to qualities; and verbs correspond to relations.

(2) A molecular proposition is one that contains ". . . other propositions which you may call their atoms."[115] It is a proposition in which truth-function words like "or," "if," "and," etc., occur. An example is: "If you stay, so will your sister."

The problem regarding molecular forms is whether there are molecular facts. Russell, at first, denies their existence:

I do not suppose there is in the world a single disjunctive fact corresponding to [the proposition] "p or q." It does not look plausible that in the actual objective world there are facts going about which you could describe as "p or q."[116]

According to Russell, then, "pvq" refers to two facts, the fact corresponding to "p" and the fact corresponding to "q."

When Russell discusses general facts, however, he reverses his decision and affirms the existence of molecular facts, because he accepts the existence of general facts, which is the genus of the molecular species.[117]

(3) An existence proposition is the traditional "I" or "O" proposition. For Russell it is a proposition which asserts the truth of at least one value of a propositional function; e.g., "Some men are brutal."

That there are existence facts, as distinct from atomic facts, Russell regards as obvious: "Of course, it is not so difficult to admit what I might call existence-facts—, such facts as 'There are men. . . .' Those, I think, you will readily admit as separate and distinct facts over and above the atomic facts."[118]

(4) A general proposition is the traditional "A" or "E" proposition, interpreted in the Boolean sense. It is a proposition

[114] P. L. A., II, 520.
[115] Ibid., III, 37.
[116] Ibid., 39.
[117] Ibid., V, 201.
[118] Ibid., 200-201.

which asserts (or denies) the truth of all values of a propositional function.

A general fact is one which corresponds to a general proposition. One cannot deny the existence of general facts or reduce them to other facts:

It would be a very great mistake to suppose that you could describe the world completely by means of particular facts alone. Suppose that you had succeeded in chronicling every single particular fact throughout the universe, and that there did not exist a single particular fact of any sort anywhere that you had not chronicled, you still would not have got a complete description of the universe, unless you also added: "these that I have chronicled are all the particular facts there are,"[119]

which, of course, is a general fact.

(5) A completely general proposition is one which occurs in logic, either as an axiom or a theorem. It contains only variables and truth-functions.[120]

Completely general propositions are analytic and *a priori* because of a ". . . certain peculiar quality which marks them out from other propositions."[121] What this quality is, Russell is not sure:

Although it is a necessary characteristic of logical propositions that they should consist solely of variables, i.e., that they should assert the universal-truth, or the sometimes-truth, of a propositional function consisting solely of variables . . . it is not a sufficient one.[122]

Russell's treatment of completely general facts is vague and,

---

[119] *Ibid.*, I, 502-503.

[120] *Ibid.*, V, 200. However, not all propositions which contain only variables and truth-functions are logical. A proposition, to be logical, must be expressed in the language of logic and deduced from the premisses of logic (or be a primitive premiss of logic). There are some propositions which are expressed logically, but not proved logically, e.g., 'There is at least one thing in the world'; see *ibid.*, 204-205.

[121] *Ibid.*, 206.

[122] *Ibid.* In *A. of Matter* (176), however, Russell accepts the analysis of Wittgenstein, that the peculiar characteristic of logical propositions is their tautological character. But in the new "Introduction" to *P. of M.* (1937), Russell gives up this analysis as being too linguistic and conventional, offering nothing in its place. Thus, so far as I know, he has no complete analysis of logical propositions; that they consist solely of variables and truth-functions, and that they are *a priori*, is clear, but that they are only that or conventional, Russell cannot believe.

unfortunately, I cannot find any adequate discussion of them in his essays on formal analysis.

(6) This brings us to positive and negative propositions and facts. These are not distinct species but two different ways of looking at the others. That is, an atomic proposition or fact, e.g., may be either positive or negative.

That there are positive and negative propositions most of us would admit. Also, the view that there are positive facts would cause little dispute. But negative facts seem to us to be in the same category as "blue centaurs," etc. Indeed, the belief in negative facts seems to violate that robust feeling of reality which is one of Russell's cardinal principles. Nevertheless, with all this against him, he insists that there are negative facts:

I think you will find that it is better to take negative facts as ultimate. Otherwise you will find it so difficult to say what it is that corresponds to a proposition. When, e.g., you have a false positive proposition, say "Socrates is alive," it is false because of a fact in the real world. A thing cannot be false except because of a fact, so that you will find it extremely difficult to say what exactly happens . . . unless you are going to admit negative facts.[123]

To sum up: Formal analysis is the examination of the world considered *abstractly*, i.e., apart from whether it is physical or mental or neutral, etc. Its concern is with the various modes of organization which are disclosed by the linguistic and non-linguistic aspects of reality. Together with ontological analysis, formal analysis comprises part of what has been traditionally called "metaphysics:" ontological analysis is concerned with the ultimate categories: the mental, the physical, the universal, etc.; formal analysis is abstract cosmology and deals with the abstract patterns in which the ontological categories are organized.

SECTION III. ANALYSIS AS LOGISTIC

Logistic, or analysis as applied to mathematical logic, is probably the best known of the species of analysis in Russell. Also, no one, I suppose, would criticize Russell here as lacking in

[123] P. L. A., III, 46; see also P: W. T. A., 5.

fundamental unity, since he has been expounding the same basic philosophy of mathematics from 1900 to the present. Because logistic is so well known and its unity in Russell's work is granted by all (and our space is limited), it will not be necessary to treat it at any length.[124] What I shall try to do in this section, therefore, is to offer the briefest sort of general picture of logistic, in order to make the exposition of Russell's philosophy in terms of analysis as complete as possible.

The best answer to the problem of the nature of logistic lies, I think, in the answer to a broader question: What is the correct philosophy of mathematics? Since the latter half of the nineteenth century when, for the first time, mathematics became a well-defined science, through the brilliant work of Weierstrass and Peano, there have been in the main three philosophies of mathematics: intuitionism, formalism, and logistic.

Intuitionism, in its modern form, stems from Kant and Poincaré, and is represented at present by Brouwer and Weyl. In the work of the latter two, according to Russell, it is characterized by two doctrines: finitism and the denial of the principle of excluded middle.[125] It claims, Russell asserts, that a mathematical proposition is neither true nor false unless there exists a method which enables us to determine which it is. When no such method is forthcoming in the consideration of a certain proposition, that proposition is regarded as literally meaningless. The first consequence of this doctrine is the denial of the principle that any proposition is either true or false; from which it further results that many hitherto accepted theorems regarding infinity are thrown out of mathematics as meaningless because they cannot be known to be either true or false.

Russell rejects intuitionism; his criticism amounts to saying that it is *too empirical*. If its thesis, that mathematics is a set of intuitive constructions governed by the principle of verification, be maintained and pushed to its logical consequences, it results in absurdity:

[124] A fuller treatment of logistic, as well as more complete discussions of many of the topics of this essay, may be found in my doctoral dissertation, *The Method of Analysis in the Philosophy of Bertrand Russell* (University of Michigan, 1943).
[125] *P. of M.* (new "Introduction," 1937), v-vi.

Men, for example, though they form a finite class, are practically and empirically, just as impossible to enumerate as if their number were infinite. If the finitist's principle is admitted, we must not make *any* general statement—such as "All men are mortal"—about a collection defined by its properties, not by actual mention of all its members. This would make a clean sweep of all science and of all mathematics, not only of the parts which the intuitionists consider questionable.[126]

Formalism, which had its royal birth in the non-Euclidean geometries of the nineteenth century and in the work of Peano, is best represented by Hilbert. Essentially, Hilbert distinguishes between two disciplines: mathematics-proper and meta-mathematics. The former is a collection of symbols about which there are certain undefined ideas and axioms, which tell us what we are allowed to do to the symbols in order to derive the propositions which we desire. Meta-mathematics consists of statements about mathematics-proper that reveal which formulae can and which cannot be derived from the axioms according to the rules.

Now, just as intuitionism is too empirical, so formalism, Russell argues, is *too rational*. Neither in the form of Peano nor Hilbert can it account for our practical uses of mathematics.

The formalists have forgotten that numbers are needed, not only for doing sums, but for counting. Such propositions as "There were 12 Apostles" or "London has 6,000,000 inhabitants" cannot be interpreted in their system. For the symbol "o" may be taken to mean any finite integer, without thereby making any of Hilbert's axioms false; and thus every number-symbol becomes infinitely ambiguous. The formalists are like a watchmaker who is so absorbed in making his watches look pretty that he has forgotten their purpose of telling the time, and has therefore omitted to insert any works.[127]

The third prevalent philosophy of mathematics is logistic, which was developed by Frege and Russell. Independently of each other, they carried on the arithmetization of mathematics to the "logicizing" of arithmetic; i.e., they reduced the theory of natural numbers to certain logical ideas and propositions.

---

[126] *Ibid.*, vii; see also "The Limits of Empiricism," *Proceedings of the Aristotelian Society* (1935-36), 141-145.
[127] *P. of M.*, vi.

Logistic, to Russell, is fundamentally the view that mathematics and logic are continuous and identical. "They differ as boy and man: logic is the youth of mathematics and mathematics is the manhood of logic."[128] It is easy to see, I think, although many modern logicians have forgotten it, that logistic represents a compromise between the complete empiricism of intuitionism and the complete rationalism of formalism. The nature of this compromise can be seen best in Russell's rejection of formalism. The *analysis* of mathematical ideas and propositions, Russell contends, must not only do justice to the bare formulae of mathematics, but also to our experiences with mathematics, e.g., in counting.

We want our numbers not merely to verify mathematical formulae, but to apply in the right way to common objects. We want to have ten fingers and two eyes and one nose. A system in which "1" meant 100, "2" meant 101, and so on, might be all right for pure mathematics, but would not suit daily life. . . . We have already some knowledge (though not sufficiently articulate or analytic) of what we mean by "1" and "2," and so on, and our use of numbers in arithmetic must conform to this knowledge.[129]

These, then, are the prerequisites of an adequate philosophy of mathematics: it must make articulate our unanalyzed knowledge of mathematical ideas and propositions and it must so define these ideas and deduce these propositions, in terms of logical ideas and propositions, that the definitions and deductions both verify mathematics as a body of abstract formulae and conform to our experience of counting. It is the contention of Russell that only logistic has satisfied these requirements. In his logical writings—*P. of M.* (1903), *P. M.* (1910-13), which was written with Whitehead, and *I. M. P.* (1919)—the determination of the basic ideas and propositions of mathematics and the reduction of them to logic has been worked out. This determination of the basic ideas and propositions of mathematics and the reduction of them to logic constitute *analysis as logistic* in the philosophy of Russell.

[128] *I. M. P.*, 194.
[129] *Ibid.*, 9.

Section IV. Analysis as the Resolution of Incomplete Symbols

What is to be called the resolution of incomplete symbols in this section is what Russell has at various stages of his writings called (1) the analysis of denoting phrases,[130] (2) the analysis of incomplete symbols,[131] (3.) constructionism,[132] (4) the principle which dispenses with abstractions,[133] and (5) the logical-analytic method.[134] In principle, all of these, I think, mean the same thing: they are all names of a technique whereby certain symbols, because they are defective, are replaced by other symbols or groups of symbols. The advantage of our term is that it emphasizes this fact: that one kind or species of analysis in Russell has to do with getting rid of, i.e., *resolving,* certain symbols in favor of certain other symbols.

Analysis as the resolution of incomplete symbols is probably the most successful attempt at semantical analysis since Plato's explication of negative judgment in the *Sophist.* The problems which it solves are tremendous in their scope; for they include not only traditional linguistic questions but also many problems which have not been considered by most philosophers to be mainly linguistic in their nature.

The setting of this fourth species of analysis in Russell's philosophy is to be found in *P. of M.* Now, in many ways, this work represents the climax of the revolt, begun in the nineteenth century by certain mathematicians, against the classical logic, e.g., in its proofs that the subject-predicate proposition is not the ultimate or the only kind of proposition. In spite of the revolutionary character of this book, however, it nevertheless proclaims one of the fundamental doctrines of the classical logical tradition: that language has its non-linguistic correlate in reality. As Russell writes:

Whatever may be an object of thought, or may occur in any true or false proposition, or can be counted as *one,* I call a *term.* This, then, is

[130] "On Denoting," *Mind* (1905), 479.
[131] *P. M.*, "Introduction," Ch. III.
[132] R. S. D. P., 157; *E. W.*, viii; and L. A., 364.
[133] *E. W.*, 44; and L. A., 364.
[134] *E. W.*, vii.

the widest word in the philosophical dictionary. I shall use as synonymous with it the words unit, individual, entity. The first two emphasize the fact that every term is *one*, while the third is derived from the fact that every term has being, i.e., *is* in some sense. A man, a moment, a number, a class, a relation, a chimaera, or anything else that can be mentioned is sure to be a term; and to deny that such and such a thing is a term must always be false.[135]

`This doctrine,—which he shared with Meinong,—Russell recognized immediately after the publication of *P. of M.*, in "On Denoting," as having one very serious difficulty, it fell into contradiction. As he expressed it later: Consider, e.g., the proposition "the round square does not exist." This is a true and significant proposition to everyone, even Meinong. But ". . . we cannot regard it as denying the existence of a certain object called 'the round square.' For if there were such an object, it would exist: we cannot first assume that there is a certain object, and then proceed to deny that there is such an object."[136]

Meinong's and *P. of M.*'s defect, Russell now points out, arises primarily from "the violation of a robust sense of reality."[137] All analysis, Russell insists, must preserve a robust sense of what is real and must not invent all *sorts of realities* to suit all occasions and to match all difficulties. Applied to propositions like "the round square does not exist," this sense of reality means that the ascription of reality to unreal and self-contradictory objects must be avoided at all costs. Analysis should no more admit as real round squares, centaurs and golden mountains than mathematics, zoology and geology do.[138]

When Russell abandoned his position of *P. of M.* and gave up Meinong's mode of analysis, he realized that his problem was to present an analysis of propositions containing symbols of unreal and self-contradictory objects which would preserve our robust sense of reality and yet allow us to discourse about these "pseudo-objects" intelligibly. This he solved in his famous

[135] *P. of M.*, 43.
[136] *P. M.*, I, 66.
[137] *I. M. P.*, 169.
[138] *Ibid.*

theory of descriptions. In essence, the theory amounts to making a fundamental distinction between two basic kinds of symbols: proper names and descriptions. A proper name, taken in an extended sense, is a simple symbol like "Scott." It designates an individual directly; that individual is its meaning, and it has this meaning in isolation, i.e., independently of all other words. A description is a complex symbol, like "the author of *Waverley*." It does not designate an individual directly, since it would then be a proper name. Because it does not refer to an actual object directly the way a proper name does, Russell calls it an "incomplete symbol," i.e., a symbol which has no meaning in isolation, but which obtains a meaning in a context with other symbols.[139] This analysis of propositions containing definite descriptions enables us to talk intelligibly about unreal and self-contradictory pseudo-objects, because all propositions about them can now be interpreted as propositions involving propositional functions and variables and not real objects which somehow are also unreal.

The theory of descriptions became very significant after it was developed in 1905, because it became a model to Russell for the treatment of other philosophical symbols. Classes, numbers, relations (in extension), points, instants, particles of matter, even ordinary objects, like tables and people, were dealt with in the same way as descriptions: each of these was reduced from an actual entity to an incomplete symbol which could be interpreted in terms of propositional functions and variables or sensible objects.

There are, it seems to me, three rather distinct kinds of incomplete symbols in Russell's work: (1) descriptions, (2) specifically mathematical symbols, and (3) the symbols of the natural sciences (including those of ordinary discourse which can be assimilated by the natural sciences, e.g., "tables," "chairs," "persons," etc.). It will be impossible to deal with all of these here; consequently I shall discuss rather fully one example from each of the three categories: (1) definite descriptions; (2) classes; and (3) points. Let us begin with definite descriptions.

[139] *Ibid.*, 173-174; *P. M.*, I, 66; and P. L. A., IV, 57.

Russell's earliest treatment of definite (and indefinite) descriptions as incomplete symbols was in the article, "On Denoting" (1905). In that article he considers descriptions as species of denoting phrases. A phrase, Russell points out, denotes

... solely in virtue of its *form*. We may distinguish three cases: (1) A phrase may be denoting, and yet not denote anything; e.g., "the present King of France." (2) A phrase may denote one definite object; e.g., "the present King of England" denotes a certain man. (3) A phrase may denote ambiguously; e.g., "a man" denotes not many men, but an ambiguous man.[140]

Denoting phrases are analyzed by Russell in the following way: he takes as fundamental the variable. He then declares that "x has C" means a propositional function in which "x" is a constituent and, as a variable, is undetermined. With this logical machinery, he can now interpret phrases containing "everything," "something," and "nothing," which are the most primitive denoting phrases. Thus, "everything has C," e.g., is to mean " 'x has C' is always true."

"Everything," "nothing," and "something" are incomplete symbols because they have no meaning in isolation. Rather, as the above example shows, a meaning is assigned to the propositions in which they occur. This is the basic thesis of Russell's theory of denoting phrases, that they ". . . never have any meaning in themselves, but that every proposition in whose verbal expression they occur has a meaning."[141]

In this same article Russell also offers analyses of other denoting phrases: those involving words like "a," "all," "no," and "the." E.g., suppose I say "I met a man." This, according to Russell's theory, becomes: "The propositional function 'I met x and x is human' is not always false." This analysis leaves the phrase "a man," by itself, without meaning, but attributes a meaning to every proposition in whose verbal expression "a man" occurs.

One can hardly exaggerate the significance of "On Denoting." Not only did it explain how we may speak truly and meaningfully about "the round square," "the present King of

---

[140] "On Denoting," 479.
[141] *Ibid.*, 480.

France," "the golden mountain," etc., without assuming that
these enter into discourse as the denotata, in the form of actual
entities, of our verbal symbols; but it also showed, by implication, how we may utter phrases like "a man," "the present King
of England," etc., without assuming that there are objects
which correspond to these phrases either. Other theories, like
Meinong's, which regard denoting phrases as designating genuine objects, fall into contradiction,—e.g., in simultaneously affirming and denying the existence of the round square,—and
can escape this difficulty only by inventing various kinds of
realities: imaginative, logical, empirical, etc., which give rise to
further difficulties centering around the denial of our robust
sense of reality.

We may now consider, somewhat systematically, Russell's
theory of definite descriptions. There are two parts to the
theory: (1) to determine why they are incomplete symbols;
and (2) to resolve them into symbolic contexts which give them
their meanings. As our example of a definite description let us
take "the author of *Waverley*."

"The author of *Waverley*" is an incomplete symbol, to begin
with, because it is not a proper name, for three reasons: (a) it is
not a simple symbol which designates a particular or an individual treated as a particular, but is a complex symbol. (b) Its
meaning is determinate; as a phrase, its meaning is fixed as soon
as we know the meanings of the separate words, whereas the
meaning of a proper name is not determined by words but by
our knowing to whom the name is applied.[142] (c) If it were a
proper name, it would render "Scott was the author of *Waverley*" either tautological or false. That is, if "the author of
Waverley" were a proper name, then one could substitute for
it any proper name. If that name were "Scott," the proposition
becomes "Scott was Scott," which is trivial; and if that name
were other than "Scott," the proposition would be false. However, the proposition is neither trivial nor false, but revealing
and true, disclosing a fact of literary history.[143]

[142] P. L. A., VI, 210-211.
[143] P. M., I, 67; and I. M. P., 174.

A second, closely related, reason why descriptive phrases are incomplete symbols is because *what* they are supposed to refer to are not really "constituents of propositions."[144] That is, there is no actual entity which we may call its denotation. When a description occurs in a proposition there is no constituent of that proposition corresponding to that description as a whole. This is a consequence of the fact that we may utter significant and true propositions which deny the existence of the so-and-so as, e.g., "the golden mountain does not exist." This proposition could not be significant and true, which it is, if the golden mountain had to be an actual constituent of the proposition, since, if there were no golden mountain, it certainly could not be a constituent of *any* proposition.

This completes our exposition of Russell's argument that definite descriptions are incomplete symbols. Our next problem is to resolve them into meaningful symbolic contexts. Now, the most important thing about the resolution or analysis of definite descriptions is that it does not consist in the analysis of the descriptions themselves, but of the *propositions* in which they occur; and the propositions themselves must be so analyzed that what were the grammatical subjects shall have disappeared.[145]

According to Russell, the best way to begin the analysis of propositions containing definite descriptions is to see what circumstances would render them false.[146] Our example, "Scott was the author of *Waverley*," is certainly false if (1) *Waverley* had never been written; (2) several people had written *Waverley*; or (3) the person who wrote *Waverley* was not Scott. In order to resolve the proposition, we need only negate these three conditions of falsity; then (1) becomes " 'x wrote *Waverley*' is not always false; i.e., at least one person wrote *Waverley*;" (2) becomes "if x and y wrote *Waverley*, then x and y are identical; i.e., at most one person wrote *Waverley*;" (3) becomes " 'if x wrote *Waverley*, then x was Scott', is always

true." Taken all together, these three propositions state that
" 'x wrote *Waverley*' is always equivalent to 'x was Scott'."[147]

We come now to our second example, the resolution of symbols which are supposed to represent classes. The theory of
classes as incomplete symbols and the resolution of them into
defined symbolic contexts was developed in 1910, in *P. M.*,
where it is stated:

> The symbols for classes, like those of descriptions, are, in our system,
> incomplete symbols; their *uses* are defined, but they themselves are not
> assumed to mean anything at all. That is to say, the uses of such symbols
> are so defined that, when the *definiens* is substituted for the *definiendum*,
> there no longer remains any symbol which could be supposed to represent
> a class. Thus classes, so far as we introduce them, are merely symbolic
> or linguistic conveniences, not genuine objects as their members are if
> they are individuals.[148]

This theory of classes, it is apparent, is the historical resultant
of Russell's treatment of descriptions, in 1905. Like most
logicians, Russell desires to abstain from making any unnecessary assumptions, without, of course, thereby rendering pre-
carious the subject-matter which is being considered. Consequently, when he succeeded in dealing with described "objects"
in such a manner that we no longer needed to assume their
existence, it was only natural for him, as a logician, to try to
do the same thing with classes. However, there is this difference
between his treatments of descriptions and classes: with described
"objects," he is quite certain that they do not exist, and that any
theory which thinks otherwise falls into contradiction. But with
classes, he is not so dogmatic. He neither asserts nor denies
their reality as actual entities. He writes: "We are merely
agnostic as regards them: like Laplace, we can say *'je n'ai pas
besoin de cette hypothèse'*."[149]

The resolution of symbols for classes, like the resolution of
descriptive symbols, does not consist in the definition of classes
themselves but in the definition of the *propositions* in which
words apparently representing classes appear. These proposi-

[147] *P. M.*, I, 68.
[148] *Ibid.*, 71-72.
[149] *I. M. P.*, 184.

tions are defined in such a manner that these class-symbols disappear. How is this resolution of a class-symbol into a symbolic complex, in which no class-symbol appears, accomplished? It is done by resolving every proposition supposedly about a class into a proposition about the values that satisfy some propositional function. For example:

Take such a statement as, "The class of people interested in mathematical logic is not very numerous." Obviously this reduces itself to, "Not very many people are interested in mathematical logic." For the sake of definiteness, let us substitute some particular number, say 3, for "very many." Then our statement is, "Not three people are interested in mathematical logic." This may be expressed in the form: "If x is interested in mathematical logic, and also y is interested, and also z is interested, then x is identical with y, or x is identical with z, or y is identical with z." Here there is no longer any reference at all to a class. [150]

In this example, then, the proposition containing the symbol for the *class* of people interested in mathematical logic is resolved into a complex statement about the *individuals* who satisfy the function "x is interested in mathematical logic." In a similar fashion, Russell insists, all propositions about classes can be resolved into propositions about the values of propositional functions.[151]

Upon the completion of *P. M.* both Russell and Whitehead reassembled the techniques which they had employed in mathematics and applied them to the *natural* sciences. The enormous success they had achieved in their treatment of descriptions, classes, numbers, relations (in extension), etc., as incomplete symbols inspired in them the hope that they might be able to deal similarly with the symbols of the other scientific disciplines. Both of them recognized in the techniques of *P. M.* a powerful instrument for the solution of many of the traditional problems

[150] *E. W.*, 224-225.
[151] *P. M.*, I, 23; *I. M. P.*, 184-193; P. L. A., VII, 359-363; and L. A., 364. In *P. M.*, Russell (and Whitehead) develop a uniform method for the resolution of propositions containing class-symbols; its distinctive feature is its reduction of propositions about classes to propositions about extensional predicative functions which are formally equivalent to certain first-order functions (*P. M.*, I, 72-78; also *I. M. P.*, Ch. 17).

of scientific philosophy: time, space, mind and matter.[152]

Whitehead was the first to turn the full force of *P. M.* upon the natural sciences. By 1914 he had persuaded Russell that the world of physics is to be regarded no longer as an inference, as in *P. of P.*, but as a construction out of empirical data.[153] From 1914 until 1928 Russell's philosophical contribution consisted, to a great extent, in the formulation and exemplification of "the method of constructionism," as applied to the fundamental natural sciences, physics and psychology.

The basic problem which led Russell to treat the symbols of the natural sciences as incomplete was the status of the entities which the symbols of science apparently designate. Physics, e.g., talks about points in space, instants of time and particles of matter. Furthermore, it asserts that it is an empirical science, i.e., based upon observation; hence its points, instants, and electrons ought to be observable. But, of course, they are not: what we observe—empiricists agree—are immediate data of sense, with certain spatio-temporal relations. If physics desires to become an empirical science, Russell advised, it must be reconciled to these sense-data. One way, the most radical, but not the only way in which this can be done is to define the objects of physics as functions of the immediate data of sense, a procedure in direct contrast to the usual one in physics:

In physics as commonly set forth, sense-data appear as functions of physical objects: when such-and-such waves impinge upon the eye, we see such-and-such colours, and so on. But the waves are in fact inferred from the colours, not vice versa. Physics cannot be regarded as validly based upon empirical data until the waves have been expressed as functions of the colours, and other sense-data.[154]

So to interpret the entities of physics means, of course, that they are no longer the denotata of proper names, as they had been in *P. of M.*, nor the denotata of descriptions, as they were in *P. of P.* They became pseudo-entities or, more correctly, *unnecessary* entities, i.e., things without which we can get along

[152] L. A., 361.
[153] E. W., viii and R. S. D. P., 157.
[154] R. S. D. P., 146.

excellently in scientific discourse, and even in the language of daily life.

The symbols for these unnecessary entities, because they are not proper names and, consequently, have no meaning in themselves, become incomplete symbols, to be dealt with along lines similar to the treatment of other incomplete symbols. That is, the propositions in which these unnecessary entities are supposedly designated are interpreted in such a manner that the symbols for these unnecessary entities are resolved into other symbolic contexts whose denotata are empirical.[155]

The earliest formulation by Russell of the method of constructionism as applied to the natural sciences was in 1914, in *E. W.* and in R. S. D. P. especially. In P. L. A. (1918-19), L. A. (1924), and *A. of Matter* (1927), he supplemented his earlier statement. However, in none of these writings does he present a comprehensive picture of constructionism. This being the case, it becomes our task here to attempt a brief synthesis of what Russell means by constructionism.

The easiest way to understand constructionism, I think, is in its historical setting, as a philosophy of science. Since the seventeenth century there have been many philosophies of science, among them the following: (1) the view that the function of philosophy is to accept completely the results of science and to generalize these results so that they embrace all aspects of reality, including human experience. The philosophy of evolutionism as championed by Spencer is perhaps the classic example of this kind of view. (2) Then there is the theory of

---

[155] As Russell says: "I do not mean that statements apparently about points or instants . . . or any of the other entities which Occam's razor abolishes, are false, but only that their linguistic form is misleading, and that, when they are rightly analyzed, the pseudo-entities in question are found to be not mentioned in them. 'Time consists of instants', for example, may or may not be a true statement, but in either case it mentions neither time nor instants. It may, roughly, be interpreted as follows: Given any event x, let us define as its 'contemporaries' those which end after it begins, but begin before it ends; and among these let us define as 'initial contemporaries' of x those which are not wholly later than any other contemporaries of x. Then the statement 'time consists of instants' is true if, given any event x, every event which is wholly later than some contemporary of x is wholly later than some initial contemporary of x" (*P. of M.*, new "Introduction," xi).

Hume, that the function of philosophy, in relation to science, is to challenge the assumptions of science, specifically: induction, causality and substance. (3) Philosophers like Berkeley, I think, regard the function of philosophy, so far as science is concerned, to be one of sharp reconstruction. Specifically, philosophy, they assert, must attempt an interpretation of the concepts and entities of science so that these harmonize with the more gross facts of human experience. (4) Finally, there is the view of philosophers like Kant, who maintain that the function of a scientific philosophy is the justification of science, either as a method or as a body of knowledge.

Now, when we come to Russell's conception of the rôle of philosophy in relation to science, we find that he has much in common with Berkeley, Hume, and especially Kant, whom he has disparaged so vehemently! Like Hume he thinks that philosophy should challenge the assumptions of science and he agrees with Berkeley that philosophy should reconcile science and experience. But, above all, I think, he considers the grand rôle of philosophy to be the justification of science. Unlike Hume he does not seek to challenge science in order to transform our knowledge into scepticism; nor does he wish, like Berkeley, to reconstruct science in terms of experience in order to establish some sort of pan-psychism. *His challenge to and his reconstruction of science is motivated by his desire to justify science.* From his debut into philosophy, when he wished ". . . to find some reason to believe in the truth of mathematics . . . ,"[156] until the present day, Russell's primary interest, it seems to me, has been the attempt to justify science.

Taken broadly and loosely, science consists of two related parts, a methodology and a body of propositions. Its methodology contains a set of operative techniques, e.g., measurement; and a set of principles or assumptions, e.g., induction and causality. Induction, of course, is the most important principle of science, and any complete justification of science must offer some validation of the principle of induction. Unfortunately, at this very point Russell has no solution, which, in itself, is a very

[156] L. A., 359.

serious gap in his attempt to justify science.[157]

Russell's great contribution has been his justification of science, considered as a body of knowledge, and not as a set of techniques or principles. It is this which distinguishes him from Kant, since the latter's energy was primarily directed toward the justification of the methodology of science, especially induction.

Before we consider the meaning of the justification of the natural sciences, let us make our general remarks more specific. The method of constructionism, Russell proclaims, has for its historical antecedent the maxim of William of Occam: "Entities are not to be multiplied beyond necessity." Russell regards this maxim as the fundamental one of a scientific philosophy.[158] He states it in a somewhat different form: "Wherever possible, substitute constructions out of known entities for inferences to unknown entities."[159] In practice, the maxim comes in in the following way:

Take some science, say physics. You have there a given body of doctrine, a set of propositions expressed in symbols . . . and you think that you have reason to believe that on the whole those propositions, rightly interpreted, are fairly true, but you do not know what is the actual meaning of the symbols that you are using. The meaning they have *in use* would have to be explained in some pragmatic way: they have a certain kind of practical or emotional significance to you which is a datum, but the logical significance is not a datum, but a thing to be sought, and you go through . . . these propositions with a view to finding out what is . . . the smallest apparatus, not necessarily wholly empirical . . . out of which you can build up these propositions.[160]

Constructionism, then, as this quotation discloses, is dependent for its use upon the existence of a body of propositions which it interprets in such a way as to preserve the truth-value of the propositions while minimizing the amount of inference to

[157] Russell's early view, that the principle of induction is *a priori*, he abandoned in 1914 (*E. W.*, 37). From 1914-27 he devoted little attention to induction, and in *A. of Matter* (1927) he states quite baldly his inability to provide a solution of the problem (398-399).

[158] R. S. D. P., 155.

[159] L. A., 363.

[160] P. L. A., VIII, 366-367.

unempirical entities. That is, constructionism, in interpreting a science, leaves alone its details; it is only the fundamental ideas which are changed. Russell calls this process the preservation of the structure of science.[161]

When a scientific philosophy functions as the justification of science, considered as an extant body of propositions, it is identical with constructionism. This is, I think, the most comprehensive definition of constructionism. As we have seen, there are to be found in any of the natural sciences certain symbols for entities which we never experience. The function of constructionism, in regard to these entities, is neither to affirm nor to deny their existence, but to replace the symbols for these entities by other symbols. That is, to substitute symbols whose denotata are either given directly in sense-experience or are similar to and continuous with what is given in sense-experience for symbols whose denotata are not given in sense-experience but are postulated as inferred entities completely unlike those given in sense-experience. This substitution of empirical for unempirical symbols means, of course, that scientific symbols are defined in sensory terms, which validates the claim of (natural) science that it is empirical. It is in this sense, I think, that constructionism is the justification of science.

This process, whereby empirical symbols replace unempirical symbols, has, it seems to me, two distinct parts: (1) to determine what are the ultimate wholly or partially empirical entities,[162] and (2) to define, by means of logic, the symbols of science in terms of the wholly or partially empirical entities.[163]

The determination of the ultimate wholly empirical entities was accomplished by Russell in *P. of P.*, before he became a constructionist. In that work, as we have seen, he employs two

[161] L. A., 367.

[162] By an ultimate *wholly empirical* entity, I mean one which is given directly in sense-experience, e.g., a sense-datum; by an ultimate *partially empirical* entity, one which is inferred as similar to and continuous with what is given directly in sense-experience, e.g., a sensible. Both of these are to be contrasted with a *wholly unempirical* entity, i.e., one which is inferred or postulated as completely unlike that which is given directly in sense-experience, e.g., an electron.

[163] To divide constructionism in such a manner is, I think, in keeping with Russell and Occam: "In dealing with any subject-matter, find out what entities are undeniably involved, and state everything in terms of these entities," *E. W.*, 113.

principles in order to establish the ultimate entities of reality: the Cartesian method of doubt and the method of hypothesis. The first gives him the ultimate empirical and conceptual entities, the second the ultimate inferred entities. Examples of the first are sense-data and universals; of the second, other minds and physical objects. The ultimate wholly empirical entities, according to the method of doubt, are sense-data: these are the most undeniable entities of sense-experience.[164]

In R. S. D. P., Russell accepts completely this doctrine that the ultimate wholly empirical entities are sense-data. Besides these, Russell regards "unsensed sensibilia" as entities which physical constructions may denote: these are inferred as similar to and continuous with sense-data, except that no one is aware of them.

Many students of Russell think that constructionism does not employ as ultimate denotata of scientific symbols any *inferred* entities. But this is not true, as the admission of unsensed sensibilia as legitimate constituents of constructions in R. S. D. P. proves. What is true is that Russell rejects inferred entities which are wholly unempirical, like Kant's *Ding-an-sich*. It is only in *E. W.* that Russell construes constructionism as the method which dispenses with *all* inferred entities as valid constituents of constructions. But in Russell's other constructionist works, at least as regards physical constructions, both wholly and partially empirical entities are employed.

In *E. W.* Russell contends that the only acceptable entities of constructions are the wholly empirical ones, sense-data. However, before we discuss his reasons for rejecting unsensed sensibilia as valid constituents of constructions, let us return our attention to the method which discloses the ultimate wholly empirical character of sense-data, the Cartesian method of doubt, since this method is an integral part of the search for the ultimate empirical entities. The method of doubt was first practiced by Russell in *P. of P.*, not upon the propositions of science, but upon ordinary common-sensical propositions. The work itself opens with the question: "Is there any knowledge in the world which is so certain that no reasonable man could doubt it?"[165] This quest for certainty is, I think, the distinctive inquiry of constructionism because it is the results of this quest which comprise the empirical and logical premisses of constructionism. As Russell expresses it in a later article:

The things we have got to take as premisses in any kind of work of analysis are the things which appear to *us* undeniable—to us here and now, as we are—and I think on the whole that the sort of method adopted by Descartes is right: that you should set to work to doubt things and retain only what you cannot doubt because of its clearness and distinctness. . . ."[166]

This, then, is the initial task of constructionism: to take a body of propositions and to practice doubt upon them in order to establish some sort of "hierarchy of dubitables," i.e., some sort of system in which the least dubious propositions constitute the premisses of the entire system of propositions.[167]

In *P. of P.* a specific hierarchy is presented: the propositions of which we are most certain, when we begin systematically to doubt, are those about sense-data and logic. Lower are propositions about immediate memory, awareness, distant memory and ethical value. Lowest in the hierarchy are propositions about inferred objects, like tables, chairs and other minds.[168]

In *E. W.* a similar hierarchy is offered: Russell characterizes as "hard data," i.e., those propositions which appear as luminously certain, our knowledge of sense-data, logic, recent memory, introspection, relations of time and space and, finally, universals; these data are contrasted with "soft data," i.e., those propositions about whose truth we are no longer certain when we practice doubt upon them, which include our knowledge of physical objects and other minds.[169]

---

[165] *Ibid.*, 9.

[166] P. L. A., I, 500.

[167] This erection of a hierarchy of dubitables is what Russell takes to be the supreme task of epistemology too. See *P. of P.*, 39-41; N. of A., IV; and *Inquiry*, 15-19. Thus, in our interpretation of Russell, epistemology plays a subsidiary rather than a preëminent rôle in his *total* philosophy.

[168] *P. of P.*, 176-178; 182-183; 217.

[169] *E. W.*, 72-77. It is a rather interesting footnote on Russell's unity, I think, that the Cartesian method of doubt and the hierarchy of dubitables, worked out in *P. of P.*, a pre-constructionist book, have been retained by him throughout his

The importance for constructionism of the method of doubt, then, is twofold: (1) it establishes the wholly and partially empirical entities; and (2) it provides a logical instrument for constructionism which is as self-evident as the empirical entities. The significance of (1) and (2), taken together, is that they furnish the ultimate, self-evident, empirical and logical elements of constructionism.

Let us now return to the basic empirical entities of constructionism in *E. W*. Like R. S. D. P., the main concern of this work is with the symbols of physics, not with those of psychology. It is Russell's most extreme exhibition of constructionism, because of his doctrine that the only valid constituents of constructions are the wholly empirical ones, sense-data. The inferred and partially empirical entities, "unsensed sensibilia," are rejected and defined as functions of "sensed sensibilia," i.e., sense-data. In fact, all the symbols of physics, in an attempt to render them completely empirical, are interpreted in terms of sense-data:

> I think it may be laid down quite generally that, *in so far* as physics . . . is verifiable, it must be capable of interpretation in terms of actual sense-data alone. The reason for this is simple. Verification consists always in the occurrence of an expected sense-datum. . . . Now if an expected sense-datum constitutes a verification, what was asserted must have been about sense-data; or, at any rate, if part of what was asserted was not about sense-data, then only the other part has been verified.[170]

As far as physics is concerned, then, *E. W*. satisfies the requirements of the constructionist ideal: all inferences to unknown entities are replaced by constructions out of known entities, i.e., sense-data.

However, in U. C. M. Russell returns to the view of R. S. D. P., that the ultimate denotata of the symbols of physics are either wholly or partially empirical.[171] He retains this view

---

writings, from *E. W*. to *Inquiry*. The only changes that have occurred are in the specific data of the hierarchy. *E.g.*, in *A. of Matter* (180-181) the facts of awareness are omitted, the reason being, of course, that Russell abandoned the belief in consciousness as an entity. See also *A. of Mind*, 262-266 and 297-299; and *Inquiry*, Chs. X-XI.

[170] *E. W*., 86; see also 117-118.

[171] U. C. M., 130, 137, 143.

in *A. of Mind*[172] and *A. of Matter*,[173] which is the last of his
major writings devoted to physics. In the latter work, the basic
wholly empirical entities are perceptual events and the basic
partially empirical entities are unperceived events. These are
inferred as (1) continuous with perceptual events, by means of
the causal theory of perception and (2) similar to perceptual
events, with the aid of the general theory of neutral monism.
Every concept of physics—"points," "space," "time," "electrons," etc.—Russell proclaims, can be interpreted as a function
of these perceptual and unperceived events.[174]

In *A. of Mind* Russell discusses fully the basic empirical
entities of the constructions of *psychology:* these are the wholly
empirical entities, sensations and images. Every concept of psychology, Russell claims, can be built up in terms of these.[175]

This brings us to the second part of constructionism, the
defining of the symbols of physics and psychology in terms of
the wholly and partially empirical entities which we have discovered. If we examine the writings of Russell in which he has
practiced constructionism in the natural sciences, we shall find
that there are about twenty constructions.[176] Space limitations
permit me to discuss only one of these and I shall choose Russell's construction of "points" in *E. W.*, because it seems to me
best to represent the sort of thing Russell does when he defines
scientific symbols in terms of empirical entities.

The definition of the "points" of mathematical physics in
sensory terms is not especially difficult. The problem is to find
". . . some complex assemblage of immediately given objects,
which will have the geometrical properties required of
points."[177] The empirical objects which have these requisite
properties are sense-data. Consider a sense-datum. What are its

[172] *A. of Mind*, 97-107, 121, 143, 306-307.
[173] *A. of Matter*, 139-140, 214-217, 270-271, 399.
[174] *Ibid.*, 275-278.
[175] *A. of Mind*, 69, 109, 121, 143.
[176] These are, in physics, "space," "time," "thing," or "matter," "points,"
"instants," "qualitative series," "space-time," "interval," and "quanta;" see
R. S. D. P., *E. W.*, Chs. III, IV, and *A. of Matter*; and, in psychology, "instinct,"
"habit," "desire," "feeling," "perception," "memory," "conception," "thought,"
"belief," "emotions," "will," and "consciousness;" see *A. of Mind* and *Phil.*
[177] *E. W.*, 121.

obvious properties? We know that it is always of some *finite* extent; that is, any visual datum, e.g., has a surface which is never ostensibly infinitesimal. Furthermore, a sense-datum, which is *prima facie* one undivided whole, may, upon strict attention, be broken up into its constituent parts. Whenever this phenomenon occurs, we have one part contained within a different part and entirely enclosed by it. This relation of "enclosure," which is given in sense-experience, is the first property of sense-data which will enable us to define "points" in terms of them.

The second requisite property has to do with certain hypotheses which are attributed to the relation of enclosure. What we desire, in order to define "points" in terms of sense-data and enclosure, is that a set of visual data, considered as volumes or surfaces, should get smaller and smaller so that ". . . of any two of the set there is always one that encloses the other."[178] This desideratum is satisfied with the aid of six hypotheses, which are as follows:

The hypotheses required for the relation of enclosure are that (1) it must be transitive; (2) of any two *different* spatial objects, it is impossible for each to enclose the other, but a single object always encloses itself; (3) any set of spatial objects such that there is at least one spatial object enclosed by them all has a lower limit or minimum, i.e., an object enclosed by all of them and enclosing all objects which are enclosed by all of them; (4) to prevent trivial exceptions, we must add that there are to be instances of enclosure, i.e., there are really to be objects of which one encloses the other. When an enclosure-relation has these properties we will call it a "point-producer."[179]

The fifth hypothesis is necessary to guarantee that space is infinite: (5) "Any object which encloses itself also encloses an object other than itself."[180] Finally, the sixth hypothesis is concerned with an enclosure-series—i.e., a set of objects in which, of any two of them, one is contained in the other—converging to a point: (6) "Let our enclosure-series be such that, given any other enclosure-series of which there are members enclosed in any arbitrarily chosen member of our first series, then there are

[178] *Ibid.*, 122.
[179] *Ibid.*
[180] *Ibid.*, 123.

members of our first series enclosed in any arbitrarily chosen member of our second series."[181] When this sixth hypothesis is realized, the first enclosure-series is called a "punctual enclosure-series."

We may now define a "point," as it is conceived by mathematical physics. It is a logical construction which has as its constituents ". . . all the objects which enclose members of a given punctual enclosure-series."[182] This definition, Russell concludes, is sufficient to express all that physics requires in regard to its use of "points;" and it validates the claim of physics that it is an empirical science.

Section V. What Does Russell Mean by Analysis?

It is a curious fact that Russell, one of the greatest modern exponents of the method of analysis, has never discussed in any detail what he means by it. Like a prodigious mathematician, who is too preoccupied doing mathematics to seek into its foundations, Russell has devoted most of his philosophical writings to the exemplification, rather than to the explication, of analysis. As we have seen, he has practiced the analytical method especially in four disciplines: (1) ontology, (2) abstract cosmology, (3) mathematical logic, and (4) semantics, or the examination of ordinary and scientific discourse. In our previous sections we have dealt with these uses of analysis in Russell, attempting, as much as possible, to discuss them in an historical manner, so that the reader might be able to appreciate more fully the significance of each use of analysis and the total unity of his philosophy. In none of these sections, however, did we venture an interpretation of what Russell means by analysis. I shall now attempt to remedy this deficiency.

The view regarding Russell's theory of analysis which I wish to present in this final section is this: that Russell means by analysis a form of definition, either real definition of a non-Aristotelian sort, or contextual definition, i.e., definition of symbols in use. I shall not attempt to show that Russell does not mean something *more* by analysis nor shall I try to prove

[181] *Ibid.*
[182] *Ibid.*

conclusively that he means by analysis either of these kinds of definition. I wish merely to present an hypothesis concerning his theory of analysis which, it seems to me at least, can explain all of his uses of analysis.

Let us begin with Russell's theory of analysis as real definition. Now, real definition, as conceived by the Aristotelian tradition, has suffered much abuse, perhaps deservedly, because its conception of real definition—that it is concerned with ascertaining the essences of species—is certainly not a credible one, especially since Darwin's refutation of the notion of fixed species. However, there is another sense of definition which, because it obviously cannot be interpreted as nominal, can be characterized as real definition: namely, the sense in which the *properties of a given complex are enumerated;* where I mean by "properties" (1) the elements of a complex, (2) their characteristics, and (3) the relations among them; and by a "complex," a group of facts, which exists independently of the way in which we use language.

Does Russell accept this conception of analysis? I think that he does. It is, however, no easy matter to prove this; the reason being that whenever Russell discusses the nature of definition he seems to reject real definition by explicitly affirming a nominalistic view. Nevertheless, if we examine closely his writings on definition, even these affirmations of nominalism, we shall see that always Russell is *also* defending real definitions. Consider, e.g., his classic statement of nominalism in *P. M.:*

A definition is a declaration that a certain newly-introduced symbol or combination of symbols is to mean the same as a certain other combination of symbols of which the meaning is already known. . . .

It is to be observed that a definition is, strictly speaking, no part of the subject in which it occurs. For a definition is concerned wholly with the symbols, not with what they symbolise. Moreover it is not true or false, being the expression of a volition, not of a proposition. Theoretically, it is unnecessary ever to give a definition. . . . [Definitions] are, strictly speaking, mere typographical conveniences. Practically, of course, if we introduce no definitions, our formulae would very soon become so lengthy as to be unmanageable; but theoretically, all definitions are superfluous.

In spite of the fact that definitions are theoretically superfluous, it is nevertheless true that they often convey more important information than is contained in the propositions in which they are used . . . [One reason for this is that] when what is defined is (as often occurs) something already familiar, such as cardinal or ordinal numbers, the definition contains an analysis of a common idea, and may therefore express a notable advance. Cantor's definition of the continuum illustrates this: his definition amounts to the statement that what he is defining is the object which has the properties commonly associated with the word "continuum," though what precisely constitutes these properties had not before been known. In such cases, a definition is a "making definite:" it gives definiteness to an idea which had previously been more or less vague.[183]

This quotation expresses exactly Russell's ambivalent theory. In the first half he affirms the nominalistic theory: a definition is a stipulation as to how one intends to use a word or symbol; it is neither true nor false; it is convenient; and it has to do merely with symbols, not with what is symbolized. All of these are among the well-worn characteristics of a nominalistic theory.

The second part of the quotation, however, tells a different story. In effect, it asserts that there are *some* definitions, e.g., of cardinal numbers or the continuum, which, even though they may be formally expressed on the printed page as statements about our intentions to use symbols in certain ways, contain implicitly analyses of given complexes. These analyses consist in the enumeration of the properties of the complex and purport to be true (or false). As Russell says: Cantor's definition of the continuum ". . . amounts to the statement that *what he is defining is the object which has the properties commonly associated with the word 'continuum'* " (my italics).

If our reading of this quotation is correct, then Russell's theory of analysis amounts to this: that in the analysis of many given complexes, what we do is (1) to enumerate the properties of our given complex and (2), if we so desire, to express these properties in a formal definition which, when it appears on the printed page, resembles a nominal definition, but which actually functions as a convenient, abbreviated expression of a real definition.[184]

---

[183] *P. M.*, I, 11-12.

[184] Russell's statement in *P. of M.* (63) bears out this view, that many apparent nominal definitions are actually abbreviations of real definitions or analyses: "It is

Let us now examine certain examples of analyses, taken from Russell's writings, which further validate our hypothesis concerning his theory of real definition. Consider, to begin with, his definition of pure mathematics in *P. of M.*:

Pure mathematics is the class of all propositions of the form "p implies q," where p and q are propositions containing one or more variables, the same in the two propositions, and neither p nor q contains any constants except logical constants.[185]

Let us ask ourselves: Is this merely a nominal definition; i.e., does this definition merely express the way that Russell intends to use the words "pure mathematics?" Consider his answer to this question:

The definition professes to be, not an arbitrary decision to use a common word in an uncommon signification, but rather a precise analysis of the ideas which, more or less unconsciously, are implied in the ordinary employment of the term.[186]

Next, let us look at the *P. M.* definition of number as a class of classes similar to a given class. Is this merely a statement as to the way in which Russell intends to use the word "number?" Or does it also embody an analysis of number, i.e., an enumeration of the constituent properties of the complex which we call "number?" Part of the answer to this question, I think, is to be sought in Russell's critique of Peano's system of arithmetic and the formalist theory of mathematics in general. What, then, is Russell's objection to Peano's conception of number? Briefly, it is this: Peano makes "number," along with "zero" and "successor," an undefined concept of arithmetic. This conception, Russell points out, allows us to interpret number in an infinite

---

a curious paradox, puzzling to the symbolic mind, that definitions, theoretically, are nothing but statements of symbolic abbreviations, irrelevant to the reasoning and inserted only for practical convenience, while yet, in the development of a subject, they always require a very large amount of thought, and often embody some of the greatest achievements of analysis." See also *E. W.* (222) for the same view.

The doctrine that analysis is the enumeration of the constituent properties of a given complex, and that such an enumeration constitutes a real definition of that complex, may be found also in *P. of M.* (141 and 466), *E. W.* (222) and *Inquiry* (160 and Ch. XXIV).

[185] *P. of M.*, 1.
[186] *Ibid.*

variety of ways, without invalidating the five postulates of Peano's system. The fact that number is amenable to such a variety of interpretations, Russell argues, reveals the inadequacy of Peano's conception. Any adequate conception of number, Russell proclaims, must correspond to our unanalyzed notion of it, especially as it is used in the experience of counting:

We want to have ten fingers and two eyes and one nose. A system in which "1" meant 100 and "2" meant 101, and so on, might be all right for pure mathematics, but would not suit daily life. We want "0" and "number" and "successor" to have meanings which will give us the right allowance of fingers and eyes and noses. We have already some knowledge . . . of what we mean by "1" and "2" and so on, and our use of numbers in arithmetic must conform to this knowledge.[187]

Our conception of number, then, whether we leave it undefined or define it, must correspond to our knowledge and experience of it. If we choose to define it, our definition cannot be merely a stipulation regarding the way we intend to use the symbol "number," but it must also contain implicitly an enumeration of the constituent properties which, in ordinary daily life, we call "number." The *P. M.* definition professes to be just that. However, when we examine the definition for the first time, it seems to be too paradoxical to be a real definition of number; and some logicians have argued that, because it is so paradoxical, it is a *false* definition. This criticism is meaningful, although not necessarily true, only if what we have asserted about the characteristics of real definitions is accepted; it is not a meaningful criticism if Russell's definition is taken to be nominal, since nominal definitions are, among other things, never true or false.

Russell's definition, however, provides for this sort of criticism. It admits the apparent paradox of the definition, but insists that the paradox arises from the fact that the definition is *empirical*; i.e., that it is an enumeration of the empirical properties of the complex we call "number."[188] The objection to Russell's definition usually springs from the belief in the doctrine that number is either a Platonic universal or an inferred

[187] *I. M. P.*, 9.
[188] *Ibid.*, 18, and *E. W.*, 222-223.

entity which is postulated as existing in the flux rather than in the realm of essence. Russell regards this objection as harmless because it is founded not upon the actual, given, experienced properties of number, but upon the inferred, unempirical properties which it is supposed to have. Consequently, Russell's definition not only claims to be an enumeration of the properties of number, but also a *true* definition, in the sense that it has exhausted all of its empirical properties. To sum up, then: Russell's definition of number as a class of classes similar to a given class is an abbreviated, formal expression of an analysis or real definition of the complex which we call "number."

The example which illustrates best Russell's use of analysis as real definition is his analysis of memory, in *A. of Mind* (Ch. IX). If we examine closely that discussion, we note certain statements, like the following:

[1] "In the present lecture I shall attempt the *analysis* of memory-knowledge . . . ;" [2] "I am only anxious to point out that, whatever the *true analysis* of knowledge may be, knowledge of past occurrences is not proved by behaviour which is due to past experience;" [3] "Perhaps a more *complete analysis* could explain the memory-belief also on lines of association . . . ;" [4] "This analysis of memory is probably extremely *faulty*, but I do not know how to improve it."[189]

Now, what is the meaning of such statements regarding memory-knowledge, which use words like "analysis," "faulty analysis," "true analysis" and "complete analysis?" This is an extremely important question, because the total meaning of Russell's analysis of mental and physical phenomena revolves about its answer, since Russell's treatment of "memory" may be regarded as a model of his treatment of "points," "matter," "habit," "perception," etc. Indeed, it was the consideration of this question which first led me to the hypothesis that Russell means by analysis, at least in some cases, real definition. It is only in terms of analysis as real definition that I can give any meaning to faulty, true, and complete analyses. Any other interpretation, e.g., that Russell's analysis consists merely in the stipulation as to how he shall use the word "memory" or as to how he shall interpret sentences containing the word "memory,"

---

[189] *A. of Mind*, 157, 167, 178, 187 respectively (my italics).

does not do even partial justice to the above phrases. If analyses are only stipulations about the use of symbols or symbolic contexts, then how can they be faulty or true or complete? No, the only way to interpret these phrases is in terms of real definition. Thus, what Russell means when he talks about the analysis of memory, etc., is primarily the enumeration of the properties of a given complex which we call "memory," but which does not depend for its existence upon the fact that it is called "memory."[190]

Enough has been said, I think, to show that Russell does accept the conception of analysis as real definition.[191] Our next problem is to determine whether or not Russell means something more by analysis. There is, I think, another meaning of analysis in Russell's philosophy which also has to do with definition, specifically, nominal definition. There are two sorts of nominal definitions, the ordinary or dictionary kind and the contextual kind, i.e., the definition of symbols in use. Both of these have in common, first, the fact that they involve the sub-

---

[190] These properties are: (1) certain *elements*, namely, sensations and images; (2) their *characteristics*, namely, the feelings of pastness, context, familiarity and respect; and (3) the *relations* among them, namely, the relation between (a) the feelings and the memory-image, (b) the belief and the content, and (c) the memory-image and the feeling of respect. See *A. of Mind.*, Ch. IX.

[191] Although I do not have the space to prove it, it seems to me that this conception is basic to at least three of the four species of analysis in Russell: ontology, abstract cosmology, and mathematical logic. That is, as an ontologist, Russell practices analysis as real definition. Both as a dualist and neutral monist, Russell's analysis consists in an enumeration of the ultimate entities of reality, with their characteristics and relations. As an abstract cosmologist, Russell is also meaning by analysis real definition: he is endeavoring to enumerate the basic forms of reality, as revealed by language and fact. Analysis as logistic is real definition, too, for it consists in the definition of the basic notions of mathematics in logical terms; specifically, it is the enumeration of the fundamental properties of "number," etc.

Furthermore, I think, Russell practices analysis as real definition in his search for the ultimate wholly and partially empirical entities, which is the first part of constructionism. The analysis of "points," e.g., consists primarily, as we have seen, in the enumeration of the empirical properties of the complexes which we call "points," but which do not depend for their existence upon the fact that they are so called. These properties are sense-data, their characteristics (e.g., they are of finite extent) and their relations (e.g., enclosure).

For a more complete discussion of the relation between real definition and the uses of analysis in Russell, see my dissertation, *op. cit.*, (*cf.* footnote 124 above) 256-276.

stitution of one symbol for another, or one set of symbols for another set; i.e., they are strictly concerned with language. Secondly, they are not propositions in the sense of truth-claims but are, rather, stipulations regarding our verbal desires. Thirdly, they are much shorter in length than the phrases that they are defined as meaning.

Nominal definitions, according to their exponents, are supposed to possess a fourth characteristic, arbitrariness. But, as we shall see, it is only the ordinary nominal definitions which have this characteristic. However, even here, I think, we must be careful. Arbitrariness is an ambiguous word and, so far as nominal definitions are concerned, at least two meanings must be distinguished: arbitrariness as capriciousness and arbitrariness as the possibility of making a choice in the presence of alternatives. Now, although all ordinary nominal definitions are arbitrary in the sense that they are choices among alternative expressions, there are few such definitions which are arbitrary in the capricious sense, since every significant ordinary nominal definition is an attempt to *answer* certain needs.

There are many examples of ordinary nominal definitions in Russell. His definitions of words like "truth-value," "atomic proposition," "emergent," "perspective," "phenomenalism," etc., are all convenient abbreviations of longer phrases and, although they are choices among alternative expressions, they are not capricious, for they are formulated to meet certain expository or stylistic requirements. As important as these definitions are in Russell's writings, they are not analyses, nor are they intended to be. When they function, as they may, as formal, resultant abbreviations of real definitions, they do serve as statements which embody analyses and, as such, they are true or false. But otherwise they are merely symbolic conveniences having the usual characteristics of nominal definitions.

Now, in the second sense in which Russell, as it seems to me, means analysis, it is not ordinary nominal definition, but contextual definition. The best example of analysis as contextual definition in Russell, and probably in the whole of philosophical literature, is his analysis of definite descriptions, which we considered in the previous section.

This analysis of definite descriptions amounts to a *definition* of the sentences in which definite descriptions occur. Consider e.g., the analysis of "the author of *Waverley*." It proceeds by defining certain sentences in which "the author of *Waverley*" appears; e.g., "Scott was the author of *Waverley*." The analysis of this sentence, then, consists in giving a definition of it, which is: " 'x wrote *Waverley*' is not always false, i.e., at least one person wrote *Waverley*; and if x and y wrote *Waverley*, then x and y are identical, i.e., at most one person wrote *Waverley*; and 'if x wrote *Waverley*, then x is Scott' is always true."

This analysis is a contextual nominal definition because (1) it is concerned with a purely linguistic complex and involves the substitution of one set of symbols for another set; (2) it consists of a declaration regarding our verbal intentions. It is saying that the symbolic complex "Scott was the author of *Waverley*" is to be defined as the symbolic complex " 'x wrote *Waverley*' is not always false, etc.;" hence the definition is neither true nor false; (3) it is typographically convenient; (4) it is a definition in use, i.e., of symbols in certain used contexts, namely, sentences; and (5) it is *not* arbitrary, for two reasons: (a) Russell contends that the definition of sentences containing definite descriptions is an *accurate* analysis of the logical structure of certain sentences; i.e., it reveals the constituent parts of the expression "Scott was the author of *Waverley*," namely, (1) at least one person wrote *Waverley*, (2) at most one person wrote *Waverley* and (3) that person was Scott. The value or purpose of this analysis, and of contextual nominal definition in general, where the logical complexity of an expression is resolved into its constituents, is that it offers a revelation of the logical structure of language. It is this characteristic, that both are concerned with the analysis of complexes, one with non-linguistic, the other with linguistic complexes, which brings real and contextual definition close together and contrasts them with ordinary definition. (b) The second reason why the analysis of sentences containing definite descriptions is not arbitrary is because it is designed to meet certain difficulties, which *no other* extant analysis or definition can meet, namely, it enables us to talk meaningfully and truly about non-existent and self-contradictory pseudo-objects, without inventing all sorts of realities to do so. Thus, e.g., the proposition "The present King of France is bald" is defined as, or analyzed into, the proposition "There is someone who is at present both king of France and bald and there is not at present two kings of France." The present King of France, whom Meinong assumed was an actual entity, having some sort of existence, because we could talk about him, is no longer mentioned in the defined symbolic complex but is replaced by a statement about a value of a variable which satisfies a propositional function. The definition also enables us to talk meaningfully and truly about things which we ordinarily regard as actual entities, like "the author of *Waverley*" or "the present King of England," etc., without assuming that they exist either. The reason why the treatment of descriptive phrases, whether they are like "the golden mountain," "the round square," or even "the author of *Waverley*," is uniform is because in each case we may wish to make statements in which these phrases appear without assuming that their non-linguistic correlates exist. If the author of *Waverley*, the round square or the golden mountain had to be actual entities in order for us to talk about them, then we could never deny their existence, as we often do, when, e.g., we say "the round square is unreal," without falling into contradiction by first assuming and then denying that these pseudo-objects exist.

This conception of analysis as contextual definition is, I think, what Russell mainly means by analysis when he practices it as the resolution of incomplete symbols. Descriptive symbols, specifically mathematical symbols and the symbols of the natural sciences, because they are incomplete, i.e., have no meanings in themselves, have to be assigned meanings in sentential contexts. It is this attribution of meaning which constitutes the analysis— in the form of a contextual definition—of the sentences in which these symbols appear.[192]

Real and contextual definitions may sometimes proceed to-

---

[192] Thus, the analysis of sentences in which symbols for classes occur consists in the contextual definition of the sentences. The sentence "there is not a class of three people interested in mathematical logic" becomes, by analysis or contextual definition: "If x is interested in mathematical logic, and also y is interested and also z, then x is identical with y, or x is identical with z, or y is identical with z." This analysis is a contextual definition because it possesses all the characteristics of such a definition.

gether. Consider, e.g., Russell's analysis of "time" or "instants." We may, in analyzing these concepts, first enumerate the empirical properties of the non-linguistic complex that we call "time" or "instants," which properties are *events*, with their characteristics and relations. This enumeration constitutes a real definition of this non-linguistic complex. Secondly, *upon the basis of this enumeration or real definition*, we may realize that these concepts are no longer simple symbols, i.e., proper names of simple particulars, but are rather incomplete symbols. In this case we may present an analysis of the sentences in which the symbols occur, where they will be resolved into whole new complexes of symbols having to do with events and not with time or instants. That is to say, the sentence "time consists of instants," upon the basis of an enumeration of the empirical properties of *what* we call "time" and "instants," is analyzed into the sentence: "Given any event x, every event which is wholly later than some contemporary of x is wholly later than some initial contemporary of x." This analysis of the sentence containing the words "time" and "instants," in which the words disappear, being replaced by phrases about events, constitutes a contextual definition of this linguistic complex. Thus, in this manner, we may offer a real definition of a non-linguistic complex and at the same time present a contextual definition of the sentences containing the symbols of that complex.

To sum up: It is our contention that Russell means by analysis two kinds of definition, real and contextual. The chief characteristics of these are: (1) real definition is concerned primarily with complexes which are non-linguistic, i.e., independent of the way in which we use language, whereas contextual definition is concerned wholly with linguistic complexes. Another way to express this difference is: that the contextual definition is concerned with symbols, real definition with *what* is symbolized. (2) Real definition is the enumeration of the properties of a given complex; contextual definition is the substitution of one set of symbols for another set. (3) Real definitions are true or false, i.e., they are truth-claims about the properties of given complexes; contextual definitions are neither true nor false, but are volitional stipulations regarding our verbal intentions.

This means that real definitions are expressed in empirical, synthetic propositions, whereas contextual definitions are *a priori* and analytic. (4) Neither real nor contextual definitions are ever arbitrary, since both are designed to cope with certain problems, and, as analyses, deny the adequacy of an alternative definition. (5) Real definitions may be expressed in statements which resemble ordinary nominal definitions, but when they are, the statements are actually formal abbreviations of analyses as real definitions; contextual definitions are always expressed in statements which resemble ordinary definitions, but these statements embody accurate analyses of linguistic complexes. (6) The value or purpose of real and contextual definitions is that they reduce the vaguenesses of certain complexes by calling attention to their various components.

MORRIS WEITZ

UNIVERSITY OF MICHIGAN

3

Kurt Gödel

RUSSELL'S MATHEMATICAL LOGIC

RUSSELL'S MATHEMATICAL LOGIC

MATHEMATICAL LOGIC, which is nothing else but a precise and complete formulation of formal logic, has two quite different aspects. On the one hand, it is a section of Mathematics treating of classes, relations, combinations of symbols, etc., instead of numbers, functions, geometric figures, etc. On the other hand, it is a science prior to all others, which contains the ideas and principles underlying all sciences. It was in this second sense that Mathematical Logic was first conceived by Leibniz in his *Characteristica universalis*, of which it would have formed a central part. But it was almost two centuries after his death before his idea of a logical calculus really sufficient for the kind of reasoning occurring in the exact sciences was put into effect (in some form at least, if not the one Leibniz had in mind) by Frege and Peano.[1] Frege was chiefly interested in the analysis of thought and used his calculus in the first place for deriving arithmetic from pure logic. Peano, on the other hand, was more interested in its applications within mathematics and created an elegant and flexible symbolism, which permits expressing even the most complicated mathematical theorems in a perfectly precise and often very concise manner by single formulas.

It was in this line of thought of Frege and Peano that Russell's work set in. Frege, in consequence of his painstaking analysis of the proofs, had not gotten beyond the most elementary properties of the series of integers, while Peano had accomplished a big collection of mathematical theorems expressed

[1] Frege has doubtless the priority, since his first publication about the subject, which already contains all the essentials, appeared ten years before Peano's.

in the new symbolism, but without proofs. It was only in *Principia Mathematica* that full use was made of the new method for actually deriving large parts of mathematics from a very few logical concepts and axioms. In addition, the young science was enriched by a new instrument, the abstract theory of relations. The calculus of relations had been developed before by Peirce and Schröder, but only with certain restrictions and in too close analogy with the algebra of numbers. In *Principia* not only Cantor's set theory but also ordinary arithmetic and the theory of measurement are treated from this abstract relational standpoint.

It is to be regretted that this first comprehensive and thorough going presentation of a mathematical logic and the derivation of Mathematics from it is so greatly lacking in formal precision in the foundations (contained in *1-*21 of *Principia*), that it presents in this respect a considerable step backwards as compared with Frege. What is missing, above all, is a precise statement of the syntax of the formalism. Syntactical considerations are omitted even in cases where they are necessary for the cogency of the proofs, in particular in connection with the "incomplete symbols." These are introduced not by explicit definitions, but by rules describing how sentences containing them are to be translated into sentences not containing them. In order to be sure, however, that (or for what expressions) this translation is possible and uniquely determined and that (or to what extent) the rules of inference apply also to the new kind of expressions, it is necessary to have a survey of all possible expressions, and this can be furnished only by syntactical considerations. The matter is especially doubtful for the rule of substitution and of replacing defined symbols by their *definiens*. If this latter rule is applied to expressions containing other defined symbols it requires that the order of elimination of these be indifferent. This however is by no means always the case ($\varphi!\hat{u} = \hat{u}[\varphi!u]$, e.g., is a counter-example). In *Principia* such eliminations are always carried out by substitutions in the theorems corresponding to the definitions, so that it is chiefly the rule of substitution which would have to be proved.

I do not want, however, to go into any more details about

either the formalism or the mathematical content of *Principia*,[2] but want to devote the subsequent portion of this essay to Russell's work concerning the analysis of the concepts and axioms underlying Mathematical Logic. In this field Russell has produced a great number of interesting ideas some of which are presented most clearly (or are contained only) in his earlier writings. I shall therefore frequently refer also to these earlier writings, although their content may partly disagree with Russell's present standpoint.

What strikes one as surprising in this field is Russell's pronouncedly realistic attitude, which manifests itself in many passages of his writings. "Logic is concerned with the real world just as truly as zoology, though with its more abstract and general features," he says, e.g., in his *Introduction to Mathematical Philosophy* (edition of 1920, p. 169). It is true, however, that this attitude has been gradually decreasing in the course of time[3] and also that it always was stronger in theory than in practice. When he started on a concrete problem, the objects to be analyzed (e.g., the classes or propositions) soon for the most part turned into "logical fictions." Though perhaps this need not necessarily mean [according to the sense in which Russell uses this term] that these things do not exist, but only that we have no direct perception of them.

The analogy between mathematics and a natural science is enlarged upon by Russell also in another respect (in one of his earlier writings). He compares the axioms of logic and mathematics with the laws of nature and logical evidence with sense perception, so that the axioms need not necessarily be evident in themselves, but rather their justification lies (exactly as in physics) in the fact that they make it possible for these "sense perceptions" to be deduced; which of course would not exclude that they also have a kind of intrinsic plausibility similar to that in physics. I think that (provided "evidence" is understood in a sufficiently strict sense) this view has been largely justified by subsequent developments, and it is to be expected that it will be still more so in the future. It has turned out that (under the

---

[2] Cf. in this respect W. V. Quine's article in the Whitehead volume of this series.
[3] The above quoted passage was left out in the later editions of the *Introduction*.

assumption that modern mathematics is consistent) the solution of certain arithmetical problems requires the use of assumptions essentially transcending arithmetic, i.e., the domain of the kind of elementary indisputable evidence that may be most fittingly compared with sense perception. Furthermore it seems likely that for deciding certain questions of abstract set theory and even for certain related questions of the theory of real numbers new axioms based on some hitherto unknown idea will be necessary. Perhaps also the apparently unsurmountable difficulties which some other mathematical problems have been presenting for many years are due to the fact that the necessary axioms have not yet been found. Of course, under these circumstances mathematics may lose a good deal of its "absolute certainty;" but, under the influence of the modern criticism of the foundations, this has already happened to a large extent. There is some resemblance between this conception of Russell and Hilbert's "supplementing the data of mathematical intuition" by such axioms as, e.g., the law of excluded middle which are not given by intuition according to Hilbert's view; the borderline however between data and assumptions would seem to lie in different places according to whether we follow Hilbert or Russell.

An interesting example of Russell's analysis of the fundamental logical concepts is his treatment of the definite article "the." The problem is: what do the so-called descriptive phrases (i.e., phrases as, e.g., "the author of *Waverley*" or "the king of England") denote or signify[4] and what is the meaning of sentences in which they occur? The apparently obvious answer that, e.g., "the author of *Waverley*" signifies Walter Scott, leads to unexpected difficulties. For, if we admit the further apparently obvious axiom, that the signification of a composite expression, containing constituents which have themselves a signification, depends only on the signification of these constituents (not on the manner in which this signification is expressed), then it follows that the sentence "Scott is the author of *Waverley*" signifies the same thing as "Scott is Scott;" and this again leads

---

[4] I use the term "signify" in the sequel because it corresponds to the German word *"bedeuten"* which Frege, who first treated the question under consideration, used in this connection.

almost inevitably to the conclusion that all true sentences have the same signification (as well as all false ones).[5] Frege actually drew this conclusion; and he meant it in an almost metaphysical sense, reminding one somewhat of the Eleatic doctrine of the "One." "The True"—according to Frege's view—is analyzed by us in different ways in different propositions; "the True" being the name he uses for the common signification of all true propositions.[6]

Now according to Russell, what corresponds to sentences in the outer world is facts. However, he avoids the term "signify" or "denote" and uses "indicate" instead (in his earlier papers he uses "express" or "being a symbol for"), because he holds that the relation between a sentence and a fact is quite different from that of a name to the thing named. Furthermore, he uses "denote" (instead of "signify") for the relation between things and names, so that "denote" and "indicate" together would correspond to Frege's "*bedeuten.*" So, according to Russell's terminology and view, true sentences "indicate" facts and, correspondingly, false ones indicate nothing.[7] Hence Frege's theory would in a sense apply to false sentences, since they all indicate the same thing, namely nothing. But different true sentences may indicate many different things. Therefore this view concerning sentences makes it necessary either to drop the above mentioned principle about the signification (i.e., in Rus-

[5] The only further assumptions one would need in order to obtain a rigorous proof would be: 1) that "φ (a)" and the proposition "a is the object which has the property φ and is identical with a" mean the same thing and 2) that every proposition "speaks about something," i.e., can be brought to the form φ (a). Furthermore one would have to use the fact that for any two objects a. b. there exists a true proposition of the form φ (a, b) as, e.g., a ≠ b or a = a. b = b.

[6] Cf. "Sinn und Bedeutung," *Zeitschrift für Philosophie und philosophische Kritik*, Vol. 100 (1892), p. 35.

[7] From the indication (*Bedeutung*) of a sentence is to be distinguished what Frege called its meaning (*Sinn*) which is the conceptual correlate of the objectively existing fact (or "the True"). This one should expect to be in Russell's theory a possible fact (or rather the possibility of a fact), which would exist also in the case of a false proposition. But Russell, as he says, could never believe that such "curious shadowy" things really exist. Thirdly, there is also the psychological correlate of the fact which is called "signification" and understood to be the corresponding belief in Russell's latest book. "Sentence" in contradistinction to "proposition" is used to denote the mere combination of symbols.

sell's terminology the corresponding one about the denotation and indication) of composite expressions or to deny that a descriptive phrase denotes the object described. Russell did the latter[8] by taking the viewpoint that a descriptive phrase denotes nothing at all but has meaning only in context; for example, the sentence "the author of *Waverley* is Scotch," is defined to mean: "There exists exactly one entity who wrote *Waverley* and whoever wrote *Waverley* is Scotch." This means that a sentence involving the phrase "the author of *Waverley*" does not (strictly speaking) assert anything about Scott (since it contains no constituent denoting Scott), but is only a roundabout way of asserting something about the concepts occurring in the descriptive phrase. Russell adduces chiefly two arguments in favor of this view, namely (1) that a descriptive phrase may be meaningfully employed even if the object described does not exist (e.g., in the sentence: "The present king of France does not exist"). (2) That one may very well understand a sentence containing a descriptive phrase without being acquainted with the object described; whereas it seems impossible to understand a sentence without being acquainted with the objects about which something is being asserted. The fact that Russell does not consider this whole question of the interpretation of descriptions as a matter of mere linguistic conventions, but rather as a question of right and wrong, is another example of his realistic attitude, unless perhaps he was aiming at a merely psychological investigation of the actual processes of thought. As to the question in the logical sense, I cannot help feeling that the problem raised by Frege's puzzling conclusion has only been evaded by Russell's theory of descriptions and that there is something behind it which is not yet completely understood.

There seems to be one purely formal respect in which one may give preference to Russell's theory of descriptions. By defining the meaning of sentences involving descriptions in the above manner, he avoids in his logical system any axioms about the particle "the," i.e., the analyticity of the theorems about "the" is made explicit; they can be shown to follow from

---

[8] He made no explicit statement about the former; but it seems it would hold for the logical system of *Principia*, though perhaps more or less vacuously.

the explicit definition of the meaning of sentences involving "the." Frege, on the contrary, has to assume an axiom about "the," which of course is also analytic, but only in the implicit sense that it follows from the meaning of the undefined terms. Closer examination, however, shows that this advantage of Russell's theory over Frege's subsists only as long as one interprets definitions as mere typographical abbreviations, not as introducing names for objects described by the definitions, a feature which is common to Frege and Russell.

I pass now to the most important of Russell's investigations in the field of the analysis of the concepts of formal logic, namely those concerning the logical paradoxes and their solution. By analyzing the paradoxes to which Cantor's set theory had led, he freed them from all mathematical technicalities, thus bringing to light the amazing fact that our logical intuitions (i.e., intuitions concerning such notions as: truth, concept, being, class, etc.) are self-contradictory. He then investigated where and how these common sense assumptions of logic are to be corrected and came to the conclusion that the erroneous axiom consists in assuming that for every propositional function there exists the class of objects satisfying it, or that every propositional function exists "as a separate entity;"[9] by which is meant something separable from the argument (the idea being that propositional functions are abstracted from propositions which are primarily given) and also something distinct from the combination of symbols expressing the propositional function; it is then what one may call the notion or concept defined by it.[10] The existence of this concept already suffices for the paradoxes in their "intensional" form, where the concept of

---

[9] In Russell's first paper about the subject: "On Some Difficulties in the Theory of Transfinite Numbers and Order Types," *Proc. London Math. Soc.*, Second Series, Vol. 4, 1906, p. 29. If one wants to bring such paradoxes as "the liar" under this viewpoint, universal (and existential) propositions must be considered to involve the class of objects to which they refer.

[10] "Propositional function" (without the clause "as a separate entity") may be understood to mean a proposition in which one or several constituents are designated as arguments. One might think that the pair consisting of the proposition and the argument could then for all purposes play the rôle of the "propositional function as a separate entity," but it is to be noted that this pair (as one entity) is again a set or a concept and therefore need not exist.

"not applying to itself" takes the place of Russell's paradoxical class.

Rejecting the existence of a class or concept in general, it remains to determine under what further hypotheses (concerning the propositional function) these entities do exist. Russell pointed out (*loc. cit.*) two possible directions in which one may look for such a criterion, which he called the zig-zag theory and the theory of limitation of size, respectively, and which might perhaps more significantly be called the intensional and the extensional theory. The second one would make the existence of a class or concept depend on the extension of the propositional function (requiring that it be not too big), the first one on its content or meaning (requiring a certain kind of "simplicity," the precise formulation of which would be the problem).

The most characteristic feature of the second (as opposed to the first) would consist in the non-existence of the universal class or (in the intensional interpretation) of the notion of "something" in an unrestricted sense. Axiomatic set theory as later developed by Zermelo and others can be considered as an elaboration of this idea as far as classes are concerned.[11] In particular the phrase "not too big" can be specified (as was shown by J. v. Neumann[12]) to mean: not equivalent with the universe of all things, or, to be more exact, a propositional function can be assumed to determine a class when and only when there exists no relation (in intension, i.e., a propositional function with two variables) which associates in a one-to-one manner with each object, an object satisfying the propositional function and vice versa. This criterion, however, does not appear as the basis of the theory but as a consequence of the axioms and inversely can replace two of the axioms (the axiom of replacement and that of choice).

For the second of Russell's suggestions too, i.e., for the zig-zag theory, there has recently been set up a logical system which shares some essential features with this scheme, namely

---

[11] The intensional paradoxes can be dealt with e.g. by the theory of simple types or the ramified hierarchy, which do not involve any undesirable restrictions if applied to concepts only and not to sets.

[12] Cf. "Über eine Widerspruchsfreiheitsfrage in der axiomatischen Mengenlehre," *Journal für reine und angewandte Mathematik*, Vol. 160, 1929, p. 227.

Quine's system.[13] It is, moreover, not unlikely that there are other interesting possibilities along these lines.

Russell's own subsequent work concerning the solution of the paradoxes did not go in either of the two afore-mentioned directions pointed out by himself, but was largely based on a more radical idea, the "no-class theory," according to which classes or concepts *never* exist as real objects, and sentences containing these terms are meaningful only to such an extent as they can be interpreted as a *façon de parler*, a manner of speaking about other things (cf. p. 141). Since in *Principia* and elsewhere, however, he formulated certain principles discovered in the course of the development of this theory as general logical principles without mentioning any longer their dependence on the no-class theory, I am going to treat of these principles first.

I mean in particular the vicious circle principle, which forbids a certain kind of "circularity" which is made responsible for the paradoxes. The fallacy in these, so it is contended, consists in the circumstance that one defines (or tacitly assumes) totalities, whose existence would entail the existence of certain new elements of the same totality, namely elements definable only in terms of the whole totality. This led to the formulation of a principle which says that "no totality can contain members definable only in terms of this totality, or members involving or presupposing this totality" [vicious circle principle]. In order to make this principle applicable to the intensional paradoxes, still another principle had to be assumed, namely that "every propositional function presupposes the totality of its values" and therefore evidently also the totality of its possible arguments.[14] [Otherwise the concept of "not applying to itself" would presuppose no totality (since it involves no quantification),[15] and the vicious circle principle would not prevent its application to itself.] A corresponding vicious circle principle

<hr />

[13] Cf. "New Foundations for Mathematical Logic," *Amer. Math. Monthly*, Vol. 44, p. 70.

[14] Cf. *Principia Mathematica*, Vol. I, p. 39.

[15] Quantifiers are the two symbols (∃ x) and (x) meaning respectively, "there exists an object x" and "for all objects x." The totality of objects x to which they refer is called their range.

for propositional functions which says that nothing defined in terms of a propositional function can be a possible argument of this function is then a consequence.[16] The logical system to which one is led on the basis of these principles is the theory of orders in the form adopted, e.g., in the first edition of *Principia*, according to which a propositional function which either contains quantifications referring to propositional functions of order n or can be meaningfully asserted of propositional functions of order n is at least of order n + 1, and the range of significance of a propositional function as well as the range of a quantifier must always be confined to a definite order.

In the second edition of *Principia*, however, it is stated in the Introduction (pp. XI and XII) that "in a limited sense" also functions of a higher order than the predicate itself (therefore also functions defined in terms of the predicate as, e.g., in p 'κ ε κ) can appear as arguments of a predicate of functions; and in appendix B such things occur constantly. This means that the vicious circle principle for propositional functions is virtually dropped. This change is connected with the new axiom that functions can occur in propositions only "through their values," i.e., extensionally, which has the consequence that any propositional function can take as an argument any function of appropriate type, whose extension is defined (no matter what order of quantifiers is used in the definition of this extension). There is no doubt that these things are quite unobjectionable even from the constructive standpoint (see p. 136), provided that quantifiers are always restricted to definite orders. The paradoxes are avoided by the theory of simple types,[17] which in

---

[16] Cf. *Principia Mathematica*, Vol. I, p. 47, section IV.

[17] By the theory of simple types I mean the doctrine which says that the objects of thought (or, in another interpretation, the symbolic expressions) are divided into types, namely: individuals, properties of individuals, relations between individuals, properties of such relations, etc. (with a similar hierarchy for extensions), and that sentences of the form: "a has the property φ," "b bears the relation R to c," etc. are meaningless, if a, b, c, R, φ are not of types fitting together. Mixed types (such as classes containing individuals and classes as elements) and therefore also transfinite types (such as the class of all classes of finite types) are excluded. That the theory of simple types suffices for avoiding also the epistemological paradoxes is shown by a closer analysis of these. (Cf. F. P. Ramsey's paper, quoted in foot-

Principia is combined with the theory of orders (giving as a result the "ramified hierarchy") but is entirely independent of it and has nothing to do with the vicious circle principle (cf. p. 147).

Now as to the vicious circle principle proper, as formulated on p. 133, it is first to be remarked that, corresponding to the phrases "definable only in terms of," "involving," and "presupposing," we have really three different principles, the second and third being much more plausible than the first. It is the first form which is of particular interest, because only this one makes impredicative definitions[18] impossible and thereby destroys the derivation of mathematics from logic, effected by Dedekind and Frege, and a good deal of modern mathematics itself. It is demonstrable that the formalism of classical mathematics does not satisfy the vicious circle principle in its first form, since the axioms imply the existence of real numbers definable in this formalism only by reference to all real numbers. Since classical mathematics can be built up on the basis of *Principia* (including the axiom of reducibility), it follows that even *Principia* (in the first edition) does not satisfy the vicious circle principle in the first form, if "definable" means "definable within the system" and no methods of defining outside the system (or outside other systems of classical mathematics) are known except such as involve still more comprehensive totalities than those occurring in the systems.

I would consider this rather as a proof that the vicious circle principle is false than that classical mathematics is false, and this is indeed plausible also on its own account. For, first of all one may, on good grounds, deny that reference to a totality necessarily implies reference to all single elements of it or, in other words, that "all" means the same as an infinite logical

---

note 21, and A. Tarski, *Der Wahrheitsbegriff in den formalisierten Sprachen, Stud. phil.*, Vol. I, Lemberg, 1935, p. 399.)

[18] These are definitions of an object α by reference to a totality to which α itself (and perhaps also things definable only in terms of α) belong. As, e.g., if one defines a class α as the intersection of all classes satisfying a certain condition φ and then concludes that α is a subset also of such classes u as are defined in terms of α (provided they satisfy φ).

conjunction. One may, e.g., follow Langford's and Carnap's[19] suggestion to interpret "all" as meaning analyticity or necessity or demonstrability. There are difficulties in this view; but there is no doubt that in this way the circularity of impredicative definitions disappears.

Secondly, however, even if "all" means an infinite conjunction, it seems that the vicious circle principle in its first form applies only if the entities involved are constructed by ourselves. In this case there must clearly exist a definition (namely the description of the construction) which does not refer to a totality to which the object defined belongs, because the construction of a thing can certainly not be based on a totality of things to which the thing to be constructed itself belongs. If, however, it is a question of objects that exist independently of our constructions, there is nothing in the least absurd in the existence of totalities containing members, which can be described (i.e., uniquely characterized)[20] only by reference to this totality.[21] Such a state of affairs would not even contradict the second form of the vicious circle principle, since one cannot say that an object described by reference to a totality "involves" this totality, although the description itself does; nor would it contradict the third form, if "presuppose" means "pressuppose for the existence" not "for the knowability."

So it seems that the vicious circle principle in its first form applies only if one takes the constructivistic (or nominalistic) standpoint[22] toward the objects of logic and mathematics, in particular toward propositions, classes and notions, e.g., if one understands by a notion a symbol together with a rule for translating sentences containing the symbol into such sentences as do

---

[19] See Rudolf Carnap in *Erkenntnis*, Vol. 2, p. 103, and *Logical Syntax of Language*, p. 162, and C. H. Langford, *Bulletin American Mathematical Society*, Vol. 33 (1927), p. 599.

[20] An object a is said to be described by a propositional function $\varphi(x)$ if $\varphi(x)$ is true for $x = a$ and for no other object.

[21] Cf. F. P. Ramsey, "The Foundations of Mathematics," in *Proc. London Math Soc.*, Series 2, Vol. 25 (1926), p. 338. (Reprinted in *The Foundations of Mathematics*, New York and London, 1931, p. 1.)

[22] I shall use in the sequel "constructivism" as a general term comprising both these standpoints and also such tendencies as are embodied in Russell's "no class" theory.

not contain it, so that a separate object denoted by the symbol appears as a mere fiction.[23]

Classes and concepts may, however, also be conceived as real objects, namely classes as "pluralities of things" or as structures consisting of a plurality of things and concepts as the properties and relations of things existing independently of our definitions and constructions.

It seems to me that the assumption of such objects is quite as legitimate as the assumption of physical bodies and there is quite as much reason to believe in their existence. They are in the same sense necessary to obtain a satisfactory system of mathematics as physical bodies are necessary for a satisfactory theory of our sense perceptions and in both cases it is impossible to interpret the propositions one wants to assert about these entities as propositions about the "data," i.e., in the latter case the actually occurring sense perceptions. Russell himself concludes in the last chapter of his book on *Meaning and Truth*, though "with hesitation," that there exist "universals," but apparently he wants to confine this statement to concepts of sense perceptions, which does not help the logician. I shall use the term "concept" in the sequel exclusively in this objective sense. One formal difference between the two conceptions of notions would be that any two different definitions of the form $\alpha(x) = \varphi(x)$ can be assumed to define two different notions α in the constructivistic sense. (In particular this would be the case for the nominalistic interpretation of the term "notion" suggested above, since two such definitions give different rules of translation for propositions containing α.) For concepts, on the contrary, this is by no means the case, since the same thing may be described in different ways. It might even be that the axiom of extensionality[24] or at least something near to it holds for

---

[23] One might think that this conception of notions is impossible, because the sentences into which one translates must also contain notions so that one would get into an infinite regress. This, however, does not preclude the possibility of maintaining the above viewpoint for all the more abstract notions, such as those of the second and higher types, or in fact for all notions except the primitive terms which might be only a very few.

[24] I.e., that no two different properties belong to exactly the same things, which, in a sense, is a counterpart to Leibniz's *Principium identitatis indiscernibilium*, which says no two different things have exactly the same properties.

concepts. The difference may be illustrated by the following definition of the number two: "Two is the notion under which fall all pairs and nothing else." There is certainly more than one notion in the constructivistic sense satisfying this condition, but there might be one common "form" or "nature" of all pairs.

Since the vicious circle principle, in its first form does apply to constructed entities, impredicative definitions and the totality of all notions or classes or propositions are inadmissible in constructivistic logic. What an impredicative definition would require is to construct a notion by a combination of a set of notions to which the notion to be formed itself belongs. Hence if one tries to effect a retranslation of a sentence containing a symbol for such an impredicatively defined notion it turns out that what one obtains will again contain a symbol for the notion in question.[25] At least this is so if "all" means an infinite conjunction; but Carnap's and Langford's idea (mentioned on p. 136) would not help in this connection, because "demonstrability," if introduced in a manner compatible with the constructivistic standpoint towards notions, would have to be split into a hierarchy of orders, which would prevent one from obtaining the desired results.[26] As Chwistek has shown,[27] it is even possible under certain assumptions admissible within constructivistic logic to derive an actual contradiction from the unrestricted admission of impredicative definitions. To be more specific, he has shown that the system of simple types becomes contradictory if one adds the "axiom of intensionality" which says (roughly speaking) that to different definitions belong different notions. This axiom, however, as has just been pointed out, can be assumed to hold for notions in the constructivistic sense.

Speaking of concepts, the aspect of the question is changed completely. Since concepts are supposed to exist objectively, there seems to be objection neither to speaking of all of them

---

[25] Cf. Carnap, *loc. cit.*, footnote 19 above.

[26] Nevertheless the scheme is interesting because it again shows the constructibility of notions which can be meaningfully asserted of notions of arbitrarily high order.

[27] See *Erkenntnis*, Vol. 3, p. 367.

(cf. p. 143) nor to describing some of them by reference to all (or at least all of a given type). But, one may ask, isn't this view refutable also for concepts because it leads to the "absurdity" that there will exist properties φ such that φ (a) consists in a certain state of affairs involving all properties (including φ itself and properties defined in terms of φ), which would mean that the vicious circle principle does not hold even in its second form for concepts or propositions? There is no doubt that the totality of all properties (or of all those of a given type) does lead to situations of this kind, but I don't think they contain any absurdity.[28] It is true that such properties φ [or such propositions φ (a)] will have to contain themselves as constituents of their content [or of their meaning], and in fact in many ways, because of the properties defined in terms of φ; but this only makes it impossible to construct their meaning (i.e., explain it as an assertion about sense perceptions or any other non-conceptual entities), which is no objection for one who takes the realistic standpoint. Nor is it self-contradictory that a proper part should be identical (not merely equal) to the whole, as is seen in the case of structures in the abstract sense. The structure of the series of integers, e.g., contains itself as a proper part and it is easily seen that there exist also structures containing infinitely many different parts, each containing the whole structure as a part. In addition there exist, even within the domain of constructivistic logic, certain approximations to this self-reflexivity of impredicative properties, namely propositions which contain as parts of their meaning not themselves but their own formal demonstrability.[29] Now formal demonstrability of a proposition (in case the axioms and rules of inference are correct) implies this proposition and in many cases is equiva-

---

[28] The formal system corresponding to this view would have, instead of the axiom of reducibility, the rule of substitution 'for functions described, e.g., in Hilbert-Bernays, *Grundlagen der Mathematik*, vol. I (1934), p. 90, applied to variables of any type, together with certain axioms of intensionality required by the concept of property which, however, would be weaker than Chwistek's. It should be noted that this view does not necessarily imply the existence of concepts which cannot be expressed in the system, if combined with a solution of the paradoxes along the lines indicated on p. 149.

[29] Cf. my paper in *Monatshefte für Mathematik und Physik*, Vol. 38 (1931), p. 173, or R. Carnap, *Logical Syntax of Language*, § 35.

lent to it. Furthermore, there doubtlessly exist sentences referring to a totality of sentences to which they themselves belong
as, e.g., the sentence: "Every sentence (of a given language)
contains at least one relation word."

Of course this view concerning the impredicative properties
makes it necessary to look for another solution of the paradoxes,
according to which the fallacy (i.e., the underlying erroneous
axiom) does not consist in the assumption of certain self-reflexiv-
ities of the primitive terms but in other assumptions about these.
Such a solution may be found for the present in the simple
theory of types and in the future perhaps in the development of
the ideas sketched on pp. 132 and 150. Of course, all this refers
only to concepts. As to notions in the constructivistic sense there
is no doubt that the paradoxes are due to a vicious circle. It is
not surprising that the paradoxes should have different solutions for different interpretations of the terms occurring.

As to classes in the sense of pluralities or totalities it would
seem that they are likewise not created but merely described by
their definitions and that therefore the vicious circle principle
in the first form does not apply. I even think there exist interpretations of the term "class" (namely as a certain kind of
structures), where it does not apply in the second form either.[30]
But for the development of all contemporary mathematics one
may even assume that it does apply in the second form, which
for classes as mere pluralities is, indeed, a very plausible assumption. One is then led to something like Zermelo's axiom
system for set theory, i.e., the sets are split up into "levels" in
such a manner that only sets of lower levels can be elements of
sets of higher levels (i.e., xεy is always false if x belongs to a
higher level than y). There is no reason for classes in this sense
to exclude mixtures of levels in one set and transfinite levels. The
place of the axiom of reducibility is now taken by the axiom

[30] Ideas tending in this direction are contained in the following papers by D.
Mirimanoff: "Les antinomies de Russell et de Buraliforte et le problème fonda-
mental de la théorie des ensembles," *L'Enseignment mathematique*, Vol. 19 (1917),
pp. 37-52, and "Remarques sur la théorie des ensembles et les antinomies Cantorien-
nes," *L'Enseignment mathematique*, vol. 19 (1917), pp. 209-217 and vol. 21
(1920), pp. 29-52. Cf. in particular Vol. 19, p. 212.

of classes [Zermelo's *Aussonderungsaxiom*] which says that for each level there exists for an arbitrary propositional function $\varphi(x)$ the set of those x of this level for which $\varphi(x)$ is true, and this seems to be implied by the concept of classes as pluralities.

Russell adduces two reasons against the extensional view of classes, namely the existence of (1.) the null class, which cannot very well be a collection, and (2.) the unit classes, which would have to be identical with their single elements. But it seems to me that these arguments could, if anything, at most prove that the null class and the unit classes (as distinct from their only element) are fictions (introduced to simplify the calculus like the points at infinity in geometry), not that all classes are fictions.

But in Russell the paradoxes had produced a pronounced tendency to build up logic as far as possible without the assumption of the objective existence of such entities as classes and concepts. This led to the formulation of the aforementioned "no class theory," according to which classes and concepts were to be introduced as a *façon de parler*. But propositions, too, (in particular those involving quantifications)[31] were later on largely included in this scheme, which is but a logical consequence of this standpoint, since e.g., universal propositions as objectively existing entities evidently belong to the same category of idealistic objects as classes and concepts and lead to the same kind of paradoxes, if admitted without restrictions. As regards classes this program was actually carried out; i.e., the rules for translating sentences containing class names or the term "class" into such as do not contain them were stated explicitly; and the basis of the theory, i.e, the domain of sentences into which one has to translate is clear, so that classes can be dispensed with (within the system *Principia*), but only if one assumes the existence of a concept whenever one wants to construct a class. When it comes to concepts and the interpretation of sentences containing this or some synonymous term, the state of affairs is by no means as clear. First of all, some of them

[31] Cf. "Les paradoxes de la logique," *Rev. de Metaph. et de Morale*, Vol. 14 (1906), p. 627.

(the primitive predicates and relations such as "red" or "colder") must apparently be considered as real objects;[32] the rest of them (in particular according to the second edition of *Principia*, all notions of a type higher than the first and therewith all logically interesting ones) appear as something constructed (i.e., as something not belonging to the "inventory" of the world); but neither the basic domain of propositions in terms of which finally everything is to be interpreted, nor the method of interpretation is as clear as in the case of classes (see below).

This whole scheme of the no-class theory is of great interest as one of the few examples, carried out in detail, of the tendency to eliminate assumptions about the existence of objects outside the "data" and to replace them by constructions on the basis of these data.[33] The result has been in this case essentially negative; i.e., the classes and concepts introduced in this way do not have all the properties required for their use in mathematics, unless one either introduces special axioms about the data (e.g., the axiom of reducibility), which in essence already mean the existence in the data of the kind of objects to be constructed, or makes the fiction that one can form propositions of infinite (and even non-denumerable) length,[34] i.e., operates with truth-functions of infinitely many arguments, regardless of whether or not one can construct them. But what else is such an infinite truth-function but a special kind of an infinite extension (or structure) and even a more complicated one than a class, endowed in addition with a hypothetical meaning, which can be understood only by an infinite mind? All this is only a verification of the view defended above that logic and mathematics (just as physics) are built up on axioms with a real content which cannot be "explained away."

What one can obtain on the basis of the constructivistic attitude is the theory of orders (cf. p. 134); only now (and this

[32] In Appendix C of *Principia* a way is sketched by which these also could be constructed by means of certain similarity relations between atomic propositions, so that these latter would be the only ones remaining as real objects.

[33] The "data" are to be understood in a relative sense here, i.e., in our case as logic without the assumption of the existence of classes and concepts.

[34] Cf. Ramsey, *loc. cit.*, footnote 21 above.

is the strong point of the theory) the restrictions involved do not appear as *ad hoc* hypotheses for avoiding the paradoxes, but as unavoidable consequences of the thesis that classes, concepts, and quantified propositions do not exist as real objects. It is not as if the universe of things were divided into orders and then one were prohibited to speak of all orders; but, on the contrary, it is possible to speak of all existing things; only, classes and concepts are not among them; and if they are introduced as a *façon de parler*, it turns out that this very extension of the symbolism gives rise to the possibility of introducing them in a more comprehensive way, and so on indefinitely. In order to carry out this scheme one must, however, presuppose arithmetic (or something equivalent) which only proves that not even this restricted logic can be built up on nothing.

In the first edition of *Principia*, where it was a question of actually building up logic and mathematics, the constructivistic attitude was, for the most part, abandoned, since the axiom of reducibility for types higher than the first together with the axiom of infinity makes it absolutely necessary that there exist primitive predicates of arbitrarily high types. What is left of the constructive attitude is only: (1.) The introduction of classes as a *façon de parler;* (2.) the definition of $\sim$, v, ., etc., as applied to propositions containing quantifiers (which incidentally proved its fecundity in a consistency proof for arithmetic); (3.) the step by step construction of functions of orders higher than 1, which, however, is superfluous owing to the axiom of reducibility; (4.) the interpretation of definitions as mere typographical abbreviations, which makes every symbol introduced by definition an incomplete symbol (not one naming an object described by the definition). But the last item is largely an illusion, because, owing to the axiom of reducibility, there always exist real objects in the form of primitive predicates, or combinations of such, corresponding to each defined symbol. Finally also Russell's theory of descriptions is something belonging to the constructivistic order of ideas.

In the second edition of *Principia* (or to be more exact, in the introduction to it) the constructivistic attitude is resumed again. The axiom of reducibility is dropped and it is stated explicitly that all primitive predicates belong to the lowest type and that the only purpose of variables (and evidently also of constants) of higher orders and types is to make it possible to assert more complicated truth-functions of atomic propositions,[35] which is only another way of saying that the higher types and orders are solely a *façon de parler*. This statement at the same time informs us of what kind of propositions the basis of the theory is to consist, namely of truth-functions of atomic propositions.

This, however, is without difficulty only if the number of individuals and primitive predicates is finite. For the opposite case (which is chiefly of interest for the purpose of deriving mathematics) Ramsey (*loc. cit.*) took the course of considering our inability to form propositions of infinite length as a "mere accident," to be neglected by the logician. This of course solves (or rather cuts through) the difficulties; but it is to be noted that, if one disregards the difference between finite and infinite in this respect, there exists a simpler and at the same time more far reaching interpretation of set theory (and therewith of mathematics). Namely, in case of a finite number of individuals, Russell's *aperçu* that propositions about classes can be interpreted as propositions about their elements becomes literally true, since, e.g., "$x \varepsilon m$" is equivalent to "$x = a_1, v\ x = a_2 v \ldots v\ x = a_k$" where the a_i are the elements of m; and "there exists a class such that . . ." is equivalent to "there exist individuals $x_1, x_2, \ldots x_n$ such that . . .,"[36] provided n is the number of individuals in the world and provided we neglect for the moment the null class which would have to be taken care of by an additional clause. Of course, by an iteration of this procedure one can obtain classes of classes, etc., so that the logical system obtained would resemble the theory of simple types except for the circumstance that mixture of types would be possible. Axiomatic set theory appears, then, as an extrapolation of this scheme for the case of infinitely many individuals or an infinite iteration of the process of forming sets.

[35] I.e., propositions of the form $S(a)$, $R(a,b)$, etc., where S, R are primitive predicates and a, b individuals.

[36] The x_i may, of course, as always, be partly or wholly identical with each other.

Ramsey's viewpoint is, of course, everything but constructivistic, unless one means constructions of an infinite mind. Russell, in the second edition of *Principia*, took a less metaphysical course by confining himself to such truth-functions as can actually be constructed. In this way one is again led to the theory of orders, which, however, appears now in a new light, namely as a method of constructing more and more complicated truth-functions of atomic propositions. But this procedure seems to presuppose arithmetic in some form or other (see next paragraph).

As to the question of how far mathematics can be built up on this basis (without any assumptions about the data—i.e., about the primitive predicates and individuals—except, as far as necessary, the axiom of infinity), it is clear that the theory of real numbers in its present form cannot be obtained.[37] As to the theory of integers, it is contended in the second edition of *Principia* that it can be obtained. The difficulty to be overcome is that in the definition of the integers as "those cardinals which belong to every class containing 0 and containing $x + 1$ if containing x," the phrase "every class" must refer to a given order. So one obtains integers of different orders, and complete induction can be applied to integers of order n only for properties of order n; whereas it frequently happens that the notion of integer itself occurs in the property to which induction is applied. This notion, however, is of order $n + 1$ for the integers of order n. Now, in Appendix B of the second edition of *Principia*, a proof is offered that the integers of any order higher than 5 are the same as those of order 5, which of course would settle all difficulties. The proof as it stands, however, is certainly not conclusive. In the proof of the main lemma *89.16, which says that every subset α (of arbitrary high order)[38] of an inductive class β of order 3 is itself an inductive class of order 3, induction is applied to a property of β involving α [namely $\alpha - \beta \neq \Lambda$, which, however,

---

[37] As to the question how far it is possible to build up the theory of real numbers, presupposing the integers, cf. Hermann Weyl, *Das Kontinuum*, reprinted, 1932.

[38] That the variable α is intended to be of undetermined order is seen from the later applications of *89.17 and from the note to *89.17. The main application is in line (2) of the proof of *89.24, where the lemma under consideration is needed for α's of arbitrarily high orders.

should read α—$\beta \sim \varepsilon$ Induct₂ because (3) is evidently false]. This property, however, is of an order > 3 if α is of an order > 3. So the question whether (or to what extent) the theory of integers can be obtained on the basis of the ramified hierarchy must be considered as unsolved at the present time. It is to be noted, however, that, even in case this question should have a positive answer, this would be of no value for the problem whether arithmetic follows from logic, if propositional functions of order n are defined (as in the second edition of *Principia*) to be certain finite (though arbitrarily complex) combinations (of quantifiers, propositional connectives, etc.), because then the notion of finiteness has to be presupposed, which fact is concealed only by taking such complicated notions as "propositional function of order n" in an unanalyzed form as primitive terms of the formalism and giving their definition only in ordinary language. The reply may perhaps be offered that in *Principia* the notion of a propositional function of order n is neither taken as primitive nor defined in terms of the notion of a finite combination, but rather quantifiers referring to propositional functions of order n (which is all one needs) are defined as certain infinite conjunctions and disjunctions. But then one must ask: Why doesn't one define the integers by the infinite disjunction: $x = 0 \lor x = 0 + 1 \lor x = 0 + 1 + 1 \lor \dots$ *ad infinitum*, saving in this way all the trouble connected with the notion of inductiveness? This whole objection would not apply if one understands by a propositional function of order n one "obtainable from such truth-functions of atomic propositions as presuppose for their definition no totalities except those of the propositional functions of order $< n$ and of individuals;" this notion, however, is somewhat lacking in precision.

The theory of orders proves more fruitful if considered from a purely mathematical standpoint, independently of the philosophical question whether impredicative definitions are admissible. Viewed in this manner, i.e., as a theory built up within the framework of ordinary mathematics, where impredicative definitions are admitted, there is no objection to extending it to arbitrarily high transfinite orders. Even if one rejects impredicative definitions, there would, I think, be no objection to extend it to such transfinite ordinals as can be constructed within the framework of finite orders. The theory in itself seems to demand such an extension since it leads automatically to the consideration of functions in whose definition one refers to all functions of finite orders, and these would be functions of order ω. Admitting transfinite orders, an axiom of reducibility can be proved. This, however, offers no help to the original purpose of the theory, because the ordinal α—such that every propositional function is extensionally equivalent to a function of order α—is so great, that it presupposes impredicative totalities. Nevertheless, so much can be accomplished in this way, that all impredicativities are reduced to one special kind, namely the existence of certain large ordinal numbers (or, well ordered sets) and the validity of recursive reasoning for them. In particular, the existence of a well ordered set, of order type ω_1 already suffices for the theory of real numbers. In addition this transfinite theorem of reducibility permits the proof of the consistency of the Axiom of Choice, of Cantor's Continuum-Hypothesis and even of the generalized Continuum-Hypothesis (which says that there exists no cardinal number between the power of any arbitrary set and the power of the set of its subsets) with the axioms of set theory as well as of *Principia*.

I now come in somewhat more detail to the theory of simple types which appears in *Principia* as combined with the theory of orders; the former is, however, (as remarked above) quite independent of the latter, since mixed types evidently do not contradict the vicious circle principle in any way. Accordingly, Russell also based the theory of simple types on entirely different reasons. The reason adduced (in addition to its "consonance with common sense") is very similar to Frege's, who, in his system, already had assumed the theory of simple types for functions, but failed to avoid the paradoxes, because he operated with classes (or rather functions in extension) without any restriction. This reason is that (owing to the variable it contains) a propositional function is something ambiguous (or, as Frege says, something unsaturated, wanting supplementation) and therefore can occur in a meaningful proposition only in such a way that this ambiguity is eliminated (e.g., by substituting a constant for the variable or applying quantification to it). The consequences are that a function cannot replace an individual in a proposition, because the latter has no ambiguity to be removed, and that functions with different kinds of arguments (i.e., different ambiguities) cannot replace each other; which is the essence of the theory of simple types. Taking a more nominalistic viewpoint (such as suggested in the second edition of *Principia* and in *Meaning and Truth*) one would have to replace "proposition" by "sentence" in the foregoing considerations (with corresponding additional changes). But in both cases, this argument clearly belongs to the order of ideas of the "no class" theory, since it considers the notions (or propositional functions) as something constructed out of propositions or sentences by leaving one or several constituents of them undetermined. Propositional functions in this sense are so to speak "fragments" of propositions, which have no meaning in themselves, but only in so far as one can use them for forming propositions by combining several of them, which is possible only if they "fit together," i.e., if they are of appropriate types. But, it should be noted that the theory of simple types (in contradistinction to the vicious circle principle) cannot in a strict sense follow from the constructive standpoint, because one might construct notions and classes in another way, e.g., as indicated on p. 144, where mixtures of types are possible. If on the other hand one considers concepts as real objects, the theory of simple types is not very plausible, since what one would expect to be a concept (such as, e.g., "transitivity" or the number two) would seem to be something behind all its various "realizations" on the different levels and therefore does not exist according to the theory of types. Nevertheless, there seems to be some truth behind this idea of realizations of the same concept on various levels, and one might, therefore, expect the theory of simple types to prove useful or necessary at least as a stepping-stone for a more satisfactory system, a way in which it has already been used by Quine.[39] Also Russell's "typical ambiguity" is a step in this direction. Since, however, it only adds certain simpli-

[39] *Loc. cit.*, cf. footnote 13 above.

fying symbolic conventions to the theory of types, it does not *de facto* go beyond this theory.

It should be noted that the theory of types brings in a new idea for the solution of the paradoxes, especially suited to their intensional form. It consists in blaming the paradoxes not on the axiom that every propositional function defines a concept or class, but on the assumption that every concept gives a meaningful proposition, if asserted for any arbitrary object or objects as arguments. The obvious objection that every concept can be extended to all arguments, by defining another one which gives a false proposition whenever the original one was meaningless, can easily be dealt with by pointing out that the concept "meaningfully applicable" need not itself be always meaningfully applicable.

The theory of simple types (in its realistic interpretation) can be considered as a carrying through of this scheme, based, however, on the following additional assumption concerning meaningfulness: "Whenever an object x can replace another object y in one meaningful proposition, it can do so in every meaningful proposition."[40] This of course has the consequence that the objects are divided into mutually exclusive ranges of significance, each range consisting of those objects which can replace each other; and that therefore each concept is significant only for arguments belonging to one of these ranges, i.e., for an infinitely small portion of all objects. What makes the above principle particularly suspect, however, is that its very assumption makes its formulation as a meaningful proposition impossible,[41] because x and y must then be confined to definite ranges of significance which are either the same or different, and in both cases the statement does not express the principle or even part of it. Another consequence is that the fact that an object x is (or is not) of a given type also cannot be expressed by a meaningful proposition.

[40] Russell formulates a somewhat different principle with the same effect, in *Principia*, Vol. I, p. 95.

[41] This objection does not apply to the symbolic interpretation of the theory of types, spoken of on p. 148, because there one does not have objects but only symbols of different types.

It is not impossible that the idea of limited ranges of significance could be carried out without the above restrictive principle. It might even turn out that it is possible to assume every
concept to be significant everywhere except for certain "singular
points" or "limiting points," so that the paradoxes would appear
as something analogous to dividing by zero. Such a system
would be most satisfactory in the following respect: our logical
intuitions would then remain correct up to certain minor corrections, i.e., they could then be considered to give an essentially
correct, only somewhat "blurred," picture of the real state of
affairs. Unfortunately the attempts made in this direction have
failed so far;[42] on the other hand, the impossibility of this
scheme has not been proved either, in spite of the strong inconsistency theorems of Kleene and Rosser.[43]

In conclusion I want to say a few words about the question
whether (and in which sense) the axioms of *Principia* can be
considered to be analytic. As to this problem it is to be remarked
that analyticity may be understood in two senses. First, it may
have the purely formal sense that the terms occurring can be
defined (either explicitly or by rules for eliminating them from
sentences containing them) in such a way that the axioms and
theorems become special cases of the law of identity and dis-
provable propositions become negations of this law. In this
sense even the theory of integers is demonstrably non-analytic,
provided that one requires of the rules of elimination that they
allow one actually to carry out the elimination in a finite number
of steps in each case.[44] Leaving out this condition by admitting,
e.g., sentences of infinite (and non-denumerable) length as intermediate steps of the process of reduction, all axioms of *Principia*

[42] A formal system along these lines is Church's (cf. "A Set of Postulates for
the Foundation of Logic," *Annals of Mathematics*, Vol. 33 (1932), p. 346 and
Vol. 34 (1933), p. 839), where, however, the underlying idea is expressed by the
somewhat misleading statement that the law of excluded middle is abandoned.
However, this system has been proved to be inconsistent. See footnote 43.
[43] Cf. S. C. Kleene and J. B. Rosser, "The Inconsistency of Certain Formal
Logics," *Annals of Math.*, Vol. 36 (1935), p. 630.
[44] Because this would imply the existence of a decision-procedure for all arithmetical propositions. Cf. A. M. Turing, *Proc. Lond. Math. Soc.*, Vol. 42 (1936),
p. 230.

(including the axioms of choice, infinity and reducibility) could be proved to be analytic for certain interpretations (by considerations similar to those referred to on p. 144).[45] But this observation is of doubtful value, because the whole of mathematics as applied to sentences of infinite length has to be presupposed in order to prove this analyticity, e.g., the axiom of choice can be proved to be analytic only if it is assumed to be true.

In a second sense a proposition is called analytic if it holds, "owing to the meaning of the concepts occurring in it," where this meaning may perhaps be undefinable (i.e., irreducible to anything more fundamental).[46] It would seem that all axioms of *Principia*, in the first edition, (except the axiom of infinity) are in this sense analytic for certain interpretations of the primitive terms, namely if the term "predicative function" is replaced either by "class" (in the extensional sense) or (leaving out the axiom of choice) by "concept," since nothing can express better the meaning of the term "class" than the axiom of classes (cf. p. 140) and the axiom of choice, and since, on the other hand, the meaning of the term "concept" seems to imply that every propositional function defines a concept.[47] The difficulty is only that we don't perceive the concepts of "concept" and of "class" with sufficient distinctness, as is shown by the paradoxes. In view of this situation, Russell took the course of considering

---

[45] Cf. also F. P. Ramsey, *loc. cit.*, (footnote 21), where, however, the axiom of infinity cannot be obtained, because it is interpreted to refer to the individuals in the world.

[46] The two significations of the term *analytic* might perhaps be distinguished as tautological and analytic.

[47] This view does not contradict the opinion defended above that mathematics is based on axioms with a real content, because the very existence of the concept of e.g., "class" constitutes already such an axiom; since, if one defined e.g., "class" and "ε" to be "the concepts satisfying the axioms," one would be unable to prove their existence. "Concept" could perhaps be defined in terms of "proposition" (cf. p. 148 (although I don't think that this would be a natural procedure); but then certain axioms about propositions, justifiable only with reference to the undefined meaning of this term, will have to be assumed. It is to be noted that this view about analyticity makes it again possible that every mathematical proposition could perhaps be reduced to a special case of a = a, namely if the reduction is effected not in virtue of the definitions of the terms occurring, but in virtue of their meaning, which can never be completely expressed in a set of formal rules.

both classes and concepts (except the logically uninteresting primitive predicates) as non-existent and of replacing them by constructions of our own. It cannot be denied that this procedure has led to interesting ideas and to results valuable also for one taking the opposite viewpoint. On the whole, however, the outcome has been that only fragments of Mathematical Logic remain, unless the things condemned are reintroduced in the form of infinite propositions or by such axioms as the axiom of reducibility which (in case of infinitely many individuals) is demonstrably false unless one assumes either the existence of classes or of infinitely many *"qualitates occultae."* This seems to be an indication that one should take a more conservative course, such as would consist in trying to make the meaning of the terms "class" and "concept" clearer, and to set up a consistent theory of classes and concepts as objectively existing entities. This is the course which the actual development of Mathematical Logic has been taking and which Russell himself has been forced to enter upon in the more constructive parts of his work. Major among the attempts in this direction (some of which have been quoted in this essay) are the simple theory of types (which is the system of the first edition of *Principia* in an appropriate interpretation) and axiomatic set theory, both of which have been successful at least to this extent, that they permit the derivation of modern mathematics and at the same time avoid all known paradoxes. Many symptoms show only too clearly, however, that the primitive concepts need further elucidation.

It seems reasonable to suspect that it is this incomplete understanding of the foundations which is responsible for the fact that Mathematical Logic has up to now remained so far behind the high expectations of Peano and others who (in accordance with Leibniz's claims) had hoped that it would facilitate theoretical mathematics to the same extent as the decimal system of numbers has facilitated numerical computations. For how can one expect to solve mathematical problems systematically by mere analysis of the concepts occurring, if our analysis so far does not even suffice to set up the axioms? But there is no need to give up hope. Leibniz did not in his writings about the *Characteristica universalis* speak of a utopian project; if we are to believe his words he had developed this calculus of reasoning to a large extent, but was waiting with its publication till the seed could fall on fertile ground.[48] He went even so far[49] as to estimate the time which would be necessary for his calculus to be developed by a few select scientists to such an extent "that humanity would have a new kind of an instrument increasing the powers of reason far more than any optical instrument has ever aided the power of vision." The time he names is five years, and he claims that his method is not any more difficult to learn than the mathematics or philosophy of his time. Furthermore, he said repeatedly that, even in the rudimentary state to which he had developed the theory himself, it was responsible for all his mathematical discoveries; which, one should expect, even Poincaré would acknowledge as a sufficient proof of its fecundity.

KURT GÖDEL[50]

THE SCHOOL OF MATHEMATICS
THE INSTITUTE FOR ADVANCED STUDY
PRINCETON, NEW JERSEY

[48] *Die philosophischen Schriften von G. W. Leibniz*, herausgegeben von C. J. Gerhardt, Vol. 7 (1890), p. 12. Cf. also G. Vacca, "La logica di Leibniz" (section VII), *Riv. di Mat.*, Vol. 8 (1902-06), p. 72, and the preface in the first volume of the first series of *Leibniz's Sämtliche Briefe und Schriften*, herausgegeben von der Preussischen Akademie der Wissenschaften (1923-   ).

[49] Leibniz, *Philosophische Schriften* (ed. Gerhardt), Vol. 7, p. 187.

[50] I wish to express my thanks to Professor Alonzo Church of Princeton University, who helped me to find the correct English expressions in a number of places.

4

James Feibleman

A REPLY TO BERTRAND RUSSELL'S INTRODUCTION TO THE SECOND EDITION OF *THE PRINCIPLES OF MATHEMATICS*

A REPLY TO BERTRAND RUSSELL'S
INTRODUCTION TO THE SECOND EDITION OF
THE PRINCIPLES OF MATHEMATICS

THE decision to reprint *The Principles of Mathematics* after thirty-four years was a most fortunate one. The work has had a tremendous influence and should be available to all interested students of the subject. Here is a landmark in the history of thought which many persons have heard about but never seen, and now the new edition will place it before the public again. The importance of *The Principles* rests to some extent upon two of its points: it is the first comprehensive treatise on symbolic logic to be written in English; and it gives to that system of logic a realistic interpretation. It is with the second point chiefly that these remarks shall be concerned. Symbolic logic as a discipline is here to stay, whatever its philosophical interpretation; but the interpretation itself is still a doubtful question. Of course, the metaphysical interpretation of symbolic logic is not strictly a problem of logic, but lies on the borderline between logic and metaphysics. In all probability, it belongs to metaphysics, more particularly to the metaphysics of logic. But it is a most important topic for all that, and moreover constitutes a field in which much yet remains to be done.

Are the foundations of symbolic logic realistic or nominalistic? A reading of *The Principles* should be sufficient to convince any sceptical person of the explanatory usefulness of the realistic philosophy. The assumption that relations are real and non-mental, if not true, has at least a pragmatic value; and since the criterion of truth cannot be anything except self-consistency and range of applicability, realism must to a large extent be true. That must have been also Russell's opinion when he wrote *The*

Principles. Since then he has altered his position sharply; for now in the new Introduction he challenges the validity of the philosophy underlying the work. He says

Broadly speaking, I still think this book is in the right where it disagrees with what had been previously held, but where it agrees with older theories it is apt to be wrong. The changes in philosophy which seem to me to be called for are partly due to the technical advances of mathematical logic. . . . Broadly, the result is an outlook which is less Platonic, or less realist in the mediaeval sense of the word. How far it is possible to go in the direction of nominalism remains, to my mind, an unsolved question. . . .[1]

The present paper takes issue with Russell on his new thesis, and is thus in the position of making out a case for an old book in order to defend it against the new rejection by its own author. In other words, the old Russell is to be defended against the new Russell.

Perhaps the simplest method of accomplishing this purpose would be to set forth all the arguments which have ever been advanced by anyone in favor of the truth of realism, and to refute all the arguments which have ever been used against it. But to attempt to defend realism in such a fashion would mean to become embroiled in a controversy which is most likely endless. There is another alternative. Russell puts forward certain specific and clear-cut objections to the validity of his former position. The simplest way would seem to be to show that these objections are groundless arguments, to demonstrate that his present reasons for acceding to the invalidity of his old work are themselves invalid. This will be the method adopted; and we shall take the arguments one by one in the order in which they are introduced.

The first attack upon realism consists in questioning the existence of logical constants. Russell asks, "Are there logical constants?" By logical constants are meant such expressions as "or," "and," "if-then," "1," "2," and so on. Russell says that "when we analyse the propositions in the written expression

---

[1] Bertrand Russell, *The Principles of Mathematics*, 2nd ed. (1938), p. xiv. All references, unless otherwise stated, will be to this work.

of which such symbols occur, we find that they have no con-stituents corresponding to the expressions in question."[2] One way in which the refutation of an opponent's arguments can be made to seem the most effective is first to overstate his position for him. This way, his position appears to be self-evidently untenable and is ripe for ridicule. Where possible, Russell has done this for himself by describing realism in a manner in which it is certain he himself never accepted it, even when as a realist he wrote down *The Principles*. Selecting as typical of the logical constants the term "or," he says, "not even the most ardent Platonist would suppose that the perfect 'or' is laid up in heaven, and that the 'or's' here on earth are imperfect copies of the celestial archtype."[3] Do there exist any longer realists who would be willing to accept such a description of their belief? To confine the realistic position to such an extreme ver-sion would be equivalent to asserting of all nominalists that they are admitted solipsists, which is very far from being the case. Even Russell has asserted that the question of how far it is possible to go in the direction of nominalism is as yet an unsolved one. Much the same defense might be given for realism.

We can accept a modified realism without asserting the exist-ence of a realm of essence, or heaven, in which perfect actual things are stored in order to cast the shadows which we mistake for them. Certainly there is no perfect "or" laid up in heaven, but this does not establish nominalism or deny a modified realism. From the position of modified realism, the logical constant "or" is *logical* because it can neither be successfully contradicted nor shown to involve self-contradiction, and is *a constant* because it involves a constant relationship. The relation "or" is that of alternativity, which is a logical possibility, an unchanging relationship which actual things *may* have (but do not have to have) and which has being (since it *can* exist) regardless of whether it exists at any special place and date or not. Thus the reply to Russell on this point must be as follows. The logical constant "or" is a symbol which occurs in some

[2] P. ix.
[3] P. ix.

propositions. When it occurs in true propositions and sometimes when it occurs in partly true propositions, "or" has an objective constituent, the constituent corresponding to the expression in question being the relation of alternativity.

Russell next argues that the theory of descriptions, as it is called in symbolic logic, dispenses with the actual particulars which do service as the constituents of some logical terms. For instance, he says that in "Scott is the author of *Waverley*" there is no constituent corresponding to "the author of *Waverley*." The argument consists in an analysis of the proposition; and the analysis reduces the proposition to the following. "The propositional function '*x wrote Waverley* is equivalent to *x is Scott*' is true for all values of x."[4] Russell is correct in his assertion that this does away with the realm of Being of Meinong, in which the golden mountain and the round square have a place. The theory of descriptions does "avoid this and other difficulties," but does it refute realism? The evidence here would seem to be quite to the contrary. The task performed by the theory of descriptions is the elimination of all *specified* actual particulars as the constituents of terms in propositions, and the substitution of propositional functions. Now propositional functions are relations, possibilities which can be specified by actual particulars. These relations or possibilities certainly exist. The relation between the *x* who wrote *Waverley* and the *x* who is Scott—one of equivalence—is "true for all values of *x*," which is to say can be assigned constituents by assigning specific values for *x*, but holds whether or not specific values be assigned for *x*.

The theory of descriptions not only refutes the realm of essence but also happily points out the enormously wide gulf which yawns between realm-of-essence realism and modified realism, a gulf as wide as that between realism and nominalism. We do not have any actual golden mountains and round squares; hence the assertion of Meinong that they must exist in a realm of being is equivalent to the assertion not of realism but of crypto-materialism, which is a form of nominalism. Nothing exists really except actual physical particulars, or so asserts

[4] P. x.

nominalism. But golden mountains and round squares *are* actual physical particulars: they are *remote* actual physical particulars, or so asserts crypto-materialism. The refutation of such contentions, accomplished logically by the theory of descriptions, argues for, rather than against, a modified realism, since it asserts that real existence means possibility of actualization, expressed in propositional functions.

Much the same argument as that employed above can be used to refute Russell's reasons for the abolition of classes. The cardinal numbers, Russell would persuade us, can be made to disappear in a cloud of propositional functions, and he accordingly performs the trick.[5] The numbers 1 and 2 are resolved into invariant relations holding between other invariant relations. The question is, have the numbers "entirely disappeared?" As numbers they have, because numbers are not and never were anything more than relations. Russell in his analysis has revealed their true nature; but he has not caused the relations which they essentially represent to disappear, nor has he given one argument in refutation of realism thereby. Any argument to show that specified things are not independent things but rather things dependent upon invariant relations which they exemplify can hardly be said to be an argument *against* realism. What are invariant relations, what are propositional functions, if not possibilities susceptible of actualization but never necessarily demanding it in order to show their being?

The fact is that Russell has not "dissolved" any numbers nor made them "disappear." He has merely shown them to be invariant relations between variables. This is very far from having disposed of their realistic character. Russell often talks about logic and mathematics as though he had never heard of any realism except the extreme realism which supposes that the Platonic Ideas are laid up forever in a heavenly realm of essence. Even Plato did not always believe this but sometimes argued for a status of possibility for unactualized as well as for actualized universals. Invariant relations, then, are what *can happen* to variables, and numbers are real possibilities as are all invariant relations which are non-contradictory.

[5] P. x.

Russell continues his argument against logical constants by carrying it over to cover "points of space, instants of time, and particles of matter, substituting for them logical constructions composed of events."[6] The substitution was made following Professor Whitehead's suggestion. Russell is appearing to present many arguments, whereas he is only presenting one. This one is the repeated assertion that, since logical constants prove to be relations, they are not fixed in the sense we once thought they were. They are not fixed because they have no constant reference; hence realism is untenable. The argument is no more valid in the case of physical relations than it was in the strictly logical field. Space, time, and matter have been resolved into relations varying from frame of reference to frame of reference, but invariant given the frame. The important point to bear in mind is that they are relations instead of actual things, relations which can be exemplified by the actual things to which they refer but not requiring actual things or any specific reference in order to be. This is an argument in favor of realism, and decidedly not one against it.

Russell is taking for granted throughout his argument concerning the disappearance of logical constants a confusion between two distinct meanings of "reference." There is (1) the reference of a symbol to its logical possibility, and there is (2) the reference of a logical possibility to its actual exemplification. Russell refers to them both by the same expression, "having a constituent," which is a source of unutterable confusion. In order to show what we mean let us give an example. (1) The letters a-u-t-o-m-o-b-i-l-e form a symbol, namely "automobile," which may refer to the possibility of constructing a horseless carriage propelled by an internal combustion engine, assuming that there already were or were not any, as in the sentence, "Let us build an automobile." (2) The letters a-u-t-o-m-o-b-i-l-e form a symbol, namely "automobile," which may refer to an actual physical object, assuming that there was at least one, as in the sentence, "This automobile runs well." The unfounded assumption that the refutation of the validity of meaning (2) also does away with the validity of meaning (1) accounts

[6] P. xi.

for most of the error responsible for Russell's change of viewpoint.

But perhaps there is more hidden beneath the surface of Russell's argument than we have been able thus far to grasp. A further quotation proves this to be the case. Russell goes on to say that "none of the raw material of the world has smooth logical properties, but whatever appears to have such properties is constructed artificially in order to have them."[7] This is only another way of saying that whenever there appears to be a one-to-one correspondence between logic and actuality it must have been faked. The argument runs that, since logic is ideal and actuality is not, logic cannot refer to anything actual. There is an assumption here which will not bear examination. Why cannot the part refer to the whole, the limited to the unlimited, the example to its exemplar, the actual to the ideal? Let us suppose that the fastest airplane would be one which could fly an infinite number of miles in zero seconds, yet we have to admit that, although no airplane flies that fast and probably none ever will, the airplane which flies four hundred miles per hour is nearer to the ideal than one which flies only one hundred and fifty miles per hour. The equivalence to four of two and two is tautological because that is what we mean by two and that is what we mean by four; yet this knowledge helps us to manipulate everything from apples to madonnas.

None of the raw material of the world needs to have smooth logical properties in order to refer to logic, so long as it is admissible for a cat to look at a king. Russell's charge that logic is an artificial construction, since nothing actual is ideal, also assumes the confusion which we have pointed out above in the example of the automobile, the confusion between two distinct levels of reference. Because Whitehead has persuaded Russell to substitute "logical constructions composed of events" for particles of space, time, and matter, Russell feels compelled to the further conclusion that logic is linguistic. This is the nominalistic view; the realist would say that language is logical. But then realism depends upon a careful segregation of the two levels of reference. Smooth logical properties are characteristic both of

[7] P. xi.

the tautologies of logic in language and thought, and of the possibilities to which they refer. Actuality exemplifies partially this logical possibility. For the raw material of the world to have smooth logical properties, there would have to be an identity between actuality and possibility, and this would be a signal that everything had happened that could happen. Until then, it is as much a requirement of actuality as it is of logic that the ideal contain more than the actual world.

It would appear that we have wandered a long way from our original point, but such is not the case. Having changed over from "points of space, instants of time, and particles of matter" to "logical constructions composed of events," Russell holds Whitehead responsible for his change from the realistic to the nominalistic interpretation of symbolic logic. But a careful inspection of Whitehead's own subsequent writings shows that what Whitehead was endeavoring to do was to change Russell over from a "substance" to a "relations" philosophy. In *Process and Reality* Whitehead himself still finds "eternal objects" (i.e., universals) consistent with the adoption of events. Whitehead's "events" upon analysis reveal themselves to consist of invariant relations, even the Platonic *receptacle* of simple spatio-temporal location having gone by the board.

The statement, "Time consists of instants," is shown by Russell to be false by means of an interpretation of time in terms of comparatively contemporary events. But the argument about the time statement is much the same as that we have given above concerning the cardinal numbers (p. 161). To demonstrate that an entity is analyzable into a process in terms of propositional functions does not invalidate its logically constant nature as an entity. A logical constant should only be expected to be *logically* constant, *not* actually constant as well. Time is actually composed of instants, as anyone who has actually tried to live by the clock can testify. Yet these instants resolve themselves, like all other actual things, into logical events, entities consisting of relations.

Russell's adversion from the view that realism is a valid metaphysical basis for symbolic logic rests chiefly upon the interpretation of the status of logical constants. Logical constants seem to Russell to disappear between actual things (the reference of language) on the one hand, and the formal properties of language itself on the other.[8] Thus by arbitrary definition of terms he has managed to argue himself out of realism. For language itself is merely a shorthand method of formulating and communicating the apprehension of ideas, and not anything in itself. It is safe to assert that everything in language refers beyond itself. Russell himself maintains that "it seems rash to hold that any word is meaningless."[9] Russell's error is the same one that we have pointed out above (p. 162), and consists in assuming that there is only one level of reference, a situation which automatically precludes realism. The seeds of this confusion were already contained in *The Principles,* where Russell assigned the distinction between intension and extension to psychology.[10]

Language has two kinds of reference: tautological propositions refer to possible things, whereas propositions about matters of fact refer to actual things. There is a third classification, and one that contains the greatest number of propositions: hypotheses, of which we do not know the exact reference, if any. Hypothetical propositions may be false, and therefore not propositions in the true sense at all, or they may belong to tautologies or matters of fact. Thus the distinction between hypotheses and the other two kinds of propositions is a matter of ignorance (psychological), but the difference between tautologies and matters of fact, or between intension and extension, is a genuine objective difference. Now, Russell's error lies in the supposition that tautological propositions are exhausted by the language in which they are expressed and do not refer to anything objective. Thus he disproves realism by first assuming its denial. Logical constants, like all other logical terms, are part of what language expresses, expressed as part of the language. So long as tautological propositions are valid and have a refer-

---

[8] P. xi. The first sentence of the last paragraph reads, "Logical constants, if we are able to say anything definite about them, must be treated as part of the language, not as part of what the language speaks about."

[9] P. 71.

[10] P. 69.

ence, logical constants are emphatically *not* confined to the choice between referring to actual things and being merely verbal (i.e., having no reference at all).

"No proposition of logic," Russell goes on to say, "can mention any particular object." And he proceeds to show that the well known syllogism involving the mortality of Socrates is a special case of a wider and more abstract formulation. The point taken here seems to be quite correct: logic is ideal, and if actual things could be mentioned in ideal propositions, it would infer that actual things were ideal. There are, however, two dangerous fallacies lying in wait upon the outskirts of this argument. One is the conclusion that if logic is ideal and actuality is not, logic can have no reference to actuality at all. This would make of logic a kind of harmless but useless exercise or game, having no application to the real world. The point is that the Socrates syllogism is an *application* of logic. Logic, like mathematics, is ideal and does not refer to any specific actual thing, but it may be applied to any and all actual things. $2 + 2 = 4$ as a proposition in mathematics does not refer to shoes or ships or sealing wax, cabbages or kings, but it may refer to any one of them. The fact is that the abstract syllogism does apply to Socrates, but the form of the argument expressed in the syllogism does not have to be a valid syllogism. The mortality of Socrates is contingent upon the agreement of the mortality of all men with established fact. When taken as so applying, the syllogism is an actual proposition and not a tautological one.

What Russell seems to be arguing against in this passage is the absoluteness of ideal possibles occurring as such in actuality. The dilemma is this. If actual things are made ideal, then logic does not seem to be a discipline akin to mathematics and independent of actuality. But if actual things have nothing logical about them, then ideal disciplines such as logic and mathematics belong to a remote realm of essence and bestow their reality only upon a world superior to our actual world. Thus, in protecting realism from the errors of extreme realism, Russell falls into the opposite extreme of nominalism. Logic in the form of "if-then" propositions is not stating anything about logical constants (by which Russell sometimes seems to mean ideal actuals). Neither Socrates nor mortality is asserted in the Socrates syllogism, but (granted the postulates) merely an invariant relation between them.

The question of contradictions is the final argument which Russell launches against his old position.[11] These are chiefly three: the mathematical, the logical, and the linguistic, and Russell offers an example of each.[12] It will be necessary, therefore, to confine our remarks to a few words about each of these specific contradictions as they are set forth in the Introduction.

Burali-Forti's contradiction rests on the assumption that N is the greatest of ordinals. But the number of all ordinals from O to N is $N + 1$, which is greater than N. Does the solution of this contradiction lie in the simple fact that O is not an ordinal number at all? Zero may be a cardinal but not an ordinal number. A symbol defined by "nothing" is perhaps required for the ordinal, corresponding to the cardinal, zero. For zero is not nothing; it represents the absence of *some*thing, namely, the cardinal number before one. Zero enumerates but does not order.

The second contradiction may be stated in Russell's words:

We know from elementary arithmetic that the number of combinations of n things any number at a time is 2^n, i.e., that a class of n terms has 2^n sub-classes. We can prove that this proposition remains true when n is infinite. And Cantor proved that 2^n is always greater than n. Hence there can be no greater cardinal. Yet one would have supposed that the class containing everything would have the greatest possible number of terms. Since, however, the number of classes of things exceeds the number of things, clearly classes of things are not things.[13]

The key to this contradiction lies in the theory of sub-classes. Russell's proof that "classes of things are not things" rests on the argument that the last and most inclusive class is not a thing. But if there are sub-classes there may be sub-classes of sub-classes and so on, so that classes form a hierarchical series of inclusiveness, and everything may be a class to the things below and a thing only to the classes above. This would make every

[11] P. xii.
[12] P. xiiif.
[13] P. xiii.

class a thing to the classes above (except the last class which would have no classes above it to make it a thing), and would make every thing a class to the things below (except the first thing, i.e., the actual unique thing, which would have no things below it to make it a class). Then there would be first (i.e., actual unique) things that were not a class, and there would be a last class that was not a thing. But all other classes of things would be things.

The third contradiction is linguistic, and, as Russell himself suggests, following Ramsey, linguistic contradictions can be solved by broad linguistic considerations, and lead to the so-called theory of types. The theory of types is a more detailed formula for which de Morgan's "universe of discourse" had already warned us we should have need. But even the theory of types must be applied judiciously. For instance, Russell wants to apply it to show that classes of things are not things. What should be asserted is that classes are not things in their relation to things but are things in their relation to more inclusive classes. He is correct, however, in asserting that the relations of a thing are not the relations of the class of which that thing is a member.

The fundamental realism of Russell hardly needs to be insisted upon at the last. Russell, as his own remarks betray, is a realist. However, it may be illuminating to show by chapter and verse what a profound realist he was, and perhaps still is. Let us run through *The Principles* for examples of realism. We shall not take the main categories of the work as evidence (although many of them are), but rather be on the lookout for more subtle remarks, on the grounds that the presence of realism in the assumptions will betray itself more clearly in observations and turns of thought, which could only have been implied by an unacknowledged though none the less real and effective fundamentally realistic viewpoint, than it would in more candid expressions.

The symbolic representativeness of words is the first indication we come across in our search. Russell said, "*Words* all have meaning, in the simple sense that they are symbols which stand for something other than themselves."[14] Surely, Russell does

[14] P. 47.

not mean here that words always refer to *actual* objects. The inference clearly is that the reference of *some* words, at least, is to possible objects. Another instance is the wholly realistic "distinction between a class containing only one member, and the one member which it contains."[15] The necessity for the viability of such a distinction is highly indicative of a fundamental position. In the same direction is the warning to beware of the extremely narrow limits of the doctrine that analysis is falsification. The whole may be more than its parts, he pointed out, but they are real parts. And, although analysis cannot give us the whole truth, it can give us truth.[16] "Where the mind can distinguish elements, there must *be* different elements to distinguish; though, alas! there are often different elements which the mind does not distinguish."[17] But just as analytic elements are real so are the synthetic wholes, or complexities. "All complexity is . . . real in the sense that it has no dependence upon the mind, but only upon the nature of the object."[18] Since the "complexities" referred to are not only meant to be those of actual objects, possible organizations alone can be intended.

". . . the whole denial of the ultimate reality of relations" is "rejected by the logic advocated by the present work."[19] These are plain words; and the feeling is unavoidable that Russell meant them. Order is reducible neither to psychology nor to Omnipotence itself.[20] Relations, and not terms, are necessary to order.[21] In a brilliant anticipation of modern macroscopic physics, Russell even went so far as to indicate the relational analysis of matter. Since "the only relevant function of a material point is to establish a correlation between all moments of time and some points of space,"[22] it follows that "we may replace a material point by a many-one relation."[23] The coupling of such a denial of actuality with the rejection of psychology already

[15] P. 130.
[16] P. 141.
[17] P. 466.
[18] *Ibid.*
[19] P. 166.
[20] P. 242.
[21] *Ibid.*
[22] P. 468.
[23] *Ibid.*

mentioned leaves nothing but the reality of a realm of possibility to be intended. This interpretation is confirmed by the assertion that "though a term may cease to exist, it cannot cease to be; it is still an entity, which can be counted as *one*, and concerning which some propositions are true and others false."[24]

As if in support of such a realistic thesis, Russell goes even farther than this in *The Principles*, in a definition of being. He says,

Being is that which belongs to every conceivable term, to every possible object of thought—in short to everything that can possibly occur in any proposition, true or false, and to all such propositions themselves. Being belongs to whatever can be counted. . . . Numbers, the Homeric gods, relations, chimeras and four-dimensional spaces all have being, for if they were not entities of a kind, we could make no propositions about them. Thus being is a general attribute of everything, and to mention anything is to show that it is.[25]

The entities of mathematics have being and truth, since "mathematics is throughout indifferent to the question whether its entities exist,"[26] and "what can be mathematically demonstrated is true."[27] Furthermore, propositions that are true are immutably true:

there seems to be no true proposition of which there is any sense in saying that it might have been false. One might as well say that redness might have been a taste and not a colour. What is true, is true; what is false, is false; and concerning fundamentals, there is nothing more to be said.[28]

But a true proposition is one which makes an assertion about that to which it refers. There is no difference between a true proposition and an asserted proposition.[29] Thus mathematically demonstrated propositions are likewise assertions. But pure mathematics, such as geometry, is likewise "indifferent to the question whether there exist (in the strict sense) such entities

[24] P. 471.
[25] P. 449.
[26] P. 458.
[27] P. 338.
[28] P. 454.
[29] P. 504.

as its premisses define."[30] What else could such non-existential propositions, as those of geometry, assert, except a realm of possibility, of potential being? Since mathematics is "merely a complication" of logic, the primitive ideas of mathematics being those of logic,[31] logic must share the non-existential reference which has been asserted by mathematics.

As a realist (and there can be little doubt that Russell was a realist when he wrote *The Principles*) he was opposed to the earlier positivists, particularly to Mach and Lotze. In the course of his opposition, it is clearly revealed that some of the doctrines of these modern nominalists, the logical positivists, are alien to his position in *The Principles*, since positivism in certain respects remains what it was.

For instance, against Mach's argument of the actual world being only what we find it,

any argument that the rotation of the earth could be inferred *if* there were no heavenly bodies is futile. This argument contains the very essence of empiricism, in a sense in which empiricism is radically opposed to the philosophy advocated in the present work.[32]

The philosophy advocated is "in all its chief features" derived from G. E. Moore,[33] and the G. E. Moore of 1902 was certainly a realist. Russell did in fact see quite clearly what the issue was. "The logical basis of the argument [i.e., the one stated above concerning the rotation of the earth] is that all propositions are essentially concerned with actual existents, not with entities which may or may not exist."[34] And on this argument, Russell had already stated his own position definitively, as we have seen.

The fate of Lotze in Russell's work is no better than that of Mach. Mach had confined reality to actuality; Lotze, so far as Russell was concerned, repeated the same error in other terms, for, after Leibniz, he had defined being as activity.[35] Russell refutes this definition by showing that if activity alone were real, only valid propositions would have being, since these and

[30] P. 372.
[31] P. 429.
[32] P. 492.
[33] P. xviii.
[34] P. 493.
[35] P. 450.

these alone would refer to active objects. But since false propositions which have no reference still have being, "being belongs to valid and invalid propositions alike."[36] Again, the Kantianism of supposing that propositions which are true are so because the mind cannot help but believe them, is an error due to the failure to make the "fundamental distinction between an idea and its object."[37] "Whatever can be thought of has being, and its being is a precondition, not a result, of its being thought of."[38] Thus Russell has, in his refutation of Lotze, rejected nominalism on two scores. He has rejected that objective form of nominalism which consists in holding that actuality alone is real, and he has rejected that subjective form which consists in holding that what the mind knows is real in virtue of being known.

Even now, although he has gone a little way with the logical positivists, he finds himself unable to go the whole way.[39] He is unable, for example, to accept the wholly linguistic interpretation of logic as that doctrine is advanced by Carnap. In rejecting Carnap's two logical languages as being too arbitrary, Russell says that "all propositions which are true in virtue of their form ought to be included in any adequate logic."[40] Indeed, the premisses of the realism which we have just succeeded in tracing in a number of passages from *The Principles* are in direct contradiction with the whole set of basic tenets set forth by the modern school of logical positivists. For instance, against the notion that complexity as well as analytical elements are real,[41] Carnap maintains that the question of reality concerns the parts of a system that cannot concern the system itself.[42] Carnap admits for the logical positivists a following of empiricism,[43] that same brand of empiricism which Russell has ex-

[36] *Ibid.*
[37] *Ibid.*
[38] P. 451.
[39] P. xii, second paragraph.
[40] P. xii.
[41] P. 169, above.
[42] Rudolf Carnap, *Philosophy and Logical Syntax* (London, 1935, Kegan Paul), p. 20.
[43] Rudolf Carnap, *The Unity of Science* (London, 1934, Kegan Paul), pp. 27-28.

plicitly rejected.[44] As for Bridgman, he seems guilty of an extreme case of the same error which afflicted Lotze, and thus would have to fall under the same ban of the Russell who wrote *The Principles.* Lotze made being into activity;[45] Bridgman narrows activity down to a matter of only a certain kind of activity, namely operations.[46] Lotze's second point: the Kantian view that those propositions are true which the mind cannot help but believe,[47] seems also to be held by Bridgman, who maintains that "our thinking mechanism essentially colours any picture that we can form of nature."[48] And finally, the Russell who derived his philosophy "in all its chief features" from the metaphysical realism of the early G. E. Moore[49] could hardly agree with the view of Wittgenstein that "philosophical matters are not false but senseless,"[50] or with Carnap that metaphysics is expressive but not assertive,[51] and that metaphysics is equivalent only to mud.[52] It is questionable whether any man who had understood realism so deeply and embraced it so wholeheartedly could ever change his position, no matter how much he wanted to. Despite Russell's rejection of realism and avowal of nominalism, he is not a nominalist but a realist, and it is the apparently insuperable logical difficulties standing in the path of a realistic interpretation of symbolic logic which shake his faith. In other words, he has not changed his early philosophy; he has merely become uncertain about the prospects of defending it.

This situation presents quite another kind of problem. We do not have any longer to pursue specifically logical answers to paradoxes; we have merely to convince Russell that there are some difficulties with *any* metaphysical interpretation of

---

[44] P. 171, above.

[45] P. 171, above.

[46] P. W. Bridgman, *The Logic of Modern Physics* (New York, 1928, Macmillan), p. 5.

[47] P. 172, above.

[48] P. W. Bridgman, *The Logic of Modern Physics*, p. xi.

[49] P. 171, above.

[50] Ludwig Wittgenstein, *Tractatus Logico-Philosophicus* (London, 1933, Kegan Paul), 4.003.

[51] Rudolf Carnap, *Philosophy and Logical Syntax*, p. 29.

[52] *Op. cit.*, p. 96.

symbolic logic. Whether these difficulties can be ironed out by an appeal to symbolic logic itself, as Russell suggests,[53] is debatable. It is not easy to see how an empirical fact can conclusively choose its own metaphysical interpretation. Relativity theory in physics seems to demonstrate for the materialists that all is material; it seems to the realists to show that all is resolvable into relations; and it seems to be an argument that the subjectivists can advance in favor of their own mentalism; and so on. Metaphysics is assuredly a world situation, and, although not arbitrary, it is at least broader than any limited empirical situation and thus not determinable in terms of the limited situation. If a metaphysical interpretation had no necessary implications to situations other than the one whose metaphysical nature was being investigated, it is likely that each situation would suggest its own. But metaphysics represents a system of universal implications in which non-contradiction is one of the essential features. Hence, where one empirical fact "seems to suggest" one broad interpretation and another another, we must conclude that at least one of the empirical facts is giving misleading suggestions.

Russell finds himself, before he has done, driven back to an immutable if as yet unknown truth. He is unwilling to accept the veiled subjectivism of the logical positivists' linguistic interpretation of logical truth. Axioms are not arbitrary, as Carnap would have them; they "either do, or do not, have the characteristics of formal truth. . . ."[54] To discover whether they do or do not have these characteristics may be a difficult task indefinitely prolonged; but when we have admitted that the question is not arbitrary we have already admitted that there is such a thing as absolute truth, the knowledge of which we seek to approximate in our limited formulations.

JAMES FEIBLEMAN

NEW ORLEANS, LOUISIANA

[53] P. xiv.
[54] P. xii.

5

G. E. Moore

RUSSELL'S "THEORY OF DESCRIPTIONS"

RUSSELL'S "THEORY OF DESCRIPTIONS"

F. P. RAMSEY, in one of his posthumously published writings, used the phrase "that paradigm of philosophy, Russell's theory of descriptions."[1] What statement or statements of Russell's was Ramsey calling "Russell's theory of descriptions?" And what reasons are there for regarding this statement, or these statements, as a "paradigm of philosophy?"

I think there is no doubt that when Ramsey spoke of "Russell's theory of descriptions" he was using the word "descriptions" in one or other of two different technical senses, in each of which Russell has, in different places, used the word. One of these two technical senses is that in which it is used in *Principia Mathematica*, where the word occurs as a title in three separate places;[2] and this sense is one which the authors, where they first introduce the word,[3] try to explain by saying: "By a 'description' we mean a phrase of the form 'the so and so' or of some equivalent form." The other is a sense in which Russell has used the word in two later writings, his *Introduction to Mathematical Philosophy* and his lectures on "The Philosophy of Logical Atomism."[4] And what this other sense is is partly explained by the following sentences from the former, "A 'description'," says Russell,[5] "may be of two sorts, definite and indefinite (or ambiguous). An indefinite description is a phrase

---

[1] *The Foundations of Mathematics and other Logical Essays* (London: Kegan Paul, 1931), 263, n.

[2] *Principia Mathematica*, I², 30; 66; 173. (My references throughout are to the paging of the second edition, which is unfortunately slightly different from that of the first: I indicate this by writing I².)

[3] *Ibid.*, 30.

[4] *The Monist*, XXIX, 2 (April, 1919), 206 ff.

[5] *Introduction to Mathematical Philosophy*, 167.

of the form 'a so-and-so', and a definite description is a phrase of the form 'the so-and-so' (in the singular)." It is clear, I think, that "description" is here being used in a much wider sense than that in which it was used in *Principia*. In *Principia* it was so used that no phrase would be a "description" unless it were what Russell is now calling a "definite description;" in fact, in *Principia* "description" was used as a perfect synonym for the new expression "definite description," in the sense which Russell is now giving to that expression. But here, quite plainly, it is being used in such a sense that immense numbers of phrases which are *not* "definite descriptions" are nevertheless "descriptions." We may say that here "descriptions" is being used as a name for a genus of which "descriptions," in the *Principia* sense, are only one species, the other species being what Russell is now calling "indefinite" or "ambiguous" descriptions.

In which of these two senses, the wider or the narrower one, was Ramsey using the word when he spoke of "Russell's theory of descriptions?" If he were using it in the narrower one, the one in which it is used in *Principia*, he would be saying that some of the statements which Russell has made about phrases of the sort which, later on, he called "definite descriptions," are by themselves sufficient to constitute a "paradigm of philosophy." But, if he were using it in the wider one (the sense in which "indefinite descriptions" are just as truly "descriptions" as "definite" ones), he would not be committing himself to this assertion. On the contrary, it might be his view that, in order to get a "paradigm of philosophy," we have to take into account not only statements which Russell has made about "definite descriptions," but also statements which he has made about "indefinite" ones. Now I think it is pretty certain that, of these two alternatives, the former is the true one. I think Ramsey was using "descriptions" in the narrower of the two technical senses, *not* in the wider one; and that he did consider that statements which Russell has made about "definite descriptions" are by themselves sufficient to constitute a "paradigm of philosophy," without taking into account any of the statements which he has made about "indefinite" ones. And that he was using "descriptions" in the narrower sense—the sense of *Principia*—I think we have *some* evidence (though not conclusive evidence) in another passage, in which he also speaks of "Russell's theory of descriptions." In this other passage,[6] he says, "A theory of descriptions which contented itself with observing that 'The King of France is wise' could be regarded as asserting a possibly complex multiple relation between kingship, France and wisdom, would be miserably inferior to Mr. Russell's theory, which explains exactly what that relation is." This looks as if he regarded Russell's theory as a theory about phrases which resemble the phrase "*The* King of France" in a respect in which the phrase "*A* King of France" does not resemble it. But whether or not (as I am pretty certain he did) Ramsey meant by "Russell's theory of descriptions" Russell's theory of *definite* descriptions, I am going to confine myself exclusively to statements which Russell makes about *definite* descriptions. Which of these could Ramsey have regarded as constituting his "theory of descriptions?" And why should he have thought them a "paradigm of philosophy?"

Now if we read the three different passages in *Principia* which are headed with the title "Descriptions;"[7] if we then read pp. 172-180 of the chapter entitled "Descriptions" in the *Introduction to Mathematical Philosophy;* and if, finally, we read pp. 209-222 in *The Monist* for April 1919, we shall find that in all those passages, taken together, quite a large number of different statements are made. Which among all those different statements are statements about "definite descriptions?" And which among those which are can be regarded as forming part of "Russell's theory of descriptions?" I propose to begin with one which is a statement about a "definite description;" which nevertheless cannot, I think, be regarded as itself forming part of Russell's theory of descriptions; but which is such that, by reference to it, two of the most fundamental propositions which do, I think, form a part of that theory, can be explained.

The statement I mean is one which is made by Russell on p.

---

[6] *Foundations of Mathematics*, 142.
[7] *P.M.*, I², 30-1; 66-7; 173-186.

177 of the *Introduction to Mathematical Philosophy*. He there writes out in a list the three following propositions:

(1) at least one person wrote *Waverley*
(2) at most one person wrote *Waverley*
(3) whoever wrote *Waverley* was Scotch

and then proceeds to make about these three propositions the following statement:

All these three are implied by "the author of *Waverley* was Scotch." Conversely, the three together (but no two of them) imply that the author of *Waverley* was Scotch. Hence the three together may be taken as defining what is meant by the proposition, "the author of *Waverley* was Scotch."

Now it is quite clear that, in making this statement, Russell has made a considerable number of different assertions. But it seems to me that the language which he has used in making them is, in some respects, such as not to make it quite clear just what he is asserting. I will mention in order the chief respects in which this seems to me to be the case.

It will be seen that he has expressed the proposition numbered (3) by the words "whoever wrote *Waverley* was Scotch." Now it seems to me that the most natural way, and even, so far as I can see, the *only* natural way of understanding these words, is as expressing a proposition which cannot be true unless somebody did write *Waverley:* i.e., is such that the proposition "whoever wrote *Waverley* was Scotch, but nobody did write *Waverley*" is self-contradictory. But, if Russell had been using the words in such a sense as this, then clearly his statement that though (1), (2) and (3) together imply that the author of *Waverley* was Scotch, yet *no two of them* do imply this, would be false: for (3) would imply (1), and hence (3) and (2) by themselves would imply everything that is implied by (1), (2), and (3) together. It is certain, I think, not only from this fact but from other things, that he was using these words in a sense such that the proposition expressed by them does not imply (1). And I think that the proposition which he was using them to express is one which can be expressed more clearly by the words, "There never was a person who wrote *Waverley* but was not Scotch." In the case of this proposition, which I will call (4), it is, I think, quite clear that it does not imply (1), but is quite consistent with the falsehood of (1); for it is quite clear that if (1) were false, (4) would necessarily be true: if nobody ever did write *Waverley*, it would follow that there never was a person who did write *Waverley* but was not Scotch. I shall assume that (4) is the proposition which Russell was intending to express (improperly, as I think) by the words "whoever wrote *Waverley* was Scotch." And I shall assume that he was intending to assert of (1), (2), and (4) all the things which he actually asserts of (1), (2), and (3).

The next point as to which there might, I think, be some doubt, is as to how he is using the word "implies." I shall assume that he is so using it that one proposition *p* can only be said, with truth, to "imply" another *q*, if it can also be said with truth that *q* follows from *p*, and that the assertion that *p* was true but *q* false would be not merely false but *self-contradictory*. It follows that the meaning with which "implies" is being used here is not what the authors of *Principia* describe[8] as "the special meaning which we have given to implication," and which they say[9] they will sometimes express by the compound expression "material implication." For this "special meaning" is such that, provided it is false that *p* is true and *q* false, then it follows that it can be said with truth that *p* implies *q*. It is clear, I think, that Russell was not here using "implies" with this special meaning; for, if he had been, his assertion that no two of the propositions (1), (2), and (3) imply that the author of *Waverley* was Scotch, would have been obviously false. For, in fact, it is true that the author of *Waverley* was Scotch, and consequently, if "implies" be used in the special sense adopted in *Principia*, it follows that not merely any *two*, but any *one* of the three propositions, (1), (2), and (3) implies that the author of *Waverley* was Scotch; it follows, in fact, that any other proposition whatever, true or false, implies it—for instance, the proposition that the moon is made of green cheese. I feel no doubt that Russell was here using "implies," not in

[8] *Ibid.*, 99.
[9] *Ibid.*, 7.

this "special" sense, but in one of the senses which the word can properly bear in English; nor yet that he was using it in that one among its common senses, in which p cannot be truly said to imply q, unless the proposition that q is false is inconsistent or incompatible with the proposition that p is true; unless it is *impossible* that p should be true and q false; unless, if p is true, q *must* be true too—is *necessarily* true too. In other words, "implies" is being used in such a sense, that a *necessary* condition for its being true that p implies q is that it shall be *self-contradictory* to assert that p is true but q is false. But I do not think it is being used in such a sense that the fact that it would be self-contradictory to assert that p is true but q false is a *sufficient* condition for its being true that p implies q. I doubt if there is any common sense of "implies" such that this is a *sufficient* condition. For, of course, the assertion that p is true but q false will necessarily be self-contradictory, if the assertion that p is true is by itself self-contradictory, or the assertion that q is false is by itself self-contradictory. But I do not think that in ordinary language "implies" is ever so used that in all cases where this is so, it would be true to say that p implies q.

Owing to the ambiguity of the word "implies," I think it is often desirable where, as here, we are concerned with what it expresses when used with that particular one among its common meanings which I have tried to describe (though, of course, I have not attempted to define it), to use another word instead, as a synonym for "implies" when used in this particular way. And I shall do that now. I shall use the word "entails." I shall express the proposition which (I take it) Russell is here expressing by saying that the proposition "the author of *Waverley* was Scotch" both implies and is implied by the proposition which is the conjunction of (1), (2) and (4) by saying that each of these two propositions *entails* the other, or that they are "logically equivalent."

The third point which seems to call for some explanation is Russell's use of the phrase "may be taken as defining what is meant by." I take it that he is here using the expression "may be taken as defining," in what, I think, is its most natural sense, namely as meaning "may, *without error*, be taken as defining:"

in other words, he is asserting that any person who should "take it" that (1), (2) and (4) do define what is meant by the proposition "the author of *Waverley* was Scotch," would not be in error—would not be making a *mistake*—in "taking it" that this was the case. But, if he is asserting this, then his whole assertion is logically equivalent to the assertion that (1), (2) and (4) *do* define what is meant by the proposition in question: if a person would not be in error in "taking it" that *p* is the case, it follows that *p* is the case; and if *p* is the case, it follows that a person would not be in error in taking it that *p* is the case. Russell is therefore implying that the conjunction of (1), (2) and (4) *does* "define what is meant by" the proposition in question. But what can be meant by saying that one proposition "defines what is meant by another?" To define, in the commonest sense in which that word is used, is to "give a definition of" in a sense in which a *person* may give a definition (true or false) but in which a *proposition* cannot possibly do any such thing. If we talk of a proposition "defining what is meant by" something else, we must be using "define" in some sense which can be defined in terms of that other sense of "define" in which persons sometimes define but propositions never do. And I think it is plain enough what the sense is in which a proposition may be said "to define." To say that the conjunction of (1), (2) and (4) defines what is meant by the sentence S means neither more nor less than that anyone who were to assert "The sentence S means neither more nor less than the conjunction of (1), (2) and (4)" would be giving a *correct* definition of what is meant by the sentence S. But if we say that anyone who were to assert that the sentence S means neither more nor less than the conjunction of (1), (2) and (4) would be giving a *correct* definition of what is meant by S, we are saying two distinct things about any such person: we are saying (a) that *what* he asserts is true, i.e., that the sentence S *does* mean neither more nor less than the conjunction of (1), (2) and (4), and we are saying also (b) that what he asserts is of such a nature that he can properly be said to be *giving a definition* of S (or of the meaning of S) by asserting it. These two things are certainly distinct, because by no means every true assertion of the form

"The sentence S means neither more nor less than p," is such that it can properly be called a *definition* of p. The assertion "The sentence '*au moins une personne a écrit* WAVERLEY' means neither more nor less than that at least one person wrote *Waverley*" is (I believe) true; but a person who asserts it is certainly not *giving a definition* of the French sentence named. And the assertion, "The sentence, 'The sun is larger than the moon' means neither more nor less than that the moon is smaller than the sun" is certainly true, and yet anybody who asserted it would certainly not be *giving a definition* of the English sentence named. To give one last example: The assertion, "The sentence 'George VI is a male sibling' means neither more nor less than that George VI is a brother" is true but is certainly not a definition of the sentence "George VI is a male sibling;" whereas, on the other hand, the assertion "The sentence 'George VI is a brother' means neither more nor less than that George VI is a male sibling," which again is true, is also such that anybody who were to assert it could be correctly said to be *giving a definition* of one correct use of the sentence "George VI is a brother." On the question what conditions a statement of the form "s means neither more nor less than p" must satisfy if it is properly to be called a *definition* of the meaning of s, it will be necessary to say something later. For the present I only wish to make clear that I shall assume that, when Russell says "The conjunction of (1), (2) and (4) may be taken as defining what is meant by the proposition "the author of *Waverley* was Scotch," he is committing himself to the two assertions, (a) that the proposition "the author of *Waverley* was Scotch" means neither more nor less than the conjunction of (1), (2) and (4), and (b) that anybody who asserts (a) can be correctly said to be "giving a definition," and (since (a) is true) a *correct* definition of the meaning of the proposition named.

But now we come to one final point. What Russell actually says is that (1), (2) and (4) may be taken as defining what is meant by the *proposition* "the author of *Waverley* was Scotch;" he does not say that they may be taken as defining what is meant by the *sentence* "the author of *Waverley* was Scotch." If, therefore, I am right in what I said in the last paragraph, he is committing himself to the assertion that the *proposition* "the author of *Waverley* was Scotch" means neither more nor less than the conjunction of (1), (2), and (4); but is he also committing himself to the assertion that the *sentence* "the author of Waverley was Scotch" means neither more nor less than the conjunction of (1), (2) and (4)? It is quite certain, I think, that an expression which consists of the words "the proposition" followed by a given sentence in inverted commas, *can* be properly used in such a way that it has *not* the same meaning as the expression which consists of the words "the sentence" followed by the same sentence in inverted commas; and I am inclined to think that it can *not* be properly used in such a way that it *has* the same meaning. The *proposition* "The sun is larger than the moon" is the *same* proposition as the *proposition "Le soleil est plus grand que la lune,"* and one would be misusing the word "proposition," if one used it in such a sense that they were *not* the same; but the *sentence,* "The sun is larger than the moon" is *not* the same sentence as the *sentence "Le soleil est plus grand que la lune,"* and one would be misusing the word "sentence" if one used it in such a sense that they were the same. If we write the words, "the sentence" before a sentence in inverted commas, we shall be misusing language unless we are using the sentence in inverted commas *merely* as a name for itself and in no other way; but if we write the words "the proposition" before the very same sentence in inverted commas, we shall certainly not be misusing language if we are *not* using the sentence in inverted commas merely as a name for itself, and I think we *shall* be misusing language if we *are* using it merely as a name for itself. If we had to translate into French the sentence "The proposition 'the person who wrote *Waverley* was Scotch' implies that at least one person wrote *Waverley,"* we should certainly not be giving an incorrect translation, if for the English sentence "the person who wrote *Waverley* was Scotch" we substituted the French sentence *"la personne qui a écrit* WAVERLEY *était une personne écossaise,"* and wrote *"La proposition 'la personne qui a écrit* WAVERLEY *était une personne écossaise' implique qu'au moins une personne a écrit* WAVERLEY,*"* and I *think* we should be giving a definitely incorrect translation, unless we *did* substitute the French sentence for the English one; but if we had to translate, "The sentence 'the person who wrote *Waverley* was Scotch' means neither more nor less than the conjunction of (1), (2) and (4)" our translation would be definitely incorrect if we did substitute a French sentence for the English sentence "the person who wrote *Waverley* was Scotch." It appears, then, that if Russell had written "The proposition 'the author of *Waverley* was Scotch' means neither more nor less than the conjunction of (1), (2) and (4)," he would not have been using language incorrectly, if the assertion which he was making by the use of these words had been precisely the same as he might have made quite correctly by substituting for the English sentence "the author of *Waverley* was Scotch" a French sentence which was a correct translation of it. But suppose he had used such a French sentence, instead of the English one: would he, in that case, have been committing himself to any statement at all about the meaning of the English one? It seems to me to be quite certain that from the proposition or assertion or statement "The *proposition 'l'auteur de* WAVERLEY *était une personne écossaise'* means neither more nor less than the conjunction of (1), (2) and (4)" *by itself* nothing whatever follows about the English *sentence* "the author of *Waverley* was Scotch;" although perhaps from the conjunction of this statement with the statement "The sentence 'the author of *Waverley* was Scotch' is a correct translation of the sentence *'l'auteur de* WAVERLEY *était une personne écossaise',"* it will follow that the *sentence* "the author of *Waverley* was Scotch" means neither more nor less than the conjunction of (1), (2) and (4). And I think, therefore, that a person who were to assert "The proposition 'the author of *Waverley* was Scotch' means neither more nor less than the conjunction of (1), (2) and (4)" would perhaps, if he were using the expression "the proposition 'the author of *Waverley* was Scotch' " correctly, *not* be committing himself to the assertion that the *sentence* "the author of *Waverley* was Scotch" means neither more nor less than the conjunction of (1), (2) and (4). But I feel no doubt that when Russell said "the conjunction of (1), (2) and (4) may be taken as defining what is

meant by the *proposition* 'the author of *Waverley* was Scotch',"
he was (whether correctly or incorrectly) using the expression
"the proposition 'the author of *Waverley* was Scotch' " in such a
way that he was committing himself to the assertion that the
sentence "the author of *Waverley* was Scotch" means neither
more nor less than the conjunction of (1), (2) and (4); and I
shall assume that this was so.

But now, assuming that in all these four respects I am right
in my interpretation of Russell's words, it follows that among
the various assertions which he was making in the statement
quoted, two are as follows:

(a) The proposition that the author of *Waverley* was Scotch
both entails and is entailed by the proposition that (1), (2) and
(4) are all of them true; or, in other words, these two propositions are logically equivalent.

(b) The *sentence* "the author of *Waverley* was Scotch"
means neither more nor less than the conjunction of (1), (2),
and (4); and any one who says that it does, will, by so saying,
be giving a definition of its meaning.

Are these two assertions, (a) and (b), true?

It is, I think, worth noticing that neither can be true, unless
the expression "is the author of" can properly be used in such
a sense that a person who is not male can be correctly said to
have been "the author" of a given work; unless, for instance,
Jane Austen can be properly said to have been "the author"
of *Pride and Prejudice*. For it is quite certain that the conjunction of (1), (2) and (4) implies nothing whatever as to the
sex of the person who wrote *Waverley*. Consequently, if nobody
who is not male can properly be called an author, (b) cannot
possibly be true, since there would then be no sense in which
the sentence "the author of *Waverley* was Scotch" can properly
be used, in which *all* that it means is the conjunction of (1),
(2) and (4): that sentence would in any proper use mean *also*
that some *male* person composed *Waverley*. And for the same
reason the assertion of (a) that the conjunction of (1), (2), and
(4) entails that the author of *Waverley* was Scotch would be
false. For if the only proper use of "author" were such that
nobody could have been the author of *Waverley* except a male,

then (1), (2) and (4) would be quite consistent with the proposition that *nobody* was the author of *Waverley*, and therefore also with the proposition that it is not the case that the author of *Waverley* was Scotch, which would necessarily be true if nobody was the author of *Waverley*. It is, therefore, only if Jane Austen can be properly said to have been the author of her novels, that (a) and (b) can be true. But I think it does not follow from this that (a) and (b) are false, since I think it is questionable whether "author" cannot be properly thus used, without any implication of male sex.

But I think that (a) and (b) are both of them unquestionably false for another reason. The reason is that there is no proper use of the word "author," which is such that the statement that a given person did not write a given literary composition is inconsistent with the statement that he was its author. Scott might perfectly well have been the author of *Waverley* without having *written* it. And my reason for saying this is not the obvious fact that he certainly might have been the author, even if he had dictated every word of it to an amanuensis and not written a word himself. I think this would have been a bad reason, because, so far as I can see, we have so extended the meaning of the word "write" that a person who has only dictated an original composition of his own may quite properly be said to have "written" it; perhaps he may be so said even if he only dictated it to a dictaphone. But it is surely unquestionable that a poet who, before the invention of writing, composed a poem or a story which was never written down, can *not* be properly said to have "written" it and yet may undoubtedly have been its *author*. There is no legitimate sense of the word "author" in which he will not have been its author, provided that he invented or composed it without the collaboration of any other person, and provided also that no other person or set of persons invented or composed the same poem or story independently. I think this shows clearly that there is no legitimate sense of the word "author" such that the proposition that a given person was the author of a given work is inconsistent with the proposition that the work in question was never written at all. It might have been true at the same time both that Scott was the author of *Waverley* and also that *Waverley* was never written at all: there is no *contradiction* in supposing this to have been the case. He certainly would have been its author, if he had composed or invented the whole of it by himself, without collaboration, and if also no other person or set of collaborators had invented it independently; and it is certainly *logically possible* that this should have happened, without *Waverley's* having ever been written. I think, therefore, that it is a sheer mistake on Russell's part to say that "the author of *Waverley* was Scotch" implies "at least one person wrote *Waverley*." It does *not* imply this: the proposition "the author of *Waverley* was Scotch, but it is not the case that at least one person wrote *Waverley*" is not self-contradictory. (a), therefore, I think, is certainly false. And (b) is false too, for the same reason. There is no legitimate use of the sentence "the author of *Waverley* was Scotch" which is such that this sentence means neither more nor less than the conjunction of (1), (2) and (4). In its only legitimate use it means *less* than this conjunction. It does mean (if "author" can be properly used without implying male sex) neither more nor less than that at least one person invented *Waverley*, at most one person invented *Waverley*, and there never was a person who invented *Waverley* but was not Scotch. But to assert this conjunction is to assert *less* than to assert the conjunction (1), (2) and (4); since to assert that at least one person *wrote Waverley* is to assert that at least one person *invented* it, *and* something *more* as well.

Russell's statements (a) and (b) are, then, certainly false; but the fact that they are so makes nothing against his "theory of descriptions," since they form no part of that theory. And, though they are false, they will, I think, serve just as well as if they were true to explain the nature of two statements, which do, as far as I can see, form part of that theory and which, I think, are true.

I. The first of these two statements is a statement with regard to a class of propositions of which (a) is a member. And what it asserts with regard to this class is *only* that enormous numbers of propositions which are members of it are true. It does not assert, with regard to any particular member of the class, that that particular member is true, nor does it assert that *all* of its members are true.

What is the class of propositions with regard to which it makes this assertion?

I think it can be defined by first defining a certain class of English *sentences,* which I will call "class C." Once we have defined this class of *sentences,* C, we can define the class of *propositions,* with regard to which I. makes the assertion that enormous numbers of them are true, by reference to this class of sentences.

What then is the class of sentences which I am proposing to call "Class C?"

It is a class of which the following sentence, which I will call "S," is a member, viz., "The proposition 'the author of *Waverley* was Scotch' both entails and is entailed by the proposition 'at least one person wrote *Waverley,* at most one person wrote *Waverley,* and there never was a person who wrote *Waverley* but was not Scotch'," and the rest of the members of class C are those sentences, and those only, which resemble S in certain respects which have now to be defined.

(This sentence, S, it will be seen, is merely another way of expressing that very same proposition of Russell's which I called (a), but which I then expressed by a different sentence.)

(1) In order to be a sentence which resembles S in the respects in question, a sentence must first of all resemble it in the following respects: it must begin with the words "the proposition;" these words must be immediately followed by an English sentence enclosed between inverted commas; this sentence must be immediately followed by the words "both entails and is entailed by the proposition;" these words again must be immediately followed by another English sentence enclosed between inverted commas—a sentence which is not identical with the earlier one enclosed between inverted commas; and this second sentence in inverted commas must complete the whole sentence. It is obviously very easy to tell whether a sentence does fulfil these conditions or not; and it is obvious that S does fulfil them.

(2) But, in order that a sentence, other than S, should belong to the class C, it is by no means sufficient that it should resemble S in the respects just mentioned under (1). It must also resemble S in other respects; and these other respects concern the two sentences in inverted commas which it must contain. These two sentences must resemble the two in inverted commas which S contains in the following respects: (α) the first of them must, like the first in S, begin with the word "the" followed by a noun in the *singular*, though it need not be *immediately* followed by such a noun—there may be an adjective in between: e.g., "the male inhabitant of London" or "the first President of the United States" will be just as good beginnings as "the author of *Waverley;*" (β) the second of them must, like the second in S, consist of three separate sentences, the last two of which are joined by the word "and;" and of these three sentences (again as in S) the first must begin with the words "at least one," the second with the words "at most one," and the third with the words "there never was" or with "there is not" or with "there will not be," while also there must be one identical phrase which occurs in all three of them, just as "wrote *Waverley*" occurs in all three of those which occur in the second in S. And finally (γ) the second of the two sentences in inverted commas must end with the same word or phrase as the first, just as, in S, they both end with the word "Scotch," though here, perhaps, it should be added that this will be only true if "stinks" is counted as the same word as "stink," and "limps" as "limp," etc., etc.

Here again, I think, there is no difficulty whatever in seeing whether a sentence, which does satisfy the conditions mentioned in (1), also satisfies these further conditions or not. S obviously does satisfy them; and they will also obviously be satisfied by each of the four sentences, satisfying the conditions of (1), in which the first and second sentences within inverted commas are the following pairs: "the chop in that cupboard stinks" and "at least one among all the things which exist at present is a chop in that cupboard, at most one among all the things which exist at present is a chop in that cupboard, and there is not any among all the things which exist at present which is a chop in that cupboard and which does not stink;" "the male inhabitant of London limps" and "at least one person is a male inhabitant of London, at most one person is a male inhabitant of London, and there is not any person who is a male inhabitant of London and who does not limp;" "the first President of the United States was called 'Jefferson'" and "at least one person was President of the United States before any one else was, at most one person was President of the United States before any one else was, and there never was a person who was President of the United States before any one else was and who was not called 'Jefferson';" "the next book I shall read will be a French one" and "at least one book will be read by me before I read any other, at most one book will be read by me before I read any other, and there will not be any book which will be read by me before any other and which will not be a French one."

There is, therefore, no difficulty in understanding what class of *sentences* I am proposing to call "class C;" and a class of *propositions*, which I will call "class Γ," can be defined by reference to C as follows: A proposition will be a member of class Γ if and only if some sentence belonging to class C will, if the word "entails" is used in the way I have explained, and if the rest of the sentence is used in accordance with correct English usage, express that proposition.

Now of the propositions which belong to class Γ enormous numbers are false. Russell, as we have seen, happened to hit upon a false one, namely (a), which he declared to be true. But, though enormous numbers are false, I think it is also the case that enormous numbers are true; and I think there is no doubt that one proposition or statement which forms a part of Russell's "theory of descriptions" is this true statement that

> *Enormous numbers of propositions which are members of Class Γ are true.*

That this is true seems to me to be quite certain. Consider, for example, the C-sentence "The proposition 'the King of France is wise' both entails and is entailed by the proposition 'at least one person is a King of France, at most one person is a King of France, and there is nobody who is a King of France and is not wise'"—a sentence in which the first sentence enclosed in inverted commas is the very sentence which Ramsey used in the statement about the theory of descriptions which I quoted above.[10] To anyone who understands English a very little reflection is, I think, sufficient to make it obvious that if, in this sentence, the word "entails" is being used in the way I explained, and if the rest of the sentence is being used in accordance with correct English usage, then the proposition which it expresses, which is, in that case, a Γ-proposition, is true. And, once this is seen, it is surely also obvious that it would be possible to go on indefinitely producing other examples of Γ-propositions which are true. That this is so, is, I think, obvious as soon as it is pointed out. But had anyone before Russell pointed it out? I do not know. But it seems to me that, in philosophy, it is often a great achievement to notice something which is perfectly obvious as soon as it is noticed, but which had not been noticed before. And I am inclined to think that it was a great achievement on Russell's part to notice the obvious fact that enormous numbers of Γ-propositions are true.

II. A second statement which seems to me to form part of the theory of descriptions is, like this last, a statement with regard to a certain class of propositions, to the effect that enormous numbers of propositions of that class are true. The class in question is a class of which the false proposition of Russell's which I have called (b) is a member, and I propose to call this class "class Δ." The statement which the theory of descriptions makes about Δ-propositions is only that enormous numbers of them are true: it does not state that all are, nor does it state with regard to any particular Δ-proposition that that one is true.

This class of propositions, Δ, can be defined by reference to a particular class of English *sentences* which I propose to call "D." A proposition will belong to Δ, if and only if it can be properly expressed in English by a D-sentence; but, of course, the same proposition may also be capable of being properly expressed by sentences which are not D-sentences. Sentences

[10] See p. 179 above.

which are exact translations of a D-sentence in a foreign language will also properly express Δ-propositions, and there may be English sentences which are not D-sentences, but which may be properly used to express the same proposition which a D-sentence expresses.

What class of sentences it is that I am proposing to call "D-sentences" can, I think, be most easily explained by reference to the class of C-sentences. A sentence will be a D-sentence, if and only if there is some C-sentence from which it differs and which it resembles in the following respects. Take any C-sentence you like: you will obtain the D-sentence which corresponds to it as follows. Substitute for the words "the proposition" with which the C-sentence begins the words "the sentence;" write down next, within inverted commas, the very same sentence which comes next in the C-sentence within inverted commas; then substitute for the words "both entails and is entailed by the proposition," which come next in the C-sentence, the words "means neither more nor less than that;" then write after those words, but *without putting it in inverted commas*, the very same sentence which is the second sentence in inverted commas in the C-sentence; and finally add at the end the words "and anyone who says that it does will be giving a definition of its meaning." Thus, if we take the C-sentence which I have called "S," the corresponding D-sentence will be "The sentence 'The author of *Waverley* was Scotch' means neither more nor less than that at least one person wrote *Waverley*, at most one person wrote *Waverley*, and there never was any person who wrote *Waverley* but was not Scotch; and anyone who says that it does will, by so saying, be giving a definition of its meaning." It will be seen that this particular D-sentence is merely another correct way of expressing the very same false proposition of Russell's which I called "(b)" above, but which I then expressed by a different sentence; and that therefore this proposition (b) *is* a member of the class of propositions which I am calling "Δ," since it *can* be properly expressed by a D-sentence.

Now it is certain that enormous numbers of Δ-propositions are false; but what this statement II of the theory of descriptions asserts is only that enormous numbers are true. And this, I believe, is a true statement.

So far as I can see, the only way of seeing that it is true, is to see, in the case of some one particular Δ-proposition, that *it* is true, and then to see that an indefinite number of others could be found which are certainly also true, if this one is.

Now the following Δ-proposition seems to me to be true: namely "The sentence 'The King of France is wise' means neither more nor less than that at least one person is a King of France, at most one person is a King of France, and there is not anybody who is a King of France and is not wise; and anyone who says that it does, will, by so saying, be giving a definition of its meaning."

Is this proposition true?

We have to consider two points; namely (α) whether the the sentence "The King of France is wise," a sentence which I will now call "T," does mean neither more nor less than what this Δ-proposition says it does, and (β) whether anybody who says it does, will, by so doing, be "giving a definition" of the meaning of T. I will consider (β) first.

(β) I have already pointed out[11] that a person who makes an assertion of the form "the sentence *s* means neither more nor less than the proposition *p*" can by no means always be properly said to be giving a definition of the meaning of *s* by so doing. And the question whether he is giving a definition or not seems to me to depend on whether or not the *sentence* which he is using to express *p* is or is not related in one or other of certain ways to the *sentence s*. Now, in stating above the Δ-proposition about T, which I said I believed to be true, the sentence which I used to state the proposition about which that proposition asserted that T meant neither more nor less than it, was the sentence "at least one person is a King of France, at most one person is a King of France, and there is not anybody who is a King of France and is not wise,"—a sentence which I will now call "U." Now U has to T the following relation: it contains words or phrases which *mention separately* a greater number of distinct conceptions or "objects" than are mentioned separately in T. Thus we can say

---

[11] See p. 184 above.

that T and U both mention separately the conceptions of kingship and wisdom and the "object" France; but U mentions separately in addition the conception expressed by "at least one . . . ," that expressed by "at most one . . . ," that expressed by "there is . . . ," and the conception of negation; and even if we can say that T mentions separately some conception or conceptions, besides kingship and wisdom, it certainly does not mention separately as many more as U does. That the sentence which expresses the *definiens* in a definition does thus, as a rule, *mention separately* a greater number of conceptions than are mentioned by the sentence which is or expresses the *definition*, is, I think, the reason why the authors of *Principia* were able to say[12] that some of their definitions "contain an analysis of a common idea." But I do not think that the mere fact that, in making a statement of the form "*s* means neither more nor less than *p*," the sentence used to express *p* mentions separately a larger total number of conceptions or objects than *s* does, is by itself a sufficient reason for saying that the person who makes such a statement is giving a definition of *s*. Consider the two following statements. "The sentence 'the sun is larger than the moon' means neither more nor less than that anyone who were to believe that the sun is larger than the moon would not be in error in so believing." "The sentence 'the sun is larger than the moon' means neither more nor less than that it is false that it is false that the sun is larger than the moon." In both these cases the second sentence used certainly mentions separately a greater total number of conceptions and objects than the sentence in inverted commas; and yet I do not think that a person who were to assert either of those things, could be properly said to be giving a definition, either correct or incorrect, of the meaning of the sentence in inverted commas. But both these cases obviously differ from the case of T and U, in the respect that the second sentence used *contains as a part* the very same sentence with regard to the meaning of which an assertion is being made; whereas U does not contain T as a part of itself. And I think that this is a sufficient reason for saying that a person who were to make either of those two assertions would not, by making them, be giving a

[12] *P.M.*, I², 12.

definition at all. It may, perhaps, be suggested that he might be giving a definition, but that, if he were, it would be a circular one. But I think it is not incorrect to say that a circular definition is not a definition at all. One may, of course, commit a *circulus in definiendo*—that is to say, one may commit a circle in *trying* to define; but I think it is not incorrect to say that, if one does, then one has not succeeded in defining at all, either correctly or incorrectly. However that may be, it is, so far as I can see, a sufficient condition for saying that, in making an assertion of the form "*s* means neither more nor less than *p*," one has *given a definition* (correct or incorrect) of *s*, that the sentence used to express *p* should (1) mention separately a greater total number of conceptions and objects than *s* does and (2) should also not contain as a part of itself either *s* or any other sentence which has the same meaning as *s*. If this is so it follows that a person who uses U to say what T means, will, by so doing, be giving a *definition* (though, perhaps not a correct one) of the meaning of T. But though this, which I have stated, seems to me a *sufficient* condition for saying that a person who makes an assertion of the form "*s* means neither more nor less than *p*" is, by so doing, giving a definition, correct or incorrect, of the meaning of *s*, I do not think that it is a *necessary* condition. For it seems to me that a person who were to say "The sentence 'It is true that the sun is larger than the moon' means neither more nor less than that the sun is larger than the moon" might be correctly said to be giving a definition of the meaning of the sentence "It is true that . . . etc.;" and here condition (1) is certainly not fulfilled. But, so far as I can see, it is only where, as in this case, the sentence used to express the *definiens*, or some sentence which has the same meaning, forms a part of the sentence which is the *definitum*, that one can be properly said to be giving a definition in spite of the fact that (1) is not fulfilled.

I think, therefore, there is no doubt that any person who says "The sentence T means neither more nor less than that at least one person is a King of France, at most one person is a King of France, and there is not anybody who is a King of France but is not wise" can be properly said to be giving a definition of the meaning of the sentence T. But will he be giving a *correct* one?

He will be doing so only if this assertion which he makes is true; i.e., if the sentence T *does* mean neither more nor less than what he says it means. But does it?

This is the question which I called (α) above (p. 195).

(α) Let us call the assertion, with regard to which we are here asking whether it is true, "P." If we want to consider whether or not P is true, it is, I think, very important to distinguish P clearly from another proposition with which it is liable to be confused. In stating P, I have, as I pointed out in discussing (β), made use of the sentence U, that is to say, the compound sentence "at least one person is a King of France, at most one person is a King of France, and there is not anybody who is a King of France and is not wise." But I was not, in stating P, using U merely as a name for itself, whereas I was using T merely as a name for itself. That I was not so using U is clearly shown by the fact that it was preceded by the words "means neither more nor less than *that*." Wherever a sentence is preceded by a "that," used in this particular way, not as a demonstrative but as a conjunction, it is, I think, a sign that the sentence in question is not being used *merely* as a name for itself, but in the way in which sentences are most often used—a way which can, I think, be not incorrectly described by saying that they are used to express propositions. It is true that I could have expressed P, not incorrectly, in another way; namely, instead of writing U preceded by "that" and *not* putting inverted commas round it, I might have written, instead of "that," the words "the proposition," and followed these words by U *in inverted commas*. The fact that U, in inverted commas, was preceded by the words "the proposition" would again have been a sign that U was not being used *merely* as a name for itself. What I could not have done, if I wanted to express P correctly, is to write instead of the word "that" the words "the sentence," and to follow these words by U in inverted commas. For the fact that U, in inverted commas, was preceded by the words "the sentence" or "the words" would have been a sign that U was being used *merely* as a name for itself; and hence this would not have been a correct way of expressing P. Yet I am afraid it is not uncommon among philosophers to make, in similar cases, a confusion, which, if they made it in this case, would consist in supposing that P is identical with the proposition "T means neither more nor less than U." In the sentence which I have just used to express this latter proposition, the words "means neither more nor less than" are, of course, used (quite correctly) as short for "means neither more nor less than *is meant by*." But in the sentence which I used to express P, the same words "means neither more nor less than" are not short for "means neither more nor less than *is meant by*," because the words which follow (i.e., the sentence U) are not being used merely as a name for themselves: "means" is being used in an equally correct and a more primitive way. It would be strange, would it not, if "means" were *always* used to mean "means what is meant by." Yet I am afraid it is not uncommon to suppose that when we give a definition by saying, e.g., "the expression 'is a triangle' *means* 'is a plane rectilineal figure, having three sides'," the statement we are making is identical with the statement "the expression 'is a triangle' *means what is meant by* the expression 'is a plane rectilineal figure, having three sides'." Mr. W. E. Johnson, in his *Logic,* seems to suppose this; but he also makes a true remark, which shows quite clearly that he was wrong in so supposing. His true remark is that, when we give a definition, a hearer or reader will not understand our definition unless he understands the expression which we use to express our *definiens.* I think this is obviously true; but if it is true, it follows that we are never giving a definition, if we merely say of one expression that it means what is meant by another. For, if this is all we are saying, a hearer or reader can understand us perfectly without needing to understand *either* of the expressions in question. I might, for instance, point to two sentences in a book, written in a language I do not understand at all, and say (pointing at the first) this sentence means what is meant by that (pointing at the second). And I might, by accident, or because somebody who knew the language had told me so, be right! The first sentence might really mean what is meant by the second, and the second might really be so related to the first that it could be *used* to give a definition of the first. Suppose this were so: then a person who saw the sentences and understood the English words "means what is meant by" would be able to understand my assertion perfectly, without understanding either of the two sentences any better than I did! Since, therefore, it is *not* necessary, in order to understand such a statement, that either sentence be understood, it follows that such a statement is *never* a definition. Now P *is* a definition: that is to say, anyone who asserts P can be properly said to be giving a definition of the meaning of T. It follows that P is *not* the same proposition as "T means neither more nor less than is meant by U;" since this latter proposition could be understood perfectly by a person who did not understand either T or U. The important point is that, when I *use* U in stating P, I am not using U merely as a name for itself; whereas if I say "T means neither more nor less than U," I *may* be using U merely as a name for itself, and, if so, am not asserting P.

Let us call the proposition "T means neither more nor less than is meant by U" "Q." Even if it be admitted that, as I have argued, Q is *not* the same proposition as P, though liable to be confused with it, there is, I think, still a great temptation to suppose that P follows from Q, and Q from P, i.e., that P and Q mutually entail one another. But this, I think, is a mistake. From P, *by itself*, Q does not follow: it is only from P, *together with another premise*, that Q follows; and why there is a temptation to think that P, *by itself*, entails Q, is because this other premise is so obviously true that people assume it without noticing that they are doing so. And similarly from Q, *by itself*, P does not follow: it is only from Q, *together with another premise*, that P follows; but here again the other premise is so obviously true, that we are tempted to think that Q, by itself, entails P. What is the other premise which must be conjoined with P in order that we may be entitled to infer Q? I have already pointed out, in another instance, that, in order to express P, it is not necessary to use the sentence U *at all;* whereas, in order to express Q, it is absolutely necessary to use U *as a name for itself,* but in no other way. We can express P by using, instead of U, any sentence which is a correct translation of U in a foreign language; e.g., if my French is correct (which perhaps it isn't), we can express P by "*Les mots* 'The King of France is wise' *veulent dire qu'une personne au moins est un roi de France, qu'une personne au plus est un roi de France, et qu'il n'y a aucune personne qui soit un roi de France et qui ne soit pas sage, et ces mots ne veulent dire ni plus ni moins que cela.*" And it seems obvious that some other premise, in addition to this proposition P, is required in order to entitle us to infer that the English sentence T means neither more nor less than what is meant by the English sentence U. *What* other premise is required? So far as I can see, the additional premise required is merely that the sentence U (which is, we remember, the sentence "at least one person is a King of France, at most one person is a King of France, and there is not anybody who is a King of France and is not wise") means neither more nor less than that at least one person is a King of France, at most one person is a King of France, and there is not anybody who is a King of France and is not wise. Let us call this premise "R." From P and R *together* Q obviously does follow; since P asserts of T that it means neither more nor less than the very same proposition with regard to which R asserts that U means neither more nor less than that very proposition: and, if T and U both mean neither more nor less than this particular proposition, it follows that T means neither more nor less than is meant by U—a consequence which is the proposition Q. But now R is a proposition which seems to be quite obviously true; and there is a great temptation to think that it is a mere tautology; and if it were, then any proposition which followed from the conjunction of it with P, would follow from P alone; and since Q does follow from the conjunction of P and R, and R seems to be a tautology, people are naturally led to suppose that Q follows from P alone. But I think it is a mistake to suppose that R is a tautology: it *is* obviously true, but that is not because it is a tautology, but because we who understand English, know so well what the sentence U does mean. The question at issue can be more conveniently discussed in the case of a shorter sentence than U. If R is a tautology, then the proposition which I will call "W," namely "The sentence 'At least one person is a King of France' means that at least one person is a King of France," is also a tautology; and if R is *not* a tautology, then W is also *not* a tautology. Is W a tautology? There is certainly a great temptation to think so; but the following reasons lead me to think that it is a mistake to think so. (1) W is the same proposition as *"Les mots* 'At least one person is a King of France' *veulent dire qu'une personne au moins est un roi de France."* But I think it is quite obvious that this proposition is not a tautology; and since it is the same proposition as W, it would follow that W is not either. It is true, of course, that the English sentence which I originally used to express W differs from this French sentence in a notable way. In the English sentence the expression "At least one person is a King of France," an expression which I will call "Z," occurs twice over, once, in inverted commas, *merely* as a name for itself,—once, without inverted commas, *not* merely as a name for itself but to express a proposition; whereas, in the French sentence, Z occurs once only, *merely* as a name for itself. And owing to this difference, if one wanted to assert W, it would always be quite useless to use the English sentence in order to do so, since nobody could possibly understand the English sentence unless he already knew what Z did mean. But from this fact that it will be useless to assert W by means of the English sentence, it does not follow that W is a tautology. I suggest that one reason why we are tempted to think that the proposition "The sentence 'At least one person is a King of France' means that at least one person is a King of France" is a tautology is for the irrelevant reason that we all see at once that we could not possibly convey any information to anybody by saying these words. (2) I think it is also obvious, on reflection, that the sentence Z *might,* quite easily, *not* have meant that at least one person is a King of France. To say that it does mean this is to say something about the correct English use of the words which occur in Z and of the syntax of Z. But it might easily not have been the case that those words and that syntax ever were used in that way: that they are so used is merely an empirical fact, which might not have been the case. There is, therefore, no *contradiction* in the supposition that Z does *not* mean that at least one person is a King of France: it *might* have been the case that it did not. Of course, if Z had not meant this, the words "Z does not mean that at least one person is a King of France" would not have been a correct way of expressing the fact that Z had not this meaning. Anybody who, in that case, had used these words to say this, would, of course, have been saying something that was true, but would have been expressing this true proposition incorrectly; since he would have been using Z, in the second place in which he used it, to mean something which it does now in fact mean, but which, in the case supposed, it would not have meant. But though no person, in the case supposed, could have expressed correctly the proposition which would in that case have been true by saying "Z does not mean that at least one person is a King of France," *we* can express correctly this proposition, which would then have been true, by saying it would then have been true that Z did not mean that at least one person was King of France. In short, it seems that, in the case supposed, the very same proposition would have been true, which, as things *are* (considering, that is, how these words and their syntax are actually used), would be correctly expressed by "Z does not mean that at least one person is King of France," but which is, as things are, false. But if this proposition would have been true, provided that a supposition which is certainly not self-contradictory had been the case, it cannot be self-contradictory. It seems, then, that the proposition "Z does *not* mean that at least one person is a King of France" is *not* self-contradictory, and therefore that the proposition "Z means that at least one person is a King of France" is not a tautology. But it must be owned that though the first of these two propositions, though false, seems not to be self-contradictory, yet there is a special absurdity in expressing it by the words I have just used. The absurdity I mean arises from the fact that when we use expressions to make an assertion, we *imply* by the mere fact of using them, that we are using them in accordance with established usage. Hence if we were to assert "Z does *not* mean that at least one person is a King of France" we should imply that Z *can* be properly used to mean what, on the second occasion on which we are using it, we are using it to mean. And this which we *imply* is, of course, the contradictory of what we are asserting. We *imply* it, by using this language to make our assertion, though we do not assert it, nor is it implied (i.e., entailed) by what we do assert. To make our assertion by the use of this language is consequently absurd for the same reason for which it is absurd to say such a thing as "I believe he has gone out, but he has not" is absurd. This, though absurd, is not self-contradictory; for it may quite well be true. But it is absurd, because, by saying "he has not gone out" we *imply* that we do *not* believe that he has gone out, though we neither assert this, nor does it follow from anything we do assert. That we *imply* it means only, I think, something which results from the fact that people, in general, do not make a positive assertion, unless they do not believe that the opposite is true: people, in general, would not assert positively "he has not gone out," if they believed that he had gone out. And it results from this general truth, that a hearer who hears me say "he has not gone out," will, in general, assume that I don't believe that he has gone out, although I have neither asserted that I don't, nor does it follow, from what I have asserted, that I don't. Since people will, in general, assume this, I may be said to *imply* it by saying "he has not gone out," since the effect of my saying so will, in general, be to make people believe it, and since I know quite well that my saying it will have this effect. Similarly, if I use the words "at least one person is a King of France" not merely as a name for themselves, but to express a proposition, people will, in general, assume that I am using the words in their ordinary sense, and hence I may be said to *imply* that I am, though I am not asserting that I am, nor does it follow that I am from anything which I am asserting. Now suppose I *am* using them in their ordinary sense when I say "Z does not mean that at least one person is a King of France." What I am asserting is then the false proposition that Z, if used in its ordinary sense, does *not* mean the very thing which, using it in its ordinary sense, I am using it to mean. But, by the mere fact of using it, I imply, though I do not assert, that, if used in its ordinary sense, it does mean what I am using it to mean. I am, therefore, *implying* a proposition which is the contradictory of what I am asserting, but which is not being asserted by me and is not entailed by what I assert. Owing to this peculiar absurdity which attaches to the asserting that Z does not mean that at least one person is a King of France, *by the use of those words,* we are tempted to think that that proposition is itself self-contradictory, when, in fact, it is not, but is only obviously false; and this, I think, is another reason why we are tempted to think that its negation, the proposition W, the proposition "The sentence 'At least one person is a King of France' means that at least one person is a King of France" is a mere tautology, when in fact it is not, but only obviously true.

But if W is not a tautology, then neither is R a tautology; and I am right in saying that Q does not follow from P by itself, but only from the conjunction of P and R. R is an extra premise required to be added to P in order to entitle us to infer Q. And the same extra premise, R, has also to be added to Q, in order to entitle us to infer P. P and Q, therefore, are not only different propositions; it is also true that neither entails the other. And it was important to bring this out, because the particular objection to P, which I want to consider, would be invalid, if P were identical with Q.

The objection is this:

P is the proposition that the sentence T, i. e., the sentence "The King of France is wise," means neither more nor less than that at least one person is a King of France, at most one person is a King of France and there is nobody who is a King of France and is not wise. But (1) it is quite certainly true that T means neither more nor less than that the King of France is wise. (2) If, therefore, P is true, we shall be expressing a true proposition both by the use of the sentence I have used to express P, and also by saying "T means neither more nor less than that the King of France is wise." But (3) if we are using "means neither more nor less than" correctly, then it cannot be said with truth both that T means neither more nor less than that at least one person is a king of France, at most one person is a king of France, and there is not anybody who is a king of France and is not wise, and also that T means neither more nor less than that the King of France is wise, unless it can also be said with truth that the proposition "at least one person is a king of France, at most one person is a king of France, and there is nobody who is a king of France and is not wise" is *the same proposition* as "the King of France is wise." But (4) if this last can be said with truth, it will follow that it can also be said with truth that P is *the same proposition* as the proposition (which I will call "X") that T means neither more nor less than that the King of France is wise. But (5) P is certainly *not* the same proposition as X; and hence (6) it cannot be said with truth that "the King of France is wise" is *the same proposition* as "at least one person is a king of France, at most one person is a king of France, and there is nobody who is a king of France and is not wise," and hence (7) since (1) is true, P cannot be true.

And a similar argument can be used against the proposition Q, i.e., the proposition that T means neither more nor less than is meant by U. This argument would be as follows. (1) T means neither more nor less than that the King of France is wise, and (this is the proposition which I previously called "R") U means neither more nor less than that at least one person is a king of France, at most one person is a king of France, and there is nobody who is a king of France and is not wise. But (2), from the conjunction of (1) with Q, it follows that the proposition "The King of France is wise" *is the same proposition as* the proposition "at least one person is a king of France, at most one person is a king of France, and there is nobody who is a king of France and is not wise." But (3) if this is so, it follows that the proposition "The proposition 'The King of France is wise' both entails and is entailed by the proposition 'at least one person is a king of France, at most one person is a king of France, and there is nobody who is a king of France and is not wise'," *is the same proposition as* "The proposition 'The King of France is wise' both entails and is entailed by the proposition 'The King of France is wise'." But (4) the conclusion of (3) is certainly false. Therefore (5) the conclusion of (2) is also false; and (6), since (1) is true, Q must be false.

Now, as regards these two arguments, it seems to me unquestionable that, in the case of the first, (1), (2) and (3) are all true, and, in the case of the second, both (1) and (2) are true; and also unquestionable that, in the case of the first, (5) is true, and, in the case of the second, (4). If, therefore, we are to avoid the conclusion that P and Q are both false, we must, in the case of the first argument, dispute (4), and, in the case of the second, dispute (3). And I think it is pretty certain that both the assertion which the first argument makes in (4), and the assertion which the second makes in (3) are false. But I don't think it's at all easy to see why they are false. Both are certainly very plausible.

To begin with, it must, I think, be admitted to those who may be inclined to say that "The King of France is wise" is *not* the same proposition as "at least one person is a king of France, at most one person etc.," that our use of "is the same proposition as" is such, that, even if it is correct to say that these two are the same proposition, it is *also* not incorrect to say that they are *not*. That this is so is implicit in the very language I have just used; for how could it be correct to say that *these two* are the same proposition, unless it were correct to say that "The King of France is wise" is *one* proposition and "at least one person is a king of France etc." is *another?* It is, indeed, not by any means always the case that where we can say with truth "the proposition '———' is the same proposition as the proposition '———'," a different *sentence* being enclosed within the first inverted commas from that which is enclosed within the second, that we can also substitute, with truth, the words "is *not* the same proposition as" for the words "*is* the same proposition." For instance, if one of the two sentences is an exact translation in a foreign language of the other, the proposition obtained by this substitution would, I think, be definitely false. "*Le roi de France est chauve*" *is* the same proposition as "The King of France is bald," and it would be definitely incorrect to say that it is a different proposition, or *not* the same. A person who were to use the first sentence, in its ordinary sense at a given time, to make an assertion, would definitely be making the *same* assertion or statement or proposition as a person who at the same time used the second sentence, in its ordinary sense, to make an assertion; and it would be definitely *wrong* to say that the one was making a *different* proposition or statement from that which the other was making, in spite of the fact that they were using different sentences. But the same would not hold, if one of them said "The King of France is bald" and the other said *"Une personne au moins est un roi de France, une personne au plus est un roi de France, et il n'y a aucune personne qui soit un roi de France et qui ne soit pas chauve."* Here even if we could (as I think we can) correctly say that they were making the same assertion or statement or proposition by the use of different sentences, on the ground that the information they were giving, if their statements were true, was exactly the same; yet it would also not be incorrect to say that the one was making a *different* proposition from that which the other was making. Any one who offered the French sentence as a translation of the English one, would be definitely giving an *incorrect* translation of it; and I think that wherever we can say that one sentence is *not* a correct translation of another, it is also not incorrect to say that it expresses a *different* proposition from that which the other expresses, though it may also be quite correct to say that it expresses the same proposition. Again, whenever, using two different sentences in the two different places enclosed by inverted commas, we can make, with truth, a proposition of the form "The proposition '——' both entails and is entailed by the proposition '——'," we can, I think, also make with truth the corresponding proposition of the form "The proposition '——' is a different proposition from the proposition '——'." If we were to say "The proposition 'The King of France is bald' both entails and is entailed by the proposition *'Le roi de France est chauve '*," we should be definitely misusing the expression "both entails and is entailed by;" it is definitely incorrect to say that "The King of France is bald" is a different proposition from *"Le roi de France est chauve,"* and therefore also definitely incorrect to say that we have here an instance of *two* propositions, which are logically equivalent—of *two* propositions, each of which entails the other. But if we say "The proposition 'The King of France is bald' both entails and is entailed by *'Une personne au moins est un roi de France, une personne au plus est un roi de France, et il n'y a aucune personne qui soit un roi de France et qui ne soit pas chauve* '," we are using "both entails and is entailed by" perfectly correctly, because it is also correct to say that we have here an instance of *two* different propositions, each of which entails *the other*. This ambiguity which attaches to the expression "is the same proposition as," and is such that, in hosts of cases, where, writing one sentence in inverted commas after the words "the proposition" the first time they occur and a different sentence after the same words the second time they occur, we can say, with truth "the proposition '——' is the same proposition as the proposition '——'," we can *also* say, with truth, "the proposition '——' is *not* the same proposition as the proposition '——'," also, it seems to me, attaches to two other expressions which are frequently used. In hosts of cases where it is not incorrect to say of one sentence that it "means the same as" another, it is also not incorrect to say of the same two sentences that the one does *not* "mean the same as" the other. And in hosts of cases where it is not incorrect to say of a given sentence that it is "merely another way of saying" that so and so is the case, it is also not incorrect to say of the very same sentence that it is *not merely* another way of saying that so and so is the case, in spite of the fact that in both cases the sentence used to express the "so and so" in question is exactly the same. And, in all three cases, I doubt if any precise rules can be laid down as to what distinguishes the cases where it is correct to say both of the two apparently contradictory things from those in which it is not correct to say both. Certainly, if we are to say of two different sentences, which we *can* say express two different propositions, that they also express the *same* proposition, a *necessary* condition for our saying so with truth, is that we should also be able to say with truth that each proposition *entails* the other; but I doubt whether this is a *sufficient* condition for saying so. In cases where, having two different *sentences* before us, we can rightly say that we have *two* propositions before us, we certainly cannot rightly say that those two propositions are the *same* proposition, unless conditions which are necessary and sufficient for the truth of the one are precisely the same as those which are necessary and sufficient for the truth of the other; and in many cases where this condition is fulfilled, we can, I think, rightly say that they are the same proposition: but I doubt whether we can in all. On the other hand, where we have two sentences, like T and U, of which we can (as I think) rightly say that they express the same proposition or have the same meaning, a *sufficient* condition for its being also correct to say that they express different propositions or have *not* the same meaning, is, I think, that we should be able to say that, for those who understand the language or languages involved, the hearing or reading of the one sentence brings before the mind of the hearer or reader ideas which the other does not bring before his mind. It can, I think, hardly be denied that to those who understand English, the hearing or reading of U will, in general, bring before the mind ideas which the hearing or reading of T will not in general bring before the mind, for the very reason which makes it right to say that you can *give a definition* of T by means of U, i.e., that U mentions separately a greater total number of conceptions and objects than T does; and this, I think, is a sufficient justification for saying that *in a sense* U does *not* "mean the same" as T, and does *not* "express the same proposition." This, I think, is the element of truth contained in the argument, often used, that two given sentences do *not* "mean the same," because, when we understand the one, "what we are thinking" is not the same as what we are thinking when we understand the other. But what those who use this argument often overlook is that even where we can rightly say, for this reason, that two sentences do *not* "mean the same," it may also be perfectly right to say that, in another, and perhaps more important sense, they *do* mean the same. Though, however, the fact that one sentence will, in general, bring before the mind of those who understand it ideas which a different sentence, though in one sense it has the same meaning, will not bring before the mind, is, I think, *sufficient* to make it correct to say that the proposition expressed by the one is a different proposition from that expressed by the other, I doubt if this is *necessary* to make it correct to say so. Consider the two sentences "The sun is larger than the moon" and "The moon is smaller than the sun." It is certainly not incorrect to say that these two sentences are different ways of expressing the same proposition, and that they have the same meaning. Yet I doubt whether it is incorrect to say that the proposition "the sun is larger than the moon" is one proposition, and the proposition "the moon is smaller than the sun" is *another* proposition. It is worth noticing that if we had to translate *"Le soleil est plus grand que la lune"* into English, it would be definitely incorrect to translate it by the second of these two sentences instead of by the first. And it is also, I think, not incorrect to say: "The proposition that the sun is larger than the moon both entails and is entailed by the proposition that the moon is smaller than the sun: these *two* propositions are logically equivalent." Whereas it would be definitely incorrect to say "The proposition *'Le soleil est plus grand que la lune'* both entails and is entailed by the proposition 'The sun is larger than the moon'," or to say that we have here *two* propositions which are logically equivalent. And yet I do not think we can say that the sentence "The sun is larger than the moon" brings before the mind any ideas which are not brought before it by the sentence "The moon is smaller than the sun," nor yet that the latter brings before the mind any ideas which are not brought before it by the former.

I think, therefore, it must be admitted to those who may be inclined to say that P and Q are false, that, so far as they are saying only that it is not incorrect to say that the proposition expressed by U is *not* the same as that expressed by T, and not incorrect to say that T and U do not have the same meaning, they are right. But the arguments which I gave, as arguments which might be used to show that P and Q are false, would seem to show more than this. For, when, in the first argument, (5) asserts that P and X are certainly not the same proposition, it seems that this is unquestionably true not merely in the sense that it is not incorrect to say that they are not the same, but in the sense that it is definitely *incorrect* to say that they *are* the same—that there is no sense whatever in which they can be correctly said to be the same. And similarly, in the second argument when (4) asserts that "the proposition 'The King of France is wise' both entails and is entailed by 'At least one person is a king of France, at most etc.' " is *not* the same proposition as " 'The King of France is wise' both entails and is entailed by 'The King of France is wise'," it seems that this is unquestionably true not merely in the sense that it is not incorrect to say so, but in the sense that it would be definitely incorrect to say that they *are* the same. And in both cases it is not at all easy to see how it can be definitely incorrect to say that the propositions in question are the same, if it is not incorrect to say that "The King of France is wise" is the same proposition as "At least one person is a king of France, at most one etc." The question is: If it is definitely *incorrect* to say that P and X are the same, and that the propositions which (4), in the second argument, declares to be *not* the same, are the same, can it possibly be correct to say that "The King of France is wise" is the same proposition as "At least one person is a king of France, etc.?" I am convinced that it can, and is. but I must confess that I am unable to see *how* it can be, and *why* it is. I must, therefore, confess that I am unable to point out where the fallacy lies in these arguments to show that what P and Q say is definitely incorrect.

But that there is some fallacy in the arguments is, I think, evident from the fact that, if there were not, then, so far as I can see, *no* definition would ever be correct. Consider, for instance, the following definition of "is a widow:" "is a widow" means neither more nor less than "was at one time wife to a man who is now dead, and is not now wife to anyone." This is, I think, clearly a correct definition of at least one way in which the expression "is a widow" can be properly used in English. And it is clearly correct to say: The sentence "Queen Victoria was a widow in 1870" means neither more nor less than that, in 1870, Queen Victoria had been wife to a man who was then dead, and was not then wife to anyone. And yet this proposition which I have just written down can certainly *not* be correctly said to be the same proposition as: The sentence "Queen Victoria was a widow in 1870" means neither more nor less than that Queen Victoria was a widow in 1870. And it can certainly not be correctly said either that the proposition "The proposition that Queen Victoria was a widow in 1870 both entails and is entailed by the proposition that, in 1870, Queen Victoria had been wife to a man who was then dead, and was not then wife to anyone" is the same proposition as "The proposition that Queen Victoria was a widow in 1870 both entails and is entailed by the proposition that Queen Victoria was a widow in 1870." But the fact that neither of these two things can be correctly said is, I think, clearly not inconsistent with the proposition that the proposition "Queen Victoria was a widow in 1870" can be correctly said to be the same proposition as "In 1870, Queen Victoria had been wife to a man who was then dead, and was not then wife to any-one," though I cannot explain *why* they are not inconsistent with this proposition.

I think, then, that what I have described as Prop. II of Russell's theory of descriptions, namely, the statement that immense numbers of propositions, which resemble, in the re-spects I specified, the proposition "The sentence 'The King of France is wise' means neither more nor less than that at least one person is a king of France, at most one person is a king of France, and there is not anybody who is a king of France and is not wise; and anyone who were to assert that this is so would be giving a definition of the meaning of the sentence 'The King of France is wise' " are true, is certainly true.

And I think it must have been this statement made by the theory of descriptions, which led Ramsey to mention, as a merit of that theory, that it explains *exactly what* multiple relation be-tween kingship, France and wisdom is asserted by "The King of France is wise." I think that if we are told that the sentence "The King of France is wise" means neither more nor less than that at least one person is a king of France, at most one person is a king of France, and there is nobody who is a king of France and is not wise, this statement, if true (as I have argued that it is), can be fairly said to explain exactly what multiple relation we should be asserting to hold between kingship, France and wis-dom, if we were to assert that the King of France is wise. And I think it is a great merit in Russell's theory of descriptions that it should have pointed out (for the first time, so far as I know) that, in the case of enormous numbers of sentences, similar in certain respects to "The King of France is wise," an explanation, similar *mutatis mutandis* to this one, of what we are asserting if we use them to make an assertion, can be given.

But it should be emphasized, I think, that from this statement, which I am calling Prop. II of the theory of descriptions, it does not *follow* that "The King of France is wise" means neither more nor less than that at least one person is a king of France, at most one person is a king of France, and there is nobody who is a king of France and is not wise. Prop. II only says that enormous numbers of Δ-propositions are true; and from this it will not follow, in the case of any particular Δ-proposition whatever, that *that* one is true. It would have been quite a different matter if Russell, or Whitehead and Russell, had somewhere, in what they say about "descriptions," presented us with a true *universal* proposition to the effect that *all* Δ-propositions, which satisfy certain specified conditions, are true. The conditions specified might have been such that from this universal proposition it *followed* that the Δ-proposition "The sentence 'The King of France is wise' means neither more nor less than that at least one person is a king of France, at most one, etc." is true, and similarly in the case of every other true Δ-proposition. But I cannot see that we have anywhere been presented with a true universal proposition of this kind. In order to find such a universal proposition, it would be necessary, so far as I can see, to do two things. Δ-propositions, as I have defined them, are propositions which make about some sentence beginning with the word "the" followed (with or without an intervening adjective) by a noun in the singular, a statement, similar in respects which I specified, to the statement made about the sentence "The King of France is wise" by the Δ-proposition which I have just mentioned. And, so far as I can see, there are many sentences beginning with "the" followed by a noun in the singular, about which *no* true Δ-proposition can be made. Take, for instance, these: "The heart pumps blood into the arteries," "The right hand is apt to be better developed than the left," "The triangle is a figure to which Euclid devoted a great deal of attention," "The lion is the king of beasts," or (to borrow an example from Professor Stebbing) "The whale is a mammal." It is obvious that no part of the meaning of any one of these sentences is (respectively) "at most one object is a heart," "at most one object is a right hand," "at most one object is a triangle," "at most one object is a lion," "at most one object is a whale." And even if (which I doubt) there could, in each case, be constructed in some complicated way a Δ-proposition which was true of that sentence, I think it is obvious that they are examples of uses of (to use Russell's phrase) *"the in the singular,"* very different from those which he had in mind in what he says about "definite descriptions." He has, it seems to me, given a true, and most important, account of at least one use of *"the* in the singular," and perhaps this use is far the commonest; but there are other quite common uses to which his account does not apply. And, if I am right in thinking that there are many sentences beginning with *"the* in the singular," about which *no* Δ-proposition is true, then, in order to get a true *universal* proposition to the effect that all Δ-propositions *of a certain kind* are true, we should need to find some characteristic which distinguishes those sentences beginning with *"the* in the singular" about which some Δ-proposition is true, from those about which none is true—some characteristic, that is to say, *other* than the mere fact that some Δ-proposition is true of each of the sentences in question. If we could find such a characteristic, say Φ, we should be able to make the true universal proposition: Of *all* sentences beginning with *"the* in the singular" which have the characteristic Φ, some Δ-proposition is true; and Φ might be such that from this universal proposition it could be deduced that of the sentence "The King of France is wise" *some* Δ-proposition is true. But I doubt whether any such characteristic can be found; and even if one could, I do not think that Russell, or *Principia,* have anywhere mentioned such a characteristic. But, even if this could be done, something more would plainly be required, if we wanted to find a universal proposition from which it followed that the sentence "The King of France is wise" means neither more nor less than that at least one person *is a king of France,* at most one person *is a king of France,* and there is not anybody who is *a king of France,* and is not wise; and from which, similarly, every other true Δ-proposition also followed. We should need, in fact, a universal rule, which would tell us, in the case of each different phrase of the form "the so-and-so" such that *some* Δ-proposition was true of any sentence beginning with that phrase, *what* phrase must follow the words "at least one," "at most one," and "there is not," in order to get a sentence which expressed a true Δ-proposition. That it is easy to make a mistake as to this is shown by the fact that Russell himself thought, falsely, as I have tried to show, that the statement "The sentence 'The author of *Waverley* was Scotch' means neither more nor less than that at least one person *wrote Waverley*, at most one person *wrote Waverley*, and there never was anybody who *wrote Waverley* and was not Scotch" was a true Δ-proposition. In order to get a sentence which does express a true Δ-proposition, in this case, we certainly need to substitute some other word for "wrote." It is, I think, clearly quite impossible to give any general rule whatever, which would ensure us against making mistakes of this kind. And hence I do not believe that it is possible to find any *universal* proposition to the effect that *all* Δ-propositions which are of a certain kind are true.

I think, therefore, that it is perhaps only by a stretch of language that the theory of descriptions can be said to explain exactly what relation we are asserting to hold between kingship, France and wisdom, if we assert that the King of France is wise. The theory of descriptions, I should say, consists only of *general* propositions. But general propositions may be of two kinds, which we may call *universal* propositions and *existential* propositions. I do not think that it contains, or could contain, any *universal* proposition from which it would follow, in the case of any Δ-proposition whatever which *is* true, that that proposition is true. And from the existential proposition that enormous numbers of Δ-propositions are true, it plainly will not follow, in the case of any particular one, that *that* one is true. But even if, as I think, the theory of descriptions only gives us a statement of the form "Enormous numbers of Δ-propositions are true" and does not give us any universal proposition of the form "All Δ-propositions, which have the characteristic Φ, are true," it is, I think, just as useful and important, as if it had given us such a universal proposition. The statement that enormous numbers are true is sufficient to suggest that, where we find a sentence beginning with "*the* in the singular," it will be wise to consider whether it is not one of which some Δ-proposition is true, and whether, therefore, the consequences which follow from its being one are not true of it. When once the question is suggested by the theory of descriptions, it is, I think, easy to see in particular cases, both that a given sentence is one of which *some* Δ-proposition is true, and *what* Δ-proposition is true of it. It is, I think, only in this sense that the theory of descriptions can be said to tell us that "The King of France is wise" means neither more nor less than that at least one person is a king of France, at most one person is a king of France, and there is nobody who is a king of France and is not wise.

III. Is there any other statement, forming a part of the "theory of descriptions," which is both true and important? I think there is at least one. But the subject which I am now going to discuss seems to me to be one about which it is very difficult to see clearly what is true, and about which I may easily be wrong.

Prop. II has told us that, in enormous numbers of cases where we have a sentence beginning with "the" followed (with or without an intervening adjective) by a noun in the singular, some Δ-proposition is true of that sentence. Now suppose we have found such a sentence, of which some Δ-proposition is true, and have also found some Δ-proposition which is true of it. We then have a correct answer to the question: What is the meaning of that sentence? Thus, e.g., a correct answer to the question: What does the sentence "The King of France is wise" mean? is "It means that at least one person is a king of France, at most one etc." But having got a correct answer to the question: What is the meaning of this sentence as a whole? we may want to raise another question, namely: What is the meaning of that part of it which consists in the words "The King of France?" This is a question which has obviously interested Russell, and about which he has said a good deal. There is no doubt, that if some Δ-proposition is true of the sentence "The King of France is wise," then the words or phrase "The King of France" are what he would call a "definite description." And the corresponding words in any sentence of which a Δ-proposition is true would also be called by him a "definite description." E.g., in the sentence "The first President of the United States who was called 'Roosevelt' hunted big game," the words "The first President of the United States who was called 'Roosevelt' " would be a "definite description," provided that some Δ-proposition is true of that sentence, as I think is obviously the case. One thing which is, I think, not clear about his use of the phrase "definite description" (or, in *Principia,* "description") is whether or not a phrase, which, when used in the way in which it is used in a sentence of which a Δ-proposition is true, is a "definite description," is also to be called a "definite description," if (supposing that were possible) in another sentence it is used in a different way. Does to say that a phrase is "a definite description" mean only that it is *sometimes* used in a particular way, so that any phrase, which is *ever* so used, will be a "definite description," even when it is not so used? or can the very same phrase be a "definite description" when used in one way, and *not* a "definite description" when used in another? However that may be, Russell is certainly interested in the question what meaning such phrases have *when* used in sentences about which some Δ-proposition is true.

And his theory of descriptions is certainly supposed by him to give an answer to this question different, in important respects, from what he himself and other philosophers had formerly held to be a correct answer to it. This appears very plainly from the first of his writings in which he put forward the views which he subsequently expressed under the heading "Descriptions." In this early article in *Mind,* entitled "On Denoting,"[13] he uses the name "denoting phrases" as a synonym for "Descriptions" in the wider of the two senses in which, as I have pointed out, he subsequently used "Descriptions," i.e., to include both what he subsequently called "definite descriptions" and what he subsequently called "indefinite" or "ambiguous" descriptions; but he says (p. 481) that "phrases containing 'the' are by far the most interesting and difficult of denoting phrases" and he is chiefly concerned with these. He points out difficulties which he finds in the views about such phrases put forward by Meinong and Frege, and says[14] that the theory which he himself formerly advocated in the *Principles of Mathematics* was very nearly the same as Frege's, and quite different from that which he is now advocating.

[13] *Mind,* N. S., XIV, 479.
[14] *Ibid.,* 480, n. 1.

Now I think it is quite clear that this change of view arose from his having noticed that, e.g., "The King of France is wise" entails and is entailed by "at least one person is a king of France, at most one person is a king of France, and there is nobody who is a king of France and is not wise;" and having further thought that this fact must be relevant to the question what "the King of France" means, or (as it is put in *Principia*) that "in seeking to define the use" of such a symbol "it is important to observe the import of propositions in which it occurs."[15] Apparently when he wrote the *Principles* it had not occurred to him that the fact that such a proposition as "The King of France is wise" cannot be true unless at least one man and at most one man is a king of France, must be relevant to the question what "the King of France" means; nor, so far as I know, had it ever occurred to any other philosopher. That the noticing that it was relevant was, at least in part, the origin of the new view, first expressed in "On Denoting," and embodied in *Principia*, is, I think, quite clear. But what *is* the new view? and how does it differ from the old?

One novelty in the new view is one which the authors of *Principia* try to express by saying that such a phrase as "The King of France" "is not supposed to have any meaning in isolation, but is only defined in certain contexts"[16] and later by saying that "we must not attempt to define" such a phrase itself, but instead "must define the propositions," in "the expression" of which it occurs. They propose[17] to use the new technical term "is an incomplete symbol" as a short way of saying that this is true of a given phrase; and accordingly declare that "descriptions" are "incomplete symbols."

Now when they say that we "must not attempt to define" such a phrase as "The King of France," as used in the sentence "The King of France is wise," I suppose their reason for saying so must be that they think that, if we did attempt to define it, we should necessarily fail to get a *correct* definition of it. If it were possible to get a correct definition of it, there would seem to be

[15] *P.M.*, I², 67.
[16] *Ibid.*, 66.
[17] *Ibid.*, 67.

no reason why we shouldn't attempt to get one. I think, therefore, their meaning must be that it is *impossible* to give a correct definition of this phrase *by itself;* and when they say that we must define "propositions" in the "expression" of which it occurs, I think what they mean might have been equally well expressed by saying that we must define *sentences* in which it occurs.

But why does Russell hold that though we can define such a sentence as "The King of France is wise" we can *not* define that part of this sentence which consists in the words "The King of France?" By introducing a new technical term for those phrases, occurring as parts of sentences, which can't themselves be defined although the sentences of which they are parts can be, he implies, of course, that there are other phrases which are parts of sentences, in the case of which we can not only define the whole sentence, but *also* define the phrase which is a part of it. And this certainly seems to be the case. To use an illustration which I gave above: we can define the sentence "Mrs. Smith is a widow" by saying that it means "Mrs. Smith was formerly wife to somebody who is now dead, and is not now wife to anybody." And we can also say that *any* sentence of the form *"x* is a widow" means that the person in question was formerly wife to somebody who is now dead and is not now wife to anybody. But in this case it seems also perfectly correct to take the phrase "is a widow" by itself, and to say "is a widow" means "was formerly wife to somebody who is now dead, and is not now wife to anybody." In this case, as in hosts of others, it seems that we can both define sentences in which a given phrase occurs, and *also* define the phrase by itself. This, which seems to be possible in so many cases, Russell seems to be declaring to be *impossible* in the case of phrases like "The King of France." *Why* does he declare it to be impossible? If we can define "is a widow" *as well as* sentences in which it occurs, why should we be unable to define "The King of France" *as well as* sentences in which it occurs?

I think there *is* a good reason for making this distinction between "The King of France" as used in the sentence "The King of France is wise," and "is a widow" as used in "Mrs. Smith is a widow;" but this, which I am going to give, is the only good reason I can see.

Let us consider a *different* definition of the sentence "The King of France is wise" from that which we have hitherto considered. Instead of considering the proposition "The sentence 'The King of France is wise' means neither more nor less than that at least one person is a king of France, at most one person is a king of France, and there is nobody who is a king of France and is not wise," let us consider the proposition "The sentence 'The King of France is wise' means neither more nor less than that there is somebody or other of whom the following three things are all true, viz. (1) that he is a king of France, (2) that nobody other than he is a king of France, and (3) that he is wise." This latter proposition is just as good a definition of the sentence in question as the former; and indeed, instead of saying that it is a *different* definition, but just as good a one, we can say, if we please, equally correctly, that it is *the same definition* differently expressed. For a very little reflection is sufficient to make it evident that the proposition "at least one person is a king of France, at most one person is a king of France, and there is nobody who is a king of France and is not wise" both entails and is entailed by "there is somebody or other of whom it is true that he is a king of France, that nobody else is a king of France, and that he is wise:" if the first is true, the second *must* be true too, and if the second is true, the first *must* be true too. And I think this is obviously a case, such as I spoke of before, in which it is equally correct to say either of the two apparently contradictory things: This is the same proposition as that; and: These *two* propositions are logically equivalent; and also equally correct to say of the two *sentences* each of the two apparently contradictory things: This sentence means the same as that, they are merely two different ways of saying the same thing; and: These two sentences have *not* quite the same meaning, they are *not* merely two different ways of saying the same thing. In support of the assertion that the two sentences have *not* the same meaning, and therefore do not express the same proposition, it may, for instance, be pointed out that the first proposition is a conjunction of three *independent* propositions, whereas the second is not: how could the *same* proposition be both?

Let us, then, consider the proposition (which is a definition): "The sentence 'The King of France is wise' means neither more nor less than that there is somebody or other of whom it is true that he is a king of France, that nobody other than he is a king of France and that he is wise." If this be true (as it is) it follows that we can correctly say: The sentence "The King of France is wise" means the same as the sentence "There is somebody or other of whom it is true that he is a king of France, that nobody else is so, and that he is wise." But now it appears that we can also correctly say that in these two sentences the words "is wise" mean the same. But since the whole sentences mean the same, and one part of each means the same as a part of the other, it seems natural to conclude that the part of the one which is left over when "is wise" is subtracted from it *must* mean the same as the part of the other which is left over when "is wise" is subtracted from it: i.e., that "The King of France" means the same as "There is somebody or other of whom it is true that he is a king of France, that nobody else is, and that he . . . ." But do those two phrases mean the same? I think we must answer: No; they certainly don't. For some reason or other, we can't do in the case of these two sentences what we could do in the case of "Mrs. Smith is a widow" and "Mrs. Smith was formerly wife to somebody who is now dead and is not now wife to anyone." There we could subtract "Mrs. Smith" from both sentences, and say correctly that what was left of the one meant the same as what was left of the other. Here we can't say correctly that what is left of the one sentence when "is wise" is subtracted from it means the same as what is left of the other when "is wise" is subtracted from it; and this in spite of the fact that the two whole sentences certainly do mean the same!

Now, so far as I can see, if you take any sentence whatever which can be used to express the *definiens* in a correct definition of "The King of France is wise," provided that the definition in question is not a definition of the sentence *only* because it yields a definition of "is wise" or of "king" or of "France," it will always be found that the part of the sentence which is left

over when "is wise," or that part of it which has the same meaning as "is wise," is subtracted from it, can *not* be said to have
the same meaning as the phrase "The King of France." And
this, I think, is a good reason for saying, as I have supposed
Whitehead and Russell intended to say, that you can't define
"The King of France" (in this usage), though you can define
sentences in which that phrase occurs. If this is what they mean
by saying that "The King of France," in this usage, is an "incomplete symbol," then I think it must be admitted that it *is* an
incomplete symbol.

In support of my contention that we cannot possibly say that
the phrase "The King of France," in this sentence means the
same as the phrase "There is somebody or other of whom it is true
(1) that he is a king of France (2) that nobody other than he is
so and (3) that he," I should like to call attention to the following point. There is no doubt that the expression "The King of
France" can be properly called, as Russell once called it, a "denoting phrase," if we agree that a phrase can be properly called
a "denoting phrase," provided it is the *sort* of phrase which
could have a denotation as well as a meaning, even if it actually
has no denotation. If a person were to assert *now* that the King
of France is wise by the use of the sentence "The King of France
is wise," it would be correct to say that "the King of France,"
as used by him, though a "denoting phrase," "does not denote
anything" or has no denotation because at present there is not a
King of France; but, if an Englishman in 1700 had used that
sentence to say that the King of France was wise, it would have
been quite correct to say that "the King of France," as used by
him, did "denote" Louis XIV, or, if we had been in the presence
of Louis, it would have been correct to point at Louis and say
"The phrase 'The King of France' denotes that person." It appears from Russell's article "On Denoting" that one of the
things which had puzzled him before he arrived at the theory
explained in that article (that is to say, his "theory of descriptions") was that it seemed to him that, in such a case as that of
an Englishman saying in 1700 "The King of France is wise,"
the Englishman's proposition would certainly have been "about"
the *denotation* of the phrase "the King of France," i.e., about

Louis, and *not* about the *meaning* of the phrase; and he was unable to see how the meaning was related to the denotation, when such a proposition was made. This puzzle his "theory of descriptions" seemed to him to solve. But the point I wish now to make is this: In the case of such an Englishman in 1700, it would certainly have been correct to say that his phrase "The King of France" *denoted* Louis XIV; but if he had said instead "There is somebody or other of whom it is true that he is a king of France, that nobody other than he is, and that he," would it have been correct to say that *this* phrase "denoted" Louis? I think nobody could possibly say so: and this seems to me a good reason for saying that his phrase "the King of France" would *not* have "meant the same" as this other phrase. And yet his whole sentence "the King of France is wise" would certainly have "meant the same" as the sentence "There is somebody or other of whom it is true that he is a king of France, that nobody else is, and that he is wise," if used at that time.

But, though in the case of sentences which resemble "The King of France is wise" in the respect that a true Δ-proposition can be made about them, there is, I think, good reason for saying that we can't define the phrase of the form "the so-and-so," with which they begin, though we can define the sentences in which the phrase occurs, it does not seem to me at all so clear that we cannot define such phrases when used in certain sentences in which they do not begin the sentence. Contrast, for instance, with "the King of France is wise," the sentence "There is a person who is the King of France," or the sentence "That person is the King of France," as it might have been used by an Englishman pointing at Louis XIV in 1700. Here, I think, we can certainly say that "is the King of France" does "mean the same" as "is a person of whom it is true both that he is a king of France and that no-one other than he is." If so, we must, I think, say that, in this usage, "the King of France" is *not* an incomplete symbol, though, where it begins a sentence about which a true Δ-proposition can be made, it *is* an incomplete symbol. It seems to me by no means paradoxical to say that the two usages are different; and even to say that, in this usage, "The King of France" never has denoted anyone, though in the other it has.

However that may be, there does seem to me to be good reason for saying that in the case of sentences about which some Δ-proposition is true, the phrase of the form "the so-and-so" with which such sentences begin, never can be defined, although the sentences in which it occurs can. And the statement that this is so should, I think, be reckoned as a third important part of "Russell's theory of descriptions."

Perhaps there are other statements, deserving to be called a part of that theory, which are also important, or perhaps even *as* important, as these three which I have distinguished. But it seems to me that these three, viz.

I. Enormous numbers of Γ-propositions are true.

II. Enormous numbers of Δ-propositions are true.

III. In the case of every sentence about which some Δ-proposition is true, the phrase, of the form "the so-and-so," with which it begins, cannot be defined *by itself*, although the sentences in which it occurs can be,——

statements, none of which, so far as I know, had ever been made before by any philosopher, are by themselves sufficient to justify Ramsey's high praise of the theory

G. E. MOORE

SWARTHMORE, PA.

6

Max Black

RUSSELL'S PHILOSOPHY OF LANGUAGE

6

RUSSELL'S PHILOSOPHY OF LANGUAGE

"The influence of language on philosophy has, I believe, been
profound and almost unrecognized." (Russell)

A. Introduction

1. Russell's influence. For the purpose of preliminary definition we might adapt a remark of William James and identify
philosophy of language as "what a philosopher gets if he thinks
long enough and hard enough about language." This characterization may serve as a reminder of the persistence and in-
tensity of Russell's preoccupation with language, displayed in
much of his philosophical writing during the past twenty-five
years.[1] The flourishing condition of present-day "semiotic"
is a sufficient testimony to the fertility of Russell's ideas; today,
some twenty years after the epigraph of this essay was composed,
it would be more accurate to say: "the influence of language
on philosophy is profound and almost universally recognized."[2]

[1] The quotation at the head of this paper is taken from the article "Logical
Atomism," in *Contemporary British Philosophy*, Vol. I (1924), which is, for all
its brevity, the best statement of Russell's early program for philosophical inquiries
into language. It is a matter for regret that the earlier lectures, published under the
title of "The Philosophy of Logical Atomism" in *The Monist* (Vol. 28 (1918),
495-527; Vol. 29 (1919), 32-63, 190-222, 345-380), have never been reprinted.
Language is a topic of central importance also in "On propositions: what they
are and how they mean" (*Aristotelian Society Proceedings*, Supplementary Vol. 2
(1919), 1-43), in *The Analysis of Mind* (1921), (especially Ch. 10: "Words
and Meaning") and *Philosophy* (1927, Ch. 4: "Language"). *An Inquiry into
Meaning and Truth* (1940) is, of course, almost entirely devoted to the same
topic.

[2] Contemporary concern with philosophy of language is most apparent in the
members and sympathizers of the philosophical movement known as "Logical
Positivism" or "Scientific Empiricism." In this instance the transmission of ideas
can be traced with rare accuracy. It is known that the Vienna Circle was much
influenced, in the post-war years, both by Russell's own work and that of his

229

If it is true that "Language has, so to speak, become the *Brenn-punkt* of present-day philosophical discussion,"[3] hardly another philosopher bears a greater share of the responsibility.

Philosophical study of language, conceived by Russell as the construction of "philosophical grammar,"[4] may have been regarded by him, at an early period, as a mere "preliminary" to metaphysics; it soon became much more than this. Philosophical linguistics may be expected to provide nothing less than a pathway to the nature of that reality which is the metaphysician's goal. To this very day the hope persists that ". . . with sufficient caution, *the properties of language may help us to understand the structure of the world.*"[5]

So ambitiously conceived, as a study potentially revealing ontological structure, philosophy of language cannot be restricted to the examination of uninterpreted formal systems, still less, as with earlier philosophers, to the rhetorical art of avoiding unintentional ambiguity. Its successful pursuit requires the use of data drawn from logic, psychology, and empirical linguistics and the formulation of reasoned decisions concerning the scope of metaphysics and the proper methods of philosophical research. Such questions as these arise constantly in Russell's discussions, even on occasions when he is most earnestly avowing the "neutrality" of his devotion to scientific method.

Since the full-bodied suggestiveness of Russell's work on language is a function of his refusal to adopt the self-imposed limitations of the mathematical logician, it would be ungrateful

---

pupil Wittgenstein. Although the *Tractatus* owes much to Russell, there can be no question but that the influence here was reciprocal, as Russell has frequently and generously acknowledged. The *Monist* articles are introduced with the words: "The following articles are . . . very largely concerned with explaining certain ideas which I learnt from my friend and former pupil, Ludwig Wittgenstein" (*The Monist*, Vol. 28, 495). A more detailed discussion of sources would call for some reference to the work of G. E. Moore (Russell's colleague at Cambridge). Cf. *The Philosophy of G. E. Moore*, 14 ff.

[3] W. M. Urban, *Language and Reality* (1939), 35.

[4] "I have dwelt hitherto upon what may be called *philosophical grammar*. . . . I think the importance of philosophical grammar is very much greater than it is generally thought to be . . . philosophical grammar with which we have been concerned in these lectures" (*The Monist*, Vol. 29, 364).

[5] *An Inquiry into Meaning and Truth*, 429 (italics supplied).

to regret the complex interweaving of themes which results. But any selection of topics, considered in abstraction from the context of Russell's general philosophical doctrines, is bound to be somewhat misleading. It must be hoped that the aspects of Russell's earlier procedures here chosen for brief critical examination so typically manifest his style of philosophic thought at this period that an understanding of their merits and defects will serve as a guide to the evaluation of the more extensive doctrines of which they are a part.

2. *The scope of this paper.* The main topics discussed in the remainder of this paper are:

(i) *The consequences of applying the theory of types to "ordinary language."* A new paradox will be presented whose resolution requires extensive reformulation of Russell's theory, and a critical judgement will be made of the value of the renovated theory.

(ii) *The search for "ultimate constituents" of the world.* The procedure here, so far as it is relevant to the criticism of language, will be shown to be, in part, susceptible of a neutral interpretation, and, for the rest, to be based upon an unproven epistemological principle, (reducibility to acquaintance), which will, after examination, be rejected.

(iii) *The notion of the "ideal language."* This branch of the investigation concerns the goal of the entire method. The construction of an "ideal language" will be condemned, for due reason presented, as the undesirable pursuit of an ideal incapable of realisation.

These headings cover most of Russell's *positive* contributions to philosophy of language.[6] There will be no space for discussion of the genesis of the whole enquiry in the destructive criticism of "ordinary language."[7] The bare reminder must suffice that the English language, as now used by philosophers, offends by provoking erroneous metaphysical beliefs. Syntax induces misleading opinions concerning the *structure* of the world (notably in the attribution of ontological significance to the subject-predicate form), while vocabulary, by promoting the hypostati-

[6] The only serious omission is reference to Russell's behavioristic analysis of meaning (cf. especially the last four works cited in footnote 1 above). I have already explained my reasons for objecting to this mode of analysis in an article (*The Journal of Philosophy*, Vol. 39, 281-290) whose arguments apply with little modification to Russell's position on this matter.

[7] *Contemporary British Philosophy*, Vol. I, 368.

zation of pseudo-entities, encourages false beliefs concerning the *contents* of the world. In either case we are "giving meta-physical importance to the accidents of our own speech."[8] It is in trying to remedy these defects of ordinary language by search-ing for what is *essential* in language that we arrive finally at the "ideal language" and its valid metaphysical implications.

B. The Consequences of Applying the Theory of Types to Ordinary Language

1. The genesis and character of the theory of types. Russell's arguments against philosophers who insist upon reducing all statements to the subject-predicate form amounts to showing that their procedure leads to contradiction.[9] But the "new logic" of relations, whose function it was to take account of complexi-ties of form neglected by syllogistic logic, proved to be infected by the new and more puzzling contradictions of the "mathe-matical and logical paradoxes." The basis of Russell's cure for this malady is the observation that each paradox involves a characteristic reflexive application of terms (as exemplified typi-cally in the notion of a class being a member of itself). The cure provided in *Principia Mathematica*, as the "theory of types," is, accordingly, a restriction upon the kind of symbols which may be inserted into a given context.[10] Entities designated by symbols all of which may be inserted into some one context are said *to belong to the same type.* There results a segregation of entities into a logical hierarchy of types, whose members are

---

[8] *The Analysis of Mind*, 192.

[9] Cf. *Our Knowledge of the External World etc.*, 58. It may be noted that the argument, as there presented, is defective in requiring the alleged defender of the universality of the subject-predicate form to propose an analysis which is not of that form. The argument could however be patched up. It would then establish that the attempt to express all relational propositions as logical products of functions of *one* variable (i.e., to assert that xRy $\equiv$ Px.Qy for all x and y) would lead to inconsistency with the theorems of the relational calculus. Russell interprets this result as a proof of the inadequacy of exclusive adherence to the subject-predicate form; but an opponent (such as Bradley, against whom the argument was directed) might regard it as one further manifestation of the "un-reality of relations."

[10] Cf. the article by Alonzo Church on "Paradoxes, logical" (in *The Dictionary of Philosophy*, 224-225) for a convenient statement of the problem and a bibli-ography.

individuals, functions of individuals, functions of functions of individuals, etc. (or an equivalent extensional hierarchy of classes and relations). Specification of the types of the entities involved is sufficient to reveal as invalid the arguments used in deriving *some* of the paradoxes.

This refutes only the paradoxes expressed in terms belonging wholly to mathematics or logic; but this is all that is required within logic itself, as subsequent logicians have emphasised. They follow Ramsey in rejecting the further subdivisions inside the types (the "branching theory of types") which were the basis of Russell's contribution to the solution of the remaining paradoxes. They agree with Ramsey that the latter are caused by "faulty ideas concerning thought and language,"[11] and, by claiming that "the fault must lie in the linguistic elements,"[12] they achieve a radical simplification of the original form of Russell's theory. This is no doubt satisfactory for those engaged in constructing a formal logic of maximum manipulative simplicity,[13] but it still leaves to be unravelled an imputed and endemic "ambiguity" of "ordinary language." Russell's discussion of this important residual problem deserves more critical attention than it has hitherto received.

2. *The definition of the logical types of entities designated by words of the ordinary language.* As contrasted with the definition of logical types in the artificial language of mathematical logic, the main point of difference which arises when the attempt is made to establish distinctions of type within "ordinary language" depends upon the fact that in the latter case modifica-

---

[11] F. P. Ramsey, *Foundations of Mathematics,* 21. In the group of logical paradoxes Ramsey puts those arguments, such as that involved in the contradiction of the greatest cardinal number, ". . . which, were no provision made against them, would occur in a logical or mathematical system itself. They involve only logical or mathematical terms . . ." The remainder ". . . are not purely logical, and cannot be stated in logical terms alone; for they all contain some reference to thought, language or symbolism, which are not formal but empirical terms." (*Ibid.*)

[12] F. P. Ramsey, *loc. cit.* (He proceeds to urge the need for further examination of the "linguistic elements.")

[13] " . . . the contradictions against which this part of type theory was directed are no business of logic anyway . . . the whole ramification, with the axiom of reducibility, calls simply for amputation." W. V. Quine (*The Philosophy of Alfred North Whitehead,* 151).

tion is introduced into a system of vocabulary and syntax *already in use*. There can be no question, therefore, of attaching unambiguous indications of type to symbols *introduced by definitions* (as in *Principia Mathematica*); the need is rather for a principle which will serve to reveal ambiguities of type within the system of grammatical rules already current.

The leading principle of the theory of types, so far as it applies to ordinary language, consists in the assertion that *grammatically* impeccable sentences often prove to be crypto-nonsense generated by a propensity for substituting in the same context words which agree in grammatical while differing in logical form. "In its technical form, this doctrine states merely that a word or symbol may form part of a significant proposition, and in this sense have meaning, without being always able to be substituted for another word or symbol in the same or some other proposition without producing nonsense."[14]

The benefit to be anticipated from an application of the theory of types to ordinary language will, therefore, consist in a set of criteria specifying *which* substitutions of words are legitimate. Since words which may so replace one another in all contexts are said to belong to the same type (by an extension of the usage of the similar expression in *Principia Mathematica*) the notion of logical types, as *here* used, will be of crucial importance.

The definition of a logical type [Russell says,] is as follows: A and B are of the same logical type if, and only if, given any fact of which A is a constituent, there is a corresponding fact which has B as a constituent, which either results by substituting B for A or is the negation of what so results. To take an illustration, Socrates and Aristotle are of the same type, because "Socrates was a philosopher" and "Aristotle was a philosopher" are both facts; Socrates and Caligula are of the same type, because "Socrates was a philosopher" and "Caligula was not a philosopher" are both facts. To love and to kill are of the same type, because "Plato loved Socrates" and "Plato did not kill Socrates" are both facts.[15]

In the form presented, this definition can be made to generate

---

[14] *Contemporary British Philosophy*, I, 371.
[15] *Op. cit.*, 369-370.

a new and instructive paradox, whose existence will demonstrate the need for further clarification of Russell's procedure.

3. *The paradox of dissolution of types.* Let it be supposed that K and L are of the same type, as defined above, and K and M are of *different* types. Then the following statements are true:

(1) "L is of the same type as K" is a fact,
(2) "M is not of the same type as K" is a fact.[16]

Now the second fact is the negation of what results from substituting M for L in the first fact. And the situation is formally analogous to that used for illustrative purposes by Russell, with L, M, and *being of the same type as* K corresponding respectively to Socrates, Caligula, and *being a philosopher*. Since L and M can replace each other in the manner specified in the definition, it follows that *L and M are of the same type*. But this clearly contradicts the initial assumption that M belongs to a type other than that to which both K and L belong. Expressed otherwise, the argument would seem to establish that, if there are at least three entities in the world, it is impossible that they should not all belong to the same type.[17]

Such a consequence would, of course, be quite intolerable. For, since it may be granted that there are at least three entities, it would be permissible to substitute any symbol for another in all contexts, and the application of the theory to ordinary language would achieve precisely nothing.

Two suggestions for the removal of this difficulty, each having a certain initial plausibility, will now be discussed.

4. *The consequences of relying upon ambiguity in the term "fact" to resolve the paradox.* It would be in the spirit of Russell's own exposition to retort that the word "fact" occurs, in the sentences (1) and (2) above, in a sense other than was intended in the definition of logical type. For, according to his account, "the following words . . . by their very nature sin against it [the doctrine of types]: attribute, relation, complex,

---

[16] The statements have been expressed in ways parallel to those used in Russell's examples.
[17] This contradiction does not seem to have been previously discovered.

fact, . . ."[18] No doubt it is required that a fact to the effect that
K and L are of the same type shall be of an order of complexity
other than that of an empirical fact in which K or L are constituents. But if this is maintained, Russell's definition of type
becomes itself ambiguous and of indefinite application.[19]

So long as the word "fact" is taken in the colloquial sense in
which to say " 'X' is a fact" is merely to say "it is true that X,"
the definition is plainly intelligible (though itself then sinning
against the theory of types). In this sense *every* true sentence
must be admitted to express a "fact," and the paradox is un-
assailable. But if the word "fact," as it occurs in the definition,
is to be so restricted in meaning that only *some* true sentences
shall be permitted to express facts in this unusual sense, it now
becomes imperative to indicate how *such* facts are to be identified. In the absence of such supplementary information the
definition will be useless.

Should such specification of the technical meaning of the
crucial term "fact," however, be possible there would remain
the further difficulty that the definition, now amended to be consistent with the theory of types, would have application only to
a restricted class of sentences, viz., those expressing "facts" in
the narrow technical sense. There would be no guarantee that
the restricted theory of types resulting would not allow paradoxes to proliferate in the area over which it exercised no
jurisdiction.

The theory is, then, indefinite and possibly self-contradictory;
at best it can hope only to be incomplete. It would seem that
Russell's own formulation leads to formidable if not insuperable
difficulties.

5. *The paradox resolved by a re-interpretation of Russell's theory.* The root of the difficulties above displayed is
to be found in Russell's interpretation of the relationship of
belonging to the same type as holding between "entities." A

---

[18] *Contemporary British Philosophy,* I, foot of 371.

[19] An alternative proposal that might deserve examination would be to render
the relation *being of the same type as* systematically ambiguous according to the
type of the entities it relates. But this proposal would itself violate the theory of
types.

direct escape is provided by substituting a parallel relation holding between *words*.

Let the locution, "K and L are of the same type," be abandoned in favor of the expression "the *words* 'K' and 'L' are *syntactically similar*" (and let it be agreed that in such cases 'K' and 'L' shall be said to belong to the same *syntactical type*). With this understanding, the sentences (1) and (2) above must be rewritten in some such form as

(3) "λ is of the same syntactical type as κ" is a fact,

(4) "μ is not of the same syntactical type as κ" is a fact,

where λ, μ, and κ are now *words*. And from this it will follow only that the *names* of all three words will be syntactically similar. Since the name of a word is not identical with the word itself, no contradiction will now result. Thus this suggestion, which is in line with Russell's own remark that "the theory of types is really a theory of symbols, not of things,"[20] would seem to provide a satisfactory resolution of the paradox.

But only at the cost of considerable increase in complexity. It may be left as an exercise to the reader to show that it will be necessary at the very least to provide an infinite hierarchy of senses of the expression "syntactically similar" corresponding to the different syntactical levels of the words it relates. There will need to be one relation of syntactical similarity between words, another between names of words, still another between names of names, and so forth. But this hierarchy has the advantage of being generated *by definition*; since the expression "syntactically similar" is specifically introduced into the language by definition, there can be no objection to the supplementary differentiation of several senses; the character of the hierarchy involved makes the identification of the level involved in any particular instance immediate and unmistakable.

6. *The need for a negative interpretation of Russell's theory.* If a linguistic translation of Russell's theory on the lines suggested above should prove feasible, there will still be required further modifications, if contradiction is to be avoided.

There are certain syntactically polygamous contexts able to

receive words of the most diverse syntactical types without degenerating into nonsense. It is proper to say both "I am thinking about Russell" and "I am thinking about continuity;" thus nothing that has so far been said would prevent the disintegrating and absurd inference that "Russell" and "continuity" are syntactically similar. Unless further inhibitory measures are instituted, a wholesale merging and dissolution (this time of syntactical types) will once again be in prospect.

There seems no solution for this kind of difficulty, which arises in connection with all sentences expressing propositional attitudes (whether of knowing, supposing or believing), except to interpret the theory of types negatively as essentially an instrument for establishing *differences* of type. It will be necessary however to add a supplementary provision for the transmission of type distinctions to the associates of the ambiguous word in every context. The new procedure consists in asserting that two typographically distinct words are syntactically *dissimilar* if there is *at least one* context in which one cannot be substituted for the other without generating nonsense. To this is added the further condition that corresponding elements of contexts capable of receiving syntactically dissimilar words are themselves to be regarded (independently of typographical similarity) as syntactically dissimilar. (The first part of this test shows "Russell" and "continuity" to be syntactically dissimilar; the second then requires the two occurrences of "thinking" in "I am thinking about Russell" and "I am thinking about continuity" to be construed as instances of *two* words belonging to different syntactical types.)

Thus the application of the theory of types to ordinary language is a more complex undertaking than Russell's own account would suggest. A single attempt at substitution may establish that "A" is not of the same (syntactical) type as "B." Suppose two sentences are typographically identical except in containing "A" in place of "B;" then the corresponding symbols, in spite of typographical identity, must be considered as belonging to different types. Implicit recognition of this consequence may have been responsible for Russell's criticism of the use of such words as "attribute," "relation," etc., and for his subsequent comment that after discriminating the type ambiguities, ". . . we usually arrive, not at one meaning, but at an infinite series of different meanings."[21]

7. *The value of Russell's application of the theory of types.* The consequences of Russell's procedure should by now be sufficiently clear. Any interpretation that will be faithful to his intentions requires the impossibility of substituting two words for one another in even a single context to be regarded as sufficient cause for their segregation into mutually exclusive types. The consistent elaboration of this leading idea involves the making of ever finer distinctions of "meaning" between words not customarily regarded as ambiguous. So stringent does the requirement prove that it becomes difficult, if not impossible, to state the theory itself without contradiction; such difficulty being only a single instance, though a striking one, of a general tendency to produce a paralysis of the general statements of which philosophical discussion so largely consists.

The case for submitting to such unwelcome consequences is something less than conclusive. It is well to recall that the theory was originally designed to purge discourse of those paradoxes which are not accounted for by the non-branching theory of types. But it may be supposed that the paradoxes in question might prove capable of a solution having less drastic consequences; indeed it is plausible to expect that prohibition of a characteristic reflexive type of *definition* might be enough to achieve this end.[22] Whether this suggestion should prove fruitful or not, it may be suspected that Russell's theory does less than justice to the success with which communication is actually achieved in *ordinary* language. The demonstration of distinctions of type, defined in terms of possibility of mutual substitution of words, is on occasion a valuable technique for exhibiting operative ambiguity whose removal is relevant to the solution of philosophical disputes. But the consequences of

---

[21] *Contemporary British Philosophy*, I, 372. It is to be noted that the quoted statement, by referring collectively to "meanings," itself sins against the theory of types.

[22] Thus the paradox of the least finite integer definable in a specified number of words depends upon the lack of definition (or the simultaneous use of contradictory definitions) of the term "definable."

an attempt to apply such techniques universally may be regarded as a *reductio ad absurdum* of a point of view which seeks to apply to ordinary language segregatory criteria appropriate to an artificially constructed calculus. And this in turn can be traced back to the inclination to regard the relation between language and the world exclusively in the light of identity of structure.

C. The Search for Ultimate Constituents of the World

1. The genesis of the theory of descriptions. For all their drastic character, the segregatory techniques of the theory of types prove insufficient to cure *all* the philosophical confusions which can be attributed to excessive confidence in grammatical structure as a guide to logical form. A notable instance of such confusion arises in connection with the syntactical properties of phrases of the form "the so-and-so."

If the phrase, "The present king of France," be compared, in respect of identity or diversity of type, with a personal name, say that of Stalin, it will be found that the noun clause may be substituted for the name without producing nonsense.[23] More generally, it is a fact that some descriptive phrases and some nouns can replace each other in some or all contexts without producing nonsense. If the theory of types were to be relied upon to provide a sufficient criticism of ordinary language, it would be necessary to conclude that "Stalin" and "The present king of France" are syntactically similar.[24] This conclusion is maintained in a more colloquial form by anybody who claims that "The present king of France" names or denotes a person.

Upon such a foundation of identification of the syntactical properties of the descriptive phrase and the name, curious arguments have sometimes been erected. Since "The present king

---

[23] This statement would need some qualification for complete accuracy. It is not easy to provide an account of the theory of descriptions that shall succeed in being tolerably brief. The best short version known to me is that of Professor L. S. Stebbing in her *Modern Introduction to Logic*, 2nd edition, 144-158 ("The analysis of descriptions") and 502-505 ("Logical constructions"). Cf. also G. E. Moore's article (in the present volume) on "Russell's 'Theory of Descriptions'."

[24] Or that Stalin and the present King of France belong to the same type.

of France" refers to a person who does not exist, it must be conceded that there are *non-existent persons* who can appear as subjects of true propositions. Though non-existent, they must accordingly be capable of sustaining predicates. Thus it is certain, by the law of excluded middle, that one of the two propositions, "The present king of France is a parent" and "The present king of France is childless," is true. And there must be countless other properties by which the non-existent present king of France is characterised (among them the property of being under discussion in this paper). It can scarcely be doubted that whatever is characterised by properties is not a mere nonentity, that in order to be a subject of which characters are genuinely predicable it is required to have some kind of objective "being," not to be confused with the vacuity of sheer nothingness on the one hand or the full actuality of "existence" on the other.

The argument culminates, then, in the assertion that the present king of France has some shadowy mode of participation in the world—some tenuous sort of "reality" compatible with non-existence. And, if so much prove acceptable, the stage is set for similar argument in defense of the right to a recognised objective status of fictions, self-contradictory entities and even nonentity itself. Hamlet and the Snark, the philosopher's stone and the round square, being all characterised by predicates, must all, in some versions of this position, have their being in a multiplicity of distinct limbos, realms of *Sosein, Aussersein* and *Quasisein* in which to enjoy their ambiguous status of partial or quasi-existence.[25] The exploration and portrayal in "a terminology devised expressly for the purpose" of such *Lebensräume* of Being, will, of course, provide philosophers of this persuasion with endless material for mystification and dialectical ingenuity.

That arguments so remarkable should have appealed to some philosophers is a matter of historical record; and many another argument in good standing to-day might be shown to involve

---

[25] The classical source of this argument is Meinong's *Ueber Gegenstandstheorie* (1904). For a sympathetic exposition cf. J. N. Findlay's *Meinong's Theory of Objects* (1933), especially Ch. 2.

patterns of thought essentially similar. The suppression of such invalid trains of inference, against which the theory of types provides no protection, is the main object of Russell's theory of descriptions.

This part of Russell's program may still be plausibly interpreted as a contribution to the reform of common syntax; improvement of the vocabulary of ordinary language (which will be remembered as the second plank of the platform) is provided rather by the doctrine of logical constructions. Although this is intimately connected both in origin and content with the theory of descriptions, it requires the use of certain epistemological considerations which need not be invoked in the case of the latter.

2. *The theory of descriptions as a metaphysically neutral technique of translation.* That the theory of descriptions can be construed as a method of logical translation, capable of justification independently of adherence to any disputable epistemology, is a point that is commonly overlooked by critics. The reader may be reminded that Russell's contribution to the interpretation of descriptive phrases consists in the circumstantial demonstration that every sentence containing a descriptive phrase can be translated into another sentence having the same meaning but a different, and normally more complex, grammatical form. Thus, to take the familiar illustration once again,

(5) The present king of France is married

becomes

(6) Exactly one thing at present reigns over France and nothing that reigns over France is not married.[26]

The features upon which the usefulness of this procedure depends is the absence in the expanded form (6) of any ostensible reference to an alleged constituent (a "non-existent person") designated by the original phrase "The present king of France." Not only has the descriptive phrase disappeared in the course of translation, but no part of the expansion of (5)

---

[26] Here again some accuracy has been deliberately sacrificed. Cf. Stebbing, *op. cit.*, foot of 157, for a better statement.

can be identified as capable of abbreviation by the original descriptive phrase. Thus the procedure is not one of definition, in the dictionary sense, of the phrase "The present king of France," but rather a method for recasting every sentence in which the original phrase occurs.[27]

Mastery of the character of the translations appropriate to the different kinds of contexts in which descriptive phrases may occur having once been achieved, a permanent protection is provided against the blandishments of grammatical analogy which lend the doctrine of Realms of Being its spurious plausibility. Reference to the expanded form (6) above shows that the original sentence (5) differs quite radically in form from such a sentence as "Stalin is married." It becomes obvious that adherence to the principle of excluded middle is consistent with the assertion that *every* ascription of a predicate to the present king of France results in a false statement; more generally, a valuable instrument is thereby provided for the expulsion of illegitimate inferences and the clarification of ideas, as the successful application of methods essentially similar to a variety of other philosophical problems amply demonstrates.[28]

It is important to recognise that the enjoyment of such welcome benefits exacts no prior commitment to any epistemological theses. The gist of the method is the proof of the equivalence in meaning of given sentences. Only if appeal to some philosophical principle is involved in verifying the truth of any such proposed translation will it be necessary to deny that the method is epistemologically neutral.

Now the manner in which the equivalence of two *English* sentences is established does not differ in principle from that involved in proving the correctness of a translation from one European language into another. In both cases there is more or less explicit and direct appeal to congruence of behavior and linguistic utterance in cognate situations. The criteria are of a sociological order and may, for that very reason, provide a

---

[27] There is no reason, however, why the notion of definition should not be extended so as to cover the kind of reduction involved in the example cited.

[28] A good example is G. E. Moore's article, "Is existence a predicate?" *Aristotelian Society Proceedings*, Supplementary Vol. 15 (1936), 175-188.

basis for agreement between philosophers elsewhere advocating very diverse epistemological or metaphysical doctrines. Since an idealist and a materialist can agree upon the correct translation of a passage from Homer, there seems to be no reason why they should have much more difficulty in coming to an understanding about the soundness of a proposed translation within their native tongue; they might both therefore make equal and equally good use of the methods provided by the theory of descriptions. It is not extravagantly optimistic to hope that, once the theory has been separated from the more specifically metaphysical components with which it is associated in Russell's presentation, it may ultimately achieve a measure of common agreement (without prejudice to eventual differences of opinion concerning the interpretation and value of the method) such as may be found in the elementary propositional calculus or the other well-established branches of symbolic logic.

3. *The doctrine of logical constructions and its reliance upon the principle of reducibility to acquaintance.* It is to be noted that the foregoing non-controversial portion of Russell's theory is concerned with the logical expansion of *logical symbols*. When sentence (5) was equated with sentence (6), such words as "present," "king," "France," etc., occurred *vacuously* (to use a convenient term of Dr. Quine's[29]); they were present merely as illustrative variables indicating how "The X of Y is Z" might, *in general*, be translated. Thus the translations offered by the theory of descriptions provide further insight into the manner in which the logical words "the," "and," "of" are used in ordinary language; but no information is yielded concerning the syntactical relationships of non-logical material words.

The shift from the consideration of logical to that of non-logical or material words corresponds exactly to the line drawn in this brief exposition between the theory of descriptions and the doctrine of logical constructions; it will now be shown that when this boundary is crossed the validity of an epistemological principle concerning the reducibility of knowledge to acquaintance becomes relevant to the criticism of Russell's method.

[29] W. V. Quine, *Mathematical Logic*, 2.

Anybody who maintains, with Russell, that tables are logical constructions, or that the self is a logical construction, is claiming *at least* that sentences containing the material words "table" or "I" submit to the same type of reductive translation as was demonstrated in connection with descriptive phrases.[30] If tables are logical constructions it is necessary that every sentence containing the word "table" shall be capable of transformation into another sentence from which that word is absent and no part of which could be abbreviated by the word. It is quite certain that *some* material words, such as "average," satisfy such a condition; and it would seem initially plausible that some elements of vocabulary do and others do not admit of such reduction. If this were the case the claim in respect of any specific X that it was a logical construction would seem to require a specific demonstration. On Russell's principles, however, it can be known in advance of specific investigation that the entities referred to by the vast majority, if not indeed the totality, of the words of ordinary language *must be* logical constructions.

For very much more than mere translation of the kind specified is implied by Russell's contention that tables are logical constructions: the procedure must, on his view, have a *direction*, determined by progressive approach towards a *final translation*. A sentence is a final translation only if it consists entirely of "logically proper names" (demonstrative symbols) for "ultimate constituents;" it may then conveniently be referred to as a *pictorial sentence*.[31] To say that X is a logical construction is to claim that sentences containing "X" may be *finally* translated, in this drastic sense, into pictorial sentences.

What are these "ultimate constituents?"[32] They are, on Russell's view, precisely those entities "with which we can be acquainted;" more specifically, sense-data (particulars) now pre-

---

[30] Russell of course did not use so linguistic a version. Cf. the statement in the text with the following typical utterance: "The real man, too, I believe, however the police may swear to his identity, is really a series of momentary men, each different one from the other, and bound together, not by a numerical identity, but by continuity and certain intrinsic causal laws." (*Mysticism and Logic*, 129)

[31] The term is due to Stebbing.

[32] "Neither the word [a proper name] nor what it names is one of *the ultimate indivisible constituents of the world*." (*Analysis of Mind*, 193. Italics supplied.)

sented to us and universals characterising sense-data with which we are or have been acquainted. The assurance that every sentence can be finally translated into a pictorial sentence is provided by the principle that "every proposition which we can understand must be composed wholly of constituents with which we are acquainted."[33]

The reasons should now be obvious for distinguishing between the theory of descriptions and the theory of logical constructions. The latter predicts that sentences containing "table" will prove to admit of translation into pictorial sentences in which each element refers to an object with which we are acquainted. But ordinary language contains no logically proper names, and can therefore provide no pictorial sentences.[34] The verification of the thesis here requires the invention of a new vocabulary departing drastically in character from that which it is to replace.

The case for the validity of the doctrine of logical constructions accordingly is quite different from that which supports the theory of descriptions. The latter is established by empirical grounds manifested in achieved success in translation; the former is, in the absence of the successful provision of the new vocabulary desiderated, rather the expression of a stubborn aspiration, whose plausibility rests entirely upon the supposed truth of the principle of reducibility to acquaintance.

No mention has hitherto been made of the metaphysical consequences of the doctrine of logical constructions. The reader will hardly need to be reminded that Russell has drawn such consequences freely, characteristically maintaining that matter, the self, and other minds (to cite some striking instances of alleged logical constructions) are "symbolic fictions" or even "myths."[35] But for these supposed consequences it is unlikely

---

[33] *The Problems of Philosophy*, 91.

[34] "We cannot so use sentences [i.e., pictorially] both because our language is not adapted to picturing and because we usually do not know what precisely are the constituents of the facts to which we refer," Stebbing, *op. cit.*, 157. ". . . no word that we can understand would occur in a grammatically correct account of the universe," Russell, *Philosophy*, 257.

[35] The following are typical statements: "The persistent particles of mathematical physics I regard as logical constructions, symbolic fictions . . ." (*Mysti-*

that Russell's theory of constructions would have received the critical attention which has been lavished upon it. If, as the next section will try to show, the principle of reduction to acquaintance has no evidential support, discussion of these alleged consequences becomes redundant.[36]

4. *Criticism of the principle of reducibility to acquaintance.* Since the various formulations of the principle which Russell has given[37] hardly vary except in unimportant details of phraseology, the version of 1905 might be taken as standard: ". . . in every proposition that we can apprehend (i.e., not only in those whose truth or falsehood we can judge of, but in all that we can think about) all the constituents are really entities with which we have immediate acquaintance."[38]

The confidence with which this principle is presented for acceptance contrasts strikingly with the baldness of the grounds offered in its defense. "The chief reason," says Russell, "for

---

cism and Logic, 128); ". . . matter, which is a logical fiction. . . ." (*Analysis of Mind,* 306); ". . . [Desire] merely a convenient fiction, like force in mechanics . . . ." (*op. cit.,* 205).

[36] The standard argument against Russell's attribution of a fictitious status to logical constructions (viz., the proof that "X is a logical construction" does not entail "X does not exist"), though accurate, does less than justice to Russell's point, however misleadingly expressed. The critics of Russell's language of "fictions" would not allow that the average man is a "fiction" or "unreal;" but they would be prepared to admit that the average *unicorn* is "unreal" (though no doubt stigmatising the choice of terms as perverse). Now there is a sense in which the plain man would want to claim that both the average man *and* the average unicorn are fictions, because the phrases referring to them can be dispensed with in a complete account of the world. And more generally, if 'X' is a dispensable symbol it is natural to say something like: " 'X' is a mere symbolic expedient, corresponding to nothing ultimate and irreducible in the world." It is this kind of statement that Russell wishes to make. Now, if all non-pictorial sentences were finally translatable, it would be natural to say that the world consists only of particular sense-data and the universals by which they are characterised, and to attribute the apparent presence of *other* entities to unwarranted inferences drawn from the nature of the symbols used in abbreviating pictorial sentences. It would, in short, be natural to say that facts about tables are *nothing but* facts about objects of acquaintance. This is the gist of Russell's position.

[37] "On Denoting," *Mind,* Vol. 14 (1905), 492; *Mysticism and Logic,* 219, 221; *The Problems of Philosophy,* 91. Cf. J. W. Reeves, "The Origin and Consequences of the Theory of Descriptions," *Proceedings of the Aristotelian Society,* Vol. 34 (1934), 211-230.

[38] *Mind,* Vol. 14, 492.

supposing the principle true is that it seems scarcely possible to believe that we can make a judgement or entertain a supposition without knowing what it is that we are judging or supposing about."[39] And in another place, after this statement is repeated almost verbatim, there is added merely the comment: "We must attach *some* meaning to the words we use, if we are to speak significantly and not utter mere noise, *and the meaning we attach to our words must be something with which we are acquainted.*"[40]

Whatever persuasiveness attaches to this defense of the principle can be shown to arise from equivocation upon the crucial words "know," "mean," and "acquaintance." It may be just permissible so to use the term "acquaintance" that the sentence "I know the meaning of X" is synonymous with "I am acquainted with X," where the word "meaning" is used in the sense it has in *ordinary language.* This is hardly a sense of "acquaintance" which can be relied upon not to engender confusion, but a philosopher may nevertheless find its introduction expedient. In this sense of the word, however, the assertion that "the meaning we attach to our words must be something with which we are acquainted" is merely the tautology that "the meaning of our words must be the meaning of our words." This can hardly be Russell's intention in the passages cited. Since we understand the word "Attila" we may be said either to "know the meaning of the word" or, alternatively and synonymously, to "be acquainted with Attila." Now Attila is neither a sense-datum nor a universal capable of characterising sense-data; it is impossible, then, for anybody to be acquainted with Attila in the narrow technical sense of acquaintance which makes Russell's principle, whether true or false, something more than a mere tautology. If his assertion is to have any content, he must be interpreted as meaning "it seems scarcely possible to believe that we can make a judgement without knowing *by acquaintance* what it is that we are judging about" and "it is

[39] *Mysticism and Logic,* 219.
[40] *The Problems of Philosophy,* 91 (italics supplied). I am not aware of any other defense of the principle by Russell.

impossible that our words should have meaning unless they refer to entities *with which we are acquainted.*"

The alleged defense of the favoured principle ("the chief reason for supposing the principle true") is now seen to be a mere repetition of that which was to be demonstrated. One of two things must be the case. Either Russell is using the term "meaning" in one of its customary senses; in that case the argument adduced in favour of the principle is refuted quite simply by pointing out that "Attila" *means* a certain person with whom we are *not* acquainted in Russell's sense. Or, alternatively, a new sense of meaning is implicitly *introduced* in which only objects with which we are acquainted can be meant by words: in that case the argument is a *petitio principii.* In the other case the principle remains unproven.

5. *Grounds for rejecting the principle of reducibility to acquaintance.* It is likely that the reasons why the principle, in default of persuasive argument in its defense, should have seemed to so many philosophers self-evident are connected with the supposed necessity of "directness" in relations of meaning and knowing. Underlying Russell's position throughout is the conviction that in all genuine knowledge or meaning there must be some such ultimate fusion of intimacy between the knower and what is known as is provided by the notion of "acquaintance."

Let the validity of such an approach be tested in some less controversial area. Suppose it were argued that "every proposition about the *possession* of material objects must be reducible to a proposition about *contact* with objects" on the ground that "it seems hardly possible to believe that we can hold an object without really being in contact with it." Would it not be clear in such a case that there was being introduced a restricted and misleading sense of "holding" or "possession," in virtue of which it becomes logically impossible to hold anything except the surface with which one is in contact? And would it not be quite as clear that the mere introduction of a stipulation concerning the meaning of a term could succeeed in demonstrating precisely nothing?

It may be objected that the analogy is unsound; and it is true that there might be *independent* grounds for supposing the relationship of *meaning*, unlike that of physical possession, to be necessarily direct. But although this may be allowed as an abstract possibility, neither Russell nor anybody else has yet provided good grounds for believing it to be anything more. And there are good opposing reasons for rejecting the principle.

Whenever sentences containing a symbol (such as "the present king of France" or "the average man") can be translated in such a manner that the symbol neither appears explicitly nor can be identified with any portion of the translation, it will be convenient to speak of the symbol as being *dispensable*. Now there is good reason to believe that "table" and "I" are not dispensable symbols, i.e., that there are truths concerning tables and the self which are not capable of being expressed without the use of these or synonymous symbols. It can be demonstrated, in connection with quite elementary examples of deductive theories, that "auxiliary" or "secondary" symbols can be introduced in such a way that they are not capable of *explicit* definition in terms of the basic experiential terms of the theory.[41] This does not render them undefined, in a wide sense of that term, since the mode of introduction of the auxiliary symbols into the system provides both for their syntactical relations with associated symbols and for inferential relations between the sentences in which they occur and the "primary" observational sentences of the system. This seems to be precisely the situation in respect of such scientific terms as "energy," "entropy," and "field," none of which are "dispensable."[42] There appears to be no *a priori* reason why this should not be the case also in respect of the names of material objects and other terms of ordinary language.

Indeed a careful scrutiny of the attempts made (especially by phenomenalists) to prove that words denoting material objects are dispensable will render this last suggestion something more than plausible. For these attempts invariably termi-

---

[41] Cf. Ramsey's discussion of the place of explicit definitions in a theory. (*Foundations of Mathematics*, 229).

[42] Further detail would be needed to prove this statement.

nate in sceptical conclusions. When Russell, in his latest book, undertakes to provide a phenomenalistic analysis of "you are hot,"[43] he arrives at a proposition which in order to be known to be true requires the speaker to know *inter alia* that the hearer is aware of a multitude of events in the same sense of "aware" in which he himself is aware of events and, further, that whole classes of events which *could* be perceived exist in the absence of such perception. Now neither of these truths could be known by acquaintance; the conclusion drawn is that the original proposition analysed is not *strictly* known to be true. At best we can "assume" its truth, "in the absence of evidence to the contrary."[44] But to assume or postulate the truth of a proposition is only to *hope* that it may be true. There are circumstances in which the truth of the assertion "you are hot" is *certain;* nothing could be more absurd than to doubt that this remark, when addressed to a philosopher in the warmest chamber of a Turkish Bath, may sometimes be both true and known to be true. Now if the truth of the principle of acquaintance requires the rejection of even a single certain truth, there would seem to be sufficient reason to abandon it.

D. The Notion of the "Ideal Language"

1. The character of the "ideal language." An examination of the character of that "ideal language" which Russell recommends as the goal of the philosophy of language provides a very precise test of the value of his early doctrines. For the "ideal language" is, by definition, the symbolism which would be entirely free from the philosophical defects which Russell claims to find in ordinary language. If language "had been invented by scientifically trained observers for purposes of philosophy and logic,"[45] just this symbolism would have resulted. And it would be "logically perfect"[46] in the sense of conforming to "what logic requires of a language which is to avoid contradiction."[47] The character of the ideal language is

---

[43] *An Inquiry into Meaning and Truth,* 280-282, 284-291.
[44] *Ibid.,* 292.
[45] *The Analysis of Mind,* 193.
[46] *The Monist,* Vol. 28, 520.
[47] *Contemporary British Philosophy,* Vol. I, 377.

calculated, then, to reveal in a vivid fashion the benefits to be expected from a successful outcome of Russell's program of reform.

The discussion of the preceding sections should have made clear the features which would be manifested by such a paradigm of philosophical symbolism. Every symbol will be a "logically proper name" denoting objects of acquaintance: "there will be one word and no more for every simple object and everything that is not simple will be expressed by a combination of words."[48] How closely will these logically proper names for ultimate constituents resemble the words at present in use? By definition, they must be unintelligible in the absence of the entities they denote. Thus no proper names, in the familiar *grammatical* sense, can qualify for inclusion in the ideal language, just because, in virtue of referring to complex series of causally related appearances, they function as logical descriptions. The descriptive character of such a name as "Napoleon" is recognised by the circumstance that the name is intelligible to persons who never met the Corsican.[49]

Similar considerations would seem to disqualify all other types of words in the ordinary language. The names of universals characterising sense-data (e.g., the name of a specific shade of colour) might seem to be exceptions; but it would be hard to deny that even these have meaning in the absence of instances of the universals they denote. Now if universals are among the ultimate constituents, as Russell claims, they must be represented in the ideal language by arbitrary noises of such a character that it is logically impossible that they should be uttered in the absence of instances of the universals concerned.

The attempt might be made to construct illustrative instances of sentences of the ideal language composed entirely of demonstratives, by inventing such words as "thet" and "thot" to supplement the present meagre stock of "this" and "that."[50] But even "This thet thot"[51] would still convey to a hearer some

---

[48] *The Monist*, Vol. 28, 520.
[49] *The Analysis of Mind*, 192-193.
[50] As suggested by John Wisdom, *Mind*, Vol. 40, 204.
[51] Somewhat more drastic than Wisdom's "This son that, and that brother thet, and thet mother thot, and thot boy, and this kissed Sylvia" (*Ibidem*).

such meaning as "Something with which the speaker is acquainted has some relation, with which the speaker is acquainted, to some other thing with which he is acquainted."[52] The proposition understood by the hearer would not then be the proposition intended by the speaker; the "perfect sentence," having meaning only to the speaker and to him only at the time of utterance, would be perfectly unintelligible. If this criticism is based upon a misinterpretation of Russell's intention, and if it were permissible for the names of such ultimate constituents as are universals to be intelligible at a variety of times and to more than a single person, it would still be necessary that the names of particulars should be private; and communication would be possible only by the grace of some kind of pre-established speaker-hearer ambiguity in virtue of which what was a logically proper name for the one functioned as a description for the other.

What becomes under such conditions of the intention that the ideal language shall be "completely analytic and . . . show at a glance the logical structure of the facts asserted or denied?"[53] Such a system, containing "no words that we can [at present] understand"[54] would be so remote from our present means of expression and so unsuited to perform the functions of unambiguous and logically accurate communication which may be desired of an efficient language, that to urge its capacity to provide "a grammatically correct account of the universe"[55] is to be extravagantly implausible. The "ideal language" in practice would resemble a series of involuntary squeaks and grunts more closely than anything it is at present customary to recognise as a language.

It is by no means certain that Russell ever seriously supposed that the ideal language could be realised; and some of his remarks suggest that he regarded it on occasion as a mere device of exposition.[56] If, as has been argued above, the ideal language is not capable of realisation, it becomes impossible seriously to

[52] Cf. Wisdom's discussion of this point, *op. cit.*, 203.
[53] *The Monist*, Vol. 28, 520.
[54] *Philosophy*, 257.
[55] *Ibidem.*
[56] Cf. *The Monist*, Vol. 28, 520.

defend indefinite progression towards such an "ideal" as a desirable procedure for the philosophical criticism of language.

It is not difficult to see, in retrospect, why Russell should have been led into this untenable position of defending as the aim of the philosophy of language the construction of a language which could never work. For the "ideal language" would satisfy perfectly the intention to make the relation of "picturing" the sole essential basis of symbolism. Whatever else Russell is prepared to regard as "accidental" in language, he is unwilling to abandon the notion that language must "correspond" to the "facts," through one-one correlation of elements and identity of logical structure. But there is no good reason why we should expect language to correspond to, or "resemble," the "world" any more closely than a telescope does the planet which it brings to the astronomer's attention.

2. *Consequences of abandoning the pursuit of an "ideal language."* To abandon the image of language as a "picture" of the world, which has, on the whole, wrought so much mischief in the philosophy of language, is to be in a position to make the most intelligent use of the products of Russell's analytical ingenuity.

For it would be both unfair and ungrateful to end without acknowledging the pragmatic value of the techniques invented by Russell. Rejection of the possibility or desirability of an "ideal language" is compatible with a judicious recourse to the methods of translation and analysis which have been criticised in this paper. It is a matter of common experience that philosophical confusion and mistaken doctrine are sometimes connected with failure to make type distinction or to reveal, by the technique of translation, the correct deductive relations between sentences of similar grammatical, though differing logical, forms. And where such confusion is manifested it is helpful to follow Russell's new way of "philosophical grammar." It will be well, however, to be unashamedly opportunistic, making the remedy fit the disease and seeking only to remove such hindrances to philosophical enlightenment as are demonstrably occasioned by excessive attachment to the accidents of grammar and vocabulary. In this way there is some hope of avoiding the temptation to impose, by way of cure, a predetermined linguistic structure—of seeking to eliminate the philosophical ills of the language at present in use by proposing an "ideal language" which never could be used. Nor need such a program be aimless. For the object will be to remove just those linguistic confusions which are actually found to be relevant to doctrines of philosophical importance.

MAX BLACK

DEPARTMENT OF PHILOSOPHY
UNIVERSITY OF ILLINOIS

7

Philip P. Wiener

METHOD IN RUSSELL'S WORK
ON LEIBNIZ

METHOD IN RUSSELL'S WORK
ON LEIBNIZ

PINOZA'S dictum that Peter's opinion of Paul tells us more about Peter than about Paul should be modified when Peter's mind is of the same cast as Paul's. Thus, Russell's *Critical Exposition of the Philosophy of Leibniz* tells us a good deal about both Russell and Leibniz, insofar as both were concerned with the central rôle of method in philosophy. We see from the following quotation that Russell in 1900, when he published his lectures on Leibniz, rejected Leibniz's attempt to base philosophy on logic, but so stealthily do ideas grow on one, that "the Ariadne's thread" of Leibniz's philosophy, logic in its most formal and mathematical sense, became for many years the chief preoccupation of Russell and the essence of philosophy for him.

As a mathematical idea—as a Universal Algebra, embracing Formal Logic, ordinary Algebra, and Geometry as special cases—Leibniz's conception has shown itself in the highest sense useful. But as a method of pursuing philosophy, it had the formalist defect which results from a belief in analytic propositions, and which led Spinoza to employ a geometrical method. For the business of philosophy is just the discovery of those simple notions, and those primitive axioms, upon which any calculus or science must be based. The belief that the primitive axioms are identical leads to an emphasis on *results*, rather than premises, which is radically opposed to the true philosophic method. There can be neither difficulty nor interest in the premises, if those are of such a kind as "A is A" or "AB is not non-A." And thus Leibniz supposed that the great requisite was a convenient method of deduction. Whereas, in fact, the problems of philosophy should be anterior to deduction. An idea which can be defined, or a proposition which can be proved, is of only subordinate philosophical interest. The emphasis should be laid on the indefinable and indemonstrable, and here no method is available save intuition.[1]

Despite the similar intellectual interests of these two versatile minds, ranging from logic and the philosophy of the sciences to ethics, history, and politics, there is the greatest difference between them as persons. Leibniz acquired his title to nobility by flattering powerful princes and church officials and by defending their feudal privileges; whereas Russell, though born an aristocrat, has always defended the democratic tradition and courageously opposed political and church authoritarianism at the cost of that very type of worldly success which was so dear to Leibniz. In their theories of education, Leibniz wrote only for powerful jurists and rulers, but Russell has tried to reach all citizens.

In what follows, I shall indicate what can be learned from Russell's work on Leibniz's philosophy about the development of Russell's philosophic views, especially on the question of method, which he himself has considered the core of philosophy. But I wish also to examine the method employed by Russell in characterizing the philosophy of an important figure in the history of modern philosophy, because this method has certain distinctive merits and some limitations, as I see them, for the critical history of thought.

At Cambridge in the late 1890's, Russell (and G. E. Moore) were powerfully reacting to the Hegelianism of Lotze and Bradley, and, as a result, the first formulations of the new logical realism appeared. Bradley had followed the Hegelian attempt to feed Platonic universals to an omnivorous Absolute which swallowed both universals and individuals in disregard of the more balanced diet of the sciences and of ethical utilitarianism. Russell himself was not to be emancipated from Platonic notions of mathematics and ethics for many years to come;

[1] B. Russell, *A Critical Exposition of the Philosophy of Leibniz*, (1st edition, 1900; 2d edition, 1937, pp. 170-171. All page references here are to second edition.) Russell declares, in his preface to the second edition, that he now believes in the analytic nature of necessary propositions. It is encouraging to know that Russell's intuitionism, which may have been due to the influence of Bradley, was not incorrigible, as is the case with so many intuitionist philosophies.

Platonism was also deeply engrained in Leibniz's philosophy. What repelled Russell in the idealism of Leibniz was not such Platonic notions in themselves, but the scholastic theology and anti-individualistic ethics which Leibniz (and Hegel) infused in their writings, notions which Russell properly regarded as inimical both to scientific inquiry and to the political freedom of individuals. The Leibnizian (and Hegelian) conception of a metaphysical logic and ethics was distinctly opposed to the empiricistic and individualistic approach of Locke, Hume, and their successors. Russell, as an heir to this individualistic tradition, submitted to sceptical scrutiny the formidable arguments which Leibniz used to buttress theology with formal logic and scholastic metaphysics with a divinely created hierarchy of monads. This task was rendered all the more difficult by the great prestige enjoyed by the distinguished Leibniz as a mathematician, logician, and classical philosopher.

It would be interesting to know whether Russell's abandonment of Platonism in ethics (which he attributes to reading Santayana's criticisms of his philosophy) was connected with his shift to nominalism in metaphysics. Historically, the belief in absolute goodness has been associated with belief in necessary empirical truths. However, Leibniz should have been an exception, insofar as he argued for analytical necessity in logic and metaphysics, but for irreducible contingency in empirical science. Although Russell was opposed to the theological ground of Leibniz's apriorism, he did not question the Platonic elements in Leibniz's metaphysics, but showed how they were inconsistent with Leibniz's doctrine of contingency. The alternative would be to put logic, ethics, and empirical science on a contingent, operational basis. But Russell, who was just beginning to study modern logic, was not yet ready for a conception which owes its contemporary development to the American logician and founder of pragmatism, Charles S. Peirce.

Regarding logic, in a Platonic way, as the core of philosophy, Russell had to separate out from the mass of Leibniz's writings a coherent logical structure in order to show that the main defects of Leibniz's philosophy were due to flaws in that structure. This procedure implied a Platonic theory of metaphysical truth such as Leibniz himself had adopted in his *a priori* proofs of God's existence, immortality, and free-will. It is only incidentally that the more purely historical considerations of Leibniz's philosophy as an expression of the science and social institutions of his day enter into Russell's work. But that is because Russell sharply distinguished, again in a Platonic way, pure philosophy from pure history, when in fact—but here I am expressing my own opinion—philosophy and history are not "pure" disciplines. I thus find myself admiring Russell's penetrating analyses of the logical structure of Leibniz's thought, as well as Russell's empirical insights into the more wordly interests of Leibniz's theology, ethics, and politics, without understanding what relation, if any, Russell meant to assert or to imply as holding between the two versions of the philosophy of Leibniz, which the latter held "one for himself and one for the admiration of princes and (even more) of princesses." It is true that mathematics, especially the infinitesimal calculus, and formal logic, especially the *characteristica universalis*, greatly influenced Leibniz. Furthermore, what elicited Russell's admiration of Leibniz as a philosopher was his discovery that "Leibniz's system does follow correctly and necessarily from five premisses," which Russell states as the basis of Leibniz's real philosophy; such rare logical rectitude "is the evidence of Leibniz's philosophical excellence, and the permanent contribution which he made to philosophy." We are also told:

What is first of all required in a commentator is to attempt a reconstruction of the system which Leibniz should have written—to discover what is the beginning, and what the end, of his chains of reasoning, to exhibit the interconnections of his various opinions, and to fill in from his other writings the bare outlines of such works as the *Monadology* or the *Discours de Métaphysique*. This unavoidable but somewhat ambitious attempt forms one part—perhaps the chief part—of my purpose in the present work. (2-3)

Yet there is a clear and explicit recognition by Russell of certain historical facts, e.g., that Leibniz's philosophy did change from a youthful scholasticism to the atomism of Hobbes and Gassendi, and finally, to his monadology (70). However, it is also clear that Russell was more interested in logical structures than in such historical questions. "Since the philosophies of the past belong to one or another of a few great types—types which in our own day are perpetually recurring—we may learn, from examining the greatest representative of any type, what are the grounds for such a philosophy." (xii) Bradley's (or Lotze's) idealism was an example of one of the types of philosophy alluded to here. In any case, Russell wished to exhibit the logical structure of a possible, and to him important, philosophy, and found the nearest exemplification of the type of idealistic arguments current in his own time in the mature views of Leibniz "held, with but slight modifications, from January 1686 till his death in 1716. His earlier views, and the influence of other philosophers, have been considered only in so far as they seemed essential to the comprehension of his final system." (3)

Just as there are for Russell two versions of Leibniz's philosophy, the one offered for the approval of state and church officials, and the other intended for more serious logicians like Russell, so there are two kinds of inconsistencies which Russell indicates in Leibniz's system: those due to Leibniz's political fears of admitting consequences necessarily entailed by his premises, but "shocking to the prevailing opinions of Leibniz's time;" secondly, those due to formal contradictions among Leibniz's premises, which for Russell form a "greater class of inconsistencies." (4)

Russell exhibits the first class of inconsistencies simply by drawing the shocking conclusions, e.g., that Leibniz's premises lead to Spinozism, and the second class by showing that Leibniz's real philosophy is reducible to five premises, the first of which (every proposition has a subject and a predicate) is inconsistent with the fourth and fifth (the Ego is a substance, and perception yields knowledge of an external world). We now have three philosophies of Leibniz: the one used to convince the princes, the one that appeared consistent to Leibniz but which he concealed from the world, and the inconsistent system which was concealed from himself, but which Russell's logical analysis has uncovered. Logical realism implied that the real Leibniz was this last inconsistent one. However, it seems meaningless to ask which is the real philosophy of Leibniz, since they are all contained in Leibniz's writings and their significance depends on the way they function in discourse. The first Leibniz belongs to seventeenth-century political history; the second to the history of logic which dates back to Aristotle;[2] and the third Leibniz belongs to the Cambridge neo-realism of Russell and G. E. Moore. These versions of Leibniz raise an important question. On Russell's analysis, Leibniz's system is inconsistent. Therefore, Leibniz could have proven *any* proposition. Then why did Leibniz in fact deduce only a certain class of propositions from five inconsistent premises? The answer cannot be given by logical analysis of the internal structure of Leibniz's thought.

Russell's logical atomism (in its earliest form) shared with Leibniz's "alphabet of knowledge" the assumption that there are absolute logical beginnings; for example, he finds in the *Discourses on Metaphysics* "the logical beginning" of Leibniz's system (7). The phrase quoted is self-contradictory, as Hegel once pointed out, and as modern logic and Russell now would claim. Given a specific text, we say that it contains statements from which the other statements are deducible, and only relative to that deductive order are the first statements "the logical beginning" of the reasoning exhibited in the text. The seventeenth-century Leibniz did employ a large variety of arguments and diverse modes of exposition which start from theological, ethical, and metaphysical as well as scientific premises Russell's success in reducing the second apparently coherent Leibniz to a system that begins with only five premises is evidence, I should say, of Russell's excellence in logic, and is his contribution to the study of Leibniz's philosophy as well as to the method of writing the critical history of philosophy. It is extremely useful to reduce a complex system of writings to a few statements, but the products of distillation will not resemble the raw materials from which they are made, because of ingredients subtracted or added by the critic or historian. Thus, there is no one-one correspondence between the simple set of five premises of Russell's Leibniz and the more complex mean-

[2] Cf. Vailati Scritti "Sul carattere del contributo apportato de Leibniz allo sviluppo della Logica Formale," 619 ff., quoted in my "Notes on Leibniz's Conception of Logic and Its Historical Context," *Philosophical Review*, vol. 48 (Nov. 1939), 567-586.

ing of Leibniz's arguments considered in their historical context. But it is true that by means of such a set of premises as Russell has made out we are able to trace more clearly a certain structure in an important part of Leibniz's arguments. The relationship here is similar to that between a mathematical system and its physical applications. But before we can know how appropriate any deductive device is to a given empirical situation, we should know how frequently we can apply it to a class of similar situations. Hence, to know the relative importance of scientific logic and theology in Leibniz's thinking, we should inquire how frequently we find him having recourse to one or the other in order to solve certain problems. The critical historian of philosophy will have first to ascertain what would constitute a solution to these problems, as Russell did.

Russell, like Aristotle in relation to his predecessors as given in the first book of the Metaphysics, but more consciously and explicitly, looked upon the writings of Leibniz as important only when they bore upon the problems with which he was himself concerned, regardless of the peculiar historical meaning these problems had for Leibniz. For example, Russell very clearly discerns five distinct meanings of matter in Leibniz's writings and two meanings of resistance (ch. VII), but is more concerned to show how Leibniz confounded them than to trace the prior and subsequent history of these meanings. Of course, the historian of ideas can do this if, and only if, he has made the preliminary analysis which Russell has made.

Russell explained later that his method of characterizing Leibniz is one he would not use in characterizing a different sort of philosopher like Santayana:

In attempting to characterize philosophers, no uniform method should be adopted. The method, in each case, should be such as to exhibit what the philosopher himself thinks important and what, in the opinion of the critic, makes him worthy of study. There are some—of whom Leibniz is the most important example—who stand or fall by the correctness of their reasoning and logical analysis; the treatment of such philosophers demands minute dissection and the search for fallacies.[3]

[3] "The Philosophy of Santayana," in Volume Two of *The Library of Living Philosophers*, ed. Schilpp, 453.

One of the subjects Leibniz himself thought important—theology—is certainly not what his critic, Russell, thinks makes him worthy of study; but the other—logic—was considered both by Leibniz and his critic as of paramount importance, and was subjected to minute dissection by Russell. It is doubtful, however, whether Leibniz would have turned atheist, if he had read Russell's criticisms, and hence, there is no *necessary* connection between Leibniz's theological beliefs and his logic. But there are, in the history of human thought, empirical or probable connections, and all the evidence points to the influence of ethics and theology on Leibniz's use of logic and even on his physics. Consider, for example, the pride Leibniz expresses in his dynamic view of matter as endowing physical bodies with direction and final causes. This theological motive in no way detracts from the soundness of Leibniz's logical criticisms of Descartes' physics (152-153).

Most historians of thought seem to regard the goal of their study as learning the language spoken or written by past thinkers, without themselves thinking through what these thinkers were writing about. Submissive "participation" in the utterances of a past thinker seems to be a substitute for thinking through the problems dealt with. Russell's more philosophical, because more critical, view regards the history of philosophy as the development of a limited number of possible types of thought represented by different individual thinkers. He could have made clearer the fact that in any one philosopher like Leibniz there is a mingling of types sometimes productive of a fruitful and new synthesis, but more often not, because of failure to note inconsistencies. It is a logical problem to note these inconsistencies, but it is not as problems *of* logic that we find them in the history of thought. I believe that Russell does treat certain logical problems in his critical exposition of Leibniz as though they were the same problems of logic which were foremost in discussions at Cambridge about 1899. However, there was no great harm done to Leibniz at this point, since Leibniz did attach a great deal of importance to the problems of logic as he conceived them, i.e., to the general nature of propositions (attributive and relational), types of reasoning (syllogistic and asyllogistic), truths (necessary and contingent, analytic and synthetic), knowledge (intuitive and symbolic, adequate and inadequate, clear and confused, distinct and obscure). But most of these so-called problems of logic were mixed up with questions of metaphysics and psychology set in a cultural context which was different in Leibniz's age than in Russell's. When Russell properly indicates the Spinozism implicit in Leibniz's premises and its incompatibility with the existence of individuals, he was aiming at the metaphysics and ethics which idealists like Bradley advocated. It was scoring against the late nineteenth-century philosophy of "objective idealism" for Russell to prove that the first premise of Leibniz's system (the subject-predicate theory of propositions) was inconsistent with the premises that the Ego is a substance and that perception gives knowledge of an external world.

Furthermore, Russell proved that Leibniz's failure to develop an adequate logic of relational propositions led Leibniz to regard relations as merely mental, with the absurd consequence that the relations in and among monads which God is supposed to know intuitively must be strictly meaningless (14). That this was not a question of pure logic, either for Russell or Leibniz, ought to be obvious to anyone who has the slightest acquaintance with the concern about God's existence which both philosophers have shown in their writings. In several passages Russell's historical sense shows itself alive to the rôle of theology in Leibniz's philosophy; for example, in a footnote to his chapter on "Leibniz's Philosophy of Matter" (78), Russell indicates how extra-logical theological questions were mixed with questions of scientific logic in Leibniz: "Leibniz appears to have been led to this discovery [that the essence of body is not extension] by the search for a philosophical theory of the Eucharist." In order to show that the Cartesian theory of matter as extension was false and inconsistent with both transsubstantiation and consubstantiation, Leibniz held to the belief in the existence of the vacuum, but was quite perturbed when he had to abandon the latter belief because it conflicted with his teleological principle of continuity and plenitude. I should add that there was in the seventeenth century no major philosophical or scientific issue that was not discussed as having theological implications. This *historical* fact does not affect the *logical* validity of the arguments advanced, many of which were repetitions of arguments dating back to Plato and Aristotle, whose theology was pagan. Russell is quite right in distinguishing, for the sake of clarity, historical from logical questions; but since there is no actual separation nor identity of the two sorts of questions, it is equally important to have a clear conception of the relation of history to logic. At about 1900 and for the many years to which he held to Platonism, Russell apparently held only necessary relations as clearly conceived; and since there is no necessary connection between Leibniz's theological beliefs and his logic, there seemed to Russell to be none but a purely adventitious relationship between the two. But I should like to offer the following general considerations in order to throw some light on the relationship between the historical and logical versions of the philosophy of Leibniz mentioned above.

Let us note that there is an historical development in logic itself as there is in the case of any science. The logical works of Aristotle, Leibniz, Russell, and Whitehead are monumental landmarks in the cumulative history of logic, despite Kant's mistaken notion that logic was a completed science. Russell's own views as to the logic of mathematics underwent considerable improvement between the first (1900) and second (1937) editions of his book on Leibniz. This sort of scientific development is correlated with the historical development of mathematics and not with the economic or religious history of modern Europe, despite Marxian and theodicic philosophies of history. But certain aberrations of logic and science, which occur in dialectical and scholastic philosophies of science, are correlated with and explained by political and theological interests. For example, there is a striking logical similarity between the totalitarianism and authoritarianism of Communist and Catholic ideologies. The violent opposition between them is correlated with and accounted for by the conflicting political interests of these systems of regimenting individual thought and conduct. Let us apply this principle, (suggested or implied by Russell,) that wherever aberrations of reason or scientific logic occur, there is some external (extra-scientific) historical factor at work, to the two versions of Leibniz's philosophy which Russell has so brilliantly expounded, but whose relation to each other he has not explained. Russell sometimes attempts an explanation by referring merely to Leibniz's dual personality, but this psychological fact is historically an effect rather than a cause. Sometimes Russell refers more illuminatingly to the pervasive conflict between the progressive work of scientific logic and the retarding influence of seventeenth-century theology and politics. These occasional references suggest inquiries into the historical Leibniz which are quite as important as deducing from the logical structure of a selected portion of Leibniz's views what Leibniz *should* have said further, if he had not let himself be influenced by external causes.

When generalized, the methodological principle involved here (and suggested by Russell's work on Leibniz) has the significance of a first law of inertia for intellectual history, which I shall express very loosely on the analogy (not to be taken too literally) of Newton's first law of motion: "Any mind at rest in certain premises or moving along certain lines of thought determined by these premises will continue to rest content with these premises or develop in lines consistent with them unless acted upon by external historical forces." It is in the light of some such principle (which assumes absolute logical beginnings as Newton assumed absolute physical space and time) that we can understand the point Russell makes so frequently in his work, namely, that Leibniz's philosophy when it departed from its major premises did so because of historical (political and theological) influences. The inconsistencies of Leibniz's system can then be explained by reference to these historical influences. For example, in attacking Leibniz's four proofs for God's existence, Russell notes that "only one of these, the Argument from the Pre-established Harmony, was invented by him, and that was the worst of the four" (172). Why so good a logician as Leibniz should have offered such vulnerable proofs is for Russell understandable only in terms of Leibniz's desire to please ecclesiastical authority. Even a theologian like Francesco

Olgiati today can see through the superficiality of Leibniz's religious arguments. In his recent scholarly work on Leibniz, Olgiati rejects the thesis of Baruzi and Carlotti that Leibniz's philosophy was essentially religious by proving that "the religiosity of Leibniz was only a magnificent pyrotechnical spectacle."[4]

Olgiati also rejects Russell's (and Couturat's) thesis, that Leibniz's philosophical system was an outgrowth of Leibniz's logical studies, by insisting on the importance of the historical works of Leibniz and his sense of historical development, expressed by Leibniz in his law of continuity (*natura non facit saltos*) and dictum "*le présent est gros de l'avenir, et chargé du passé.*" Olgiati was impressed by Louis Davillé's work on *Leibniz historien, essai sur l'activité et la méthode de Leibniz* (1909) and article "Le développement de la méthode historique de Leibniz" (*Revue de Synthèse historique,* 1911). But Davillé and Olgiati forget that time and historical development were subsumed by Leibniz under preformationist and immanent mathematical rules supposed by Leibniz to govern biological heredity as well as continuous series. Leibniz's idea of internal development of individual organisms was extended to cultural history in the subsequent romantic philosophies of history of Lessing and Herder, Goethe, Fichte, Schelling, and Hegel. In any case, an organic philosophy of history is as inconsistent as Leibniz's Platonism is with an empiricist study of the diverse factors that make for specific historical changes.[5] The dynamics of intellectual history requires the delineation and analysis of empirical factors that accelerate certain ideas.[6] Such a factorial

---

[4] F. Olgiati, *Il Significato Storico di Leibniz* (Pubblic. della Università Cattolico del Sacro Cuore, Milano 1938): "La religiosità di Leibniz fu solo un magnifico spettacolo pirotecnico." (p. 62) Olgiati may not be as detached as Russell in judging a Protestant.

[5] Cf. my "Methodology in the Philosophy of History," *Journal of Philosophy* (June, 1941). Also J. Rosenthal, "Attitudes of Some Modern Rationalists to History," (*Journal of the History of Ideas,* IV, 4 [Oct. 1943], 429 ff.) contains a most penetrating and critical analysis of Leibniz's anti-historicism.

[6] As a possible 'second law of motion' for intellectual history, following Gabriel Tarde and C. S. Peirce, the acceleration of the spread of ideas, it may be said, varies directly with the extra-logical social needs which determine the evolutionary survival value of ideas, and inversely with the mass of established conventions that resist change.

and empirical analysis is suggested by Russell in his preface to the first edition of his work on Leibniz:

Questions concerning the influence of the times or of other philosophers, concerning the growth of a philosopher's system, and the causes which suggested his leading ideas—all these are truly historical: they require for their answer a considerable knowledge of the prevailing education, of the public to whom it was necessary to appeal, and of the scientific and political events of the period in question.[7]

The rather sharp separation of formal from historically empirical considerations in Russell's treatment of Leibniz's philosophy often appears by sudden juxtaposition of the results of Russell's logical analysis of Leibniz's views alongside of Russell's historical insight. Consider, for example, the following two statements:

"A monism is necessarily pantheistic, and a monadism when it is logical, is as necessarily atheistic. Leibniz, however, felt any philosophy to be worthless which did not establish the existence of God." (p. 170) Why Leibniz felt this way we are left to surmise from the casual references Russell makes to Leibniz's political career. Now Russell, who is undoubtedly much more honest intellectually and morally than the successful Leibniz, was able to see through the duplicity of the German diplomat. A very clear example of Leibniz's dishonesty is seen in his relations to the philosophy of Spinoza (who had with some reluctance shown Leibniz the manuscript of his *Ethics*). Leibniz in private correspondence with Spinoza praised his work, but in correspondence with prominent officials, condemned Spinoza as atheistic and immoral. Yet he borrowed Spinoza's central notion of metaphysical substance and the internality of relations. Russell not only exposed Leibniz's plagiarism but also showed how it led to inconsistencies with Leibniz's attempt to save the individual soul and grant it freedom and immortality. For it is logically impossible to adopt Spinoza's notion of substance and endow individuals with any but a transitory and absolutely determined existence. A similar objection may be

---

[7] Cf. A. O. Lovejoy, "Reflections on the History of Ideas," *Journal of the History of Ideas*, I, 1 (1940) for a similar but more detailed analysis of the method of historiography.

made against Hegelian and Marxian theories of freedom, but most historians of philosophy are either baffled or overcome by dialectics.

Russell's method of formal analysis is best suited to finding hidden premises and inconsistencies in a system like Leibniz's. The limitation of that method consists in its inability to correlate the formal structure of thought with its historical genesis and setting. Couturat had set out to trace the history of Leibniz's logical studies by a minute search and examination of unpublished manuscripts of Leibniz at the same time that Russell was performing his anatomy of the published works and letters of Leibniz. It was not a mere coincidence that Couturat should have found independent corroboration of Russell's thesis by discovering the key to Leibniz's entire metaphysics in his notions of a universal mathematics and alphabet of human thought in extension of the syllogism. For Couturat like Russell was a logician and was bound to select from a huge mass of unpublished manuscripts (still not edited completely) exactly those writings of Leibniz dealing with logical questions. Cassirer, who wrote his book on Leibniz after Russell and Couturat had finished theirs, aimed at a different interpretation of Leibniz's conception of logic. Having in mind the controversy between Cartesians and Leibnizians over *vis viva*—and no historian of science can minimize the significance of this dispute over the foundations of seventeenth-century physics—Cassirer pointed out the dynamic and teleological character of the physical world for Leibniz. He was thus led to criticize Russell and Couturat for having divorced the *formal* structure of Leibniz's philosophy of science from its *material* content, given by Leibniz's theory of activity and entelechy as the essence of things. Dewey in his work on *Leibniz's New Essays* (1888), written under Hegelian influence, also had regarded organic development and unity as the key concepts of Leibniz's philosophy, thus overlooking Leibniz's contribution to formal logic. Leibniz did try to base physical and moral contingency upon the ambiguous teleological principle of sufficient reason; e.g., he applies the latter to the law of least action in his deduction of the law of the refraction of light, and to proving free-will in ethics. But Leibniz also warned against resorting in physical theory to any but mechanical causes. The inconsistency of Leibniz's attempt to base physics both on a metaphysical principle of final causes and on an empirical doctrine of contingency enables one to find passages in Leibniz to justify both the formal and material interpretations of Leibniz's theory of science offered by Russell and Couturat, on the one hand, and by Dewey and Cassirer on the other. The real issue here is between the logical and Platonic realism of Russell and the neo-Kantian spiritualism of the Marburg school to which Cassirer belonged. The latter school, founded by Hermann Cohen and Natorp, sought to improve Kant's theory of knowledge, which separated the method of physical sciences from that of ethics, by providing an idealistic synthesis. Russell should think Kant was sounder than the neo-Kantians on this point. However, I believe that Russell's logical atomism is too absolute a pluralism for the methodology of the physical and social sciences (under which I should include ethics), for it makes scientific method or rational criticism useless in evaluating human needs and goals.

The absolutism of Leibniz and Russell proceeded from erecting the scientific knowledge of their times into eternal truths. For example, Leibniz had three orders of space and time: (1) in the mind of God, (2) in the perceptions of each monad, and (3) objective space and time among monads after they are created. In Russell's *Essay on the Foundations of Geometry* (1897), we find three absolute orders of space: (1) in the pure constructions of geometry, (2) in psychology, and (3) in physical space which was Euclidean; with respect to time, Russell regarded simultaneity as "obviously" an irreducible relation between perceptions (130). Thus it is evident that the limitations of Leibniz's and Russell's theory of knowledge consisted in converting the science of the times into eternal principles of knowledge. A theory of knowledge can be no more general in its validity than the scope of the scientific knowledge it claims to comprehend. Russell has himself abandoned the absolutistic view of space and time and the

Kantian view that necessary propositions of mathematics are synthetic, which he held when he wrote on Leibniz. Now, since he admitted that his own ideas about philosophy were inseparable from his interpretations of Leibniz's philosophy,[8] we cannot regard all of his interpretations of Leibniz as final.

Russell started as a Platonist but turned to a more empiricistic nominalism under the influence of operationalist developments in the logic of the sciences. Leibniz, on the other hand, started as an atomist, but turned to a more "realistic" metaphysic in keeping with the seventeenth-century belief that science like art held the mirror of man's mind up to nature. In Russell's theory of knowledge, logical analysis has broken the mirror into so many atomic sense-data that it makes no sense to talk about mind as a mirror at all. The analysis of meaning becomes a matter of logical construction in which sense-data and universals serve as neutral and transparent building blocks, and truth involves a rather obscure relation of logical correspondence. Thus, Russell has effectively criticized the simple mirroring relation that Leibniz's monads have to each other in their divinely pre-established harmony. But a certain sort of Platonism still haunts Russell's theory of truth by logical correspondence in which atomic statements stalk like ghosts of eternal truth.

By the thesis of absolute logical beginnings, I mean the assumption that a deductive system of ideas *must* start with certain unique premises which "contain" the system. Plato and his followers obtained unique premises by intellectual intuition. Plotinus added a touch of mystical ecstasy to the Platonic intellectual act of apprehending the Form of the Good. Even Aristotle with his empirical naturalism found it necessary to postulate that the order of logical demonstration was fixed by the unalterable zoological order of natural species which was inverse to the order of knowledge "for us." The seventeenth-century philosophers repeated these Greek patterns of thought in various forms expressed by Italian and Cambridge neo-

---

[8] "For unless we have clear ideas about philosophy, we cannot hope to have clear ideas about Leibniz's philosophy." (*Op. cit.*, 11.)

Platonists, by Descartes' clear and distinct ideas, by Spinoza's identification of the order and connection of ideas with the order and connection of things, which we have already seen was adopted by Leibniz in the doctrine of absolute simples and his universal alphabet of knowledge. This thesis was not the exclusive property of so-called rationalists; for in the British empiricists we find psychological entities (Locke's ideas, Berkeley's sensations, Hume's impressions) playing the same logical rôle of absolute beginnings. Mach and the early logical positivists (Wittgenstein, Carnap), also postulated protocol and atomic propositions as absolute logical beginnings. It was only the development of an operational logic implicit in Leibniz's notion of a "calculus ratiocinator" and furthered by methodological studies of the foundations of geometry and arithmetic (Boole, Peirce, Poincaré, Hilbert, Tarski) which enables us to abandon the thesis of uniquely determined and privileged axioms as absolute logical beginnings. The methodology of deductive systems permits one to start with any statements that obey a consistent set of rules of formation and transformation. The variety of deductive systems thus generated gives the scientist a richer choice of systems to apply to a given problem. Preference for any one of these becomes a problem relative to pragmatic considerations rather than a quest for absolutely predetermined, self-evident premises. All of these now obvious logical considerations were lacking in Russell's first analysis of Leibniz; but I was surprised to find no mention of them in Russell's preface to the second edition of his work.

Without these vestiges of absolute logical beginnings Russell's method could have more effectively divested Leibniz's organic hierarchy of its theological and political arrogance. But much of Russell's insight into Leibniz's thought proceeds from a profounder source in Russell than his method of logical atomism. It seems to me to have its roots in an historical and political soil, richer and freer than the one in which Leibniz flourished. A few years ago I eagerly looked forward to learning from Russell himself, within the public halls of a municipal college, the answers to the questions which had disturbed me in reading his treatise on Leibniz's philosophy. But the very sort of persons, to whom Leibniz had always catered for support, intervened and insisted on the divine prerogative of their pre-established harmony.

PHILIP P. WIENER

DEPARTMENT OF PHILOSOPHY
COLLEGE OF THE CITY OF NEW YORK

8

Albert Einstein

REMARKS ON BERTRAND RUSSELL'S
THEORY OF KNOWLEDGE

BEMERKUNGEN ZU BERTRAND RUSSELLS ERKENNTNIS-THEORIE

ALS die Schriftleitung mich aufforderte, etwas über Bertrand Russell zu schreiben, bewog mich meine Bewunderung und Verehrung für diesen Autor sogleich Ja zu sagen. Der Lektüre von Russells Werken verdanke ich unzählige glückliche Stunden, was ich—abgesehen von Thorstein Veblen —von keinem andern zeitgenössischen, wissenschaftlichen Schriftsteller sagen kann. Bald aber merkte ich, dass es leichter sei, ein solches Versprechen zu geben als zu erfüllen. Ich hatte versprochen, etwas über Russell als Philosophen und Erkenntnis-Theoretiker zu sagen. Als ich vertrauensvoll damit angefangen hatte, erkannte ich schnell, auf was für ein schlüpfriges Gebiet ich mich gewagt hatte, als ein Unerfahrener, der sich bis jetzt vorsichtig auf das Gebiet der Physik beschränkt hatte. Der Physiker wird durch die gegenwärtigen Schwierigkeiten seiner Wissenschaft zu Auseinandersetzung mit philosophischen Problemen in höherem Masse gezwungen als es bei früheren Generationen der Fall war. Von diesen Schwierigkeiten wird zwar hier nicht gesprochen, die Beschäftigung mit ihnen ist es aber in erster Linie, die mich zu dem im Nachfolgenden skizzierten Standpunkt geführt hat.

In dem Entwicklungsprozess des philosophischen Denkens durch die Jahrhunderte hat die Frage eine Hauptrolle gespielt: Was für Erkenntnisse vermag das reine Denken zu liefern, unabhängig von den Sinneseindrücken? Gibt es solche Erkenntnisse? Wenn nein, in was für einer Beziehung steht unsere Erkenntnis zu dem von den Sinnes-Eindrücken gelieferten Rohmaterial? Diesen Fragen und einigen andren mit ihnen innig verknüpften Fragen entspricht ein fast unübersehbares Chaos

REMARKS ON BERTRAND RUSSELL'S
THEORY OF KNOWLEDGE*

WHEN the editor asked me to write something about Bertrand Russell, my admiration and respect for that author at once induced me to say yes. I owe innumerable happy hours to the reading of Russell's works, something which I cannot say of any other contemporary scientific writer, with the exception of Thorstein Veblen. Soon, however, I discovered that it is easier to give such a promise than to fulfill it. I had promised to say something about Russell as philosopher and epistemologist. After having in full confidence begun with it, I quickly recognized what a slippery field I had ventured upon, having, due to lack of experience, until now cautiously limited myself to the field of physics. The present difficulties of his science force the physicist to come to grips with philosophical problems to a greater degree than was the case with earlier generations. Although I shall not speak here of those difficulties, it was my concern with them, more than anything else, which led me to the position outlined in this essay.

In the evolution of philosophic thought through the centuries the following question has played a major rôle: What knowledge is pure thought able to supply independently of sense perception? Is there any such knowledge? If not, what precisely is the relation between our knowledge and the raw-material furnished by sense-impressions? An almost boundless chaos of philosophical opinions corresponds to these questions and to a few others intimately connected with them. Nevertheless there is visible in this process of relatively fruitless but heroic endeavours a systematic trend of development, namely

* Translated from the original German by Paul Arthur Schilpp.

philosophischer Meinungen. In diesem Prozess relativ unfrucht-
barer heroischer Bemühungen ist doch ein systematischer Zug
der Entwicklung erkennbar, nämlich eine steigende Skepsis gegenüber jedem Versuch, durch reines Denken etwas erfahren zu
können bezüglich der "objectiven Welt," der Welt der "Dinge"
im Gegensatz zu der Welt blosser "Vorstellungen und Gedank-
en." In Parenthese sei gesagt, dass hier wie bei einem echten
Philosophen das Anführungszeichen (" ") gebraucht wird, um
einen illegitimen Begriff einzuführen, den der Leser für den
Augenblick zu gestatten ersucht wird, obgleich er der philosophischen Polizei suspekt ist.

Der Glaube, dass es möglich sei, alles Wissenswerte durch
blosses Nachdenken zu finden, war im Kindeszeitalter der
Philosophie ziemlich allgemein. Es war eine Illusion, die ein
jeder leicht begreifen kann, wenn er für einen Augenblick
davon absieht, was er von der späteren Philosophie und der
Naturwissenschaft gelernt hat; er wird sich nicht darüber
wundern, wenn Plato der "Idee" eine Art höhere Realität
zuschrieb als den empirisch erlebbaren Dingen. Auch bei
Spinoza und noch bei Hegel scheint dies Vorurteil als belebende
Kraft die Hauptrolle gespielt zu haben. Es könnte sogar einer
die Frage aufwerfen, ob ohne etwas von solcher Illusion überhaupt Grosses auf dem Gebiet des philosophischen Denkens
geschaffen werden kann—wir aber wollen so etwas nicht fragen.
Dieser mehr aristokratischen Illusion von der unbeschränkten
Durchdringungskraft des Denkens steht die mehr plebejische
Illusion des naïven Realismus gegenüber, gemäss welchem die
Dinge so "sind," wie wir sie mit unseren Sinnen wahrnehmen.
Diese Illusion beherrscht das tägliche Treiben der Menschen
und Tiere; sie ist auch der Ausgangspunkt der Wissenschaften,
insbesondere der Naturwissenschaften.

Die Überwindung dieser beiden Illusionen ist nicht unabhängig voneinander. Die Überwindung des naïven Realismus
ist verhältnismässig einfach gewesen. Russell hat diesen Prozess
in der Einleitung seines Buches *An Inquiry into Meaning and
Truth* (Seiten 14-15) in wunderbar prägnanter Form so
gekennzeichnet:

We all start from "naïve realism," i.e., the doctrine that things are an increasing scepticism concerning every attempt by means of pure thought to learn something about the "objective world," about the world of "things" in contrast to the world of mere "concepts and ideas." Be it said parenthetically that, just as on the part of a real philosopher, quotation-marks are used here to introduce an illegitimate concept, which the reader is asked to permit for the moment, although the concept is suspect in the eyes of the philosophical police.

During philosophy's childhood it was rather generally believed that it is possible to find everything which can be known by means of mere reflection. It was an illusion which any one can easily understand if, for a moment, he dismisses what he has learned from later philosophy and from natural science; he will not be surprised to find that Plato ascribed a higher reality to "Ideas" than to empirically experienceable things. Even in Spinoza and as late as in Hegel this prejudice was the vitalizing force which seems still to have played the major rôle. Someone, indeed, might even raise the question whether, without something of this illusion, anything really great can be achieved in the realm of philosophic thought—but we do not wish to ask this question.

This more aristocratic illusion concerning the unlimited penetrative power of thought has as its counterpart the more plebeian illusion of naïve realism, according to which things "are" as they are perceived by us through our senses. This illusion dominates the daily life of men and of animals; it is also the point of departure in all of the sciences, especially of the natural sciences.

The effort to overcome these two illusions is not independent the one of the other. The overcoming of naïve realism has been relatively simple. In his introduction to his volume, *An Inquiry Into Meaning and Truth*, Russell has characterized this process in a marvellously pregnant fashion:

We all start from "naïve realism," i.e., the doctrine that things are what

what they seem. We think that grass is green, that stones are hard, and that snow is cold. But physics assures us that the greenness of grass, the hardness of stones, and the coldness of snow, are not the greenness, hardness, and coldness that we know in our own experience, but something very different. The observer, when he seems to himself to be observing a stone, is really, if physics is to be believed, observing the effects of the stone upon himself. Thus science seems to be at war with itself: when it most means to be objective, it finds itself plunged into subjectivity against its will. Naïve realism leads to physics, and physics, if true, shows that naïve realism is false. Therefore naïve realism, if true, is false; therefore it is false.

Abgesehen von der meisterhaften Formulierung sagen diese Zeilen etwas, an was ich vorher nie gedacht hatte. Bei oberflächlicher Betrachtung scheint nämlich die Denkweise von Berkeley und Hume in einem Gegensatz zu der Denkweise der Naturwissenschaften zu stehen. Aber Russells obige Bemerkung deckt einen Zusammenhang auf: Wenn Berkeley darauf fusst, dass wir nicht "Dinge" der Aussenwelt durch unsere Sinne direkt erfassen, sondern dass nur mit der Anwesenheit der "Dinge" kausal verknüpfte Vorgänge unsere Sinnesorgane erreichen, so ist dies eine Überlegung, die ihre Überzeugungskraft aus dem Vertrauen auf die physikalische Denkweise schöpft. Wenn man nämlich die physikalische Denkweise auch in ihren allgemeinsten Zügen bezweifelt, so besteht keine Notwendigkeit, zwischen das Objekt und den Akt des Sehens irgend etwas einzuschieben, was das Objekt von dem Subjekt trennt, und die "Existenz des Objekts" zu einer problematischen macht.

Dieselbe physikalische Denkweise sowie deren praktische Erfolge waren es aber auch, welche das Vertrauen in die Möglichkeit erschüttert hat, die Dinge und ihre Beziehungen auf dem Wege blossen spekulativen Denkens zu verstehen. Allmählich setzte sich die Überzeugung durch, dass alles Wissen über Dinge ausschliesslich eine Verarbeitung des durch die Sinne gelieferten Rohmaterials sei. In dieser allgemeinen (und absichtlich etwas verschwommen redigierten) Form wird dieser Satz gegenwärtig wohl allgemein akzeptiert. Diese Überzeugung beruht aber nicht etwa darauf, dass jemand die Unmöglichkeit des Gewinnens von Realerkenntnissen auf rein

they seem. We think that grass is green, that stones are hard, and that snow is cold. But physics assures us that the greenness of grass, the hardness of stones, and the coldness of snow, are not the greenness, hardness, and coldness that we know in our own experience, but something very different. The observer, when he seems to himself to be observing a stone, is really, if physics is to be believed, observing the effects of the stone upon himself. Thus science seems to be at war with itself: when it most means to be objective, it finds itself plunged into subjectivity against its will. Naïve realism leads to physics, and physics, if true, shows that naïve realism is false. Therefore naïve realism, if true, is false; therefore it is false. (pp. 14-15)

Apart from their masterful formulation these lines say something which had never previously occurred to me. For, superficially considered, the mode of thought in Berkeley and Hume seems to stand in contrast to the mode of thought in the natural sciences. However, Russell's just cited remark uncovers a connection: If Berkeley relies upon the fact that we do not directly grasp the "things" of the external world through our senses, but that only events causally connected with the presence of "things" reach our sense-organs, then this is a consideration which gets its persuasive character from our confidence in the physical mode of thought. For, if one doubts the physical mode of thought in even its most general features, there is no necessity to interpolate between the object and the act of vision anything which separates the object from the subject and makes the "existence of the object" problematical.

It was, however, the very same physical mode of thought and its practical successes which have shaken the confidence in the possibility of understanding things and their relations by means of purely speculative thought. Gradually the conviction gained recognition that all knowledge about things is exclusively a working-over of the raw-material furnished by the senses. In this general (and intentionally somewhat vaguely stated) form this sentence is probably today commonly accepted. But this conviction does not rest on the supposition that anyone has

spekulativem Wege tatsächlich bewiesen hätte, sondern darauf, dass der im obigen Sinne empiristische Weg allein sich als Quelle der Erkenntnis bewährt hat. Galilei und Hume haben diesen Grundsatz zuerst mit voller Klarheit und Entschiedenheit vertreten.

Hume sah, dass von uns als wesentlich betrachtete Begriffe, wie z.B. kausale Verknüpfung, aus dem durch die Sinne gelieferten Material nicht gewonnen werden können. Er wurde durch diese Einsicht zu einer skeptischen Einstellung gegenüber jeglicher Erkenntnis geführt. Wenn man seine Bücher liest, wundert man sich, dass nach ihm viele und zum Teil hochgeachtete Philosophen so viel Verschwommenes haben schreiben und dankbare Leser finden können. Er hat die Entwicklung der Besten nach ihm nachhaltig beeinflusst. Man spürt ihn durch bei der Lektüre von Russells philosophischen Analysen, deren Scharfsinn und schlichte Ausdrucksweise mich oft an Hume erinnert hat.

Die Sehnsucht des Menschen verlangt nach gesicherter Erkenntnis. Deshalb erschien Humes klare Botschaft niederschmetternd: Das sinnliche Rohmaterial, die einzige Quelle unserer Erkenntnis, kann uns durch Gewöhnung zu Glauben und Erwartung aber nicht zum Wissen oder gar Verstehen von gesetzmässigen Beziehungen führen. Da trat Kant auf den Plan mit einem Gedanken, der zwar in der von ihm vorgebrachten Form gewiss unhaltbar war, aber doch einen Schritt zur Lösung des Hume'schen Dilemmas bedeutete: Was an Erkenntnis empirischen Ursprungs ist, ist niemals sicher (Hume). Wenn wir also sichere Erkenntnis besitzen, so muss dieselbe in der Vernunft selber begründet sein. Dies wird z.B. behauptet bezüglich der Sätze der Geometrie und bezüglich des Kausalitätsprinzips. Diese und gewisse andere Erkenntnisse sind sozusagen ein Teil des Instrumentariums des Denkens, müssen also nicht erst aus den Sinnesdaten gewonnen werden (d.h. sind Erkenntnisse "a priori"). Heute weiss natürlich jeder, dass die genannten Erkenntnisse nichts von der Sicherheit, ja inneren Notwendigkeit, an sich haben, wie Kant geglaubt hat. Was mir aber an seiner Stellung dem Problem gegenüber richtig erscheint, ist die Konstatierung, dass wir uns mit gewisser

actually proved the impossibility of gaining knowledge of reality by means of pure speculation, but rather upon the fact that the empirical (in the above mentioned sense) procedure alone has shown its capacity to be the source of knowledge. Galileo and Hume first upheld this principle with full clarity and decisiveness.

Hume saw that concepts which we must regard as essential, such as, for example, causal connection, can not be gained from material given to us by the senses. This insight led him to a sceptical attitude as concerns knowledge of any kind. If one reads Hume's books, one is amazed that many and sometimes even highly esteemed philosophers after him have been able to write so much obscure stuff and even find grateful readers for it. Hume has permanently influenced the development of the best of philosophers who came after him. One senses him in the reading of Russell's philosophical analyses, whose acumen and simplicity of expression have often reminded me of Hume.

Man has an intense desire for assured knowledge. That is why Hume's clear message seemed crushing: The sensory raw-material, the only source of our knowledge, through habit may lead us to belief and expectation but not to the knowledge and still less to the understanding of law-abiding relations. Then Kant took the stage with an idea which, though certainly untenable in the form in which he put it, signified a step towards the solution of Hume's dilemma: Whatever in knowledge is of empirical origin is never certain (Hume). If, therefore, we have definitely assured knowledge, it must be grounded in reason itself. This is held to be the case, for example, in the propositions of geometry and in the principle of causality. These and certain other types of knowledge are, so to speak, a part of the instrumentality of thinking and therefore do not previously have to be gained from sense data (i.e., they are *a priori* knowledge). Today everyone knows of course that the mentioned concepts contain nothing of the certainty, of the inherent necessity, which Kant had attributed to them. The

"Berechtigung" beim Denken solcher Begriffe bedienen, zu welchen es keinen Zugang aus dem sinnlichen Erfahrungs-material gibt, wenn man die Sachlage vom logischen Stand-punkte aus betrachtet.

Nach meiner Überzeugung muss man sogar viel mehr behaupten: die in unserem Denken und in unseren sprach-lichen Äusserungen auftretenden Begriffe sind alle—logisch betrachtet—freie Schöpfungen des Denkens und können nicht aus den Sinnes-Erlebnissen induktiv gewonnen werden. Dies ist nur deshalb nicht so leicht zu bemerken, weil wir gewisse Begriffe und Begriffs-Verknüpfungen (Aussagen) gewohn-heitsmässig so fest mit gewissen Sinnes-Erlebnissen verbinden, dass wir uns der Kluft nicht bewusst werden, die—logisch unüberbrückbar—die Welt der sinnlichen Erlebnisse von der Welt der Begriffe und Aussagen trennt.

So ist z.B. die Reihe der ganzen Zahlen offenbar eine Erfindung des Menschengeistes, ein selbstgeschaffenes Werk-zeug, welches das Ordnen gewisser sinnlicher Erlebnisse erleichtert. Aber es gibt keinen Weg, um diesen Begriff aus den Erlebnissen selbst gewissermassen herauswachsen zu lassen. Ich wähle hier gerade den Begriff der Zahl, weil er dem vorwissenschaftlichen Denken angehört, und an ihm der konstruktive Charakter trotzdem noch leicht erkennbar ist. Je mehr wir uns aber den primitivsten Begriffen des Alltags zuwenden, desto mehr erschwert er uns die Masse einge-wurzelter Gewohnheiten, den Begriff als selbständige Schöp-fung des Denkens zu erkennen. So konnte die für das Ver-ständnis der hier obwaltenden Verhältnisse so verhängnisvolle Auffassung entstehen, dass die Begriffe aus den Erlebnissen durch "Abstraktion," d.h. durch Weglassen eines Teils ihres Inhaltes, entstehen. Ich will nun zeigen, warum mir diese Auffassung so verhängnisvoll erscheint.

Hat man sich einmal Humes Kritik zu eigen gemacht, so kommt man leicht auf den Gedanken, es seien aus dem Denken alle jene Begriffe und Aussagen als "metaphysische" zu ent-fernen, welche sich nicht aus dem sinnlichen Roh-Material her-leiten lassen. Denn alles Denken erhält materialen Inhalt ja durch nichts anderes als durch seine Beziehung zu jenem sinn-

following, however, appears to me to be correct in Kant's statement of the problem: in thinking we use, with a certain "right," concepts to which there is no access from the materials of sensory experience, if the situation is viewed from the logical point of view.

As a matter of fact, I am convinced that even much more is to be asserted: the concepts which arise in our thought and in our linguistic expressions are all—when viewed logically—the free creations of thought which can not inductively be gained from sense-experiences. This is not so easily noticed only because we have the habit of combining certain concepts and conceptual relations (propositions) so definitely with certain sense-experiences that we do not become conscious of the gulf—logically unbridgeable—which separates the world of sensory experiences from the world of concepts and propositions.

Thus, for example, the series of integers is obviously an invention of the human mind, a self-created tool which simplifies the ordering of certain sensory experiences. But there is no way in which this concept could be made to grow, as it were, directly out of sense experiences. It is deliberately that I choose here the concept of number, because it belongs to pre-scientific thinking and because, in spite of that fact, its constructive character is still easily ·recognizable. The more, however, we turn to the most primitive concepts of everyday life, the more difficult it becomes amidst the mass of inveterate habits to recognize the concept as an independent creation of thinking. It was thus that the fateful conception—fateful, that is to say, for an understanding of the here existing conditions—could arise, according to which the concepts originate from experience by way of "abstraction," i.e., through omission of a part of its content. I want to indicate now why this conception appears to me to be so fateful.

As soon as one is at home in Hume's critique one is easily led to believe that all those concepts and propositions which cannot be deduced from the sensory raw-material are, on account of their "metaphysical" character, to be removed from

lichen Material. Letzteres halte ich für völlig wahr, die darauf gegründete Vorschrift für das Denken aber falsch. Denn dieser Anspruch—wenn er nur völlig konsequent durchgeführt wird— schliesst überhaupt jedes Denken als "metaphysisch" aus.

Damit Denken nicht in "Metaphysik" bezw. in leeres Gerede ausarte, ist es nur notwendig, dass genügend viele Sätze des Begriffssystems mit Sinnes-Erlebnissen hinreichend sicher verbunden seien, und dass das Begriffssystems im Hinblick auf seine Aufgabe, das sinnlich Erlebte zu ordnen und übersehbar zu machen, möglichste Einheitlichkeit und Sparsamkeit zeige. Im übrigen aber ist das "System" ein (logisch) freies Spiel mit Symbolen nach (logisch) willkürlich gegebenen Spielregeln. Dies alles gilt in gleicher Weise für das Denken des Alltags wie für das mehr bewusst systematisch gestaltete Denken in den Wissenschaften.

Es wird nun klar sein, was gemeint ist, wenn ich Folgendes sage: Hume hat durch seine klare Kritik die Philosophie nicht nur entscheidend gefördert, sondern ist ihr auch ohne seine Schuld zur Gefahr geworden, indem durch diese Kritik eine verhängnisvolle "Angst vor der Metaphysik" ins Leben trat, die eine Krankheit des gegenwärtigen empirizistischen Philosophierens bedeutet; diese Krankheit ist das Gegenstück zu jenem früheren Wolken-Philosophieren, welches das sinnlich Gegebene vernachlässigen und entbehren zu können glaubte.

Bei aller Bewunderung für die scharfsinnige Analyse, die uns Russell in seinem letzten Buche *Meaning and Truth* geschenkt hat, scheint es mir doch, dass auch dort das Gespenst der metaphysischen Angst einigen Schaden angerichtet hat. Diese Angst scheint mir nämlich z.B. der Anlass dafür zu sein, das "Ding" als "Bündel von Qualitäten" aufzufassen, wobei nämlich die "Qualitäten" dem sinnlichen Rohmaterial zu entnehmen gesucht werden. Der Umstand nun, dass zwei Dinge nur ein und dasselbe Ding sein sollen, wenn sie inbezug auf alle Qualitäten übereinstimmen, zwingt dann dazu, die geometrischen Beziehungen der Dinge zu einander zu ihren Qualitäten zu rechnen. (Sonst wird man dazu genötigt, den Eiffelturm in Paris und den in New York als "dasselbe Ding"

thinking. For all thought acquires material content only through its relationship with that sensory material. This latter proposition I take to be entirely true; but I hold the prescription for thinking which is grounded on this proposition to be false. For this claim—if only carried through consistently— absolutely excludes thinking of any kind as "metaphysical."

In order that thinking might not degenerate into "metaphysics," or into empty talk, it is only necessary that enough propositions of the conceptual system be firmly enough connected with sensory experiences and that the conceptual system, in view of its task of ordering and surveying sense-experience, should show as much unity and parsimony as possible. Beyond that, however, the "system" is (as regards logic) a free play with symbols according to (logical) arbitrarily given rules of the game. All this applies as much (and in the same manner) to the thinking in daily life as to the more consciously and systematically constructed thought in the sciences.

It will now be clear what is meant if I make the following statement: By his clear critique Hume did not only advance philosophy in a decisive way but also—though through no fault of his—created a danger for philosophy in that, following his critique, a fateful "fear of metaphysics" arose which has come to be a malady of contemporary empiricistic philosophizing; this malady is the counterpart to that earlier philosophizing in the clouds, which thought it could neglect and dispense with what was given by the senses.

No matter how much one may admire the acute analysis which Russell has given us in his latest book on *Meaning and Truth*, it still seems to me that even there the spectre of the metaphysical fear has caused some damage. For this fear seems to me, for example, to be the cause for conceiving of the "thing" as a "bundle of qualities," such that the "qualities" are to be taken from the sensory raw-material. Now the fact that two things are said to be one and the same thing, if they coincide in all qualities, forces one to consider the geometrical relations between things as belonging to their qualities. (Otherwise one is forced to look upon the Eiffel Tower in Paris and that in

anzusehen.[1]) Demgegenüber sehe ich keine "metaphysische" Gefahr darin, das Ding (Objekt im Sinne der Physik) als selbständigen Begriff ins System aufzunehmen in Verbindung mit der zugehörigen Zeit-räumlichen Struktur.

Im Hinblick auf solche Bemühungen hat es mich befriedigt, dass im letzten Kapitel des Buches doch herauskommt, dass man ohne "Metaphysik" nicht auskommen könne. Das einzige, was ich daran zu beanstanden habe, ist das schlechte intellektuelle Gewissen, das zwischen den Zeilen hindurchschimmert.

ALBERT EINSTEIN

SCHOOL OF MATHEMATICS
THE INSTITUTE FOR ADVANCED STUDY
PRINCETON

[1] Vergl. Russells *An Inquiry into Meaning and Truth*, S. 119-120, Kapitel "Proper Names."

New York as "the same thing.")[1] Over against that I see no "metaphysical" danger in taking the thing (the object in the sense of physics) as an independent concept into the system together with the proper spatio-temporal structure.

In view of these endeavours I am particularly pleased to note that, in the last chapter of the book, it finally crops out that one can, after all, not get along without "metaphysics." The only thing to which I take exception there is the bad intellectual conscience which shines through between the lines.

ALBERT EINSTEIN

SCHOOL OF MATHEMATICS
THE INSTITUTE FOR ADVANCED STUDY
PRINCETON

[1] Compare Russell's *An Inquiry Into Meaning and Truth*, 119-120, chapter on "Proper Names."

9

John Laird

ON CERTAIN OF RUSSELL'S VIEWS CONCERNING
THE HUMAN MIND

ON CERTAIN OF RUSSELL'S VIEWS CONCERNING
THE HUMAN MIND

HAD I had the time and the nerve I should have liked to discuss what I took to be most significant in Russell's philosophical achievement and not, as I am going to do, certain of his views which happen to be nearest the perspective of my own limited interests. I should also have liked to make a comprehensive survey of the chosen theme and not, as I mean to do here, to confine myself, in the main, to one particular volume. Mr. Schilpp, however, when he cabled me his request for the present paper had to impose a time limit, although otherwise leaving me as free as a man could wish to be. The time limit was not ungenerous, but it was a restriction. So I think I may say that I had certain solid reasons for the choice I have made and was not actuated wholly by sloth and timidity.

I am going to discuss some of the arguments in Russell's *Analysis of Mind*—not all, since I have not the space for that, but some which are not unimportant. This seems to me a legitimate undertaking. Russell may have changed a good many of his opinions on the subject since 1921, when the book appeared. It looks to me as if his latest book *An Inquiry Into Meaning and Truth* is rather different in some of its implications. On the whole, however, the *Analysis of Mind* is an adequate and tolerably stable account of an important part of Russell's middle or late-middle philosophy. It is a full-dress or, at least, a fairly dressy statement of the results of his conversion from English to American "new realism" *in re* the human mind, that is, of a very radical conversion, in respect of mental analysis, as compared with the confident and debonair statements of so late a book as *The Problems of Philosophy* (1912). Its main contentions regarding the human mind are very similar indeed to those of his *Outline of Philosophy* (English edition, 1927). It is mentioned with approval in his Tarner Lectures (*The Analysis of Matter*, 1927, p. 240n). So it cannot reasonably be regarded as an ephemeral thing, a *livre de circonstance*, the outcome of a mood.

The book begins with an investigation into the Brentano-Meinong schema of act-content-object. Realists, Russell says, either suppress both "act" and "content" (if they are of the American type) or suppress the content but not the act (if they are of the British type, as represented by Moore in his early "Refutation of Idealism" or by Russell himself in *Problems*). Russell himself, he now says (p. 20), "remains a realist as regards sensation but not as regards memory or thought." In so far, however, as he remained a realist he had become converted to the new realism of the Americans.

Some remarks may be made about this schema.

It seems to fit memory, belief, and propositional "thought," and I shall postpone discussion of this matter. *Prima facie*, however, it seems to be very ill-adjusted to what we call "feeling" and emotion, and also to sensing, perceiving, and imaging unless we hold, with some philosophers, that all these processes, including even sensing, necessarily involve some sort of judgment or belief.

Take the first point first. With regard to feeling and more generally to emotion, most analytical psychologists find no difficulty at all in the conception of objectless feelings, feelings that refer to nothing. You need not (they say) be pleased *at* or *with* anything. You may just be pleased in the particular way in which you *are* pleased. If you allow that in general you are pleased *with* something, or in other words that your feelings are seldom if ever wholly blind, this circumstance need not be explained by anything intrinsically pointing in the feeling. It is quite sufficient if the feeling is accompanied by (or at any rate if it is interfused with) something in the way of cognition. Again, even if you may attend to your sorrow, and give an introspective description of what it feels like to be in the dumps, it is preposterous to hold (they say) that you cannot feel sad without attending to your sadness in this way. Therefore the feeling may, and commonly does, exist without an act of that kind. If it does not require *such* an "act," why should it require any "act" at all?

As regards perceiving and other such cognitive processes, the most plausible sort of "act" would be an "act" of attention or, as Russell has recently said (*Inquiry*, p. 51), of "noticing." It seems difficult to deny that, if you attend, you must attend *to* something, that is, that the very meaning of attention includes attention *to* some "object." It would be strange, however, if this "object" were a "content" *of the "act,"* if when you attend to what you describe as a blue patch, the patch were contained in your "act." The "act" seems to be essentially alio-referent. The natural and the plausible analysis in this case is Locke's, that is, a doctrine of "operations of the mind" directed upon certain "immediate objects" (cf. Russell in *Problems*, p. 73). According to this analysis it would be a question for further inquiry whether these "direct" or "immediate" objects were either mental states, or "in the mind" in some special sense (cf. Berkeley, *Principles*, para. 49) or in *no* sense. They are not "in" the *act* in any plausible sense, and, although some of them (or most of them in certain respects) may refer, directly or obliquely, to some physical object, this may be reasonably held to be an extrinsic property, and therefore additional to the original analysis, not properly a part of its core.

We may next consider why, in those respects in which he remained a realist, Russell abandoned his British (new) realism and naturalised himself, in a spiritual way, on the American continent. The reasons he gives are that cognitive "acts" in sensing or imaging cannot be observed empirically and are not required on theoretical grounds. The "content" suffices.

The first of these reasons is blunt. In *Problems* (e.g., p. 77) Russell had spoken quite gaily of "my seeing the sun" as "an object with which I have acquaintance." Now he abolishes all such alleged "objects" and says they are fictions of malobservation.

The thing, one might suppose, could be very easily tested. Let anyone try whether he can "see" (i.e., observe) his seeing as something empirically distinguishable from the speck or the patch which he sees. There is, however, at least one empirical obstacle. When one sees (to keep to vision) one can certainly observe certain muscular and other bodily sensations connected with the process of seeing. These, however, Russell and others would correctly say, are just sensa and are not "acts" in the relevant sense. Eliminate them analytically and it may be very difficult to say with any confidence what is observably left. Still, many competent philosophical psychologists have made the attempt in good faith and with an adequate knowledge of this particular snag. Some of them, though not the majority, say that "acts" are observed in such cases. The others give an unqualified "No."

This is unsatisfactory. If one attributes sinister motives (i.e., theory-bred mal- or non-observation), one can attribute such motives to either party. It would be pleasanter if there were something better to offer than the counting of "Ayes" and "Noes." Here, however, the requirements of theory (of which I shall speak later) are irrelevant. For theory might require something unobservable. Let us stick to the question of possible empirical observation.

Sometimes it is said that acts, being essentially alio-referent, could not *also* be self-referent and so that the alleged empirical observation must be a fiction. This, I think, is not a good argument; and Russell, if I have not mistaken his meaning, does not use it. Grant that an act of inspection could not inspect itself and you have still no good reason for denying that another act belonging to the same self might inspect the said act of inspecting. The Ego, according to most psychologists, is quite sufficiently complex for that. Again the inspecting and the inspected acts might be simultaneous. So there is no need to appeal to memory.

A much more important type of question arises, I think, when we ask whether *if* we "see our seeing" we *inspect* our seeing in the same general way as we inspect black dots or blue patches, and indeed whether, although "conscious" of it, we inspect it at all. In other words, we have to ask whether we should not distinguish between self-acquaintance and self-inspection.

In the main European philosophical tradition "reflexive" knowledge (more accurately, self-acquaintance) was distinguished from and contrasted with non-reflexive other-knowledge, and the contrast was very seriously intended. Locke was a rebel when he said that reflexive self-acquaintance, "though it be not sense, yet it is very like it and might properly enough be called internal sense" (*Essay*, II, 1, para. 4), and described it as "that notice which the mind takes of its own operations and the manner of them" (*ibid.*) or (ch. 6) as what happens when the mind "turns its view inward upon itself and observes its own action," even if none of these statements is quite as definite as "seeing our seeing." The rebel may have been wrong and the traditionalists right. If they were right, their analysis would be not that "operations of the mind" can be inspected like colours, or are the objects of a distinct alio-referent act of awareness, but that our acquaintance with them is of a totally different order, not involving any duality of act and object and yet, like our feelings, something which not only may be but also (as many would say) *must* be a part, or at least an empirically experienced modality, of what we commonly call our "consciousness." We feel sorrow in the sense in which we run a race or construct a construction, not in the sense in which we hit or miss a target; but, when we feel it, we feel it "consciously" and may very well doubt whether an "unconscious" feeling (so-called) is anything other than an unfelt feeling, that is to say, anything other than a piece of nonsense.

If this analysis of reflexive acquaintance be allowed to be possible, several consequences follow. I shall mention two of them here.

The first concerns cognitive acts, and its general purport is that we might be reflexively acquainted with cognitive acts, even in such simple instances as sensing, although we could not inspect them in any ordinary sense of inspection. I think myself that we *are* so acquainted with attentive acts of sensing and do not agree with Russell (*Inquiry*, p. 50) that "noticing consists mainly in isolating from the sensible environment." However, I'm not at all confident about that.

The second is that, if our empirical self-acquaintance is most accurately described in the way in which we describe conscious feelings (which may be more or less discriminating, and less or more vague), we should have to do in that case with a part or modality of what we commonly call our "consciousness," in which the referential sense of "conscious of" may be wholly absent and in which an adverbial description is usually more appropriate. It is generally better to say "I am painfully conscious" than "I am conscious of a pain," although the latter, of course, is quite good current English. The question would then arise whether, in the case of sensing, if "acts" are suspect, "objects" are not suspect too, whether instead of renouncing both "acts" and "contents" in this case, as Russell the convert proposes to do, we should not instead renounce "acts" *and "objects,"* retaining "content" and interpreting "content" in the way in which *feeling* would be interpreted in the reflexive fashion. If so, the correct analysis would be neither "I am conscious of a blue patch" nor "blue patch here-now" but "I am blue-patchily conscious." This sounds awkward, but is not an unusual philosophical analysis, though it is seldom stated quite in that way. One question is whether there is anything against it *except* its linguistic awkwardness. Another question is whether, if there are serious objections to it in the case of sensed blue patches, there are not equally serious objections to any other analysis of, say, toothache. If so, different sensations would have to be analysed in fundamentally different ways; and that is not impossible.

When he deals with the question whether acts, even if they were beyond any possible sort of empirical observation, are required for any tenable theory of philosophical psychology, Russell says (p. 18) that "Meinong's 'act' is the ghost of the subject or what was once the full-blooded soul" and denies that either the ghost or its former incarnation is needed for the theory of knowledge. This large question has several parts, some of which I may mention here.

In general, if anyone set about to discuss Soul, or Self, or Ego, he would suppose that he was discussing something existent which had various intrinsic characteristics and also had extrinsic connections. He would not be exclusively concerned, and, very likely, would not be chiefly concerned with the problem of the minimum that is needed for a theory of *cognition* to be viable. The nature of the latter question may be indicated roughly by asking, "What is the very least that must be assumed about 'I' if sense is to be made, e.g., of the statement: 'I' who am now watching and hearing these actors on the stage believe that 'I' am the same 'I' that recently arrived at the theatre in a taxi?" That is a legitimate and an important question. It is not, however, the only important question in this matter, and most Ego-investigators would be equally interested in a host of other statements in which "I" occurs, whether or not such statements had any direct bearing upon the minimal assumptions an epis-temologist has to make, and even if the epistemological irrelevancies in such statements (or what seemed to be irrelevancies) were a positive embarrassment to epistemologists. Thus, with regard to the dispute about reflexive self-acquaintance mentioned above, the question is not primarily whether such reflexive self-acquaintance must be assumed if epistemology is to work, but whether it occurs or not.

One of the questions which Russell briefly mentions here (p. 18) and examines more fully in some other places is whether the inveterate grammatical use of the first personal pronoun (e.g., "I noticed this") implies, when it is fully examined, that there must be an entity called "I" additional to what philosophers often call "its" acts and experiences. He replies in the negative, and, since I should like to agree with him, my inclinations are all in favour of a purr of joyful assent. In view of what I have just said, however, I am bound to remark that the question, for me, refers to *all* that, to use F. H. Bradley's terms, can reasonably be regarded as the "psychical filling" of the Ego and is not exclusively cognitive. I think that selves are very peculiar and very highly integrated "bundles" of what Broad calls "sympsychic" experiences. Even if, as Russell has recently maintained in *Inquiry* (e.g., chap. VII), it would be possible to give a consistently impersonal account of "egocentric particulars," I should not believe that, in fact, any human experience *was* impersonal.

But perhaps I am running on too fast. What Russell, in the context, is most anxious to say is that in the crucial instance of sensation, the sensum is all that need be supposed to exist, and that there is no need whatever to suppose that the analysis of sensation requires either an act of sensing as well as the sensum, or an Ego to apprehend the sensum. The sole fact in the case (he thinks) is the *occurrence* of the sensum.

This is vital to Russell's position and is a cornerstone of the metaphysical theory (a form of neutral monism) which he advocates. I do not know whether it is feasible to discuss the problem directly and in itself without any metaphysical frills. But I shall try to say something on that head.

I do not know whether anyone ever held that an occurrence *as such* implied a "mental" act, i.e., that the mere fact that something occurs had this analytical implication. If there are such people I shall not try to argue with them. Many would say, however, that when an occurrence is an appearance there is some such implication.

More elaborately, what such people say is often something like this: If you assert that "*x* appears" you imply (a) that *x* shows itself and (b) that it shows itself *to* an observer. As regards (a) there is no contradiction in something (a potato, say) existing without showing itself. Therefore, if anything is such that it shows itself by the mere fact of existing, it must be a quite special sort of thing. As regards (b), that particular consequence would follow from the assumptions that "showing itself" means showing itself to inspection and that inspection is always a case of something inspecting something *else*.

In view of what I have said about "feeling" and about "reflexive self-acquaintance," I should deny the inevitability of the assumptions contained in (b); but I think that what is asserted in (a) has to stand. An occurrence, I should say, need not be an apparition. Therefore, if an occurrence is an apparition, it *may* be, and I think it *is*, a very special sort of occurrence. Indeed, I don't see any good ground for denying that an apparition is or implies a *mental* occurrence, this statement allowing either that the apparition is a feeling which shows itself reflexively by the mere fact of being a *feeling* (i.e., felt), or that it is shown nonreflexively to something else, whether act, or bundle of sympsychic personal experiences, or Ego in some other sense.

I do not see that there is much more to be said in terms of the direct methods I am here attempting to use. There is very little point in saying, Russell-wise, that visual sense-appearances are very like the appearances on a sensitive photographic plate. By calling the plate "sensitive" you are importing quite a strong analogy; and as for the "appearances," it is clear, in any ordinary sense of language, that the appearances of a star in some astronomer's photograph are appearances in the same sense as the star itself, that is to say, they "appear" when some one looks at them. Otherwise, they do not appear at all. Again, direct methods are not very easy in the particular case of sensation because, according to Russell and most other good authorities, pure sensations are never observed by adults who are capable of telling the tale. What is observed by grown-up people is *perceived*; and percepts are overlaid and/or fused with images, associations, interpretations, etc. You can prove that there must *be* a sensational core or "datum" in your percept; but you cannot observe it in its native innocence.

In any case there is surely nothing odd or paradoxical about the conclusion that sense-occurrences are a very special class of occurrences. There are no other occurrences which are at all likely to hearten a neutral monist, that is, a philosopher who is disposed to maintain that certain entities (alleged to be ultimate and the only ultimates) are amphibious, being capable of being "material" in one context and "mental" in another.

Consider a number of philosophical disputes about sensation. Berkeley says, "There was a sound, that is, it was heard." The plain man, if naïvely realistic, would say, "Not at all; hearing the sound gives evidence of the sound's existence, but winds might roar and waves splash on the beach although no living creature heard them." Philosophers retort, "Is there any likelihood at all that an unheard sound would be a *sound*? Some of our misguided colleagues speak as if the only conceivable difference between *sensibile* and *sensum* were the irrelevance that someone is aware of the sensum, which awareness (they say) is extrinsic to the sensum and does not affect its intrinsic characteristics in any way. They are wrong. Unsensed green is just like unfelt toothache, a meaningless conjunction of words. Try to apply your distinction between *sensa* and *sensibilia* to *passiones* and *patibilia*, and see where you get."

Let us turn to the metaphysical side of Russell's contentions in this place.

Russell's metaphysical contention on its negative side is that there is no mind-stuff, and, more particularly, that "consciousness" is not a stuff but a function. We may keep to the negative argument for the time being, since the positive argument is a general sketch of Russellian neutral monism.

The terms Russell uses in this context were largely derived from certain of William James's later essays, now very well known. Some of them are more provocative than instructive. Among these is the term "stuff." Russell seems to like it, and returns to it in various parts of his argument. So far as I have noted, he does not define it, and his readers may be excused if they have some little curiosity about how he would or could define it.

If it is fair to say with Russell that "acts" are the ghosts of the Subject or Ego, it would be equally fair, I opine, to say that "stuff" is the dust of "substance." Russell's metaphysical theory of substance, as I understand him, is that "substance" is a name for specific clotting of events. That doesn't help us much in these stuffy arguments. There might easily be clots of mental events. In certain senses Russell would hold that there were. So we need something more than this to have "stuff." What more?

If "stuff" meant the classical ὕλη, there never would *be* any stuff that was just "stuff" and nothing more. "Stuff," according to this interpretation, is that without which "forms" would be void. If pure "stuff" existed it would be utterly formless stuff, which is impossible, however flocculent the "stuff" might be supposed to be. Even differentiated "stuff" would be meaningless; for to be differentiated in any degree is to be formed in that degree. Hence mental stuff would contain a *contradictio in adiecto*, and could not help us here.

I gather from several of Russell's statements (e.g., on p. 113) that he holds, "If no stuff, then no intrinsic characteristics." This is interesting in various ways. In general one would suppose that x' and x'' cannot be identical if anything is true of x' which is not true of x''. This would include extrinsic properties as well as intrinsic characteristics. Russell's affection for intrinsic characteristics at this point seems to me to be rather odd. Despite his objections to the "axiom of internal relations" he does commit himself in this book to the statement (p. 247) that if x' and x'' had no intrinsic difference their effects must be "precisely similar."

From "if no stuff, then no intrinsic characteristics" one can infer, "If intrinsic characteristics, then stuff." This principle seems to me to lead to strange conclusions. It would entail, for instance, that what Russell calls "belief-feeling" (which, he says, *has* observable intrinsic characteristics) has "stuff" in it.

The entire line of argument seems odd to me. Take the following propositions: "Jones has mechanical characteristics, since he will fall precisely like a stone if dropped from an aeroplane." "Jones has vital characteristics, for he is alive, not dead." "Jones has mental characteristics because he reflects, infers, loses his temper, and so on." All these propositions about Jones are true, and the three sets of characteristics are not the same. Can it seriously be inferred that Jones is composed of mechanical "stuff" *plus* vital "stuff" *plus* "mental" stuff? I cannot think I am bound so to conclude; but the only respect in which I have cooked this affair when I stated these three true propositions about Jones is my omission of the adjective "intrinsic" as qualifying "characteristics." That omission *might* be crucial. But is it? I have shown, with regard to the third proposition about Jones, that Russell does hold that Jones's belief-feelings *have* intrinsic characteristics. I find it difficult to believe that Jones's mechanical and vital characteristics are in no respect "intrinsic" or how, if they weren't intrinsic, they could be wholly extrinsic in view of Russell's statement on p. 247.

Sometimes, instead of speaking about "stuff," Russell speaks about "ingredients" (or "ultimate ingredients") and about "ultimate constituents." These terms also would be the better for definition. It is hardly enough to call them "items in stuff" (e.g., p. 284). In view of Russell's elaborate accounts of "logical atoms," "hard data," and the like, this request may seem pretty cool; and perhaps it is. Let me say then that I am puzzled about Russell's argument concerning "stuff" and do not find it easy to translate the term either into his technical language or into any other.

Since I am so doubtful about "stuff" and "mind-stuff," I am not inclined to go on with the discussion whether or not "consciousness" is stuffy. Anything I have to say about its functional analysis had best come later.

Up to the present, my readers may complain that I have started a few hares, some of them pretty lethargic, but have done little or nothing that is either downright destructive of Russell's argument, or at all promising as a basis for alternative construction. I agree. In the main, if I could show that the situation is more fluid than Russell says it is, I should be well content. In a positive way the chief, if not the only, contention I have advanced is that reflexive self-acquaintance (particularly in feeling) has escaped, or very nearly escaped, Russell's attention. It is time, therefore, to consider what Russell has to say about feelings.

His discussion of them occupies two chapters, the third on "Desire and Feeling," the fourteenth on "Emotions and Will." The gist of these chapters, I think, may be stated, not inaccurately, as follows:

If by "feeling" one means pleasure and pain, local bodily pains like toothache or bellyache are organic sensations proper, "items" as separable as any sensation is. In contrast with these, all pleasures, whether (as we say) "bodily" or "mental," and all "discomforts" (most of which are commonly regarded as "mental pains") are neither separable items nor an algedonic (i.e., pleasure-pain) tone suffusing certain processes. On the contrary, they are merely names for the success or failure, temporary or final, of an impulsive, instinctive, desiring or other such process which, having started, moves restlessly towards quiescence. We are "conscious" of these, Russell says, if we hold correct beliefs about what would, in fact, induce such quiescence. If, on the other hand, "feeling" is interpreted more widely to include emotions, the James-Lange theory of emotion or something very like it, is readily defensible. According to Russell, emotions, almost certainly, are organic sensa.

As regards pleasure-pain Russell's contention that local aches are sensations is widely accepted, but it is not clear to me that local bodily pleasures (call them "titillations," if you are nervous about ambiguity) are not on precisely the same footing. As regards what are often called "mental" pleasures and pains, it seems likely that these are not "separable items"—the phrase, I allow, may be something obscure—and that the language of algedonic tone is much more appropriate to them. Such "tonic" descriptions, however, seem to me to be quite obviously correct as a piece of description; and Russell's alternative account appears to omit what should not be omitted.

It has long been a subject of brisk philosophical discussion whether all pleasures and pains presuppose and, so to say, merely register the success or failure of antecedent impulsive process, understood or misunderstood. The usual answer is that some do and some don't. The pleasures arising unexpectedly from fragrance in the air, or from unsought beauty in the landscape, might be supposed to prove the reality of the negative case. The same would be true of the pleasure one may have on seeing one's favourite author praised by a judicious critic, especially if the writer be caviare to the general public. These instances might be challenged, however, on the ground that the unexpected delights of sweet smells or of charming landscapes are *general* exhilarants, and that, in the case of the applauded writer, the general mass of tendencies that are bound up with our own pride and self-esteem are stimulated quite a lot. (*Mutatis mutandis*, this would hold of depressing surroundings well enough.)

Let us suppose then that Russell's account of the matter is correct in what it includes. Is there the least reason for supposing that it is also correct in its exclusions? Allow that there is a one-one correlation between the success or failure of impulsive process and our feelings of pleasure and of pain. Does that tell us what pleasures and pains *feel like?* And don't we know what they feel like? If there is any hard datum in these matters, this one would seem to me to be adamantine.

I think that similar comments should be made about "feeling" in the wider sense which includes emotions and also desires in so far as these are felt and are not simply defined as "motions towards." No doubt, if emotions *are* organic sensa, Russell would be fully entitled to say, as he does (p. 279), that they have intrinsic characteristics which may be described. He is also fully entitled to accept the James-Lange theory with as little diffidence as an admittedly controversial subject allows. But he doesn't say much in support of the James-Lange theory. It is hardly impressive to say that Angell may have answered Sherrington. And few who accept the James-Lange theory would have the effrontery to aver that the surge of organic sensa which, according to the theory, *is* the emotion, evinces separable sensation-items. At the most what would be evinced would be a vague tumult of organic sensa impossible to identify as such except by an act of faith together with an obstinate incredulity about what the devil they could be if they weren't organic sensa.

Most psychologists, including plain men when they turn psychologists, have no difficulty at all in distinguishing between many of the intrinsic characteristics of many emotions and the cruder, more isolable organic sensa which may be intertwined with them. Poets, for instance, have been heard to say that the pit of the stomach is where they are hit hardest when the Muse is not propitious; but they are never supposed to mean that this sensitive area exhausts these very trying emotions. There is a rich descriptive literature about the *feel* of emotions, the best of it coming from writers who are not professional psychologists, but who, in spite of that (?), are gifted observers of human nature. If it is just conceivable that they may be describing subtle cadences of organic resonance it is quite impossible to say with justified confidence that they *are* doing so—except on grounds of a theory which is very unconvincing if any credible alternative can be offered.

Russell himself quite happily accepts what he calls belief-feelings, familiarity-feelings, and others of the kind because, he says (e.g., p. 233), these are not postulated but "actual experienced feelings." It is incredible to me that a familiarity-feeling is a separate or separable sensation or, for that matter, a sensation at all. In other words, I submit that Russell accepts *certain* feelings and allows that they have observable intrinsic characteristics although they are *not* sensations and are *not* images. I suggest that much in the descriptive literature of emotions describes emotional feelings on the same sort of evidence as Russell accepts in the case of belief-feelings. It is quite irrelevant to say that such descriptive work may have led psychologists to a dead end and that behaviourism, for the moment at least, has a more promising programme. The question is whether these things are so, not whether they are useful for the architectural purposes of a theorist.

This is all I mean to say about the preamble to Russell's metaphysics of neutral monism. In rough outline the theory itself proceeds as follows: Sensations and images are the stuff of all that there is, and there is no intrinsic characteristic invariably present in sensations but absent from sensory images. That is all that is stuffy in the theory. The rest is function, context, and relation (principally causal) and not "stuff." More in detail, both mind and matter are "logical constructions," not substantial things or even shadows. Matter is a logical construction from sensations (not from images) and, still more specifically, a logical construction from those sensations which come nearest (in a very Pickwickian sense) to being "public" to many observers and are most amenable, functionally, to transmogrifications that suit the laws of physics. These same sensations, and any others which like organic sensa may seem rather more private, and images are the stuff of minds, the said minds being logical constructions taking their cue from their *biographical* causal context.

A good deal might be said about this. It might be argued, for instance, that, even if mind and matter were reached by construing the implications of sensa, there is no sufficient justification for reifying the cognate accusative, that is to say, for calling them "constructions" *tout court;* and I shall have something more to say about "stuff" versus "function." For the moment, however, the most urgent job would seem to be an investigation into Russell's views about the biographical relationships of his neutral stuff.

This includes habit and association; but I don't think Russell gives a very close analysis of habit, and his account of association seems to me to be a good deal less precise than the account many associationists were accustomed to give before the days of the logical-analytical method. Russell's more resolute analysis in this matter is given to the term "mnemic," borrowed from Semon and flattered perhaps by a certain unearned increment derived from a learned language.

Semon's mnemic philosophy eventually reached a theory of engrams, that is, of permanent traces in the brain. Russell admits, as Semon himself did, that physiological engrams are largely conjectural at the present stage of our knowledge. Therefore he does not assert their existence. But he hankers after them rather ardently. In principle, if they exist in sufficient quantity and detail, the biographical relationships of neutral stuff would be physiological, and "mind," in nearly all important ways, if not quite in all, would be a behaviouristic, that is a materialistic, construction. Psychologists would come nearer to the ultimate stuff of things than physicists commonly do, but the palm would go to materialism. If, on the other hand, mnemic connection is not physiologically engrammatic, there is room for the logical construction of minds which are not material.

Supposing then that we decline to take shelter in hypothetical modifications of brain tissue, Russell asserts that the simple straight-forward thing to say is that in mnemic causation the past (some would prefer to say *our* past) is a part cause of the effect. That is the mnemic explanation of the difference between burnt and unburnt children when next they are near a fire. The statement must be taken literally. "I do not mean merely," Russell says (p. 78) "—what would always be the case—that past occurrences are part of a *chain* of causes leading to the present event. I mean that, in attempting to state the *proximate* cause of the present event, some past event or events must be included."[1] This is Russell's alternative to Bergson, whom he calls "obscure and confused" (p. 180) or a trafficker in "mere mythology" (*Outline*, p. 206).

Bergson may have been confused; and Russell seems to be clear. What many people would say, however, is that Russell's

[1] *Italics*, Russell's.

clear account is clearly an impossibility. The past is dead and so cannot act. Old-fashioned British realists (like myself) would say that past events may be observed, not as they exist now (for now they don't exist), but as they *were*, and any historian would say that they could sometimes be investigated by later inquirers. But few would maintain that they could operate after they had ceased to be. No doubt if you say, as Russell does, that causes and "operations" are only uniformities of sequence you would, on any theory, have certain correlations if the past, even remotely, had anything to do with the present. Many believe, however (and I confess I retain the prejudice), that causes and effects must be temporally continuous. If this be so, Russell's doctrine falls.

If it were suggested that the conception of persistent psychical as distinguished from persistent physiological engrams, however difficult it may be, is easier to accept than this doctrine of a dead past yet acting, Russell's answer is that, if the psychical be the conscious, conscious "acts" and the like do in fact vanish without observable trace. Thus, casting about for examples, I can attend now to the fact that *papillon* is the French for 'butterfly' and *Schmetterling* the German. I am not always attending to these names. When I'm not attending to them they seem just to disappear from my consciousness, and when I am soundly asleep or anaesthetised it may seem that my sympsychic bundle is a complete non-entity. The same would seem to be true of my feelings. When I don't feel my toothache it stops.

I don't deny that these difficulties are very serious, despite the insouciance of psychoanalysts about them. What is not clear to me, however, is that, on Russell's theory, physiologists, behaviourists, and materialists are in better case. Their explanations, according to Russell, are in terms of a logical construction construed from sensory data which, as given, are momentary and perishing. If sensa are feelings, as the toothache example shows, the problem is precisely the same for the logical construction "mind" as for the logical construction "matter." If, not being feelings, they are apparitions which exhaust their nature in appearing and don't exist when they don't appear, I can see no relevant difference between the two logical constructions.

In certain passages in his various works Russell shows a wistful sympathy with the attempt to construct a universe for himself from his own private evanescent sense data. If he could do this for his heaven and for his earth he could also do it for his "mind."

As I said at the beginning of this essay, I did not intend to make a comprehensive survey of Russell's *Analysis of Mind*, but only to examine certain parts of it. I have now said most of what I wanted to say, and the remainder of the essay will be slighter and more general in its character.

The last few chapters of Russell's book are busied about the "meaning of 'meaning'" in cases in which Russell is not a realist, i.e., in cases in which (as he thinks) we neither *are* what we are said to "mean" nor are able to inspect it directly. Thus in memory we remember *now* but mean or refer to what is gone. Russell, as we have seen, rejects the contention of some British realists that we can directly inspect past events we formerly experienced, and so has to provide a theory of extrinsic reference to what is meant in the memorial way. Similarly in the case of belief he uses the "act-content-object" schema in a modified form which substitutes "feelings" for "acts." In the believer, he says (p. 233), there are two present occurrences, the believing and what is believed. From these the "objective" of the belief must be distinguished, e.g., Caesar's crossing of the Rubicon, which could not conceivably be a present occurrence in any twentieth century mind.

In this matter I should like to repeat the comment I made before, namely that the first term in Russell's threefold schema is neither a sensation nor an image but in Russell's words (*ibid.*) "an actual experienced feeling." The point, I think, runs pretty deep. On p. 243, for instance, Russell gives an account of a series of "attitudes that may be taken towards the same content," doubting, believing, supposing, expecting, and so forth. These would commonly be described as "mental" attitudes, and of course Russell would have every right so to describe them, at this late stage of his argument, provided that they squared with his own account of "mind." If, however, as I am maintaining, these attitudes are *not* sensations and are *not* images but *are* "actual experienced feelings," I submit that he is peopling the "mind" with stowaways whose very existence he began by denying.

A comment I should like to make upon Russell's general theory of "meaning" is much more likely than its predecessor to be a prejudice of my own. Such as it is, however, I propose to make it. The brunt of Russell's argument here, I think, is behaviouristic. There is "meaning," he says, when something acts as a sign, and it acts as a sign when it causes appropriate action. (The term "appropriate" needs definition and receives some.) My comment would be similar to what I said about "appearances." In my opinion Russell gives us *Hamlet* without the Prince of Denmark. The behaviouristic view, to put it crudely, is that the clouds mean rain because they cause you to take out your umbrella. I should deny both that the clouds mean rain and that they cause you to take out your umbrella. The clouds don't "mean" at all. It is you who invest them with significance, you who are a mental being as they are not. Again, they don't cause you to take out your umbrella any more than a red light at a traffic junction causes motor cars to stop. The drivers do that when they *notice* the red light. If what they noticed was a figment of their own imaginations they would still stop their vehicles. I admit, of course, that Russell's behaviourism is not crude, and that, since it is based upon sensations and images, and not upon physical clouds, etc., much of the above criticism is *prima facie* irrelevant. But I think that the gist of it remains.

However that may be, Russell's analysis of meaning is mainly functional. The circumstance gives one an excuse for some further comments upon functional theories of the human mind.

On page 195 Russell says:

The notion that actions are performed by an agent is liable to the same kind of criticism as the notion that thinking needs a subject or ego. . . . To say that it is Jones who is walking is merely to say that the walking in question is part of the whole series of occurrences which is Jones. There is no *logical* impossibility in walking occurring as an isolated phenomenon, not forming part of any such series as we call a person.

Allowing for the slap-dash brevity of his statement, I should like, cordially and respectfully, to agree. But if this, in outline, be the correct analysis, why not go all functional and dispense with "stuff?" There is a place for "stuff" in certain analyses. It seems reasonable to say that, if a brownish fluid which looks like treacle acts like mustard gas, the stuff in it is not the stuff of treacle. Metaphysics, however, does not seem to me to be the place for these stuffy arguments, any more than for discussions about raw and manufactured articles. In a metaphysical sense you must be able to say, "There is," i.e., to distinguish between the actuality of functioning and its mere conception. That, however, is much more recondite than "stuff;" and it should be more recondite. As it seems to me, if you begin to ask, metaphysically, "What kind of stuff could alone function in such and such a way?," you are setting yourself an impossible task because you are mixing up two antagonistic questions.

Let us apply this to the human mind. The answer in general would be, "Mental is as mental does. There are mental doings, usually if not invariably sympsychic and clotted so far as we know. If these doings have intrinsic characteristics reflexively self-manifesting, why not? Let us describe them as best we can."

It may still be asked, "Even if you are rather sniffy about 'stuff', are you not holding that *'conscious* is as mental does'? And what evidence have you for *that* opinion?"

I agree that so far as my various statements are not merely critical they would amount to saying that "consciousness," that very complex phenomenon, has ultimately to be defined by the possibility of reflexive self-acquaintance, such reflexive self-acquaintance being frequently very dim. I agree further that I don't see how I could begin to attempt to prove that mental functions (such as "inferring," let us say) *could* only occur where there is conscious doing. I doubt very much whether an "unconscious wish," say, really is a *wish* and also whether an "unconscious *inference*" really is an inference; but if psychoanalysts and other friends of the "unconscious" were to say that *something* unknown could arrive pretty much where conscious doings seem to arrive, without itself being conscious in any ordinary sense, I don't know how to gainsay them. I am like Locke who didn't see his way to denying that an omnipotent God *could* "superadd" thinking to "matter." If God could do the trick, the thing might occur. And if I were asked, "What happens to your knowledge of the French or German for 'butterfly' when you are not consciously thinking about French or German or butterflies?"; or again, "How do saints differ from sinners when both are sound asleep?", I should not be able to say very much in terms of actual consciousness. I shall conclude these remarks with two observations, the first of a type usual in histories of philosophy, the second wholly personal.

The parallel between Hume's statement, at the beginning of his *Treatise*, that "all the perceptions of the human mind resolve themselves into two distinct kinds, which I shall call impressions and ideas," and Russell's doctrine that the stuff of existence consists without remainder of sensations and images, is too close to escape anyone's attention. Where the two differ in this fundamental matter is chiefly in this, that Hume professed to operate with impressions and ideas of reflexion as well as with sense-impressions and the ideas that mimic them, whereas Russell professes to operate with the latter only. Whether the extensive use that Hume made of impressions of reflexion (e.g., in providing the impression from which the idea of necessary connection was derived) is plausible or not, he had tactical advantages in being able to use them at all, advantages that are scarcely offset by Russell's superior logical weapons and by the greater flexibility of twentieth as opposed to eighteenth century science. In any case I have tried to argue that "reflexiveness" *is* a property of mental events. Another point that should be noted is that Hume, like Russell, accepted stowaways which, according to his principles, had no official existence. Thus time, according to Hume, was not an impression (or copy of one) but a "manner" of impressions, and belief was neither an impression nor an idea but "that certain *Je-ne-sais-quoi*, of which 'tis impossible to give any definition or description but which every one sufficiently understands."

My personal remark is just this: Over thirty years ago I had the privilege of being, in some sort, Russell's pupil at Trinity

College in Cambridge—I say "in some sort," because it was no part of his duty to teach me or of mine to be taught by him. I could not try to compute the extent of this privilege. It meant discussion after discussion with one, who, young as he was, was already one of the three or four preëminent philosophers of Europe; and that was but a part of what it meant to us. I can make no return for his patience or for the generosity with which he gave me so much of his time. But I should not like to miss the chance of expressing my gratitude. So I never thought of declining Mr. Schilpp's invitation. I regret the inadequacy of what I have said, and the limited range of its theme; but my intentions in writing this essay are as grateful as my recollections of that year in Cambridge.

JOHN LAIRD

UNIVERSITY OF ABERDEEN
ABERDEEN, SCOTLAND

10

Ernest Nagel

RUSSELL'S PHILOSOPHY OF SCIENCE

RUSSELL'S PHILOSOPHY OF SCIENCE

RUSSELL'S writings on the philosophy of science exhibit one persistent feature: his explicitly avowed use of the maxim "Whenever possible, substitute constructions out of known entities for inferences to unknown entities,"[1] a maxim which elsewhere he calls "the supreme maxim in scientific philosophising." Acting upon this precept, he has attempted to show that the ostensible objects of science are "logical fictions," capable of definition in terms of appropriately selected elements. I wish in this essay to examine the type of analysis which Russell has brought to bear upon the logical problems of physics as a consequence of his adoption of this maxim. However, Russell has repeatedly called attention to the fact that it was the fruitfulness of certain logical techniques in the foundations of mathematics which led him to adopt the maxim as the supreme guide in philosophy. I shall therefore briefly consider those techniques, as they are employed in the context of Russell's reconstruction of pure mathematics, preliminary to the discussion of his analysis of physics.

I

1. Russell's by now classic studies on the foundations of mathematics brought to a conclusion what was, at the time

[1] *Contemporary British Philosophy*, First Series, edited by J. H. Muirhead, London and New York, 1925, p. 363. Subsequent references to this book will be abbreviated to *CBP*.

In this essay the following abbreviations will be used for the titles of books by Russell: *FG* for *An Essay on the Foundations of Geometry*, Cambridge, England, 1897; *IMP* for *Introduction to Mathematical Philosophy*, London and New York, 1920; *P* for *Philosophy*, New York, 1927; *AM* for *The Analysis of Matter*, London, 1927; *OKEW* for *Our Knowledge of the External World*, Second Edition, New York, 1929; *PM* for *The Principles of Mathematics*, Second Edition, New of their publication, a revolution in traditional conceptions of mathematics. As is well known, the explicit thesis for which those studies supply overwhelming evidence is the essential identity of logic and pure mathematics. In exhibiting that identity, Russell also established the untenability of certain influential theories of knowledge which were based upon historically wide-spread views as to the nature of mathematics. For by clearly distinguishing between pure mathematics, whose propositions contain only logical terms, and applied mathematics, whose propositions contain descriptive (or empirical) as well as logical terms, he cut the ground from under the claims of dogmatic rationalism, Kantian apriorism, and types of sensationalistic empiricism. On the other hand, Russell's own analyses seemed to require the adoption of an extreme form of Platonic realism, since his detailed justification of mathematics as a body of valid propositions appeared to be cogent only on the hypothesis of the "independent reality" of universals and relations. Indeed, it was in considerable measure because of this supposed connection between such a realism and Russell's major thesis about mathematics, that the logico-symbolic techniques he employed so brilliantly were believed to require definite philosophical commitments, so that the use of those techniques became the center of philosophic controversy.

Nevertheless, some of Russell's most notable achievements in the analysis of mathematical notions exemplified a tendency opposed to Platonic realism. His analysis of the notion of cardinal number, for example, showed that it was unnecessary to assume the "existence" (or "subsistence") of a specific type of entity to correspond to the notion; and, accordingly, he showed that, without affecting the structure or validity of mathematics, the "ultimate population" of Platonic objects may be supposed to be smaller than had been thought.

In effecting such economies, Russell was in fact carrying on a great tradition in mathematics. Thus, the "extension" of the number-concept in the history of mathematics was first accompanied by the postulation of special *kinds* of number (the ra-

York, 1938; *ABC* for *The ABC of Relativity*, London, 1925; and *IMT* for *An Inquiry into Meaning and Truth*, New York, 1940.

tional fractions, the signed numbers, the irrationals, the imaginaries, the infinitesimals, and so on) to serve as the objects "discovered" by mathematicians. But the subsequent work of such men as Hamilton, Von Staudt, and Weierstrass made it evident that the postulation of such numbers as distinctive sorts of entities was unnecessary, since the required "entities" can all be defined in terms of familiar arithmetical notions and operations. Accordingly, when Russell declared

> Every one can see that a circle, being a closed curve, cannot get to infinity. The metaphysician who should invent anything so preposterous as the circular points [at infinity], would be hooted from the field. But the mathematician may steal the horse with impunity,[2]

and when, years later, commenting on the mathematician's occasional practice of postulating what is required, he noted that "The method of 'postulating' what we want has many advantages; they are the same as the advantages of theft over honest toil,"[3] he was doing less than justice to the tendency which the history of mathematics illustrates of eventually supplanting dubious "inferences" by suitable "constructions." Russell's maxim of philosophizing simply makes explicit a long-range trend of mathematical development.

2. For the sake of definiteness, the operation of Russell's technique for avoiding needless postulations in mathematics will be illustrated in three cases. First, the cardinal numbers. The cardinal numbers are generally admitted to be predicable of classes, two classes being assigned the same number when they are similar (i.e., when their members can be correlated in a one to one fashion). It seems natural, therefore, to regard the cardinal number of a class as the property which that class has in common with classes similar to it; and, on this view, a cardinal number is sometimes said to be obtained "by abstraction" from the classes possessing it. However, there seems no good reason for supposing that similar classes have *just one* property in common rather than a *set* of properties. There is even room for doubt whether at least one such property "exists;" for in as-

[2] *FG*, 45–6.
[3] *IMP*, 71.

suming the existence of such a property we are assuming, according to Russell, "a metaphysical entity about which we can never feel sure that it exists or that we have tracked it down."[4] In order to avoid these difficulties he therefore defined the number of a class as the *class* whose members are classes similar to the given class. Since it can be proved that there is only one such class of classes, the first difficulty vanishes; and since this class possesses all the formal characteristics expected of cardinal numbers, while at the same time its existence is "indubitable," it no longer is necessary "to hunt for a problematic number which must always remain elusive."[5]

Consider next Russell's definition of the real numbers, for example, of the irrational number which is the square-root of two. It is well known that the square-root of two is not an integer and that it cannot be a rational number. What, then, is it? Prior to Russell's analysis it was customary to regard it as the *limit* of certain series of rational numbers, or more generally, as a distinct kind of entity whose "existence" was assumed for the sake of satisfying certain mathematical relations. For example, the rational numbers, if ordered according to magnitude, form a series. In many cases this series can be decomposed into two ordered classes, such that one of the rational numbers separates their members; thus, the two classes, rationals less than two-thirds and rationals greater than two-thirds, are separated by the rational number two-thirds. On the other hand, consider the two ordered classes of rationals, rational numbers whose squares are less than two and rational numbers whose squares are greater than two; in this case, no rational number effects the separation. It again seems "natural" to suppose that there must be a number, though not a rational one, which "lies between" these two classes. But what cogent grounds have we for assuming the "existence" of such a number? Russell argued that we have none, and that it is only the influence of irrelevant spatial imagination or the seductiveness of certain algebraic operations which lends an air of plausibility to such an assumption. The assertion of the "existence" of a new kind of number is thus an unwar-

[4] *IMP*, 18.
[5] *IMP*, 18.

ranted "inference," and introduces something problematic and elusive into mathematics. On the other hand, the existence of the *class* of rationals whose squares are less than two is *not* disputable, for this class is "constructed" out of "known" elements. Accordingly, since the mathematical properties usually attributed to irrational numbers can be shown to belong to that class, Russell defined the square-root of two as identical with that class of rational numbers.

The notion of class plays a fundamental rôle in these two examples. But, according to Russell, classes, like cardinal and real numbers, are not part of "the ultimate furniture of the world" (since they are neither "particulars" nor properties or relations of particulars), and must thus be regarded as "logical constructions." He therefore required a definition of classes

which will assign a meaning to propositions in whose verbal or symbolic expressions words or symbols apparently representing classes occur, but which will assign a meaning that altogether eliminates all mention of classes from a right analysis of such propositions. We shall then be able to say that the symbols for classes are mere conveniences, not representing objects called "classes," and that classes are in fact . . . logical fictions.[6]

Russell achieved his objective by devising as translations for statements explicitly about *classes* other statements which mention only certain *properties* possessed by the individuals that would ordinarily be said to be members of those classes. Before illustrating Russell's procedure, a certain difficulty in effecting such translations must be mentioned. A given property (e.g., being human) determines uniquely just one class (i.e., the class of men); but the same class will be determined by two or more non-identical properties, if those properties are formally equivalent—that is, if every individual which possesses one of the properties also possesses the other, and conversely. Thus, the two non-identical properties of being human and being a featherless biped determine the same class. Hence, in order to effect the desired translation of a statement about a class, some device must be introduced so that in the new statement no one special property is mentioned *in exclusion* of other properties which also may determine the class in question. With this explanation in mind, but omitting fine points, Russell's general procedure may be illustrated as follows. The statement "The class of points in a plane is as numerous as the class of lines in a plane" is explicitly about two classes, one of which is certainly determined by the *property* of being a point in a plane and the other by the *property* of being a line in a plane. The approximate translation proposed for this statement is:

There exist at least two properties such that one of them is formally equivalent to the property of being a point in a plane, the other is formally equivalent to the property of being a line in a plane, and such that for every individual which has the first property there is just one individual with the second property, and conversely.

Although for the statement here chosen a somewhat simpler translation of the requisite kind can be given, the indicated translation illustrates the sort of complexity which Russell believed is required in general. In any event, the proposed translation makes no mention of any classes; and, accordingly, the assumption that classes "exist" as special kinds of entities is not required.

Let us finally state what appears to be the general pattern of the procedure of substituting "constructions" for "inferences." Let "S_1" be a statement, employed in some definite context T_1, which contains explicitly the expression "C," where this expression symbolizes some entity C; that is to say, "S_1" would normally be supposed to be about C. Under what circumstances is C (the *entity*, not the *expression* "C") to be regarded as a "logical construction" or "logical fiction?" Suppose there exist a set of entities $a_1, a_2, a_3, \cdots$, and a set of relations $R_1, R_2, \cdots$; suppose, further, that a statement "S_2" can be formed which contains mention of these entities and relations but does not contain the expression "C;" and suppose, finally, that in the context T_1 the statement "S_2" is logically equivalent to "S_1." If these conditions are satisfied, C is a logical construction out of the specified entities and relations. It will be noted that the above three examples conform to this schematism. It is clear that the statement "S_2" cannot, in general, be obtained from "S_1" by simply replacing "C" in the latter by a more complex expression without altering the rest of "S_1;" the formulation of "S_2" involves, in general, a radical recasting of "S_1."

3. A number of observations can now be made on Russell's use of his maxim of philosophizing in his reconstruction of mathematics. Although Russell substitutes "constructions out of known entities for inferences to unknown entities," he can maintain an attitude of theoretical neutrality with respect to the existence or non-existence of such things as numbers and classes. As he himself says, "When we refuse to assert the existence of classes we must not be supposed to be asserting dogmatically that there are none. We are merely agnostic as regards them: like Laplace, we can say, '*je n'ai pas besoin de cette hypothèse*'."[7] The maxim thus expresses a principle of caution and economy, and the techniques which implement it cannot by themselves help to decide what "exists" and what does not. Those techniques assume that certain entities and relations are in some sense "given."

It is well known, however, that in developing a mathematical system there is usually considerable leeway as to what materials may be taken as primitive and what is to be defined. From a formal point of view, the characterization of something as a "construction" must always be viewed as *relative* to the base selected. Accordingly, it seems as correct to regard the cardinal numbers as *primitive* (relative to a system, like Hilbert's, in which certain concepts of logic as well as of mathematics proper are taken as basic) as it is to regard them as *constructions* (relative to a system, like Russell's, in which concepts of logic are the sole primitives). Which base is in fact adopted will in general depend on matters that are not exclusively logical: upon issues of technical efficiency, upon certain more inclusive practical requirements, and often upon antecedent commitments as to what is "metaphysically" or "epistemologically" ultimate. From such a formal point of view, Russell's reconstruction of mathematics is primarily the systematization of a large body of propositions, in which remarkable economy is achieved in showing the various relations of dependence between different por-

[7] *IMP*, 184.

tions of mathematical doctrine; and Russell's claim that the concepts and propositions of general logic are sufficient for developing formally the rest of mathematics is hardly debatable. But, seen in this light, his technique for avoiding needless postulations is simply one device among others for attaining a maximum of inclusiveness and generality with a minimum of special assumptions. From this point of view at least, the issue he frequently raises as to whether numbers and classes "exist" in some ontological sense does not appear to be relevant to the problem under consideration.

On the other hand, Russell's reconstruction of mathematics may also be viewed as an attempt to *analyze* mathematical notions so as to exhibit their relevance to everyday affairs and science. It is this point of view which is paramount when Russell declares that that sort of definition of cardinal number is required which will make possible the "interpretation" of statements like "There were twelve Apostles" or "London has six million inhabitants." And he maintains that his logical definition of the cardinals "makes their connection with the actual world of countable objects intelligible."[8] Accordingly, the fundamental issue which arises in this connection is whether Russell's analyses state what is "meant" by mathematical expressions, not simply in the context of the formal development of mathematics, but in the context of statements about the empirical world; in other words, the issue is whether Russell's analyses explicate the *use* of mathematical expressions in the context of procedures such as counting and measuring.

Unfortunately, Russell does not always keep this issue at the center of his concern, and as a consequence it is often most puzzling to know just what he is doing when he says that he is "defining" the various concepts of mathematics. Thus, in commenting on the definition of cardinal number which he and Frege developed, he declares:

The real desideratum about such a definition of number is not that it should represent as nearly as possible the ideas of those who have not gone through the analysis required in order to reach a definition, but

[8] *PM*, Introduction to the Second Edition, vi.

that it should give us objects having the requisite properties. Numbers, in fact, must satisfy the formulae of arithmetic; any indubitable set of objects fulfilling this requirement may be called numbers.[9]

Russell is surely right in saying that a definition of number need not reproduce the "ideas" of those who use numerical expressions, since most people do not know *how* they use them. But it seems to me a serious blunder to maintain that "any indubitable set of objects" which satisfy the formulae of arithmetic may be called numbers—*if* the business of "logically constructing" numbers is to be something other than a purely formal exercise, and *if* the resultant analyses are to express the way or ways in which "number" is employed. From the point of view of the present approach, it is important to bear in mind the observation that an analysis or "logical construction," which is adequate for one context in which an expression is used, is not necessarily adequate for another context, and is unlikely to be adequate for all contexts. It does not follow, therefore, that definitions of the various numbers which are suitable for developing mathematics formally and systematically are suitable as analyses of them in other domains where they are used.

Two special difficulties which aggravate the analysis of mathematical concepts are worth noting in this connection. In the first place, many mathematical expressions are employed only within some more or less formalized system of mathematical statements, and have no clear or direct connections with statements which formulate matters in the actual world. The *use* of such expressions within the symbolic system may be governed by fairly explicit rules of operation, although no interpretation for those expressions may be feasible which would make the latter symbolical of anything known to occur in any part of the environment. In other words, such expressions may have an important function within what may be called a "calculus," without being "in themselves" in any way "representative." Many students (like Hilbert and Hermann Weyl) have accordingly eschewed the doubtless "natural" desire to interpret them in terms of something familiar, and have been content to

[9] *OKEW*, 222.

exhibit the rôles which specific calculi (containing such expressions) play in the system of scientific formulations. In any event, the interpretation of such expressions as denoting entities, allegedly "constructed" out of "indubitable" elements, appears to be a gratuitous enterprise. The second difficulty is that in actual practice many mathematical expressions have no *precise* use, however precisely they may be defined in terms of the basic notions of a formalized system. Analyses of what such expressions "mean," when such analyses yield something "constructed" in a precise way out of definite things or operations, must therefore be viewed as *proposals* as to how those expressions *might* be used. A proposal, however, is not to be judged in terms of truth or falsity, but in terms of its convenience and effectiveness in achieving specific objectives. And if Russell's definitions are such proposals, as I think some of them are, the issue he raises with respect to them, whether the "entities" corresponding to them are "inferred" or "constructed," does not appear to have much point.[10]

One final observation. If an entity is a logical construction, then a symbol representing that entity is theoretically capable of elimination from any statement in which that symbol occurs. It has already been noted that, if an entity can be shown to be a logical construction, considerable economy can be effected in developing mathematics. However, it is also worth noting that a gain in economy in one detail may have to be bought at the price of complicating the structure of mathematics in other details—perhaps even at the price of requiring dubious assump-

---

[10] Whether Russell's definitions of the various kinds of numbers do explicate the use which is made of the latter in everyday affairs and science, is a highly debatable question. I think that his definitions of the specific finite cardinals do express satisfactorily at least part of what is involved in the use of such statements as "I have ten fingers," "There is only one even prime," or "New York is more than 200 miles from Boston," although I am less sure than he appears to be that certain *ordinal* notions are not involved in that use, as Norman R. Campbell and Hermann Weyl have suggested. On the other hand, I am quite unconvinced that Russell's analysis of the irrationals is the appropriate one for "interpreting" such statements as "The diagonal of this square is equal to the square-root of two inches." For, although in explicating the sense of such a statement reference to a set of rational numbers is required, I do not think that this reference is to an *infinite series* of rationals.

tions concerning "the ultimate furniture of the world." Now in fact some of Russell's definitions, when these are taken as exhibitions of the structure of mathematical objects in terms of "indubitable" elements of the "actual world," do seem to me to have this dubious character. If the "existence" of a real number is doubtful when it is conceived as a special *kind* of thing, is its "existence" better warranted when it is identified with an *infinite series* of rationals? Again, Russell is not sure that classes "exist." But, in his translations of statements ostensibly about classes, he does not hesitate to introduce existential quantifiers with respect to *properties*—a procedure which requires him to assume the existence of an indeterminate *range* of properties. Is this assumption, construed in the "realistic" fashion that Russell adopts, so obvious that it may safely be taken as a metaphysical foundation for mathematics? I am not suggesting that Russell's definitions are not adequate for the purposes of systematizing formal mathematics; and fortunately I am not required on this occasion to propose a more satisfactory "metaphysics" for mathematics than his. I raise these questions only to call attention to the complex issues which await us when we employ his supreme maxim of philosophizing in a metaphysical rather than a methodological spirit.

II

1. Russell's concern with the positive sciences is dominated almost exclusively by "the problem of the relation between the crude data of sense and the space, time, and matter of mathematical physics."[11] Like many of his contemporaries, he has been impressed by the highly abstract character of physical theory, and by the *prima facie* difference between the manifest traits of the world which are exhibited in our daily experience with it and its constitution as reported by the theoretical sciences. The theories of classical physics already provided ample materials for embroidering this difference; those theories employed such notions as that of instantaneous velocities, point-particles, mathematically continuous motions, and perfectly rigid and elastic bodies, although there appears to be nothing in our

[11] *OKEW*, viii.

common experience to which these notions are applicable. But it was the advent of relativity theory and quantum mechanics, with their novel geometries and chronometries and their revolutionary conceptions of matter and causality, which supplied the chief stimulus to Russell's preoccupation with the problem.

However, the "critique of abstractions" for which the problem apparently calls may take several different forms. Russell's conception of the task of such a critique is controlled entirely by his view that the familiar concrete objects of daily life, no less than the abstract and remote entities of theoretical physics, are logical constructions. His approach to the problem must be clearly differentiated from so-called "operational" or "functional" analyses of scientific concepts—analyses which take "common-sense" knowledge and "common-sense" objects for granted. Something must therefore be said at the outset about the general pattern of Russell's views.

Like most philosophers, Russell believes that any discussion of the relation between theoretical physics and experience starts with admitting the familiar facts of common knowledge. But he maintains that on the one hand this knowledge is vague, complex, and inexact, and that on the other hand some types of its "data" are more certain and more "indubitable" than others. In order to obtain a secure foundation for knowledge we must therefore separate out those beliefs which are "inferred" from or "caused" by other beliefs, from the beliefs which are both logically and psychologically prior to all others. The "hardest" or "most certain" of all data (that is, data which "resist the solvent influence of critical reflection") are the truths of logic and the particular facts of sense.[12] The logical starting point of a philosophical inquiry into physics must therefore be with our immediate, direct perceptions. The problem of the relation of theoretical physics to the facts of experience can therefore be amplified as follows:

The laws of physics are believed to be at least approximately true, though they are not logically necessary; the evidence for them is empirical. All empirical evidence consists, in the last analysis, of perceptions; thus the world of physics must be, in some sense, continuous

[12] *OKEW*, 75.

with the world of perceptions, since it is the latter which supplies the evidence for the laws of physics. . . .

The evidence for the truth of physics is that our perceptions occur as the laws of physics would lead us to expect—e.g., we see an eclipse when the astronomers say there will be an eclipse. But physics never says anything about perceptions; it does not say that we shall see an eclipse, but something about the sun and the moon. The passage from what physics asserts to the expected perception is left vague and casual; it has none of the mathematical precision belonging to physics itself. We must therefore find an interpretation of physics which gives a due place to perceptions; if not, we have no right to appeal to the empirical world.[13]

Russell's problem has therefore a two-fold aspect. One phase of it consists in finding an "interpretation" for physics which will make its propositions relevant to the crude materials of sense; and, as will appear, this concern leads Russell to adopt the view that all the objects of common-sense and developed science are logical constructions out of *events*—our perceptions being a proper sub-class of the class of events. The other phase of the problem consists in justifying the truth-claims of physics; and this concern leads Russell to examine what data may serve as the most indubitable foundation for our knowledge, and to a discussion of the causal theory of perception as the ground for assuming the existence of events that are not perceptions. The two aspects of the problem are not independent, since the resolution of the second depends in part on the answer to the first, whereas the first requires that the "indubitable entities" (which it is the business of the second to specify) are already available. However, in the remainder of the present section I shall briefly examine some of Russell's views on perceptive knowledge; the discussion of his analysis of scientific objects will be left for the final section.

2. According to Russell, the original datum of experience consists of perceptions which are held to be known "non-inferentially;" included in this original datum are such items as specific shapes and colors, and relations like something being earlier than something else or something being above something

else. Common-sense objects like tables and books, on the other hand, must be regarded as in some sense "inferred." They are said to be "inferred," not because we have actually inferred them, but because our knowledge of them rests upon correlations between perceptions. These correlations are not invariable, and since we may be led to entertain false expectations by relying on them we do not "genuinely know" common-sense objects.[14] The proper comment upon this conclusion, so it seems to me, is to insist that we sometimes *do* know physical objects like tables and chairs, in a perfectly good and familiar sense of "know," in spite of the fact that we may sometimes be deceived about them. But this is not the issue I now wish to raise, important though it is. The question I want to put is whether, in distinguishing between perceptions as primitive and physical objects as derivative from perceptions, Russell is doing logic or psychology. Russell's *problem* certainly requires the distinction to be one of logic, for his aim is to *define* physical objects in terms of sensory qualities. From this point of view it is clearly *irrelevant* whether in the genesis of our knowledge the apprehension of discrete sensory qualities comes before or after the apprehension of configurations of qualities. Russell himself frequently makes it plain that it is not questions of psychology with which he is concerned.[15] Nevertheless, he also says that the primitive data of knowledge must not only be logically but also psychologically prior to the knowledge he regards as derivative. Thus, he declares that the "space" into which all the percepts of one person fit is a "constructed space, *the construction being achieved during the first months of life.*"[16] And here Russell is obviously talking psychology. However that may be, the empirical evidence drawn from modern psychology is certainly unfavorable to the notion that perceptions are psychologically primitive. On the contrary, that evidence supports the view that sensory qualities and relations are obtained only as the end-products of a

---

[14] *AM*, 186.

[15] See, for example, his quite explicit statement on this point in his "Professor Dewey's 'Essays in Experimental Logic'," *The Journal of Philosophy*, Vol. XVI (1919), 8 ff.

[16] *AM*, 252, italics not in the text.

deliberate process of discrimination and analysis, a process which is carried on within the framework of a "common-sense" knowledge of physical objects.

What reasons are there for regarding perceptions as the most indubitable data of knowledge? As far as one can ascertain, Russell rests his case on the simple dictum that what is more primitive is also the more certain. Thus, he asserts that

> When we reflect upon the beliefs which are logically but not psychologically primitive, we find that, unless they can on reflection be deduced by a logical process from beliefs which are also psychologically primitive, our confidence in their truth tends to diminish the more we think about them.

And he concludes that "There is . . . more need of justifying our psychologically derivative beliefs than of justifying those that are primitive."[17] Why should this be so? Russell's answer is: because the derivative beliefs are non-demonstratively "inferred" from the primitive ones and are therefore less certain than the premises from which they are drawn, and because a belief is the more certain the "shorter" is the causal route from the cause of a belief to the belief.[18]

These views seem to me to rest on unsatisfactory evidence. Russell calls those data "hard" which resist the solvent influence of critical reflection. But in order to undertake such reflection, it is necessary to employ *some* principles in terms of which the attribution of "hardness" to specific data is to be evaluated; and such principles, if their authority is to count for anything, must be better warranted than the materials under judgment. However, such principles can themselves be warranted only by the outcome of our general experience, and their certainty—of whatever degree this may be—cannot therefore be a consequence of their being psychologically primitive. Russell's entire argument, moreover, is based on a principle of reasoning which I find most debatable—the principle that the conclusion of a non-

---

[17] *OKEW*, 74-5.

[18] *IMT*, 164, 200. He also says: ". . . A given reaction may be regarded as knowledge of various different occurrences. . . . The nearer our starting point [in the process leading to a certain event in the brain] is to the brain, the more accurate becomes the knowledge displayed in our reactions." *P*, 132.

demonstrative inference cannot be more certain than any of its premisses. Quite the contrary appears to be the case in general. To take a simple illustration, if a number of witnesses testify to the occurrence of some event, the proposition that the event did occur may be more certain than any single item in the testimony, provided those items are independent. It is indeed partly in terms of the principle embodied in this example that the credibility of scientific theories is augmented. And if one accepts it as generally valid, little ground remains for the view that our psychologically primitive beliefs are also our most certain ones.[19]

Russell is not unaware of how difficult it is to identify primitive, "non-inferred" data. Thus, he notes that the records of any observation or experiment always involve an "interpretation" of the facts by the help of a certain amount of theory. He also acknowledges that "perceptions of which we are not sufficiently conscious to express them in words are scientifically negligible; our premisses must be facts which we have explicitly noted."[20] And elsewhere he insists that "a form of words is a social phenomenon," so that a person must know the language of which it is a part, as well as be exposed to certain stimuli, if he is to make true assertions.[21] The admission of the socially conditioned character of significant perception would normally be considered as a good ground for rejecting the view that perceptions are psychologically primitive. Nevertheless, Russell believes that it is possible to whittle away the element of interpretation in perceptive knowledge, and that "we can approach asymptotically to the pure datum."[22] But if pure data can be reached only asymptotically—and that means they are never *actually* reached—why is it important to try to base all our knowledge upon them? Moreover, Russell admits that some "interpretations" which accompany perceptions "can only be

---

[19] On some of the difficulties in the view that the "shortness" of the causal route between a belief and its cause can be taken as a measure of the certainty of the belief, see my "Mr. Russell on Meaning and Truth," *The Journal of Philosophy*, Vol. XXXVIII (1941).

[20] *AM*, 200.

[21] *P*, 262.

[22] *IMT*, 155.

discovered by careful theory, and can never be made intro-spectively obvious;" and he thinks that such interpretations, at any rate, "ought to be included in the perception."[23] One cannot therefore help asking: If our actual data involve an element of "interpretation" and "inference," how in principle can we exclude physical objects as objects of knowledge on the ground that physical objects involve an element of "inference?" The distinction between the primitive and the "inferred" cer-tainly shows the mark of being irrelevant to a working epis-temology.

In any event, by his mixing up questions of logic with those of psychology Russell compromises at the very outset his pro-gram of exhibiting common-sense and scientific objects as logical constructions. That program presumably requires the analysis of these objects as structures of elements which are experien-tially accessible. If such an analysis is to be more than a formal logical exercise, those elements cannot simply be *postulated* to exist; and Russell's psychologically primitive "pure data" apparently have just this status.

3. Russell introduces another distracting confusion when, in order to establish the importance of regarding physical objects as constructions, he argues the case for an epistemological dual-ism and against "naïve realism." The truth or falsity of epis-temological dualism does not seem to me germane to the question whether physical objects are analyzable into structures of specified entities. I shall therefore comment only briefly on the following views central to Russell's epistemology: that our percepts are located in our brains; that the causal theory of perception is the ground for inferring the existence of un-perceived events; and that our knowledge of physical objects is "inferred" from percepts in our brain.

Russell maintains that, although it may be natural to suppose that what a physiologist sees when he is observing a living brain is in the brain he is observing, in fact "if we are speaking of physical space, what the physiologist sees is in his own brain."[24] This seems to me incredibly wrong if the word "see" is being

[23] *AM*, 189.
[24] *P*, 140.

used in the ordinary sense in which we talk about seeing a physical object; and it is this ordinary sense of the word which Russell is employing when he supposes a physiologist to be observing a brain. There might indeed be a sense of "see" in which I see my own brain, though I have not the slightest inkling as to what that sense is. I do know, however, that I have never seen any portion of my own brain, and that I have seen many physical objects—where the statement that I have not seen one but seen the other is to be understood in the customary sense of "see." To deny the facts expressed by the statement seems to be absurd; and such a denial can be understood only if we suppose that the person making the denial is misusing language. Moreover, such facts seem to me basic for every sound epistemology and every sound interpretation of science; and, however difficult it may be to do so, the findings of physics and physiology must be interpreted so as to square with them.

The evidence Russell offers for the causal theory of perception derives whatever plausibility it has from the tacit assumptions of common-sense knowledge; accordingly, it is not this theory which can justify such common-sense assumptions as that our perceptions may have unperceived causes. Russell's chief argument for that theory consists in showing that if we accept the theory we can formulate the course of events in "simple causal laws." For example, he declares that if many people see and hear a gun fired, the further they are situated from it the longer is the interval between the seeing and the hearing. He thinks it is therefore "natural to suppose that the sound travels over the intervening space, in which case something must be happening even in places where there is no one with ears to hear."[25] But why does it seem "natural" to suppose this? Does not the "naturalness" receive its support from the experimental confirmations which are found for such assumptions in the context of our manipulating physical objects? Russell also thinks that, although the phenomenalist view (that there are no unperceived events) is not logically impossible, it is an implausible view, because it is incompatible with physical determinism.[26] But why is the assumption implausible that

[25] *AM*, 209.
[26] *AM*, 214.

"imaginary" or "fictitious" entities are causally efficacious? If the implausibility does not rest upon the findings of disciplined experience, embodied in common-sense knowledge, upon what can it rest?

Though Russell speaks much of "inferring" things, it is not clear in what sense he believes physical objects to be "inferred" from perceptions. He uses the term "inference" in at least the following distinct ways: in the ordinary sense of logically deducing one proposition from another; in the familiar sense of asserting a proposition on evidence which makes that proposition probable; in the sense in which something which is perceived with an "accompanying interpretation" is obtained from something else that is supposed to be perceived directly or without interpretation; and finally, in the sense in which something that is a logical construction is obtained from entities out of which it is constructed. It is evident that when Russell says that the sun is inferred from our percepts, he does not mean that it is inferred in either of the first two senses specified, and he repeatedly asserts that he does not mean it in these senses. On the other hand, he declares that

So long as naïve realism remained tenable, perception was knowledge of a physical object, obtained through the senses, not by inference. But in accepting the causal theory of perception we have committed ourselves to the view that perception gives no immediate knowledge of a physical object, but at best a datum for inference.[27]

In this passage Russell is apparently using the third sense of "inference;" and when he uses the term in this way he sometimes talks of an inference as an unconscious physiological process. But elsewhere he also says that "Modern physics reduces matter to a set of events. . . . The events that take the place of matter in the old sense are inferred from their effect on eyes, photographic plates, and other instruments. . . ."[28] And in this passage what is "inferred" is a physical object,

[27] *AM*, 218. Cf. also: "Our knowledge of the physical world is not at first inferential, but this is only because we take our percepts to *be* the physical world." *P*, 130.

[28] *P*, 157.

viewed as a construction out of such events as perceptions. Russell does not therefore distinguish between the last two senses of "inference" listed above, and as a consequence it is difficult to extract a coherent formulation of how physical objects are inferred from percepts. However that may be, if our knowledge of the sun is "inferred" in the third sense of the term, the inference is presumably grounded in the causal theory of perception, and therefore in the procedures involved in common-sense knowledge of things. On the other hand, if that knowledge is "inferential" in the fourth sense, the fact that the sun is a logical construction (if it is a fact) in no way prejudices the claim that we do have knowledge of it; for the exhibition of the sun as a construction out of events like perceptions obviously requires knowledge of the sun.

III

1. It is a common error of Russell's critics to interpret his view that the physical world is a logical construction, as if he intended to deny that there are physical objects in the ordinary sense of this phrase. For this misunderstanding he is at least partly to blame. Thus he declares: "Common sense imagines that when it sees a table it sees a table. This is gross delusion."[29] Again, commenting on Dr. Johnson's refutation of Berkeley, he maintains that "If he had known that his foot never touched the stone, and that both were only complicated systems of wave-motions, he might have been less satisfied with his refutation."[30] And elsewhere he says that on the view he is recommending, "the 'pushiness' of matter disappears altogether. . . . 'Matter' is a convenient formula for describing what happens where it isn't."[31]

There are indeed several not always compatible tendencies struggling for mastery in Russell's use of his supreme maxim for philosophizing. One of them is that represented by the conception of experience according to which the objects of what is immediately "known" are in the brain; a second is the view

[29] *ABC*, 213.
[30] *P*, 279.
[31] *P*, 159.

that if something is a logical construction, it is *we* who have constructed it in time; another is stated by the conception that so long as some "indubitable set of objects" can be specified which will satisfy given formulae, then any object in that set may be substituted for the "inferred" object satisfying those formulae; and a fourth is the view that an object is a construction when it is *analyzable* into a structure of identifiable elements.

It has already been argued that the first of these tendencies is essentially irrelevant to (or at any rate, can be kept distinct from) the use of Russell's maxim. The second is often explicitly disavowed by Russell himself, though he often betrays his disavowal. But before examining the incidence of the remaining two tendencies upon his reconstruction of physical theory, I want to comment on the passages cited from Russell in the opening paragraph of this section. Is it a delusion when, under appropriate circumstances, we claim to see a table? A table may indeed be a logical construction; but in the sense in which we ordinarily use the words "see" and "table," it may be quite true that we do see a table: this mode of expressing what is happening is the appropriate way of putting the matter. Again, if when Dr. Johnson kicked a stone his foot never touched the stone, what *did* his foot do? To say that his foot never touched the stone, because both his foot and the stone were systems of radiation, is to *misuse* language; for in the specified context the words "foot," "stone," "kicked," and "touched" are being so used that it is correct to say Dr. Johnson kicked a stone and therefore his foot touched it. To be sure, under some other circumstances, and for the sake of certain ends, it might be advisable to use a different language in describing what had happened. But it obviously cannot be wrong to employ ordinary language in accordance with ordinary usage. And finally, it seems to me grotesque to say that the "pushiness" of matter can disappear as a consequence of a new analysis or redefinition of matter. We have learned to apply the word "pushy" to certain identifiable characteristics of material objects; and such a use of the word is correct, simply because that is the usage that had been established for it. Whatever may be the outcome of analyzing material objects, their identifiable properties will remain their identifiable properties, and it will be correct to apply the standardized expressions to them. It will certainly not be correct to designate a physical body as a formula.

2. Let us turn to Russell's re-interpretation of physics. The first question I want to ask is what marks, if any, distinguish something which is a construction from something that is not. Russell seems to suggest at least two. One is the suggestion that something is a construction when it has properties which satisfy some mathematical formula or equation. He says, for example,

The electron has very convenient properties, and is therefore probably a logical structure upon which we concentrate attention just because of these properties. A rather haphazard set of particulars may be capable of being collected into groups each of which has very agreeable smooth mathematical properties; but we have no right to suppose Nature so kind to the mathematician as to have created particulars with just such properties as he would wish to find.[32]

One doesn't know how seriously to take such statements, especially since they imply, what is questionably the case, that it is we who invariably manufacture the properties which are convenient for the purposes of mathematical physics. It is certainly not evident what right we have to suppose that we have no right to suppose that Nature created at least some of them. It is one thing to say that for the sake of developing mathematical physics we have *isolated* certain features of things and ignored others; it is quite another thing to maintain that what we have selected we have also manufactured. Moreover, it is not clear why, on this criterion, the events out of which electrons and other objects are said to be constructions should not themselves be regarded as constructions. After all, as will be seen presently, they too have remarkably smooth mathematical properties: they fall into groups having exquisitely neat internal structures.

The second suggestion is more important. According to it, something is a construction when it is complex. Accordingly, since physical bodies as well as scientific objects like electrons

[32] *AM*, 319. At another place Russell proposes as a supplement to Occam's razor the principle "What is logically convenient is likely to be artificial." *AM*, 290.

are analyzable—indeed, on Russell's view into relations between ultimate simples—whereas perceptions and other events are not, the former are constructions out of the latter. The "ultimate furniture of the world" thus consists of a very large, perhaps infinite, number of events which have various specific relations to each other. When described in terms of spatio-temporal characteristics, these "particulars" are assumed to have quite small spatial and temporal dimensions. Moreover, some of these particulars (though not all) are perceived, and at least some of their qualities and relations are also immediately apprehended. Events, their simple qualities and their relations, are thus the building materials, the "crude data," in terms of which physics is to be "interpreted."

Russell admits that, although he believes his particulars are simples, in the sense that they have no "parts" or internal "structure," it is impossible to prove once for all that they are such. And although he also admits that simples are not directly experienced "but known only inferentially as the limit of analysis," he maintains it is desirable to exhibit objects as constructions out of simples. His belief in the existence of simples rests on self-evidence: "It seems obvious to me . . . that what is complex must be composed of simples, though the number of constituents may be infinite."[33] Against such a view it is arguable that simplicity is a relative and systemic notion, and that the justification for taking anything to be a simple rests on the clarification, the systematization, or the control of subject-matter which follows from a given mode of analysis. The issue is, however, not of great importance for the sequel. An issue of more serious concern is raised by Russell's admission that simples can be known only as the limits of analysis. For in the first place, he must also admit that we cannot in consequence literally *begin* with simples, trace through sequentially the complex patterns of their inter-relations, and so finally reach the familiar objects of daily life. And in the second place, it becomes difficult to understand, even if we did succeed in exhibiting objects as constructions out of simples, just what such an analysis contributes to bridging the gulf between the propositions of physics and the familiar world

[33] *CBP*, 375.

of daily experience. However, Russell's subsequent analyses are not vitally affected by these doubts: whether events are ultimate particulars or not, the important part of his claim is that at least some of them are perceptions, and that they are relevant to the analysis only because of their relations to other things, and not because of a demonstrated lack of internal structure.[34]

One point is clear: Russell does not exhibit the logical structure of the physical world *entirely* in terms of entities which he regards as "known," since his particulars include events that are not perceptions. Such events are held by him to be "inferred," largely on the strength of the causal theory of perception and in order to avoid the "implausible" consequences of a radical phenomenalism. Russell's own remark on the inclusion of unperceived (and therefore "inferred") events into the ultimate furniture of the world is one that many of his readers must have whispered to themselves: "If we have once admitted unperceived events, there is no very obvious reason for picking and choosing among the events which physics leads us to infer."[35] How many needless excursions into sterile epistemological speculations could have been avoided if this remark had been taken seriously! But the remark does make it plain that the significance of exhibiting things as constructions does not consist in circumventing the need for making inferences or in denying the existence of physical objects. The remark shows that the importance of the enterprise lies in *analyzing* or *defining* the sense of such expressions as "physical object," "point," "electron," and so on.

3. Russell's definition of physical object as a class of classes of events, related by certain laws of "perspective" and causal laws, is well known. It is unnecessary to dwell upon it here. It is sufficient to note that his analysis is motivated by the desire to show the otiose character of the traditional assumption of

[34] Russell declares in this connection: "Atoms were formerly particulars; now they have ceased to be so. But that has not falsified the chemical propositions that can be enunciated without taking account of their structure." *AM*, 278. The first sentence in this passage is seriously misleading, since it suggests that whether something is a particular or not depends on the state of our knowledge, and that therefore a construction is something made by us.

[35] *AM*, 325.

permanent, indestructible substances which mysteriously under-
lie the flux of events. I shall, however, examine his analysis of
points (or point-instants), in order to suggest what seems to
me a fundamental criticism of the approach to the "critique of
abstractions" which Russell credits to, and shares with, Whitehead.

There is an obvious need for an analysis of points, if we are
to become clear about the way in which the formulations of
theoretical science are applied to matters of concrete experience.
The term occurs in physical geometry, mathematical dynamics,
and many other theories; and these theories are admittedly
successful in organizing and predicting the course of events. At
the same time, there seems to be nothing in our experience
which corresponds to the term. The postulation of points as
unique types of existences will not solve the problem, since
such a postulation does not answer the question just how points
are connected with the gross materials of experience. As Russell
says, "What we know about points is that they are useful technically—so useful that we must seek an interpretation of the
propositions in which, symbolically, they occur." His own answer
to the problem consists in specifying certain "structures having
certain geometrical properties and composed of the raw material
of the physical world."[36]

In outline, Russell's definition of point-instants is as follows:
Every event is "compresent" with a number of others; i.e.,
every event has a common "region" with an indefinite number
of other events, although the latter do not necessarily overlap
with each other. If five events are compresent with each other,
they are said to be related by the relation called "co-punctuality."
If in a group of five or more events every set of five events
has the relation of co-punctuality, the group is said to be co-
punctual. And finally, if a co-punctual group cannot be enlarged
without losing its co-punctual character, the group is called a
"point." It only remains to show that points so defined exist;
and to show this it is sufficient to assume that "all events (or at
least all events co-punctual with a given co-punctual quintet)
can be well-ordered"—an assumption that Russell proceeds to

[36] *AM*, 290, 294.

make.[37] And since it turns out that points thus specified satisfy all the usual mathematical requirements, Russell believes he has satisfactorily exhibited the logical construction of points.

Nevertheless, the analysis is to me very perplexing. Let me first call attention to an observation already made. Events, in the sense in which Russell uses the term, are the *termini* of analysis, and if they are apprehended by us at all they are not apprehended as psychological primitives. In this sense, therefore, events are not the "raw materials" of adult experience, whatever else might be the case for infants and other animals. If a point is what Russell defines it to be, the physicist who wishes to make a concrete application of statements about points must therefore first proceed to *isolate* the material (events) in terms of which points are to be eventually identified. In order to carry through this process, the physicist will certainly have to make use of the distinctions and findings of gross, macroscopic experience. But this is not all. Assuming that events have been isolated, co-punctual groups of events must next be found. However, since a co-punctual group may have an indefinite number of event-members, the assertion that a given group is co-punctual will in general be a *hypothesis*. The situation does not become easier when the physicist next tries to identify those co-punctual groups which are points: the assertion that a class of events is a point will be a conjecture for which only the most incomplete sort of evidence can be available. If, as Russell believes, the existence of physical objects involves "inference," those inferences pale in comparison with the inferences required to assert the existence of points.

I now come to the serious basis of my perplexity: Russell's definition exhibits no concern whatever for the way in which physicists *actually use* expressions like "point." In the first place, it is certainly not evident that physicists do in fact apply the term to structures of events. On the contrary, there is some evidence to show that they employ it in a somewhat different fashion, using it in connection with bodies identifiable in gross experience and whose magnitudes vary from case to case ac-

---

[37] *AM*, 299. A class is said to be well-ordered if its members can be serially arranged in such a way that every sub-class in this series has a first member.

cording to the needs of specific problems. To be sure, the application of the term is frequently sloppy and vague, and its rules cannot in general be made precise. But the vagueness and sloppiness are facts which a philosophy of science must face squarely, and they cannot be circumvented by an ingenious but essentially irrelevant proposal as to how the term *might* be used.

This brings me to another phase of the difficulty. It has already been noted that Russell does not always distinguish between two distinct views as to what is required in order to exhibit the logical structure of an object: on one of them, the logical construction of an object is exhibited when some "indubitable set of objects" is specified which satisfies a given formula; on the other view, the logical construction of an object is exhibited when statements about that object are so interpreted that the interpretations make explicit how those statements are *used* (or alternately, what those statements "mean"). The difference between these views is profound; and if the supreme maxim of philosophizing is to eventuate in clarification and not simply in a highly ingenious symbolic construction, it is the second view which must be adopted. Certainly Russell himself must have imagined himself to be acting upon this second view when he claimed that his account of the cardinal numbers made intelligible their application to the world of countable objects. On the other hand, his definition of points and other scientific objects conforms only to the requirements of the first view, and thereby offers no indication of the connection between the abstractions of physics and the familiar world. Like the definitions given by Whitehead with the aid of the principle of extensive abstraction, Russell's definitions formulate what are in effect another set of abstract formulae, quite out of touch with the accessible materials of the world. His "interpretation" of the equations of physics thus yields only another mathematical system, with respect to which the same problems that initiated the entire analysis emerge once more.[38]

---

[38] One need only compare Russell's definitions of points with such analyses as those of Mach concerning mass and temperature or those of N. R. Campbell concerning physical measurement, to appreciate the difference between an analysis which is quasi-mathematics and an analysis which is directed toward actual usage.

4. One further set of general issues remains to be discussed. One of these issues arises in connection with Russell's redefinition of matter (common-sense objects, electrons, etc.) so as to avoid the hypothesis of an underlying permanent substance. He declares:

The events out of which we have been constructing the physical world are very different from matter as traditionally understood. Matter was expected to be impenetrable and indestructible. The matter that we construct is impenetrable as a result of definition: the matter in a place is all the events that are there, and consequently no other event or piece of matter can be there. This is a tautology, not a physical fact. . . . Indestructibility, on the other hand, is an empirical property, believed to be approximately but not exactly possessed by matter. . . .[39]

And elsewhere he asserts that "Impenetrability used to be a noble property of matter, a kind of Declaration of Independence; now it is a merely tautological result of the way in which matter is defined."[40] Russell is of course right in calling attention to the fact that many propositions in physics as well as in everyday discourse are not contingent, since they are definitional in nature. It is not always clear which propositions have this character, and the difficulty in identifying them arises partly from the fact that the body of our knowledge can be organized in different ways. For example, if the equality in weight of two objects is defined in terms of their being in equilibrium when placed at the extremities of a lever which is supported at its midpoint, the law of the lever is a truistic consequence of this mode of measuring weights. But if the principle of the lever is now

---

It is also interesting to note that Russell criticizes one of Eddington's interpretations of certain equations in relativity theory in a spirit analogous to the criticism which the above paragraph makes of him. Eddington reads these equations to signify that electrons adjust their dimensions to the radius of curvature of the universe, and maintains that this adjustment can be ascertained by "direct measurement." Russell's remarks are as follows: "Now the electron may be, theoretically, a perfect spatial unit, but we certainly cannot compare its size with that of larger bodies *directly*, without assuming any previous physical knowledge. It seems that Prof. Eddington is postulating an ideal observer, who can see electrons just as directly as . . . we can see a metre rod. In short his 'direct measurement' is an operation as abstract and theoretical as his mathematical symbolism." *AM*, 92.

[39] *AM*, 385.

[40] *P*, 279. See also *ABC*, 185, and *CBP*, 366.

a definition, the law of spring balances (Hooke's law) is not, and is empirically contingent. It is, however, possible to define the equality of weights in terms of Hooke's law, so that, although this law now becomes a definition, the law of the lever acquires the status of a contingent physical principle. Accordingly, to say that a law is a convention or tautology requires supplementation by a specification of its function in a particular systematization of physics, where the system of physics as a whole is not itself accepted on definitional grounds. It is thus not obvious that in every use of the words "impenetrability" and "matter," the impenetrability of matter is a logically necessary truth. For example, it is an empirical fact that a mixture of equal volumes of alcohol and water occupies a volume less than the arithmetical sum of the two, whereas a mixture of two equal volumes of water occupies a volume equal to this sum. If the concept of impenetrability is applied to this case, the impenetrability of matter appears to be a contingent truth. The point is, of course, that an "interpretation" of physics which leads to equating a logically necessary proposition with one that is contingent cannot be correct.[41]

[41] Russell is often careless in some of his judgments as to which propositions are definitional. His definition of physical object leads him to say that "Things are those series of aspects which obey the laws of physics," (*OKEW*, 117), from which it would seem to follow that the laws of physics are definitions. Indeed, he does say that "Almost all the 'great principles' of traditional physics turn out to be like the 'great law' that there are always three feet to a yard," (*ABC*, 221). This is palpably absurd when taken without serious qualifications, and in this connection one must remind Russell of one of his own jibes against certain philosophers: "Dr. Schiller says that the external world was first discovered by a low marine animal he calls 'Grumps', who swallowed a bit of rock that disagreed with him, and argued that he would not have given himself such a pain, and therefore there must be an external world. One is tempted to think that, at the time when Professor Dewey wrote, many people in the newer countries had not yet made the disagreeable experience which Grumps made. Meanwhile, whatever accusation pragmatists may bring, I shall continue to protest that it was not I who made the world." In "Professor Dewey's 'Essays in Experimental Logic'," *The Journal of Philosophy*, Vol. XVI (1919), 26. On the other hand, Russell himself recognizes the limitations in the view that physics is a huge tautology. In a penetrating brief critique of Eddington, he notes that the allegedly tautological character of the principles of the conservation of mass and of momentum holds only "in the deductive system [of physics]: in their empirical meanings these laws are by no means logical necessities." *AM*, 89.

A second general issue arises in connection with a technical detail in Russell's interpretation of physics. If the objects of theoretical physics are all constructions, then the symbols referring to them in the statements of physics are theoretically *eliminable.* Unfortunately, Russell has not formulated the translations of the requisite sort for specific statements which occur in treatises (e.g., statements like "Zinc arsenite is insoluble in water"), although he has of course indicated the general procedure to be followed in constructing such translations. There are, however, fairly good reasons for doubting whether the elimination of symbols for constructs can be carried through without introducing assumptions of a dubious character. These reasons are based on the fact that in various parts of mathematics as well as in the empirical sciences certain expressions are usually so defined that in general they cannot be eliminated by the help of methods customarily accepted. For example, so-called "functor-expressions" like "the sum of," are often defined recursively, so that such expressions cannot be eliminated from statements like "The sum of x and y is equal to the sum of y and x." And if the so-called "dispositional predicates," like "soluble," are introduced into physics by the help of conditional definitions, as Carnap has suggested, an analogous difficulty arises with respect to them. To be sure, the desired elimination can be effected, provided we are willing to employ variables of a sufficiently high type; but the use of such variables appears to involve an "ontology" which it is not easy to accept. In particular, if we recall Russell's definition of classes and his view that a physical body is a class of classes of events, a statement about a body must finally be replaced by a statement about a property of properties—that is, about a property which is at least of type two. But does the assumption that there is such a property contribute much toward "assimilating" physics to the crude materials of perception? It seems to me, therefore, that, instead of making the elimination of symbols for constructs the goal of the logical analysis of physics, a more reasonable and fruitful objective would be the following: to render explicit the pattern of interconnections between constructs and observations, on the strength of which these latter can function as relevant evidence for theories about the former.

I have been stressing throughout this essay the limitations of Russell's approach to the logical problems of science, and I have not thought it worth while to underscore their well-known excellencies. No student of his writings can fail to acknowledge the great service Russell's analyses have rendered to an adequate understanding of the mathematical sciences. He has made plain the highly selective character of physical theories, as well as the intricate transformations and reorganizations of sensory material which are involved in their use. He has exhibited the semi-arbitrary character of many symbolic constructions and the definitional nature of many physical propositions; and he has devised powerful techniques for isolating, and in some measure reducing, such arbitrariness and conventionality. Russell has not said the last word upon these matters; but he has certainly inspired a great multitude of students to try to say a better one. If the example of his own splendid devotion to independent thinking counts for anything, it is safe to believe that he would not prefer to have a different estimate placed upon his efforts.

ERNEST NAGEL

DEPARTMENT OF PHILOSOPHY
COLUMBIA UNIVERSITY

II

W. T. Stace

RUSSELL'S NEUTRAL MONISM

11

RUSSELL'S NEUTRAL MONISM

I. NEUTRAL MONISM IN GENERAL

BY neutral monism I understand the theory that mind and matter are not two radically different kinds of entities, but that both are constructed out of the same "stuff." It is not, of course, denied that there is *some* difference between the mental and the physical; since to deny this would be a patent absurdity. But it is alleged that the difference is one of *relations*, not of *stuffs*. The neutral stuff, or the bits of it which may be called neutral entities, may be arranged in different ways according to different types of relation. A group of neutral entities arranged in one way, by virtue of one set of relations, will be a piece of matter. The same neutral entities arranged in another way, by virtue of another set of relations, may constitute a mind or a series of mental events. The neutral entities considered by themselves, apart from either set of relations, are neither mental nor physical. That is why they are called neutral. Out of a given set of dominoes one may make either a square or a rectangle of unequal sides. There is, of course, a difference between the square and the rectangle. But the "stuff" of which each is made is the same, namely the dominoes. The difference lies in the spatial relations which order the dominoes in the two cases. This analogy with neutral monism is correct except that in the case of the square and the rectangle the two sets of relations are both spatial, whereas there is no version of neutral monism according to which the differentiating relations of the mental world are merely spatial. *What* are the ordering relations of the mental and material worlds respectively is one of the great questions for neutral monism—a question to which different versions of the theory may give different answers.

It follows from what has been said that any neutral monism must contain three parts:

(1) *A Theory of the Neutral Stuff*. This must tell us what kind of entities the neutral entities are.

(2) *A Theory of Matter*. The main question which this theory will have to answer will be: what kind of relations are the relations which, when they hold between a set of neutral entities, constitute that set a material object? It will have to show how the material object is constructed out of the neutral stuff by virtue of these relations.

(3) *A Theory of Mind*. The main question to be answered here will be: what kind of relations are those which, when they hold between a set of neutral entities, constitute that set a mind or a mental phenomenon? It will have to show how mental phenomena are constituted by these relations out of the neutral stuff.

There are different versions of neutral monism, and they differ just in the answers they give to these three questions. The most important versions are those of William James, the American neo-realists, and Russell. James, so far as I know, was the original inventor of the whole idea, and he set forth his version of it in his book *Essays in Radical Empiricism*.

Neutral monism appears to be inspired by two main motives. The first is to get rid of the psycho-physical dualism which has troubled philosophy since the time of Descartes. The second motive is empiricism. The "stuff" of the neutral monists is never any kind of hidden unperceivable "substance" or *Ding-an-sich*. It is never something which lies *behind* the phenomenal world, out of sight. It always, in every version of it, consists in some sort of directly perceivable entities—for instance, sensations, sense-data, colours, smells, sounds. Thus, if matter is wholly constructed out of any such directly experienceable stuff, there will be nothing in it which will not be empirically verifiable. The same will be true of mind.

II. The Development of Russell's Neutral Monism

The most complete single exposition of Russell's version of neutral monism is found in his book, *The Analysis of Mind*, published in 1921. But, as the title implies, the book is mainly concerned to develop that half of the theory which seeks to construct mental phenomena out of the neutral stuff. The theory of matter, which is the other half of Russell's neutral monism, is rapidly sketched in the same book; but for its more elaborate exposition we have to go back to Chapters 3 and 4 in his earlier book *Our Knowledge of the External World*, written in 1914. These two books will therefore be the chief sources on which I shall rely in this essay.[1] It is not certain that the theory of matter elaborated in the earlier book and that outlined in the later book are quite identical. But the differences, if any, are slight, and will not affect any of the contentions which I shall put forward in this paper.[2]

I shall not be concerned to discuss any opinions which Russell developed after 1921. I do not know whether he now maintains any of the views which will be the subject of examination here. And the question need not trouble us. For even if he should now repudiate the whole of his neutral monism, yet the opinions which constitute it, and which found expression between 1914 and 1921, were important in the development of twentieth century philosophy and, as such, are profoundly interesting and worthy of study.

[1] *The Analysis of Matter* (1928), though it is true that it contains some elements of neutral monism, belongs on the whole to a later phase of Russell's thought, in which scientific realism and the causal theory of perception have finally gained the upper hand. I understand that Russell himself does not recognize that there is any important difference between what I would thus distinguish as two phases of his thought. But I find it impossible to reconcile the emphatic assertion of the causal theory of perception which marks *The Analysis of Matter* with such a passage as the following, taken from *The Analysis of Mind* (98): "Why should we suppose that there is some one common cause of all these appearances? As we have just seen, the notion of 'cause' is not so reliable as to allow us to infer the existence of something that, by its very nature, can never be observed. . . . Instead of supposing that there is some unknown cause, the 'real' table, behind the different sensations of those who are said to be looking at the table, we may take the whole set of these sensations (together possibly with certain other particulars) as actually *being* the table." For these reasons I have excluded *The Analysis of Matter* from consideration in this article.

[2] One difference is that in the earlier book the account of matter is put forward tentatively as a "hypothetical construction" which is to fulfill certain functions, but does not necessarily claim to be true; whereas in the later book the same account is put forward as a theory claiming truth.

On the other hand Russell's writings before he published his neutral monism are of great interest to us since they disclose how it gradually developed. I shall briefly trace this development in the present section.

In *The Problems of Philosophy* (1912) Russell advocated theories which were remote from neutral monism. In the first place, he accepted Moore's distinction between the mental act of being aware and the sense-object *of* which one is aware. The former he called the *sensation*, the latter the *sense-datum*. This means that Russell was then a psycho-physical dualist, not a monist at all. In the second place, the theory of matter which this book contained was that of generative realism. When we perceive a material object, what we directly sense consists of sense-data. The qualities of these sense-data, both primary and secondary, are dependent upon two factors, the physical object on the one hand and our sense-organs, brain, nervous system, etc., on the other. Thus the redness of a red object is the effect of two joint causes, the physical object and the optical apparatus of the perceiver. And the apparent shape or size of the thing seen is likewise the effect of two joint causes, one of which is the physical object, the other the position in space of the body of the perceiver relatively to the object. And since the perceived qualities are thus dependent for their existence as much on the presence of a perceiving organism as on that of the physical object, it follows that the physical object *by itself* has none of these perceived qualities, either primary or secondary. It must, however, have some intrinsic properties, since otherwise it would be nothing at all. What can we know of its intrinsic properties? Nothing, except that they *correspond to* the perceived properties. There must be one quality corresponding to red, another to green. There must be one property corresponding to roundness, another to squareness. We may call these latter characters "shapes" if we like, but they can be no more like the sort of shapes we perceive than redness is like the intrinsic quality which corresponds to it. Presumably if we perceive one thing as larger than another, there must be between the two physical objects some real relation which corresponds to, but is quite unlike, what we mean by the perceived relation of "larger than." Of what sort these intrinsic qualities and relations are in themselves we cannot form the slightest idea.

To transform the ideas of *The Problems of Philosophy* into neutral monism two revolutionary changes are required. First, as regards the theory of matter, the physical object conceived as the cause (or part-cause) of sense-data must be got rid of, and we must be left with nothing but the sense-data, "aspects" or "appearances," themselves. The sum total of these must then be declared to *be* the piece of matter. (Russell never did arrive at *exactly* this phenomenalistic standpoint, but as a first rough approximation to a statement of his later position it will do.) The second change required will concern the theory of mind. It must consist in the repudiation of the mental act of awareness (or any other kind of mental act) as distinguished from the sense-datum, in other words the repudiation of "consciousness." Mind and the mental will then have to be identified with some arrangement of the sense-data, aspects, or appearances which also, in the new scheme, are to be constitutive of matter.

Russell did not make both these leaps at once. In the first edition of *Our Knowledge of the External World* (1914) the dualistic belief in consciousness is retained. But there now appears for the first time the more or less phenomenalistic theory of matter which was later, in *The Analysis of Mind,* to be incorporated into the author's neutral monism. Thus one half of his neutral monism, namely the theory of matter, was thought out first, and the second half, namely the theory of mind, came seven years later. He was not yet, in 1914, a neutral monist.

The new theory of matter is complicated and I do not propose to expound it in detail here. I shall assume that my reader is acquainted with it. I shall merely tabulate those essential features of it which are necessary to the understanding of what is to follow.

The theory of matter expounded in *The Problems of Philosophy* conceived that there are, in regard to every piece of matter, two things to be taken into account. The first is the physical object itself with its intrinsic properties, the nature of which we can never know. The second is the sense-data, aspects, or appearances which we perceive. It may help us imaginatively if we conceive of the physical object as a centre or nucleus, with the sense-data, aspects, or appearances existing in rings all around it. We now strike out the nuclear physical object and we declare the rings of sense-data to *be* the piece of matter. It just *is* the sum of its appearances. But a peculiar and essential part of Russell's new view is that the appearances or aspects which now constitute the material object do not exist at the place where the material object is (i.e., at the place where it is ordinarily supposed to be) but rather at the places where they are, or could be, perceived. The circular brown sense-datum which is the appearance of a penny as seen by an eye one foot from "the place where the penny is" is, not at "the place where the penny is," but on the contrary at the place where the eye or brain of the perceiver is. A foot to the right of his head there exists in empty space an unseen elliptical aspect of the penny, and if he moves his head there he will see that aspect. Ten feet away from "the place where the penny is," along the straight line passing through the centre of the penny at right angles to its flat surfaces, there will be a circular aspect of the penny, which will be considerably smaller than the one the perceiver saw when his head was a foot from the penny. When he moves his head to this more distant point in space he will see this smaller round appearance. Thus the aspects of the penny are spread out all over space. And at "the place where the penny is" (in ordinary speech) there is nothing, only a "hollow centre." In this account I have, for the sake of simplicity, neglected the fact that the public space in terms of which the account is given, is, according to Russell, "constructed" by us out of private spaces.

Russell does not tell us why he abandoned the theory of matter of *The Problems of Philosophy* and adopted this new theory. But the reason is easy to guess. He has become more empirical. He is dissatisfied with the *Ding-an-sich*-like character of the physical object of the first theory. So he gets rid of it from his philosophy. Matter is now to be constituted out of empirically verifiable elements, namely sense-data and unperceived aspects which are somehow or other *like* sense-data. It is a movement away from realism towards phenomenalism, although, as we shall see, it never arrives at a pure phenomenalism.

The second of the two revolutionary changes, or leaps, which Russell had to make in order to pass from the position of *The Problems of Philosophy* to neutral monism, was the abandonment of "consciousness." This change is made in the *Analysis of Mind* (1921), which was written under the influence of the American neo-realists. In 1928 a second edition of *Our Knowledge of the External World* was issued, and in that edition Russell struck out all references to the distinction between sensations and sense-data, thus bringing the theory of that book in line with his neutral monism.

I shall assume that the reader is, in general, acquainted with Russell's neutral monistic theory of mind and shall only outline those points which are relevant to what I want to say. For the sake of simplicity let us imagine a material universe consisting of only two objects, a penny, which we will call A, and a square table, which we will call B. They will be some distance apart, say ten feet. Then A will consist of a vast number of circular and elliptical aspects ($a_1a_2 \ldots a_n$) radiating outwards from "the place where A is;" and B will consist of a vast number of square and various perspectivally distorted squarish aspects ($b_1b_2 \ldots b_n$) radiating from "the place where B is." At any other point in space a radiating line of aspects from A will intersect with a radiating line of aspects from B. At any such point of intersection there will be one aspect of A, say a_{12}, and one aspect of B, say b_{20}. This collection of aspects, namely, one of A and one of B, will constitute a "perspective" of the universe. At every other point in space there will be some other perspective. If we now increase the number of material objects in our universe from two to any number we please, this will make no difference to the fact that at every point in space there will be a perspective of the universe.

If now we add that the aspects (of all things) are the neutral entities of Russell's monism, we shall see that there are two ways in which these neutral entities may be collected into groups or bundles. We may collect together in one group all the aspects which radiate from a common centre and which are related to one another by the laws of perspective. Such a bundle will constitute a momentary material object. Or we may collect together all the aspects (of all things) which exist together at any point in space, i.e., at any point of intersection of the radiating lines. Such a bundle will constitute a perspective. Thus a material object and a perspective are both constructed out of the same neutral stuff, the aspects, and they differ from one another only by virtue of the different kinds of relations which subsist between their members. And this, as we saw, is the essential idea of neutral monism.

But a perspective is not yet a mind. If it were, there would be a mind at every point in space. To transform a perspective into a mind two further steps are necessary. First, at the point in space where the perspective is there must be a brain, nervous system, and sense-organs. Secondly, there must be added "mnemic phenomena" which apparently arise at that point because there is an organism at that point. "We will give the name of 'mnemic phenomena'," says Russell,

> to those responses of an organism which, so far as hitherto observed facts are concerned, can only be brought under causal laws by including past occurrences in the history of the organism as part of the causes of the present response. . . . For example: You smell peat-smoke, and you recall some occasion when you smelt it before. The cause of your recollection, so far as hitherto observed phenomena are concerned, consists both of the peat-smoke (present stimulus) and of the former occasion (past experience).[3]

In other words, mnemic causation is a peculiar kind of causation in which there is an interval of time between the cause and the effect without (so far as is known) any intervening chain of causes. It is action at a distance, the distance, however, being a time-interval instead of a space-interval. Thus at any point where there is a perspective, plus an organism, plus mnemic causation, there is a mind.

This gives us, however, only a *percipient* mind, a mind capable so far of nothing but perceptions of material objects. What is still required is an account of mental phenomena other than perception, e.g., desire, instinct, general thinking, believing,

---

[3] *The Analysis of Mind*, 78.

reasoning, emotion, etc. Russell, in a series of further chapters, attempts to analyse all these in such a way as to do away in each case with the necessity for "consciousness." Some of them are explained behaviouristically, others by attempting to reduce them to sensations and images. The up-shot of the whole is that there is nothing in mind except sensations (= aspects) connected by mnemic causation, and images. I shall not go into the detail of these various reductions.

I shall now comment on this scheme under the heads of the three parts which must, as we saw, be included in any neutral monism, namely its theory of the neutral stuff, its theory of matter, and its theory of mind.

III. The Theory of the Neutral Stuff

Russell's neutral stuff consists of "aspects." In the *Analysis of Mind* he generally calls the neutral entities "sensations." It must be remembered that he has now given up the distinction between sensations and sense-data, and that in consequence he uses the word sensation for such entities as coloured patches and sounds. An aspect of a material object, when it is being perceived, consists, of course, of sense-data or sensations, so that we may say indifferently that neutral entities are aspects or sensations. This is plain sailing so long as the aspect is perceived. But we shall find that there is grave difficulty in understanding the nature of an unperceived aspect, and the identification of it with sensations will become very doubtful. For the moment, if we stick to the idea that both the material object and the mind consist of sensations grouped according to different relations, the main tenor of Russell's neutral monism is clear enough.

This theory of the neutral stuff differs both from that of James and that of the American neo-realists. James included what Russell calls sensations, and also at least some universals, such as mathematical entities. The neo-realists included sensations, universals, propositions, mathematical and logical entities. Russell includes only sensations, i.e., particulars, not universals or propositions of any kind. Concerning universals he says very little in *The Analysis of Mind*. On page 228 he writes "I *think* a logical argument could be produced to show that universals are part of the structure of the world, but they are an inferred part, not a part of our data" (a doctrine quite different from that offered in *The Problems of Philosophy*). Since they are not data, they are not experienced, and therefore cannot be parts of the neutral stuff. Nor are they ever mentioned as such in the elaboration of the theory.

We have now to note that Russell's neutral monism is not a *pure* neutral monism at all. For according to a purely neutral monistic theory of the world there is *nothing*, either in mind or in matter, which is not wholly constructed out of the neutral stuff. Russell departs from this formula in two respects. In the first place, although sensation, which is the neutral stuff, is the most important component of mind, it is not the only component. He also admits "images." Mental phenomena are not reduced sheerly to sensations, but to sensations and images. Now images are not part of the neutral stuff at all. They are never found in the physical world. They are purely subjective. In a pure neutral monism there should, of course, be nothing which is purely subjective. It is true that images are like sensations, and may be derived from them. Still, as being found solely in the realm of mind, they constitute a departure from the strict program of neutral monism.

On the other side of the picture it is, to say the least, doubtful whether, on Russell's theory, matter can be said to be composed solely of the neutral stuff of sensation. Is the unperceived "aspect" in any sense a sensation? I shall discuss this in the next section and we shall find that the whole theory is, at this point, involved in grave difficulties, if not in actual inconsistencies. At this point I will merely quote a passage which includes reference to Russell's departures from neutral monism in regard to both mind and matter.

The American realists are partly right, though not wholly, in considering that both mind and matter are composed of a neutral-stuff which, in isolation, is neither mental nor material. . . . But I should say that images belong only to the mental world, while those occurrences (if any) which do not form part of any "experience" belong only to the physical world.[4]

[4] *Analysis of Mind*, 25.

The reference in the last clause of this sentence is presumably either to unperceived aspects, or to the "scientific objects" of the physicist, or to both. I shall have more to say on this topic later. For the moment I wish only to note that the admission of physical entities which are not composed of the neutral stuff is—as Russell himself of course realizes and intends—a second departure from neutral monism. It is true that the words "if any" seem to throw doubt on this. In a later passage he writes "I contend that the ultimate constituents of matter are not atoms and electrons, but sensations, and other things similar to sensations as regards extent and duration."[5] I shall not stop at this point to unravel these obscurities, but will simply note that Russell's philosophy at this period seems to fall into a scheme of the following kind.

Purely Physical Entities	Neutral Entities	Purely Mental Entities
Occurrences (if any) which do not form part of any experience.	Sensations (which enter into both mind and matter)	Images

The neutral monist part of Russell's theory appears in the middle column, the departures from it in the columns on the left and the right.

It should not be necessary to explain that the statement that Russell's theory is not *pure* neutral monism is not in any sense a criticism of it. It is mere description. Russell simply thinks that neutral monism is partly right and partly wrong. And this, of course, might be true.

IV. THE THEORY OF MATTER

1. The theory of matter may be considered as aiming at three objectives, and our estimate of it will depend partly on what we consider to be the value of these objectives if reached, partly upon whether we consider that Russell successfully reaches them. The first objective (which the theory of matter shares, of course, with the theory of mind) is to abolish psycho-physical dualism. The second is to give an account of material objects in terms of verifiables only. There is to be no hidden substrate, no mysterious *Ding-an-sich*. The thing is to be composed of sensible

[5] *Ibid.*, 121.

appearances and aspects only. The third objective is to solve the ancient epistemological problem of the relativity of sensation.

2. Most of what I have to say about the attempt to abolish dualism will fall more naturally under the head of the theory of mind; I will postpone full discussion of it to the next section. Here I shall content myself with two remarks. First, it is quite obvious that the "impurity" of Russell's neutral monism, referred to in the previous section, renders it impossible for him to abolish dualism. For if there are in the physical world "occurrences which do not form part of any experience," and which never fall within the circle of any mind, it is clear that we have dualism again. Secondly, I do not myself regard this as the slightest objection to Russell's theory. This is because I regard dualism as both inevitable and unobjectionable. I do not know why philosophers want to make out that as few as possible kinds of things exist in the world, if possible only one; and I regard this as a mistaken objective of philosophy. The point, however, is that I do not see how Russell can have it both ways; can have one foot in the dualist camp and the other in the monist. The most that can be said is that if Russell is able to show that matter consists largely, though not wholly, of sensations, and that mind also consists largely, but not wholly, of sensations, then he will have "lessened the gulf" between them, or "thrown a bridge" from one to the other—whatever these metaphorical expressions may mean, and whatever this achievement may be worth.

3. The second objective is to give an account of matter in terms of verifiables only. The importance of doing this will be obvious to any empiricist. Let us consider only the question whether Russell succeeds in it.

The material object is constructed out of perceived and unperceived aspects. As regards the perceived aspects there is no difficulty. They are complexes of sense-data or, as Russell now calls them, sensations. Hence they are, of course, verifiables. But what sort of entities are the unperceived aspects?

It might be possible to hold that the unperceived aspects are in all ways exactly like perceived aspects, except that they do not happen to be perceived. The unperceived red patch would then be red in the same sense as the perceived red patch is red.

In that case the unperceived aspect might fairly be regarded as a verifiable. For although it would not, of course, be possible to observe it when it is unobserved, yet it would, even when unobserved, be an entity of exactly *the same sort* as observed entities are. It would be the sort of thing which we do constantly observe, although, at certain times, it does not happen to be observed. Apparently Russell has at times attempted to think of "sensibilia" in this way.

But this is not the theory which is maintained in *Our Knowledge of the External World,* and I do not find any signs of it in *The Analysis of Mind.* It is important to notice that it is only possible to hold such a view if we adopt the selective type of realism. We may briefly distinguish generative and selective realism as follows. According to generative realism—it will be remembered that Russell advocated this in *The Problems of Philosophy*—the perceived qualities of sense-data are effects of two joint causes, the physical object and the perceiving organism. Hence this type of realism must hold that the perceived qualities of things cease to exist when we are not perceiving them. The view of selective realism is quite different. The sense-organs are not in any way concerned in causing sense-qualities to exist. The sense-qualities actually exist in the object, whether it is perceived or unperceived, just as common sense supposes. What the sense-organ does is to *select* which of the sense-qualities we shall perceive. Thus when my colour-blind friend sees as green what I see as red, we are to suppose (apparently) that the object itself really is both green and red; and that my optical apparatus shuts out the green, allowing me to see only the red, whereas my friend's optical apparatus shuts out the red and allows him to see only the green.

There are grave objections to selectivism, but that is not the present point. The point is that this theory does allow one to hold that things objectively have all the qualities which we perceive in them, and that they have them even when they are not perceived by any organism. The generative theory renders any such belief *impossible,* since it holds that the presence of a sense-organ is necessary for the coming into existence of the sense-qualities.

Hence Russell could not consistently hold that unperceived

aspects have the same characters as perceived aspects, unless he first abandoned the generative theory of his earlier days and adopted selectivism. Not only is there no evidence of such a change, but certain passages in *Our Knowledge of the External World* render it clear that he still holds the generative view. Thus he writes, "it must be admitted as probable that the immediate objects of sense depend for their existence upon physiological conditions in ourselves, and that, for example, the coloured surfaces which we see cease to exist when we shut our eyes."[6] Some pages later he points out that two men sitting in a room will see "two somewhat similar worlds," i.e., two different aspects of the same room. If a third man enters and sits between them he will see a third intermediate world, i.e., a third aspect. "It is true," he goes on,

that we cannot reasonably suppose just this world to have existed before, because it is conditioned by the sense-organs, nerves, and brain of the newly arrived man; but we can reasonably suppose that *some* aspect of the universe existed from that point of view, though no one was perceiving it.[6a]

Both passages say plainly that Russell is adopting the generative hypothesis. The second passage says, though less plainly, that the unperceived aspect does not possess the same sort of characters as do the perceived aspects. Hence the interpretation that the unperceived aspects are verifiables because they are exactly the same sort of things as the perceived aspects, except that they do not happen to be perceived, falls to the ground.

There are many passages in Russell which suggest an entirely different interpretation. According to this view the unperceived aspects are to be identified with the etheric or spatial radiations of the physicist. This would render intelligible the above-quoted statements that sense-qualities arise only where there is a sense-organ, for this appears to be the view commonly held by physicists. To quote from Russell. "The definition of a 'momentary thing' involves problems concerning time, since the particulars constituting a momentary thing will not all be simul-

---

[6] *Our Knowledge of the External World* (second edition), 68.
[6a] *Ibid.*, 93.

taneous, but will travel outward from the thing with the velocity of light."[7] And from a later page,

What it is that happens when a wave of light reaches a given place we cannot tell, except in the sole case when the place in question is a brain connected with an eye which is turned in the right direction. In this one very special case we know what happens: we have the sensation called "seeing the star." In all other cases, though we know (more or less hypothetically) some of the correlations and abstract properties of the appearance of the star, we do not know the appearance itself.[8]

The unseen occurrence is called in the last sentence an "appearance"—although it is not appearing to anyone—and the word appearance is sometimes used by Russell as synonymous with aspect.

If one wishes to adopt this interpretation one may be puzzled by another passage which I have already quoted. "I contend that the ultimate constituents of matter are not atoms or electrons, but sensations and other things similar to sensations as regards extent and duration." At first sight this looks as if Russell is rejecting all such "scientific objects" as atoms, electrons, and the radiations which proceed from them. It looks like a pure phenomenalism according to which matter is nothing but complexes of sense-data and other entities similar to them in extent and duration, and in which "scientific objects" will presumably have to be regarded as pragmatic fictions justified only by their predictive value. This would, of course, be inconsistent with the identification of unperceived aspects with radiations.

But the passage can be interpreted otherwise. Russel *may* mean that he does not believe in atoms and electrons but *does* believe in the radiations which are commonly said to issue from them. This would suggest the view that there is no solid entity (atom or electron) which radiates vibrations. There is nothing but the vibrations themselves radiating from a "hollow centre." The electrons and atoms—if one wishes to reintroduce the terms—may now be identified with the radiations themselves. And this view of atoms and electrons has actually been quoted

---

[7] *Analysis of Mind*, 126.
[8] *Ibid.*, 134.

with approval by Russell elsewhere.[9] In that case the vibrations may be identified with the unperceived aspects, and the statement that "the ultimate constituents of matter are not atoms or electrons" may be meant to reject only the something-at-the-centre-which-emits-vibrations theory of atoms and electrons.

Further, the statement that the real constituents of matter are sensations "and other things similar to sensations *as regards extent and duration*" (italics mine) provides another clue. It seems to mean that the unperceived aspects have in common with the perceived aspects only the characters of "extent and duration," in short, the so-called primary qualities. In a sentence already quoted, he has told us that "the coloured surfaces which we see cease to exist when we shut our eyes." Putting the two passages together we get the result that Russell is apparently simply supporting the scientific tradition which bifurcates the primary and secondary qualities. The perceived aspects have the primary and secondary qualities, the unperceived aspects have only the primary. Epistemologically this might be rendered possible by supposing that the generative hypothesis is correct as regards secondary qualities whereas the selective hypothesis applies to primary qualities. Two men see the table top as having different shapes because the positions of their bodies select different shapes. But they see it as having different colours because the optical apparatus of one differs from that of the other. This combination of generativism and selectivism is in many ways attractive. It seems to agree with science and with a sophisticated common sense.

We may briefly sum up the interpretation of Russell which is here suggested. The material object is nothing but the collection of all its aspects, perceived and unperceived. The perceived aspects are sensations, or complexes of sense-data having primary and secondary qualities. The unperceived aspects are simply the radiations of the physicist. They have the primary, but not the secondary, qualities. When we perceive an object, the spatial position of our body selects the shape and size, and the sense-organs acted on by the radiations generate the colour

[9] See *Philosophy*, 157.

and other secondary qualities. At the centre from which the aspects radiate there is nothing, and this accords with that interpretation of atoms and electrons which identifies them with what would otherwise be considered their effects, i.e., with the radiations which are supposed to issue "from them." The electron, on this view, is what it does.

I do. not know whether all this *is* what Russell means. It *might* be nothing but a fancy of mine which I have thrust upon him. The truth is that Russell's writings are extremely obscure. The beautiful prose which he writes carries one easily along and gives rise to the delusion that what he is saying is extremely simple. Actually it is far otherwise. In the present case I can only say that the interpretation which I have offered seems to me the most likely. It harmonizes a number of tendencies and passages which on the surface seem bafflingly inconsistent with one another. It brings together in a self-consistent view his phenomenalism, his realism, and his strong desire to reconcile his philosophical views with the doctrines of physical science.

But now, if this interpretation is accepted, how shall we evaluate his theory of matter? The first thing to note is that it lays itself open to Berkeley's criticism that it is impossible to separate primary and secondary qualities. The unperceived aspect has the primary qualities but not the secondary. This objection, however, might be cured. The real point which Berkeley made was not, as he supposed, that primary qualities cannot exist without secondary qualities, but that they cannot exist without *some* other qualities. To say of a material object that it has no characters other than shape, size, duration, and motion, is to make it equivalent to a region of empty space, i.e., to nothing, and moreover to a nothing which is supposed to be in motion. To make it *something*, Berkeley supposed, it must have some other characters, for instance colour. But Berkeley's point could be met if we supposed that the unperceived aspect, besides having the primary qualities, has intrinsic qualities which are unknowable to us but which *correspond to* perceived secondary qualities. *Perhaps* this is what Russell means. I am aware of no passage in his writings which definitely supports the supposition, but it accords with the views advocated in *The Problems of*

Philosophy, and it seems the only course open to Russell to make sense of his doctrine.

The next question to ask is whether Russell's theory, thus interpreted, achieves his objective of constructing matter out of verifiables only. The answer is that it most certainly does not. The whole object of the theory, we understood at the beginning, was to get rid of hidden substrates, *Ding-an-sich*-like physical objects with unknowable intrinsic qualities. But now all this, which we were to get rid of, is back again on our hands. The only advance made on the theory of *The Problems of Philosophy* is that for the solid *Ding-an-sich*-like *thing* at the centre with its intrinsic qualities, we have substituted *Ding-an-sich*-like *aspects,* with their intrinsic qualities, radiating from the centre throughout space. This change in no way makes the theory more empirical. The unverifiable character of the old solid "physical object" is simply transferred to the new airy and fluttering "aspects."

Thus viewed, the supposed effort of this second phase of Russell's career to be more empirical and phenomenalistic, the supposed intent to construct matter out of verifiables only, turns out to be nothing but a fraud. There is a great blowing of trumpets. There is a great air of being empirical and of having no traffic with unverifiable entities. There is conjured up before our mind's eye the picture of a piece of matter composed of nothing but sensations or sense-data, of sensible aspects spreading out through space. It is true, one is given to understand, that some of these aspects are not perceived. They are, however, very much the same sort of things as sensations. If we are simple enough, we may be satisfied with this and suppose that we have an empirical and phenomenalist account of matter. We shall not notice that the whole subject of the unperceived aspects is hastily glossed over in a few very brief and evasive passages; and that when we press our question regarding them, the subject is quickly changed. But we must sternly insist on pressing the question: are these unperceived aspects entities having verifiable characters like the perceived aspects, or are they not?

It seems that only two replies are possible. One is that unperceived aspects are exactly like perceived aspects except that they do not happen to be perceived. The second is along the lines of the interpretation which I have offered as being the most likely and the most consistent with what Russell actually says. If the first alternative is chosen, then it necessitates a thorough-going selectivism. This is inconsistent with what Russell says. What is more serious, it will involve us in all the grave troubles of the selective theory. I have no space to expound these here. I have discussed them elsewhere,[10] and Professor H. H. Price's book *Perception*[11] may also be consulted on the subject. If the second alternative is chosen, it completely destroys the empirical character of the theory and the claim to construct matter out of verifiables.

It seems to me that actually Russell has a hankering for both interpretations. Always his philosophy wavers unhappily between phenomenalism and scientific realism. In the end the scientific realism always wins. The theory of *Our Knowledge of the External World* has at first sight the appearance of being a revolutionary change from that which was offered in *The Problems of Philosophy*. Actually the two theories are, if our interpretation has been correct, almost identical, save that unverifiable aspects spread throughout space are now substituted for an unverifiable physical object at the centre. From the position of scientific realism Russell has from time to time held out fluttering and ineffectual hands towards phenomenalism. But he has never embraced it. His traffic with phenomenalism has been no more than a mild and insincere flirtation.

4. We have still to enquire whether Russell achieves his objective of solving the problem set by the relativity of sensation. This question can be answered very shortly. "Difficulties have arisen" he writes "from the differences in the appearance which one physical object presents to two people at the same time." After adding that these differences have been made the basis of arguments in favour of the view that we cannot know the real nature of objects, he claims that "our hypothetical con-

---

[10] *The Nature of the World*, 118-120.
[11] *Perception*, 40-53.

struction"—i.e., his theory of matter—"meets these arguments"[12]—i.e., it solves the problem of the relativity of sensations.

Let us briefly state the problem which has to be solved. When two people simultaneously view an object, it is assumed by common sense that they both see the same identical thing. But the appearance which one of them sees may be red and circular, the appearance which the other sees may be green and elliptical. The common sense view that they are seeing the same thing entails that the circular red thing exists *at the same point of space* as the elliptical green thing. This is, however, impossible, since green and red exclude one another, and round and elliptical exclude one another. Suppose we symbolize by x_1 and x_2 any two mutually exclusive and clashing characters, (such as red and green, round and elliptical, loud and soft characters of sound, large and small appearances of the object close to us and far away respectively, etc.) then the problem arises from the fact that the common sense view of the world entails that x_1 and x_2 exist simultaneously at the same place, and that this seems to be plainly impossible.

Obviously there is only one possible principle for solving the problem, namely to suppose that x_1 and x_2 *do not exist at the same place*.

Berkeley successfully solved the problem by using this principle. According to him x_1 and x_2 are not in the same place, because they exist only as sensations *in two different minds*. Two different minds are not, of course, in two different places. Minds, according to Berkeley, are not in space, but different spaces are in different minds. Hence for him x_1 is in the private space of one mind, whereas x_2 is in the private space of another mind. Therefore they are not in the same place and they do not clash. When I say that Berkeley "successfully" solved the problem, I do not of course mean that his solution is "true." I mean only that, whether true or false, it is an hypothesis which does account for the facts.

Russell's solution proceeds on the same principle—that x_1 and x_2 are not in the same place. That is the whole point of his

[12] *Our Knowledge of the External World*, 102.

supposition that the aspects which constitute the material object are spread out through space and do not all exist together at the centre, i.e., at the place where common sense supposes the object to be. The circular aspect which I see (x_1) exists at the place where my head is. The elliptical aspect which you see (x_2) exists ten feet away at the place where your head is. Thus x_1 and x_2 exist at two different places where they cannot clash. One might say that Russell merely varies Berkeley's solution by substituting "in your head" for "in your mind." Russell's theory, accordingly, does succeed in solving this problem.

It might be objected that, although Russell's theory does explain the relativity of shape, size, and all those characters whose sensed variations are correlated with *variations in the spatial position of the sense-organ,* it fails to explain the relativity of colours, tastes, and all those characters whose sensed variations are correlated with *variations, not in the position, but in the physiological structure or condition of the sense-organ.* For, although on Russell's theory two different shapes will be in two different places, yet two different colours, such as the red which I see and the green which my colour-blind friend sees, may have to be located in the same place. For if I make way for my friend so that his head can occupy the very same position which mine occupied a moment ago, then he will see a green aspect in the very same position as that from which I saw a red aspect a moment before. Hence the green and the red must really be in the same place.

But the objection is capable of being answered if we assume, as previously suggested, that Russell is a selectivist as regards primary qualities and a generativist as regards secondary qualities. The aspect which I and my friend see has a shape (which appears the same to us both), but it has in itself no colour. When my eye is in position to see it, red colour is generated on it; and when, a moment later, my friend's eye is in that position, green colour is generated on it. Thus the green and the red, though they both exist in the same place, exist there successively and not simultaneously. Hence there is no clash.

Any theory which holds that x_1 and x_2 are not in the same place is bound to be "queer" and to seem absurd to common sense. For the proper definition of queerness in a philosophical (or scientific) theory is "departure from the beliefs of common sense." The further a theory is from those beliefs the queerer it is. This is all we *mean* by queer. Hence Berkeley's theory is queer and so is Russell's. But if it is realized that *any* solution of the epistemological problem *must* proceed on the principle that x₁ and x₂ do not exist simultaneously at the same place, and that this principle flatly contradicts common sense, and that queerness means nothing but departure from common sense beliefs—if, I say, all this is realized, it will be seen to follow that any true solution of the epistemological problem must necessarily be queer. "The truth about physical objects," Russell has said, *"must* be strange."[13] It is easy to poke fun at Russell's theory of matter on the grounds that, according to it, the penny exists at every part of the universe except where the penny is, and that Russell's brain, being a material object, is all over the universe, and that he, consequently, is "a terribly scatter-brained fellow." All such criticisms I regard as cheap and worthless, for they all depend merely on the queerness of the theory. But queerness is not a fault in an epistemological theory. The absence of it is.

V. The Theory of Mind

1. The second half of Russell's neutral monism, the theory of mind, is designed to show that—apart from images—the constituents of mind are the neutral entities of sensation. His avowed object is to get rid of "consciousness," to give an account of all mental phenomena, such as perception, memory, thinking, reasoning, desire, emotion, will, without postulating anywhere the element of consciousness.

In one sense it is manifestly ridiculous to deny the existence of consciousness. It is plain that the word consciousness is a good English word which means *something*. It is not a noise which fails to refer to anything whatever in the world, and which people sometimes make without any reason while they talk, like a grunt or a wheeze. It is plain that when I say "I am conscious of the things around me" I am not saying nothing. I

[13] *The Problems of Philosophy,* 59.

am saying something, and something which is certainly true. And it is plain that there is some difference between a man who is awake and in possession of his faculties and the same man when he has been knocked senseless by a hammer-blow on the head. We express this difference, whatever its nature, by saying that the man in the first case is "conscious" and in the second case "unconscious." Obviously this is a real, and not an imaginary, difference. In this sense there plainly is such a thing as consciousness, and no sensible philosopher, least of all Russell, would deny it. If there are any philosophers who do deny it, they cannot be refuted by any argument. They can only be advised to see their doctors.

What is it, then, that the neutral monist is denying when he denies the existence of consciousness? The answer is that he is denying that consciousness is an "entity," or "stuff," or "substance," or even an "event," of a radically different kind from the entities, stuffs, substances, or events which make up the physical world. He is repudiating that sort of absolute qualitative difference between mind and matter which has been asserted by many philosophers since the time of Descartes. To suppose, for instance, that matter is in essence spatial and non-thinking, whereas mind is in essence thinking and non-spatial, is to suppose a complete gulf between the two. They have, on this view, absolutely nothing in common.

What is the objection to such a view? Of course to Descartes's particular version of dualism it may be objected that it involves the unempirical notion of substance. But dualism can easily be purged of this. We might well construct a dualistic theory of mind and matter on purely phenomenalistic lines. Matter might be constructed out of sense-data, and mind might be constructed out of introspective data. These latter might be radically different from sense-data. They might, for example, be non-spatial. Substances would be got rid of, but we should still have a completely dualistic theory.

Of course neutral monists would deny that any such introspective data, wholly distinct from sense-data, can ever be detected, or that they exist. That is a question of fact on which opinions differ. But it is not this which is the root-objection to dualism as such. There is no doubt that at the bottom of the common dislike of dualism there is believed to be some sort of *a priori* objection. It is thought that, apart from questions of fact, dualism is in some way philosophically or logically objectionable.

It is very difficult to understand why philosophers should feel this. There certainly are a very great number of quite different kinds of data in the world. For instance, visual data are radically different from the data of sound, and these again from the data of smell. Visual data are certainly spatial, whereas it is at least doubtful whether the data of smell are (though I do not claim that this makes them 'spiritual'). There is an impassable gulf set between the different data of the different senses. The connection between them is only that of correlation. So far as I can see, it is just as much "dualism" to admit the existence of two such radically different kinds of data as those of smell and sight as it is to admit the existence of both visual data and introspective data. The connection between introspective data and visual data (or other data of sense) might well be that of correlation, as is the connection between the different kinds of sense-data. So where in the world is the *a priori* objection to admitting the possibility of introspective data alongside the others?

It may be said: The sense-data all have it in common that they are *sense*-data. They are all, in that respect, alike. But the so-called introspective data would not be sensuous at all. They would be utterly different from any data given in sense. Hence it is not true that there is as great a gulf between visual data and olfactory data as there would be between introspective data and those of sense. Sense-data all belong in one general category, but introspective data would fall outside it in some radically different category.

This argument assumes that there is some character common to all sense-data which may perhaps be called "sensuousness." I cannot, however, find in data any quality of sensuousness. They seem to be all called sense-data owing to the extrinsic and accidental fact that they are all perceived normally through one or other of the physical senses. I cannot myself see that there is anything at all in common between, say, sounds and smells. And if they are thus utterly unlike, if the gulf between them is absolute, then introspective data cannot be more unlike sense-data than "utterly unlike," nor can the gulf be greater than an absolute gulf.

Perhaps the objection really is that the introspective data are suspected of being 'spiritual', in some way, whereas the sense-data are 'merely' sensuous. This seems to put a gulf between them; and of course claims to superior spirituality are apt to be irritating. Personally I should put forward no such claims on behalf of introspective data—not at any rate as part of the theory of knowledge. For spirituality is a value-category, and epistemology is not concerned with values. Spirituality is not, at any rate in my opinion, a quality which data may have on a par with colour, hardness, and the like. It may be that, as moralists have always declared, the mind is in some way more noble than the body. But this nobility, however it is to be interpreted, must surely belong to the mind as an organized whole, not to the humble data out of which it is constructed. However that may be, the alleged nobility of mind cannot surely be made the basis of a reasonable objection to dualism.

I can therefore find absolutely no rational ground for objecting a priori to dualism. Accordingly I conclude that the strong feeling that, apart from any question of fact, there is some logical or philosophical objection to dualism as such, must have its source in some kind of prejudice. And it is quite easy to suggest the possible sources of an anti-dualistic bias.

First, as a matter of history, dualism has come down to us loaded with religious associations. And I believe that anti-dualistic philosophers are largely motivated by a feeling of fear, perhaps largely subconscious, that the admission of a psychophysical dualism will entrap them again in what they regard as discarded superstitions. Dualism suggests the "soul," and everybody now knows that we don't have souls. It further suggests that the soul may be independent of the body, and might be made the basis of a claim to immortality—another out of date idea. There is no knowing where an admission of dualism might not end. It might even land us—though I hesitate to suggest anything so indecent—in belief in God.

It is plain that in all this there is no rational argument, nothing but anti-religious prejudice. A belief in introspective data has no implications of the kind suggested. For instance, if the introspective data are correlated with sense-data—as they certainly are, if they exist at all—then the mind constructed out of introspective data will be no more independent of the body than the data of one sense are independent of the data of another. Let me remind the reader that it is just as unphilosophical to allow one's opinions to be dictated by anti-religious feelings as it is to allow them to be dictated by a pro-religious bias.

A second source of prejudice is the medieval idea that a cause must *resemble* its effect, that cause and effect cannot be radically different in kind. Descartes expressed one aspect of this idea when he said that a cause must have in it as much reality as its effect. The idea that cause and effect must be alike is a piece of pure prejudice, not born out by facts. Lightning is the cause of thunder, yet the two are totally unlike, one being a complex of visual data, the other a complex of auditory data. Cold is utterly unlike the solidity which it causes in water. It was this baseless medieval belief which gave rise to the supposed "impossibility" of interaction between mind and body, and to the whole rubbish heap of literature about parallelism, epiphenomenalism and the like. And this supposed impossibility of interaction between two radically different kinds of entity has been one of the strongest influences working against dualism. I am not saying that Russell has himself been directly influenced by this second kind of prejudice, though I should not be surprised if he has been unconsciously influenced by the first. I have been discussing the question of the causes of the prejudice against dualism quite generally.

In the light of these considerations it does not seem to me that Russell's aim of reducing mind to a conglomeration of sensory neutral stuff constitutes in any way a valuable or important objective. Of course if there *is* only one kind of stuff in the world, not two, it is important that we should know this fact—assuming that any philosophical knowledge is important. But if a survey of the facts shows that there exist two, or many, kinds of stuff, this should be accepted with natural piety. There is nothing especially valuable or meritorious in aiming at a monistic theory.

2. But now we have to consider whether Russell actually does succeed in getting rid of 'consciousness'. I hold that not only Russell's but *any* neutral monism, past, present, or future, is foredoomed to failure in this attempt. This can be shown by considering the general program of neutral monism, without taking into account the particular versions of James, the American realists, or Russell. For the neutral monist is not a crude materialist. He admits a difference between mind and matter; only he says that it is a difference of relations and not of stuffs. He must therefore face the question: what sort of relation, or relations, holding between neutral entities, constitute them mental events? Let us call this relation, or relations, R. Different versions of neutral monism may give different accounts of R. But they must all necessarily admit that R is a *unique* relation. By a 'unique' relation I mean one which cannot be reduced to physical relations and which cannot be found in the physical world. R must be a unique relation, for if it were not, it would fail to differentiate between mind and matter, which is precisely its function in the theory. R is to be the sole *differentium* of the species 'mental phenomenon' as distinguished from the species 'material phenomenon'. And this *differentium* cannot of course be found among material phenomena.

R, then, must be a unique non-physical relation. It cannot be itself a neutral entity. It must be purely subjective. But, when we have admitted this, we have admitted the existence of something which is purely mental, subjective, and non-physical as the essential characteristic of mind. This is to admit to dualism. Why now trouble to deny the existence of other subjective factors of consciousness? At most neutral monism, if accepted, shows that what is peculiar and essential to mind is not a unique non-sensory stuff but rather a unique non-sensory relation. Over this I no longer care to dispute. It may be of academic interest to decide whether what is unique in mind ought to be classified as a 'relation' or a 'stuff'. But in either case the uniqueness (= non-physicality) remains, and we have a clear dualism.

It may be asked how this purely general argument applies to Russell's particular version of neutral monism. It is not difficult to find the answer. To begin with, the type of relation which makes the difference between a piece of matter and a "perspective" is a spatial, i.e., a physical relation. For the "bundles" of aspects which respectively constitute material objects and perspectives are collected together merely on two different spatial plans. Those which radiate from a common centre and are related to each other by the laws of perspective are pieces of matter. Those which are found at points of intersection of lines of aspects radiating from different centres are perspectives. But a perspective is not a mind. There must be added a brain and nervous system. These too are purely physical, and we do not yet get a mind. Mind arrives only with the addition of "mnemic causation" and "mnemic phenomena." One might simply point out that mnemic phenomena are merely what most people call memory, and that to introduce memory here is simply to introduce a non-physical or mental event or relation. But if we have to talk Russell's language we shall say that what is introduced here is a kind of causation which skips over periods of time, so that the cause may exist today, the effect twenty years hence, with no intermediate causal links. This is certainly a relation never found in the physical world. It is a wholly peculiar and unique character found only in mind. Personally I should hold that this is an utterly inadequate account of what is unique in mind. But it is certainly sufficient to establish the point of this discussion, namely that the relation R must be a unique relation never found in the physical world.

3. Of the much-debated question whether one *can* introspect consciousness, i.e., whether introspective data actually ever are observed, I do not propose to write at length here. My own opinion is that introspective data are observable. I have discussed this matter elsewhere. I shall content myself on this occasion by asking two questions.

First, how does any neutral monist know that the relation R exists? Since it is not found in the physical world it cannot have been discovered by external observation, and I do not see how it can have been discovered at all except by introspection. If so, it is an introspective datum of an entirely non-physical and non-sensuous kind. It is true that it is a relation and not a stuff, but that does not prevent it from being a datum. Many relations are data. In the particular case of Russell the question becomes: how does Russell know that "mnemic phenomena" exist?

My other question depends upon a different point. Suppose that I hold a false opinion. I may believe, for example, that Russell is now President of the United States. Now I certainly do *know* that I hold this opinion. My question is how do I know this? It is impossible to answer that "knowing that I hold this opinion" is simply identical with "holding this opinion," and that holding this opinion can be analysed into sensations and images. "Knowing that I hold this opinion" cannot be identical with "holding this opinion," because the first is a case of knowing, and is *true*, whereas the second, the opinion, is *false*.

A behaviourist may say that I know my opinion because I hear myself say the words which express it or otherwise notice some of my own behaviour. But this explanation, though it may *sometimes* be true, is very implausible if taken as the whole explanation.

I fail to see how the question can be answered except by admitting that I do, sometimes at least, introspect my opinions.

4. There is one feature of human thought, namely its *generality*, which can never be explained by any theory which sees in mental phenomena nothing but a conglomeration of sensations and images. The reason why no such theory can explain generality is obvious. Every sensation and every image is nothing but a particular. One cannot make sensations and images general either by adding to their number (a million images are no more general than one image) or by making them vague (= having shadowy outlines).

This is what Berkeley failed to see, and Russell's theory of general ideas is only Berkeley's brought up to date. According to Berkeley what happens when I use the word "man" as a general term is that I have an image of a particular man, who will be either white or black, tall or short, etc., and that this particular image *represents* to me all other men. It is not clear how the factor of "representing" is to be explained on this theory. Is it another image? But we may suppose that point to be explained. The real difficulty lies in understanding my knowledge, or belief, that this image represents "all other men." I must, in order to know or believe this, somehow have in my mind the idea of "all other men." And I do not see how, on the theory, I can have this except by having in my mind the images of all other men—millions and millions of images. And this is certainly preposterous.

It will not do to say that in addition to the original particular image I have the images of *some* other men, perhaps one or two. For I shall then have to know that these additional images represent all the other men of whom I have no images. And how can I know this without having images of them?

But these difficulties, great as they are, do not yet bring us to the problem of generality. For the idea of "any man" is not the same as the idea of "all men." And even if we could carry in our minds images of all the actual men who have lived, will live, or are alive now, we should not have achieved the general idea of "any man." For any number of particular images, however great, still lie in the region of particularity. In order to have, in the form of images, the idea of any man, I should have to have images, not only of all actual men, but of all *possible* men also. And this is plainly an absurdity.

Russell's theory is more sophisticated than Berkeley's. But its fundamental principle is the same, and it is subject to the same criticism. Russell improves on the image which, according to Berkeley, represents other men, by making it vague in outline like a composite photograph. He admits this does not solve the problem, for the vague is not the general. In addition to this vague image, he says, you must have

particular images of the several appearances . . . you will then not feel the generalized picture to be adequate to any one particular appearance, and you will be able to make it function as a general idea rather than a vague idea. If this view is correct, no new general content needs to be added to the generalized image. What needs to be added is particular images compared and contrasted with the generalized image.[14]

This is no solution at all. I am to have in my mind one vague image and several other images more precise and with sharper outlines. I compare these and realize that the vague image is not adequate to the others. This gives me only the knowledge that this particular image (the vague one) is vaguer, less precise, than the others. I still only have *particular* ideas. Russell says that we shall then "not feel the generalized image to be adequate to *any* one particular appearance" (my *italics*). He only seems to have solved the problem because he cunningly, and without the slightest warrant, slips in the word "any" here. By doing this he just jumps the problem. It is evident that by comparing the vague image with the other two or three less vague ones I can only learn that it is inadequate to those two or three less vague ones. How can I learn that it is inadequate to other particular men of whom I have no image? How can I learn that it is inadequate to *any* particular image? It is Berkeley's problem over again, and Russell's additions and sophistications do nothing to solve it. I conclude that Russell's theory is incapable of explaining the generality of thought, and that no torturing and twisting of particular images or sensations, whether vague or clear, can ever produce anything except particular images and sensations.

5. The greater part of this paper has consisted in adverse criticisms. And it is true that in my opinion Russell's neutral monism has to be rejected both on the side of its theory of matter and on the side of its theory of mind. This does not, of course, mean that we learn nothing from it. It is profoundly suggestive and instructive. I take it as self-evident that Russell's thought on these matters has contributed vastly to the philosophical achievement of our generation, that it has profoundly stimulated enquiry, that it is full of interesting and fruitful ideas, and that it is likely to remain a landmark in the history of philosophy. This, I have no doubt, is the opinion of most

[14] *The Analysis of Mind*, 221.

of Russell's contemporaries. If it were not so, the publication of this volume could hardly be justified. And if I have dwelt more on what I consider to be the faults of his philosophy than on its merits, this is because the merits of his work are obvious and well-known to everyone.

W. T. STACE

DEPARTMENT OF PHILOSOPHY
PRINCETON UNIVERSITY

12

Andrew Paul Ushenko

RUSSELL'S CRITIQUE OF EMPIRICISM

RUSSELL'S CRITIQUE OF EMPIRICISM

1. INTRODUCTION

THIS Essay is concerned exclusively with *An Inquiry into Meaning and Truth*, to be referred to as the *Inquiry*, for I understand that Russell is not prepared to defend his comments on empiricism in the form in which they appeared in earlier publications. The restriction does not make my task much easier, even quantitatively; although the Index of the *Inquiry* refers under the heading of "Empiricism" to fifteen pages only, the fact is that the whole book is essentially about empiricism. Russell's general position is not unlike the attitude which modern mathematical logicians take towards the theory of intuitionism in mathematics: they cannot accept this theory because this would mean throwing overboard important branches of mathematics, yet they want a minimal departure from the logical rigour of the intuitionist standards. An examination of Russell's *Inquiry* will show that this work is a systematic search for points where empiricism does not do justice to what is generally taken to be knowledge, together with an attempt to provide justification for these points with the least deviation from empiricism. Thus viewed the book is a unified whole. This is important to note, because so many critics, among them myself in *Philosophy and Phenomenological Research* (September, 1941), have complained of conflicting tendencies or of a lack of unity in the *Inquiry*. These complaints are unjust, and I, for one, have no more doubts that the book under consideration is one of Russell's best.

I am unreservedly in agreement whenever Russell finds a fault with current empiricism. With characteristic critical efficacy he can find defects along such divergent lines of empiricism as Neurath's linguistic coherence theory of truth, Dewey's instrumentalism, or Carnap's identification of truth with verifiability, and he is also able to detect the basic shortcomings of the ideas which have inspired all these theories. The constructive parts of the *Inquiry*, where Russell lays the foundations of a liberal empiricism, are, I think, more doubtful than his arguments of adverse criticism, and at several points I was tempted to take issue with the author. I did not yield to the temptation, because I do not consider the existing alternative theories any more plausible; and I have neither space nor desire to work out in this paper an alternative statement of my own. Thus I am ready to go with Russell as far as he leads us, but I believe he does not go far enough; and at the crucial point where he stops, in dealing with reference to events that are not experienced, I recommend a further step toward conceptualism.

An exposition of Russell's criticism of the principles which are characteristic of modern empiricism will be found in Section 4. The preceding two sections take up the preliminary matters of terminology. Sections that follow the exposition, except the last one, clear up certain misunderstandings which the text of the *Inquiry*, in spite of its excellent style, has not prevented. In the last section a theory of concepts is outlined as a further development in a direction which Russell's work has left open for exploration.

2. TERMINOLOGICAL COMMENTS

For a better understanding of all philosophical terms, with the exception of "proposition" and "logical analysis," which are used in the expository section, the reader is referred to the original text of the *Inquiry*; the explanations below may be of some help, but are in many respects insufficient.

An "experience" must be understood as a personal experience, yet, except when it is so stated, not as an experience of one's mental states, but as a set of sense-data or sensible facts, which, although private to an observer, are his only means of building up a conception of an external world. In other words, in dealing with experiences our concern is primarily the sensible field, the data of observation, and not those of introspection. Furthermore the word "experience" designates non-linguistic sensible occurrences, at least when sentences describing experiences are contrasted with the experiences described. An experience can be contrasted with a sentence describing it, because the former can be known, in the sense that it is capable of being noticed, without the aid of words. For example, in listening attentively to a symphony I have auditory experiences; I notice and, in this sense, I know each sound as it comes in due course, and I know such things without using words. So much for a sensible experience. Experience, however, is a broader concept than sensible experience. For an experience of a sensible fact is usually accompanied or even transformed by intervention of memory-images and expectations. Hence a complete experience under the name of "perceptive experience" is contrasted with an experience which is its sensory core:

I do not like to use the word "perception" for the complete experience consisting of a sensory core supplemented by expectations, because the word "perception" suggests too strongly that the beliefs involved are true. I will therefore use the phrase "perceptive experience." Thus whenever I think I see a cat, I have the perceptive experience of "seeing a cat," even if, on this occasion, no physical cat is present. (p. 151)

The word "fact" stands for any occurrence or event whether experienced or not. Some writers use "fact" when they want to state that such and such is the case; for instance, they might refer to the fact that Caesar was assassinated. This is not Russell's use; to Russell the fact is the event of Caesar's assassination.

There are two kinds of perceptual judgments: first, sentences describing perceptive experiences, as in "There is a cat;" second, sentences describing the sensible core of perceptive experiences, the latter are called "basic propositions." "There is a feline patch of colour" is a basic proposition corresponding to the perceptual judgment "There is a cat."

In the preceding paragraph the words "sentence" and "proposition" are interchangeable, but in many contexts of the *Inquiry* they are not. I shall indicate Russell's distinction between them in an independent discussion of propositions.

3. The Proposition and Logical Analysis

A proposition can be defined as the meaning of a declarative sentence; but this definition, to be acceptable, must be cleared of a certain ambiguity. There is more than one sense in which a declarative sentence may be said to have a meaning. Suppose you assert something true, then there is a fact which accounts for the truth of your sentence. The sentence, as the *Inquiry* puts it, indicates the fact, and the latter may be said to be the meaning of the sentence. This is not the sense of meaning in my definition of a proposition. Then again a declarative sentence is an expression of one's personal belief that such and such is the case. The state of mind which a sentence can thus express is identified in the *Inquiry* with "the proposition expressed by the sentence," or with "the significance of the sentence." I am not using "the meaning of a sentence" for "the significance of a sentence" thus understood. Finally, the utterance of a sentence may be accompanied by images which may be said to form at least a part of the meaning of the sentence. I am not concerned with meaning in the sense of images either. The main reason why I do not want to identify a proposition either with what a sentence indicates or with mental states or images that go with it is communicability. A proposition is communicable if it can be conveyed by means of print to any qualified person, if necessary with the aid of translation. A perceptual judgment, such as "This is blue," is not a proposition in my sense because it can be communicated, if at all, only to those who perceive the thing that I am pointing to in uttering the judgment. A typical proposition is something which is understood as one reads a printed sentence. I pick out at random a book which opens on an article on "Biology," and I notice the following sentence: "The rediscovery of the Aristotelian biology is a modern thing." The author may or may not have images associated with this sentence; if he has, they are not constituents of the proposition, since I can understand the sentence without, I believe, any image coming along with the understanding. And, of course, since I happen not to know who the author is, I do not know, and don't care to know, in what frame of mind he has published his statement. Furthermore, not being a student of the history of biology, I cannot tell whether the statement indicates any fact. What is it then that I, or any other reader, who knows the dictionary meanings of the words involved and does not enrich them with private associations or information that may come with professional training, can understand when reading the quoted sentence? First of all, the statement is understood as a claim to truth or an assertion. I don't mean that the sentence is taken to be asserted by its author; for all I know the writer might have introduced his sentence in order to proceed to disagree with it. Nor do I mean that the reader must assert the sentence as he reads it. Even if the reader were qualified, as I am not, to accept (or reject) the sentence, he would merely be agreeing (or disagreeing) with an assertion that is already there and is not his. The sentence "asserts itself," although this is a metaphorical way of explaining the fact that the reader can interpret a declarative sentence as claiming truth and at the same time disown its claim. Since then, in order to understand a sentence, one must interpret it as an assertion, what one understands, the proposition, must be distinguished from the sentence itself. A sentence, as so many typographical marks on paper, cannot assert or do anything; to become a vehicle of assertion it must be invested, by means of a mental projection on the part of the reader, with the conceptual function of reference to fact, a function of which there is no likeness in the modes of operation of extra-mental occurrences such as marks on paper. For a claim to truth, being a reference from discourse to things outside discourse or from language to non-linguistic facts, is reference beyond words and therefore cannot be just words; it involves a conception of a relation between linguistic and non-linguistic occurrences. To illustrate the point by the sentence quoted above, there is an assertion there because the sentence is interpreted as referring the description "Modern rediscovery of Aristotelian biology" to a non-linguistic fact. The illustration is typical. A proposition can be defined as a claim to truth, to the effect that a certain description or descriptive phrase has (or does not have) realization, i.e., describes (or does not describe) some non-linguistic fact. Hence any proposition is an "existence-proposition" (or a contradictory of an "existence-proposition"), that is to say, it can always be formulated by a sentence of the following kind: "There exists (or there does not exist) something, i.e., some fact, which corresponds to (or is described by) the description concerned." And logical analysis shows that all "existence-propositions" and therefore all communicable propositions involve apparent variables when stated by means of symbolic formulas.

Logical analysis is a procedure to determine the structure of a proposition in the course of which a given sentence is replaced by another. Since overtly nothing but sentences appear in this procedure, the view that there is no need for propositions may appear to have an empirical basis, but only if one overlooks the point that replacement of one sentence by another is stultified unless it is understood that, whereas the original sentence does not do justice to the proposition, the sentence which completes the analysis renders the form of the proposition explicit and thereby brings out its full import. In other words, the purpose of logical analysis is to establish an adequate formulation of a proposition, which presupposes the existence of propositions as distinct from their verbal embodiment in sentences. Any analysis requires enumeration of the undefined or ultimate elements in terms of which the complexes to be analyzed can be resolved or accounted for. Accordingly, in logical analysis there are basic logical forms which singly or in combination with one another must be capable of exhibiting the structure of any proposition. We are in a position, in the main due to Russell's works, to give a list of basic logical forms. They are: the conjunctive "and" (symbolized by a dot), the operation of negation "It is false that. . . ." (symbolized by the curl), and the existential prefix "There exists an x such that. . . ." Let me now illustrate the use of these basic logical forms in analysis. First, all compound forms can be transformed into a conjunction or a negation or a combination of both. For instance, the implication "If it is warmer, the thermometer will rise" can be transformed into "It is false that it is warmer and the thermometer will not rise." Second, any non-compound proposition can be formulated in terms of a single or multiple occurrence of the existential prefix and of the curl. "Men exist" can be analyzed into "There is an *x* such that *x* is human." "I bought a book" becomes "There is an *x* such that *x* is book-like and *x* was bought by me." "All men are mortal" is translated into "It is false that there is an *x* such that *x* is human and not mortal." One of Russell's most striking achievements in logic is his treatment of singular propositions. Thus "The moon is bright" is to be analyzed into "There is an *x* such that *x* is lunar and it is false that there is a *y* which is both lunar and distinct from *x* and it is false that there is an *x* which is lunar and not bright." Logical analysis is complete if and only if the sentence arrived at cannot be transformed into another sentence with a greater number of existential prefixes.

My use of the term "proposition" is more in accord with the terminology of Russell's earlier writings than with the *Inquiry*, although a definition which brings out the element of assertion may be likened to the view that the proposition is a state of possible belief expressed by a sentence. The difference remains in that I do not take assertion in a subjective psychological sense, but as an impersonal conceptual act. I do not know whether Russell would approve of my way of presenting the matter of logical analysis, but it seems obvious that I have said nothing that does not agree with his own practice of analysis in his publications on logic.

4. Empiricism

Russell rejects two principles of modern empiricism, the identification of truth with verification and the identification of meaning with verifiability. The principle that only an experience can determine the truth or falsehood of an empirical (non-analytic or non-tautologous) statement is the basis of "pure empiricism," and Russell doubts whether anyone accepts it without qualification or modification, because the objections against it are overwhelming. The main difficulty of pure empiricism is its conflict with scientific common sense; pure empiricism does not do justice to knowledge, "if our knowledge is to be roughly coextensive with what we all think we know." For in matters which we take to be knowledge we rely not only on our personal observations, but, with due caution, on judgments of memory and on the testimony of other people. Of course, a veridical memory is an after-effect of a personal observation and a veridical testimony of another person may be derived from his experience; but the point is that the pure empiricist cannot admit the truth of these statements, since they do not describe any of *his* personal experiences.

"For me now, only my momentary epistemological premisses [assertions of what I now perceive and, perhaps, remember] are really premisses; the rest must be in some sense inferred. For me as opposed to others, my individual premisses are premisses, but the percepts of others are not." (p. 168)

In order to adjust pure empiricism to what is generally recognized as empirical knowledge, one may try to supplement pure empiricism not only with the principles of demonstrative inference but also with the principles of probable inference, induction and analogy. Induction and analogy will indeed save an empiricist from epistemological momentary solipsism, but they are insufficient to account for the procedure of science. For science assumes the existence of unperceivable events, such as sound-waves in the air. The proof that such unperceivable events are not inferred by induction is the fact that they can be, and have been, treated by some writers, at the cost of great theoretical complication and awkwardness, as fictions convenient for prediction and correlation of experiences. Science, however, as practiced by the great majority of scientists, accepts the existence of unperceived events precisely because this position allows for much simpler explanation than the alternative hypothesis of convenient fictions. This means that science makes use of the principle of simplicity, which in some cases involves such non-demonstrative premisses as the stipulation of a continuous causal chain of events from the physical source to observation (cf. p. 379). The *Inquiry* mentions two more instances of what may turn out to be non-demonstrative principles or premisses: "what is red is not blue," "if A is earlier than B, B is not earlier than A." Pure empiricism is untenable for yet another reason: to establish the truth of a sentence by verification one must confront this sentence with another whose truth is seen directly. To take an example, while working in my study, I can assert that "there is a piano in the living room;" to verify this assertion I walk into the living room and, at the sight of the piano, I say: "This is the piano." This latter statement verifies the original sentence, but need not itself be verified; at least if taken in the sense of "This looks like a piano," it is known to be true directly.

"But if an observation is to confirm or confute a verbal statement, it must itself give ground, in some sense, for one or more verbal statements. The relation of a non-verbal experience to a verbal statement which it justifies is thus a matter which empiricism is bound to investigate." (p. 19)

Failure to undertake this investigation is not peculiar to pure empiricism; it also undermines the second principle of empiricism, i.e., the thesis that the meaning of an empirical sentence is the method of its verification.

Again, when it is said that "the meaning of a proposition is the method of its verification," this omits the propositions that are most nearly certain, namely judgments of perception. For these there is no "method of verification," since it is they that constitute the verification of all other empirical propositions that can be in any degree known. . . . All those who make "verification" fundamental overlook the real problem, which is the relation between words and non-verbal occurrences in judgments of perception. (p. 387)

However, the principle that meaning is verification, when stated unguardedly, has a peculiar and conspicuous weakness of its own, viz., there is no distinction drawn in it between words and sentences.

. . . All necessary *words* . . . have ostensive definitions, and are thus dependent on experience for their meaning. But it is of the essence of the use of language that we can understand a sentence correctly compounded out of words that we understand, even if we have never had any experience corresponding to the sentence as a whole. Fiction, history, and all giving of information depend upon this property of language. Stated formally: Given the experience necessary for the understanding of the name "*a*" and the predicate "P," we can understand the sentence "*a* has the predicate P" without the need of any experience corresponding to this sentence; and when I say that we can understand the sentence, I do not mean that we know how to find out whether it is true. If you say "Mars contains inhabitants as mad and wicked as those of our planet," I understand you, but I do not know how to find out whether what you say is true. (p. 386f.)

In a more guarded version of empiricism the meaning of a sentence is identified with the statement of its truth-conditions. "If we knew what it would be for a given sentence to be found true, then we would know what its meaning is." (Carnap, quoted in *Inquiry*, 387f.) But even in this formulation the principle remains essentially the same. For what would be the meaning of a statement of a truth-condition? It cannot be said, without an infinite regress, that this meaning consists of *its* truth-conditions. One might suggest that to state truth-conditions is to give more or less specific directions of how to verify the statement. In fact in a passage, quoted on p. 391 of the *Inquiry*, Carnap speaks of experiments as conditioning the truth of a scientific statement. Yet he does not seem to realize that before the relevance of an experiment to a statement can be established, this experiment must be recorded in a judgment of perception. "He does not tell us what it is that we learn from each experiment." (p. 392) Thus Carnap's version, like the outright identification of meaning with methods of verification, suffers from a disregard of sentences which describe a single experiment or a single observation.

And so empiricism is forced back upon undertaking an examination of the relation between a single non-verbal experience and a sentence describing it. The question is, can this relation be accounted for in terms of empiricism, i.e., must all the words involved in a sentence which describes an experience have their meanings derived from experience. Russell answers "No," if experience is to be limited to sense-experience, because sense-data have nothing to do with the meaning of logical constants such as "or" and "not." But Russell's own extension of empiricism, arrived at by including introspection with experience, gives a plausible empirical derivation to "or" and "not" as well as to the remaining elements of logical analysis, with a possible exception of the existential prefix.

As regards meaning: we may, on the usual grounds, ignore words that have a dictionary definition, and confine ourselves to words of which the definition is ostensive. Now it is obvious that an ostensive definition must depend upon experience; Hume's principle, "no idea without an antecedent impression," certainly applies to learning the meaning of object-words . . . it applies also to logical words; "not" must derive its meaning from experiences of rejection, and "or" from experiences of hesitation. . . . (p. 368)

There remain existential prefixes or apparent variables to be explained on the basis of empiricism. Now we may observe that these elements of logic have a double function in empirical statements: (1) they make explicit the element of generality connoted by general words,—as Russell puts it, ". . . the function of variables is exactly that of general words" (p. 302); (2) they are used to refer to events outside experience. The element of generality can be derived from the data of introspection; according to Russell, it corresponds to what is common to reactions to specific instances which are of the same kind designated by a general word (cf. the argument on p. 382 of the *Inquiry*). Many judgments of perception which involve existential prefixes appear to introduce into description nothing but generality. For example, when you look at a drawing of a circle, you say "This is circular" or "There is an *x* such that *x* is circular," and either of these sentences is fully justified by perception; the second sentence expresses less than, and is a part of, what is expressed by the first. But when a judgment of perception refers to something which is not experienced, the understanding of this reference can hardly be reducible to any actual datum within experience. "This is a cat," for instance, goes beyond what could really be given in perception and what would be adequately described as "This is a feline patch of colour;" logical analysis shows that the former statement is to the effect that "There is an *x* such that *x* is feline and is perceived through this particular patch of colour" (cf. pp. 173, 271f., 278). What is true only about some judgments of perception is invariably true with regard to communicable empirical propositions, since the latter describe events that are absent.

Let me now enumerate Russell's conclusions about empiricism. The principles identifying truth with verification and meaning with verifiability are both false; contemporary empiricism unduly ignores judgments of perception; these judgments cannot be justified by experience unless experience includes introspective as well as sense-data; whereas words to be meaningful must be derived from experience, their combinations in a sentence can be understood even if the sentence as a whole does not describe any fact; finally, reference to events that are not experienced is a problem which needs to be further analyzed.

5. Is Empiricism Self-Refuting?

The observation that theoretical propositions go beyond experience leads Russell to say that the theory of empiricism is "self-refuting." I do not think, however, that "self-refuting" is meant to be taken literally. But let me quote the relevant passage.

I will observe, however, that empiricism, as a theory of knowledge, is self-refuting. For, however it may be formulated, it must involve *some* general proposition about the dependence of knowledge upon experience; and any such proposition, if true, must have as a consequence that itself cannot be known. While, therefore, empiricism may be true, it cannot, if true, be known to be so. This, however, is a large problem. (p. 207)

If empiricism were literally self-refuting, it could not be true. Nor could Russell say, if he meant to employ "self-refuting" literally, that empiricism is "not logically refutable." (p. 382) But the main point to note is that, if the theory of empiricism is to conform to Russell's own doctrine of types, it must be concerned with knowledge of a lower type than itself, i.e., it is not intended to apply to itself. Hence, "self-refuting" is to be taken rather as "self-stultifying." Let the empiricist thesis (to the effect that knowledge depends on experience) be of the nth order or type, then knowledge, to which this thesis is supposed to apply, will consist of propositions of various orders lower than the nth order. Now the empiricist thesis is an empirical proposition and its only relevant difference from the empirical propositions with which it is concerned is that of logical type. And since the empiricist thesis, as the empiricists themselves must admit, is not reducible to a description of experiences, it would be *unreasonable* to insist that among other empirical propositions, which also differ in logical type from one another, every single one must be reducible to experience. They may be in fact so reducible, but there is no reason to believe it.

But if empiricism, at least in the radical version of momentary empiricism or solipsism, is unreasonable, if, as Russell says, "no one is willing to adopt so narrow a theory," can it really be logically irrefutable? At one time I used to think solipsism to be verbally inconsistent, because, I argued, to assert that "Everything is my experience," one must use the words "my" or "I" with a meaning which is correlative to "non-I," which, in its turn, would be meaningless unless there were something other than myself. I knew of no convincing refutation of this argument until Russell pointed out to me that solipsism can be stated without recourse to personal pronouns, by first giving an enumeration of one's own personal experiences and then adding: "And there are no other events." Russell's assertion that solipsism is not logically refutable is found on p. 376 of the *Inquiry*. Nevertheless, I think that solipsism would be logically irrefutable only to a person who can himself take the part of the solipsist. And I, for one, can not. For knowing myself I *know* that I could not originate such an absurd view as solipsism. Therefore I know that I must have learned of solipsism from someone else.

6. MEANING AND TRUTH IN MATHEMATICS

The *Inquiry* has refuted the empiricist identification of truth with verification and of meaning with verifiability and not the analogous assertion of the finitists that proof constitutes both the truth and the meaning of a mathematical statement. But there is no reason to expect the finitist to be in a better position than the empiricist. Consider as an example of a mathematical statement which is not only meaningful but generally believed to be true, although no one has yet been able to prove it, the famous four-color problem, the statement, that is, that "given any division of the plane into co-exclusive regions, one can always mark the regions with one of the numbers 1, 2, 3, 4 in such a way that no two adjacent regions will have the same number." Another example is Fermat's last theorem. If the finitists should argue that neither the four color proposition nor the Fermat theorem are fully understood so long as they remain without proof, one can retort that, however imperfect one's understanding of the theorems in question, it is undoubtedly some understanding, which amounts to saying that the theorems have *some* meaning. If examples are not sufficient to convince the empiricist, let him turn to a formalized postulational system of logic and mathematics. The postulates of such a system are given without proof, and, as Gödel has shown, within the system, if it is to be consistent, there are formulas which cannot be either proved or refuted. A further contention, which some finitists have combined with the claim that meaning and truth are identical with demonstration, and which, perhaps, follows from their claim, is the assertion that a description of a proof would result in, and therefore be identical with, an actual demonstration. This additional assertion is no more plausible than the main claim, as can easily be shown by means of an example. Consider the formula for the sum of the first n integers; we may know that this formula is proved by mathematical induction and understand this method of demonstration without going into the proof itself.

7. Truth-Conditions and Logical Analysis

Russell's rejection of the identification of meaning with truth-conditions may be confronted with the observation that his own practice of analysis consists in the employment of a method whereby one arrives at the truth-conditions of the sentences to be analyzed. Thus, one might say, Russell's analysis of "The moon is bright" would result in specifying three truth-conditions: that there exists at least one moon, that there exists at most one moon, and that the condition of brightness is satisfied. But analysis, so understood and illustrated, is logical analysis, and logical analysis stops short at unanalyzed meanings once the elementary forms of logic have been reached. Logical analysis aims at exhibiting the structure of propositions, although of course as the form becomes explicit so does the content enframed in it. Now it may well be that each time an elementary logical form is made explicit, the corresponding content turns out to be a statement of one truth-condition, so that logical analysis can be carried on so long as more truth-conditions of the statement remain to be stated; nevertheless, when all truth-conditions which can be given in terms of elementary logical forms are established, logical analysis comes to an end and the resulting statements of truth-conditions must be taken as meaningful, even though they are not resolvable into a set of further truth-conditions. In other words, logical analysis must perforce leave unanalyzed, and therefore without a statement of their truth-conditions, those component meanings of the analyzed proposition which have acquired in the process of analysis an elementary logical form of existence-propositions. On the other hand, these elementary existence-propositions may still be analyzable in epistemology or from some other extra-logical point of view. For example, the elementary existence-proposition "there is an x such that x is guilty of murder" can be further analyzed by a criminologist,—to take one extra-logical standpoint,—who could say that the proposition means that "there is an x such that x is guilty of poisoning or of stabbing to death or of shooting, or etc." But suppose someone attempts a further logical analysis by enumerating the conditions under which "there exists an x such that x is guilty of murder" would be true. Suppose, for the sake of argument, that the necessary and sufficient truth-condition is the existence of an eye-witness to the murder. Then, one might argue, the sentence "there exists an x such that x is guilty of murder" can be transformed into "there is a y such that y was a witness to the murder." This transformation, however, is no advance in logical analysis, for both sentences exemplify the same logical form of an existence-proposition.

"Thus to know what it would be for the sentence to be found true is to know what it would be for some man to see some other man committing the murder, i.e., to know what is meant by another sentence of the same form." (p. 389)

This discussion explains the sense in which a sentence is said to "involve" an apparent variable: if complete logical analysis transforms the sentence into an existence-proposition, no other analysis can change its logical form, i.e., eliminate the apparent variable or introduce another in addition to it. How badly this point has sometimes been misunderstood can be seen from the following quotation from Dr. E. Nagel's article, "Mr. Russell on Meaning and Truth," (*The Journal of Philosophy*, v. 38, No. 10, p. 266):

Mr. Russell's argument is difficult to follow, and I am not clear as to what he thinks he has established. Taken quite strictly, the sentence "this dog is ten years old" surely does not *contain* an apparent variable, and the issue then is just what Mr. Russell means when he says that it nevertheless "involves" one. He may simply mean that a sentence of the form "There is an x such that x is ten years old" follows from the sentence "This dog is ten years old" . . . ; but . . . the above two sentences are not logically equivalent, for the second does not follow from the first; and yet Mr. Russell gives the impression that the first sentence formulates an analysis of what is said by the second. . . .

I hope the reader will see that Dr. Nagel's first sentence would be, in Russell's theory, only a component in the logical analysis of the second; that a full analysis of the latter would be given by some such sentence as "There is an x such that x is perceived by means of this canoid patch of colour and is ten years old;" and that "This dog is ten years old" *involves* an apparent variable in the sense that the outcome of the full logical analysis of the proposition *contains* an apparent variable.

8. Perceptual Judgment and Causation

Perceptual judgments, especially "basic propositions" such as "redness-here," form the foundation of Russell's justification of empirical knowledge. According to Russell "basic propositions" cannot be false, except for the trivial reason of misusing words, because their utterance is caused by what they mean, by sensible experience. Some competent critics think that this validation of perceptual judgments assumes scientific causation, and is not fit to serve in any endeavor to justify science, since the principle of causation is not only one of the empirical propositions but needs justification more than any other. In a general way I can answer these critics by pointing out that in his account of "basic propositions" Russell does not use "causation" in the sense of scientific causation. However, in order to make this answer more specific let me develop it in connection with Dewey's adverse criticism in an article on "Propositions, Warranted Assertibility, and Truth" (*The Journal of Philosophy*, v. 38, No. 7). On p. 171 of the article Dewey writes:

If I understand Mr. Russell aright, he holds that the ultimacy and purity of basic propositions is connected with (possibly is guaranteed by) the fact that subject-matters like "redness-here" are of the nature of perceptual experiences, in which perceptual material is reduced to a direct *sensible* presence, or a *sensum*. . . . However, Mr. Russell goes on to ask "What can be meant when we say a 'percept' causes a word or sentence? On the face of it, we have to suppose a considerable process in the brain, connecting visual centres with motor centres; the causation, therefore, is by no means direct." It would, then, seem as if upon Mr. Russell's own view a quite elaborate physiological theory intervenes in any given case as condition of assurance that "redness-here" is a true assertion. And I hope it will not appear unduly finicky if I add that a theory regarding causation also seems to be intimately involved.

Dewey overlooks here several passages of the *Inquiry* which warn the reader that "causation" can be used in different senses. (Cf. pp. 72f., 173, 280, and 291). Thus the scientific sense of "causation," i.e., the unobservable functional correlation of observable as well as unobservable events, which is explained in a discussion of "continuous intermediate causal chains" (on p. 379f. and in an account of perception on p. 146), must be contrasted with "causation" in the sense of a "transaction," which is observable within experience, between a sensum and a sentence which describes this sensum. The second sense of "causation" is fully explained on pp. 72ff. of the *Inquiry*, and it is the only sense which is relevant to the assurance that a basic proposition is a true assertion. When Russell, in the passage quoted by Dewey, explains that causation, which leads from visual to motor centers, is indirect, he obviously cannot mean observable causation, since he is concerned with a physiological causal correlation of events within the body of the person who asserts the sentence "redness-here;" throughout the passage in question Russell *assumes* the principle of scientific causation and is not aiming at its justification. Dewey's lack of understanding of Russell's distinction between scientific causation and observable causation leads him to further wrong observations on p. 178 of his article:

In the case, previously cited, of *redness-here*, Mr. Russell asserts, as I understand him, that it is true when it is caused by a simple, atomic event. But how do we know in a given case whether it is so caused? . . . The event *to be* known is that which operates, on his view, as . . . verifier; although the proposition is the sole means of knowing the event!

The answer to Dewey's "How do we know?" is, of course, "By direct observation." And it is not true that, for Russell, "the proposition is the sole means of knowing the event." On the contrary, Russell explains on p. 58f. that one can know an event by noticing it and without using words. Dewey's remarkable disregard for the relevant texts culminates in his "verdict" that "any view which holds that all complex propositions depend for their nature of *knowledge* upon prior atomic propositions, of the nature described by Mr. Russell, seems to me the most adequate foundation yet provided for complete scepticism."

9. WORDS AND CONTEXT

Russell's principle, that although isolated words must have ostensive definition, there need be no experience corresponding to the sentence as a whole, can be challenged on the grounds that words have no meaning, i.e., cannot be used with a meaning— except as abbreviations of complete sentences—in isolation from the context of a sentence. The "contextualist thesis," from which this challenge may spring, is opposed to the view that, even in complete isolation from the context of sentences, a word may be used with some such intersubjective meaning as a class-concept or a composite-image. The issue is not concerned with subjective images which may be associated with words; nor is there a denial that words can be considered in isolation, and that when someone so considers them he can know that they are meaningful in the sense of capable of being used with meanings in certain contexts. This may still be vague, but I do not know of any contextualist argument which is either precise or conclusive. There is, to take one example, H. Reichenbach's argument (in *Experience and*

Prediction, p. 20), which is short enough to be quoted in full:

... Indeed, if we speak of the meaning of a word, this is possible only because the word occurs within propositions; meaning is transferred to the word by the proposition. We see this by the fact that groups of isolated words have no meaning; to utter the words "tree house intentionally and" means nothing. Only because these words habitually occur in meaningful sentences, do we attach to them that property which we call their meaning; but it would be more correct to call that property "capacity for occurring within meaningful sentences."

I do not see, however, how this argument proves anything more than that words are meaningful in meaningful contexts, and meaningless in meaningless contexts; nothing has been proved concerning the meanings of words isolated from any verbal context. Perhaps the following argument will appear more convincing. We observe that a word has different uses, senses, or shades of meaning in different contexts; also except for the context we cannot tell with which of its possible meanings a word is being employed; hence we conclude that, since a meaning cannot combine several incompatible things, a word in isolation cannot be used with a meaning. For instance, when I say "My belief lasted a second," the word "belief" designates a mental state of believing; whereas "belief" in the sentence "My belief has been generally accepted" means the object of my belief. And since without the aid of a context the sense with which "belief" is used cannot be determined, it would seem that in isolation this word cannot be used with a definite meaning. Much more, of course, remains to be said before this kind of argument can be called a proof.

But even if we assume without proof that words have no meaning in isolation, the assumption does not seriously endanger Russell's position. In the first place, the "contextualist thesis" is dealing with reified meanings of words, i.e., with entities of some kind; whereas Russell's phrase "the meaning of an object-word" may be just "short-hand" for some such convention as follows: "A word is said to have a meaning when one has acquired, by means of conditioned reflex, the habit of taking the same overt or incipient attitude towards the word which one would take in the presence of the object designated by this word." Secondly, Russell's "words in isolation" are not independent of sentences, since, on the contrary, they stand for implicit basic propositions. For example, "Lightning!" functions like the sentence "There is lightning!" On p. 32 of the *Inquiry* we read:

At the lowest level of speech, the distinction between sentences and single words does not exist. At this level, single words are used to indicate the sensible presence of what they designate. It is through this form of speech that object-words acquire their meaning, and in this form of speech each word is an assertion.

And again on p. 92: "Every single word of this language [i.e., of the object-language] is capable of standing alone, and, when it stands alone, means that it is applicable to the present datum of perception."

Thus it would seem that Russell's principle, that words in isolation must derive their meaning from sensible experience, amounts to the statement that words which function as basic propositions describe experience, which is hardly anything more than a tautology.

Derivation from experience is a condition of the primitive use of the object-words, and Russell is aware of the fact that "words are used in many ways." (p. 29) In order to explain other uses of words Russell has recourse to sentences about sentences and to mental attitudes, and his explanation appears to be as plausible as any other theory of meaning of which I know, except when it comes to the analysis of existence-propositions and their reference to events that are not experienced. The analysis, I believe, requires the admission of concepts.

10. CONCEPTS AND EXISTENCE-PROPOSITIONS

Russell points out that "Empiricists fail to realize that much of the knowledge they take for granted assumes events that are not experienced." (p. 272) But if all object-words derive their meaning from experience, how can anyone assume or even speak of unexperienced events? The feat is performed by means of apparent variables in existence-propositions. With this answer both Russell and I agree, but I believe that much more has to be added to protect our opinion from Dr. Nagel's criticism, who, at the end of the passage quoted earlier, writes as follows:

"By transforming a sentence without variables into a sentence with variables, the relation of the latter to what it indicates is no less a problem (if it is a problem) than the relation of the former to what it formulates." (267)

I am not sure whether I fully understand Russell's position, but it would seem that he wants the apparent variable to take the place of external reference in the sense of dispensing with the latter. My position, on the other hand, is that an apparent variable takes the place of conceptual reference only in the sense of symbolizing it.

To argue for concepts I must give some explanation of what I mean by a pure concept, and I hope the following will suffice for the purpose of this section. Take a sentence in which every object-word is derived from experience; replace one of these words by a symbol whose meaning is not dependent on experience; if, after the substitution, the sentence remains a meaningful assertion, the meaning of the symbol is a pure concept. Let the reader use the letter 'a' to name or designate this page; then he can say "a is rectangular." Now let "a" in this sentence be replaced by the complex symbol "There is an x such that x . . .;" within the context of the resulting sentence the meaning of this complex symbol is a concept. As may be seen from this example, a concept need not be a meaningful entity in isolation; but I think that in the context of a sentence it must be meaningful if the sentence as a whole, and all constituents (other than the concept) within it, are meaningful. Yet to admit the presence of pure concepts might appear to be giving up the grounds of empiricism altogether; and I should not be surprised if Russell's procedure were found to be an attempt to get along without pure concepts.

As the reader asserts (1) "a is rectangular," he can also describe his perception, less specifically, by (2) "There is an x such that x is rectangular." Since (2) is deducible from (1), but not vice versa, the former must say less than the latter; also, unlike (1) which can be understood only in the presence of a, (2) is communicable to outsiders without loss of meaning. Now since (1) has no external reference, i.e., no reference outside the perception of *a*, that part of (1) which finds its expression in (2) should likewise be free from external reference, even if to an outsider (2) seems to refer to something beyond experience. Next let the reader observe that statements about events that no one has experienced are of the same form as (2), and therefore, like the latter, only seem to refer to something outside experience. "We may say generally: when I am in a state of believing, that aspect of the believing which seems to refer to something else does not really do so, but operates by means of apparent variables." (p. 278)

The argument of the preceding paragraph, which I take to be a summary of pp. 276 ff. of the *Inquiry*, depends on the premiss that (2), in being asserted by the percipient of *a*, has no external reference. But there is an ambiguity here. A reference to *a* is not external to the reader's experience, but it is external to that part of his experience which is described by (2). His assertion of (2) involves a reference external to statement (2), since *a* is not a constituent of this statement. Bearing in mind this ambiguity I should expect the correct argument to proceed rather in the reverse direction: Since to an outsider (2) involves external reference and since to a percipient of *a* (2) means the same thing as to an outsider, it only seems that the percipient understands (2) as if it were free from external reference. Furthermore, to say that a sentence seems to refer to something external, we must understand what it would be like to refer to something beyond our experience; and since the question is not whether the reference happens to be true, but whether it is possible in the sense of being meaningful, an intelligible apparent reference is no different from a real one.

But, perhaps, Russell's denial of real external reference means no more than a denial that one can actually reach absent events, i.e., that events outside experience can nevertheless be within the experience that one has in referring to them; in other words, Russell may have merely meant that in the complex relationship of reference one of the terms, which is the object that one refers to, must be a substitute for the actual but absent event, since one cannot relate within a proposition entities to one another unless they are present to be so related. If this is Russell's position, it is mine also; furthermore, although a substitute for an absent event may be an apparent variable, the understanding that the apparent variable functions as a substitute can be hardly anything but a conception. It is noteworthy that Russell is not satisfied with resting his case on apparent variables, but is trying to explain how they operate; and his explanation, I think, leads to a purely conceptual construction.

Let us revert to the illustration "you are hot," which avoids irrelevant difficulties. This may be taken to mean "there is a hotness related to my percept of your body as, when I am hot, the hotness of me is related to my percept of my body." When I am hot I can give a proper name to my hotness; when you are hot, your hotness, to me, is an hypothetical value of an apparent variable. There are here two stages. Suppose I represent my percept of my body by a, my percept of your body by b, my hotness by h, the relation which I preceive between a and h by H, then "you are hot" is "there is an h', such that bHh'."

There is here a hypothetical sentence "bHh'," which I cannot utter, because I have no name "h'" in my language. But there is also, if you are hot, an actual occurrence, which is hypothetically named by the hypothetical name h', and this occurrence is actually so related to b that its relation to b would be a verifier of the sentence "bHh'" if I could pronounce this sentence . . . . (p. 280f.)

Thus to explain how an apparent variable operates in a sentence which seems to refer to someone else's hotness, I must introduce another variable, a hypothetical name, which I might use as a real name, if I only could directly experience another person's sensations. Is there any real progress towards elimination of pure concepts in this procedure; and isn't a hypothetical name, a would-be name, just as much a concept as the notion of an unexperienced event? There is a difference. Although I can assume that an unexperienced event is an actual occurrence, a hypothetical name is only a possible name, not supposed to be used by anyone else outside my experience. Whether this difference is a progress depends on whether, first, Russell means to reduce reference to actual but unexperienced events to experienced words that are only possible names, and, secondly, if such reduction is intended, whether what appears to be a concept of a possible or hypothetical entity can be explained without residue in terms of sensible experiences. This raises the difficult question of the meaning of "possibility."

11. Possibility and Subjunctive Conditionals

A way of defining "possibility" in terms of observations or actual values of a variable is explained on p. 43 of the *Inquiry:*

> I maintain that, in all cases of possibility, there is a subject which is a variable, defined as satisfying some condition which many values of the variable satisfy, and that of these values some satisfy a further condition while others do not; we then say it is "possible" that the subject may satisfy this further condition. Symbolically, if "φx and χx" and "φx and not χx" and each true for suitable values of x, then, given φx, χx is possible but not necessary.

Let us see how this method of dealing with possibility applies in the case of a hypothetical name 'h'.' We can use φx to represent the condition "x is a letter," and χx to stand for the further condition "x is a name of an event." Then, if we have used the letter 'a' to name an event in our experience, we can say "$\varphi'a$' and $\chi'a$';" and, if we know that no one has ever used 'c' as a name of an experience, we shall say "It is false that $\varphi'c$' and $\chi'c$';" but we can only treat 'h'' as we treat the variable x, i.e., we can only say that some such letters as 'h'' name events while others don't. In other words, to say that "h' is a possible name" is no more than saying that "x is a possible name," which, in its turn, amounts to the existence-proposition "There is an x such that φx and χx." Thus, since Russell's treatment of possibility must end with an existence-proposition, although possible names have been introduced in order to dispense with external reference of existence-propositions, the conclusion is that the treatment is not effective for the latter purpose.

I think that the difficulty of accounting for possibility in terms of actual data without falling back on a reference to unexperienced events can be most clearly shown as the difficulty of translating a subjunctive conditional into a material implication. To say that 'h'' is a hypothetical name is to assert the subjunctive conditional "If I were perceiving a certain event, I would name it h'." The corresponding material implication is "If I perceive a certain event, I shall name it h'." The two conditional forms are not equivalent, i.e., they do not convey the same proposition. The consequent of the material implication can be actually verified at the time when the event to be named by 'h'' occurs; but the subjunctive conditional is asserted with no expectation of an eventual verification, and it would still be asserted even if one knew that verification were impossible. Again, the material implication is a truth-function of its two component-propositions, "I perceive a certain event" and "I shall name the event h';" whereas the subjunctive conditional is an indivisible whole, since neither "I were perceiving a certain event" nor "I would name the event h'" are complete meanings or propositions. The difference seems to me to be sufficiently essential to make the task of translating the subjunctive conditional form into a truth-function hopeless; but I am not sure whether the *Inquiry* would unreservedly support this conclusion.

The introduction of the subjunctive conditional form on p. 35 of the *Inquiry* suggests the possibility of reduction to a truth-function:

Consider next such a sentence as "I should be sorry if you fell ill." This cannot be divided into "I shall be sorry" and "you will fall ill"; it has the kind of unity that we are demanding of a sentence. But it has a complexity which some sentences do not have; neglecting tense, it states a relation between "I am sorry" and "you are ill." We may interpret it as asserting that at any time when the second of these sentences is true, the first is also true.

The neglect of tense suggests an intention to treat the sentence in question as a material implication. On the other hand, although such an intention may be there, the same passage provides some grounds for an objection against taking the subjunctive form to be a material implication. The material implication "If you are ill, I am sorry" is the contradictory of the conjunction "You are ill and I am not sorry," and either of these compound propositions has as much unity as the other, each being a truth-function of the same components. Yet Russell points out that the subjunctive conditional has the unity of a single sentence, whereas, as he puts it in the paragraph immediately preceding the quoted passage, a conjunction consists of two assertions. Whatever Russell's real position at this stage of his *Inquiry*, there are other passages where a tendency to distinguish subjunctive conditionals from material implications takes an almost definite shape. Already on p. 87 we come across the following contrast:

"It seems, therefore, that it is impossible for a mortal to give verbal expression to every observable fact, but that, nevertheless, every observable fact is such that a mortal could give verbal expression to it."

The contrast can perhaps be paraphrased as follows. Whereas the subjunctive conditional form "If *x* were observable, *x* would be nameable" is true for every value of *x*, the material implication of the form "If *x* is observed, *x* is named" must be sometimes false. Even more decisively, and in a much more important connection, the opposition between the two conditional forms is brought out, at a later stage, in its bearing upon the different interpretations of empirical knowledge by a phenomenalist and a common-sense scientist. Only the phenomenalist, in order to eliminate the notion of unobserved occurrences, attempts a translation of all sentences about unobservables into material implications whose terms are without exception observable:

Some philosophers might argue that, when I say "the book is in the drawer," I only mean "if any one opens the drawer he will see it"— where "opening the drawer" must be interpreted as an experience, not as something done to a permanent drawer. This view, right or wrong, is one which would only occur to a philosopher, and is not the one I wish to discuss. (p. 293)

Recourse to material implication in phenomenalism is then contrasted with the use of subjunctive conditionals by common sense and science:

Common sense imagines travelling round the moon (which is only *technically* impossible), and holds that, if we did so, we should either see or not see the mountains in question . . . [The question is whether there are mountains on the other side of the moon.] . . . The astronomer may say: mountains on the further side of the moon would have gravitational effects, and might therefore conceivably be inferred. In both these cases, we are arguing as to what would happen in the event of a hypothesis which has not been verified in our experience. The principle involved is, in each case: "In the absence of evidence to the contrary, we shall assume the unobserved portions of the universe to obey the same laws as the observed portions." But unless we have an independent definition of truth concerning what is unobserved, this principle will be a mere definition, and the "unobserved portions" will be only a technical device, so long as they remain unobserved. The principle only says something substantial if it means "what I shall observe will be found to resemble what I have observed," or, alternatively, if I can define "truth" independently of observation. (p. 306f.)

The second half of this passage shows, among other things, that unless one is ready to fall back on the material implication "If I shall observe events, they will be found to resemble my past experience," one makes use of subjunctive conditionals to assert that physical laws operate beyond the field of observation, which involves reference to unobserved events; and it would seem that we must therefore admit that in a sense reference to unobserved events is an ultimate or unanalyzable concept. My impression that Russell is close to drawing this conclusion is further confirmed by his observation, on p. 274, that it is possible to distinguish between realism and phenomenalism, even though experience gives no ground for preferring one hypothesis to the other. The understanding of the difference between the two hypotheses must be a pure concept, since it cannot be derived from anything in experience.

The differentiation between subjunctive conditionals and material implications can be used to add one more point to Russell's score against the uncompromising empiricists. Russell has pointed out that empiricists are forced to extend the denotation of the word "experience" from momentary personal perception to the experience of mankind, and he also noted that they speak of events which are in principle observable. But to speak of events which are in principle observable is to use the subjunctive conditional form "*x* would be observed if certain conditions were satisfied," and now that we know this form to be, in effect, another way of referring to unobserved events, we can say that empiricists, who admit verifiability in principle, are, without knowing it, converted into full-fledged realists.

The main point of this section can be given in one statement. If a subjunctive conditional proposition is not translatable into a material implication, if, therefore, the former contains something which is not a description of perceptive experiences, this untranslatable residue must be either a conception of pure disposition or, although this may be essentially the same, a conceptual reference to actual but unexperienced events.

12. Concepts and Empiricism

Since by definition pure concepts are independent of sensible experience, there are at least three interrelated questions which must be answered before conceptualism can be made plausible: How can concepts be relevant to empirical knowledge, how can they refer beyond conceptual context to actual occurrences, and how can one concept be distinguished from another with nothing in experience to illustrate their difference? The answer given below is in the main a summary recapitulation of what has been set forth at much greater length in Ch. 4 of my book *The Problems of Logic* (1941).

Although pure concepts are not derived from sensible experience, they are derived from our experience with empirical propositions, from the understanding, that is, of the structure or form of an empirical existence-proposition. In the first place, we can distinguish the logical types of the formal elements within the structure of a proposition, and the distinctions of logical types must be purely conceptual, since, as Russell himself shows in the quotation to follow, they cannot be established as distinctions among the words within the sentence which is a sensible embodiment of the proposition.

"All symbols are of the same logical type: they are classes of similar utterances, or similar noises, or similar shapes, but their meanings may be of any type, or of ambiguous type, like the meaning of the word 'type' itself." (p. 44)

Consider the form of an empirical existence-proposition, "There is an x such that fx," based on the propositional function "fx," where f is a first-order function. The purely formal difference of type between f and x, together with the understanding that the propositional function is to be applied to empirical matters, makes it clear that x symbolizes a thing and f some property or relation between x and other things. Thus we establish that the existential form is the form of an assertion that the property or relation f is realized in the thing symbolized by x; the concept, basic to conceptual reference, is that of a thing. The word "thing," as I use it here, must be taken in a very general sense, so that "This thing is a material thing" is not a tautology and "This thing is a sense-datum" may be a true statement. And the concept thing, when so generally understood, is part of the meaning of any object word when the latter is used with a meaning. For example, we mean by a sphere "a thing which is spherical" and by a plant "a thing which is vegetable." To show that an object word breaks up in this manner is important as a corrective against the widely spread prejudice that the sole function of a word or concept is description. The function of the word "spherical" or of any other adjective is indeed purely descriptive; but the modus operandi of the concept thing is entirely different; its function is to supply the object of description, a thing is that which is to be described by adjectives. The distinction between the descriptive and the "objective" functions of words and concepts helps us to understand how external reference is possible: reference as a constituent of a proposition is not external to the proposition, since a proposition cannot transcend itself, but it is external to the purely descriptive elements within the proposition, i.e., reference is from the description to the thing described. The concept thing is more than a substitute for events which are not concepts, and it can function as a substitute, because the concept is also a mode of presentation in perceptual judgments. Although pure concepts by definition cannot describe sensible experiences, they are involved, as the analysis of the sentence "There is a dog" shows, in descriptions of perceptive experiences. And even a basic proposition can be contrasted with the sensible experience which it describes, because the proposition, unlike the experience, involves concepts.

Let me explain this by means of an illustration. Imagine a diagram of a cross-section of a ring or doughnut and use the letter 'a' to name your image; you then can say "a looks like a ring." The image, which you designate by the name 'a,' could be noticed without using words or symbols, but, as you single it out by the judgments "This is a" and "a looks like a ring," you really mean that "This thing is a" and "The thing a looks like a ring." The implicit presence of the concept thing in your judgments is betrayed through a further analysis of the image, as when you observe that "a consists of one thing which is inside another thing" (i.e., of two concentric circles). The office of the concept thing within a basic proposition is even more conspicuous in the case of indistinct perception, when we say "There is something there," and, upon closer examination, add "That thing was a picture of two concentric circles." But again the concept thing in these statements does not describe the corresponding sense-datum; if it did, the datum itself would contain a conceptual element; the function of the concept is to present the datum, or elements within it, for description and further analysis, and also for subsequent reference in exist-ence-propositions. The concept can represent an experience or event in an existence-proposition because it could present it in an antecedent perceptual judgment. Experiences are pre-sented as things, i.e., in the conceptual form or frame of thing-hood, and the concept thing is more than a substitute for an absent event, since it literally is a part of the event as subject to discursive thought, i.e., a formal mode in which the event can be thought of and described. Also because of being a formal mode of entry into thought, the concept thing is discoverable within the form or structure of an empirical proposition.

Conceptualism, as sketched here, is not hostile to a liberal empiricism or realism; there is no implication of arbitrary or Kantian imposition of concepts upon experience which is intrinsi-cally foreign to them; conceptual articulation of facts is under-stood to conform to an antecedent disposition in them (to be analyzed into a definite pattern of things with properties and relations). But of course articulation or analysis is a mode of presentation which is not the mode of pre-analytic data. The

Inquiry takes a step towards conceptualism by recognizing that the structure of existence-propositions, although meaningful, is not a duplicate of the structure of sensible experience. I do not know whether Russell is ready to accept the further point, that there are non-descriptive elements of form symbolized by apparent variables; but I believe that an assimilation of this point within the context of the ideas of the *Inquiry* would prove to be to their advantage.

A. USHENKO

DEPARTMENT OF PHILOSOPHY
PRINCETON UNIVERSITY

HARPER TORCHBOOKS / The University Library

John R. Alden	THE AMERICAN REVOLUTION: 1775–1783. Illus. TB/3011
Ray A. Billington	THE FAR WESTERN FRONTIER: 1830–1860. Illus. TB/3012
Kenneth E. Boulding	CONFLICT AND DEFENSE: *A General Theory* TB/3024
Crane Brinton	A DECADE OF REVOLUTION: 1789–1799. Illus. TB/3018
J. Bronowski & Bruce Mazlish	THE WESTERN INTELLECTUAL TRADITION: *From Leonardo to Hegel* TB/3001
Edward P. Cheyney	THE DAWN OF A NEW ERA: 1250–1453. Illus. TB/3002
Foster Rhea Dulles	AMERICA'S RISE TO WORLD POWER: 1898–1954. Illus. TB/3021
Harold U. Faulkner	POLITICS, REFORM AND EXPANSION: 1890–1900. Illus. TB/3020
Carl J. Friedrich	THE AGE OF THE BAROQUE: 1610–1660. Illus. TB/3004
Leo Gershoy	FROM DESPOTISM TO REVOLUTION: 1763–1789. Illus. TB/3017
Myron P. Gilmore	THE WORLD OF HUMANISM: 1453–1517. Illus. TB/3003
Lawrence Henry Gipson	THE COMING OF THE [AMERICAN] REVOLUTION: 1763–1775. Illus. TB/3007
L. C. Goodrich	A SHORT HISTORY OF THE CHINESE PEOPLE. Illus. TB/3015
Arthur S. Link	WOODROW WILSON AND THE PROGRESSIVE ERA: 1910–1917. Illus. TB/3023
George E. Mowry	THE ERA OF THEODORE ROOSEVELT AND THE BIRTH OF MODERN AMERICA: 1900–1912. Illus. TB/3022
Wallace Notestein	THE ENGLISH PEOPLE ON THE EVE OF COLONIZATION: 1603–1630. Illus. TB/3006
Joseph A. Schumpeter	CAPITALISM, SOCIALISM AND DEMOCRACY. Third edition. TB/3008
Frederick L. Nussbaum	THE TRIUMPH OF SCIENCE AND REASON: 1660–1685. Illus. TB/3009
Penfield Roberts	THE QUEST FOR SECURITY: 1715–1740. Illus. TB/3016
John B. Wolf	THE EMERGENCE OF THE GREAT POWERS: 1685–1715. Illus. TB/3010
John B. Wolf	FRANCE: 1814–1919: *The Rise of a Liberal-Democratic Society.* TB/3019
Louis B. Wright	THE CULTURAL LIFE OF THE AMERICAN COLONIES: 1607–1763. Illus. TB/3005
M. D. Zabel, *Ed.*	LITERARY OPINION IN AMERICA. 3rd Edition. *Vol. I*, TB/3013; *Vol. II*, TB/3014

HARPER TORCHBOOKS / The Academy Library

[*Selected Titles*]

Jacques Barzun	THE HOUSE OF INTELLECT TB/1051
H. J. Blackham	SIX EXISTENTIALIST THINKERS TB/1002
Crane Brinton	ENGLISH POLITICAL THOUGHT IN THE NINETEENTH CENTURY TB/1071
Ernst Cassirer	ROUSSEAU, KANT AND GOETHE. Intro. by Peter Gay. TB/1092
Cochran & Miller	THE AGE OF ENTERPRISE: *A Social History of Industrial America* TB/1054
G. G. Coulton	MEDIEVAL VILLAGE, MANOR, AND MONASTERY TB/1022
St. Clair Drake & Horace Cayton	BLACK METROPOLIS: *Negro Life in a Northern City. Vol. I*, TB/1086; *Vol. II*, TB/1087. Intros. by Richard Wright & E. C. Hughes
Peter F. Drucker	THE NEW SOCIETY: *The Anatomy of Industrial Order* TB/1082
W. K. Ferguson, et al.	THE RENAISSANCE: *Six Essays* TB/1084
F. L. Ganshof	FEUDALISM TB/1058
Etienne Gilson	DANTE AND PHILOSOPHY TB/1089
W. K. C. Guthrie	THE GREEK PHILOSOPHERS: *From Thales to Aristotle* TB/1008
John Higham, *Ed.*	THE RECONSTRUCTION OF AMERICAN HISTORY TB/1068
Dan N. Jacobs, *Ed.*	THE NEW COMMUNIST MANIFESTO *and related documents* TB/1078
Hans Kohn, *Ed.*	THE MIND OF MODERN RUSSIA TB/1065
Samuel Noah Kramer	SUMERIAN MYTHOLOGY. Illustrated TB/1055
Paul Oskar Kristeller	RENAISSANCE THOUGHT: *Classic, Scholastic, Humanist Strains* TB/1048
Arthur O. Lovejoy	THE GREAT CHAIN OF BEING: *A Study of the History of an Idea* TB/1009
Paul Mantoux	THE INDUSTRIAL REVOLUTION IN THE EIGHTEENTH CENTURY TB/1079
Miller & Johnson, *Eds.*	THE PURITANS: *A Sourcebook of Their Writings. Vol. I*, TB/1093; *Vol. II*, TB/1094
Sir Lewis Namier	VANISHED SUPREMACIES: *Essays on European History*, 1812–1918 TB/1088
Erwin Panofsky	STUDIES IN ICONOLOGY: *Humanistic Themes in Renaissance Art.* Illus. TB/1077
Priscilla Robertson	REVOLUTIONS OF 1848: *A Social History* TB/1025
Ferdinand Schevill	THE MEDICI. Illustrated TB/1010
Ferdinand Schevill	MEDIEVAL AND RENAISSANCE FLORENCE. Illus. *Vol. I*, TB/1090; *Vol. II*, TB/1091
C. P. Snow	TIME OF HOPE. A novel. TB/1040
Paul A. Schilpp, *Ed.*	PHILOSOPHY OF BERTRAND RUSSELL: *Vol. I*, TB/1095; *Vol. II*, TB/1096
Dorothy Van Ghent	THE ENGLISH NOVEL: *Form and Function* TB/1050
W. Lloyd Warner	SOCIAL CLASS IN AMERICA: *The Evaluation of Status* TB/1013

HARPER TORCHBOOKS / The Bollingen Library

HARPER TORCHBOOKS / The Cloister Library

HARPER TORCHBOOKS / The Science Library